Date Due

Dec 19 '51			
UL			
Demco 293-5			

UNFINISHED CATHEDRAL

UNFINISHED CATHEDRAL

T. S. Stribling

THE LITERARY GUILD

New York

PRINTED AT THE *Country Life Press*, GARDEN CITY, N. Y., U. S. A.

UNFINISHED CATHEDRAL

T. S. Stribling

THE LITERARY GUILD

New York

PRINTED AT THE *Country Life Press*, GARDEN CITY, N. Y., U. S. A.

UNFINISHED CATHEDRAL

CHAPTER ONE

Wᴇɴ the Reverend Jerry Catlin and Professor J. Adlee
Petrie fell into conversation on the southbound train going
into Florence, Alabama, it began for them their disturbed, un-
comfortable, and mutually disparaging acquaintance which
lasted for the rest of their lives.

At the moment, however, these two widely diverse gentle-
men had common grounds for friendly approach. They were
the only passengers on the long crowded train who had no
financial interest in the real estate boom which was then
ballooning prices of everything in and around Florence.

All up and down their day coach, for both men found it
expedient to travel as cheaply as possible, above the rattle
of the train and the clacking of wheels on rails, these two
seat mates could catch snatches of the excited and anticipa-
tory conversation of their fellow passengers:

"Building a big four-story apartment house on the lot
next to mine" . . . "Robert E. Lee Boulevard will pass right
by" . . . "Mine's only two blocks from the Tri-City golf
course they're going to build." . . .

But these remarks were mere grace notes tinkling forth
details of personal property already purchased, sight unseen,
by these Argonauts in search of the Golden Fleece. Behind
these expectations, upholding and sustaining the same,
sounded the leitmotif of their collective hope:

"Big power dam at Wilson Lake, two hundred and sixty-
five thousand horse power" . . . "I thought it was two million
six hundred and fifty thousand horse power" . . . "Well now,
maybe . . . maybe you're right about that." . . .

"When the whole Tennessee Valley is electrified, bound to

be the biggest industrial concentration south of the Mason and . . ."

"I tell 'em, they got to do something with it . . . got to use it somehow . . . can't just let it go to waste!"

"Listen . . . take it from me, friend, one of these days they're going to deepen a ship's canal from Florence to the Gulf . . . they'll haff to do it . . . trade'll force 'em . . . load our exports at the docks of Florence and ship 'em straight to Eurp . . ."

It was at this point that Professor Petrie glanced at the Reverend Mr. Catlin and observed in a serious tone:

"These gentlemen seem not going to build these great things themselves?"

"Not from what I gather," agreed Jerry.

"It seems they are expecting another set of men to come after them and perform all these wonderful works."

"That's the idea."

"And their plan is to sell out their holdings to this second set of supermen who are coming later, make their private fortunes, and . . . go away?"

The faces of both travelers took on the quizzical look of persons inwardly amused.

"I take it you haven't bought any town lots in Florence . . . so far," said Jerry.

"I perhaps won't," returned Petrie; "I'm a school teacher."

"Don't let that discourage you. I am sure they have partial payment plans to take care of school teachers . . . and ministers."

The younger man came to some sort of interior pause in his badinage.

"Are you a minister?"

"I am."

"Well, I wouldn't have taken you for one . . . still, I don't know now that you tell me you are one . . . no, no, I really wouldn't. . . ." He sat appraising the older man.

"I wouldn't have guessed you were a school teacher either," said Jerry; and the feeling between the two travelers was that each of them had definitely complimented the other.

The two men rode on in silence with a faint subconscious gratefulness that they did not appear to be what they were. With Petrie this was like poulticing, accidentally, an old and painful wound. Presently, out of his thoughts came apparently a quite disconnected observation:

"Do you notice the hammering of that left front car wheel?"

"I hadn't observed it."

"It's flattened just a little. It'll crack eventually . . . start with a microscopic fissure that will look like a rabbit's hair lying in the steel. . . ."

"Rabbit's hair?"

"That's the finest hair I know."

"How came you to think of that . . . I mean the car wheel cracking?"

"I've looked at steel from a lot of railroad wrecks. I was always interested in the strain and stresses of metals. I majored in metallurgy."

"You are not coming to Florence as a metallurgist?"

"Oh no, I teach in the Florence High School. I got off half a day to run up to Iron City for a sample out of an old-time charcoal furnace."

The science teacher who did not look his profession leaned forward and drew from under his seat a lump of iron covered with dull red rust.

An enthusiasm in Petrie's voice which suggested that the lump held something precious caused Catlin to give it another glance.

Petrie divined that he had pressed his private hobby beyond its normal interest for a stranger. He tried to make amends by encouraging his fellow passenger to talk about himself.

"You are not coming to Florence as a minister, not at this time?"

"Why not at this time?"

"Well . . . the boom in full blast . . . everybody in such a stir and rush. I shouldn't think the people would have time for . . . for . . ."

Petrie paused, unable to find words with a rational and at the same time a respectful significance wherewith to end his sentence.

"You mean they wouldn't have time to consider death and eternity in the midst of their stir?" supplied Catlin.

"Y-yes," agreed Petrie with the usual lay feeling of the emptiness of such a consideration.

The man of cloth rode for a space conscious of the gap that had opened up in their brief talk. He said in a different voice:

"Well, some of these hustling high-powered business men are very likely to take time off to die before the boom's over . . . and laborers, there'll be scores of laborers killed in building and digging and blasting . . . but you probably were not considering labor as men I would be interested in?"

This perfectly serious irony of his seat mate amused Petrie, and he thought to himself, "Well, now, I'll bet you are not at that." And he wondered if the Reverend Mr. Catlin even suspected the quiet setting aside of all his tenets concerning death and eternity by the more cultivated members of society. Petrie suspected he did not. The clergy were like children before whom men and women avoided mentioning certain facts of belief. Aloud he said with a touch of hidden retaliation:

"Of course, your services are just as necessary during a boom as at any other time. I hope you find a place in Florence."

"I already have one."

"You mean you have one somewhere else and are just visiting Florence?"

"No, in Florence itself. I have just been appointed assistant minister to Dr. Blankenship of the Pine Street Methodist Church."

Petrie was really surprised.

"Calling in an outside man?"

"I obtained the appointment through an uncle of mine who has some influence."

"May I ask the name of your uncle? . . . I probably know him."

"Vaiden . . . Miltiades Vaiden."

Petrie made a slight movement of surprise. His face changed at some rearrangement of his thought.

"Why, of course I know Colonel Vaiden perfectly well. I do a little business at his bank . . . and he had Dr. Blankenship make a place for you?"

"I rather imagine that he did as I told you, but I had no hint from him. I simply received a letter from Dr. Blankenship inviting me to come."

Petrie watched his companion with a ghost of odd amusement in his eyes. He did know Colonel Miltiades Vaiden very well indeed. Everybody in Florence, except the rawest newcomers, knew him. He was extremely wealthy; the only man in Florence reputed to be a millionaire, whatever that means in a small town. But the thing that titivated Professor Petrie was to learn that Colonel Miltiades Vaiden had chosen who should be the assistant minister to Dr. Blankenship of the Pine Street Methodist Church when Petrie knew that Colonel Vaiden had come by his great fortune through theft.

Church and property.

CHAPTER TWO

THE ODD and rather ironic recollection which flitted through the thoughts of Professor Petrie formed, for a few minutes, a kind of puzzle for his seat mate. The Reverend Catlin saw that Petrie was amused and wondered why. He felt his tie to see if it were straight, then glanced down at himself. A moment later, however, the possibility of some personal dishevelment was driven from his thoughts by the train slowing up for the Florence station.

The passengers in the crowded day coach began gathering up their belongings and peering out of the car windows for their first glimpse of this promised land on whose future their fortunes were staked.

A crowd had collected at the station to meet the train. Two hotel buses were backed up in the parking space north of the depot. A red-capped and a blue-capped porter were yodeling the attractions of their respective hostelries.

"Rat dis way gemmun fo' yo' ol' stan'by, de Flaunts Hotel! Evah room gotta bath; evah bath got soap, tow'ls, hot'n' col' wattah. All you need is a toothbresh. Rooms twenty-fi' dollahs a day wid meals an' co'spondin' reductions widout! Come to de Flaunts Hotel!"

The red-capped porter, who had nothing especial to offer, was hallooing:

"Step heah gemmun fuh de Plantahs' Res' Hotel! Dis bus take you-all to de Plantahs' Res' Hotel! Beds fuh de sleepy; chai's fuh de tiahed; meals fuh de hongry; cheap prices fuh evahbody wid de brains to lop onto 'em! Clam in dis bus fuh de Plantah's Res' Hotel. Fi'teen dollahs a day wid all ixpenses paid!"

The porters need not have exerted their lungs, as both buses would have been filled anyway. Each negro, however, enjoyed using his talent. As the fortune hunters swarmed out of the train, they followed their national habit of patronizing the funniest. So the red-capped porter filled his bus a few minutes before his rival and triumphantly clattered away.

While the rest of the Argonauts bespoke taxicabs or started afoot from the depot to old Florence, Jerry Catlin lingered on the railway platform expecting either Dr. Blankenship or his uncle Miltiades Vaiden to send a motorcar for him. Not only was a car probable, but there was a vaguely discomforting possibility that if the Vaiden car came it would be driven by his uncle's pretty wife, Sydna Vaiden. This particular combination Mr. Catlin distinctly did not want to happen. His reluctance to meeting Sydna again amounted almost to aversion. It had been, in fact, a vague emotional objection to his acceptance of Dr. Blankenship's offer of the post of assistant minister. Why he had such a feeling he did not analyze. He had tried to throw it off as irrational, but now, as he stood waiting on the platform, he glanced apprehensively up the road toward Florence and hoped that if a car did come for him it would not be driven by Sydna Vaiden.

A man's voice asking doubtfully:

"Partner, ain't yore name Vaiden?" brought Jerry out of his faint trepidation. He explained that his name was not Vaiden, it was Catlin, but that he was a nephew of Colonel Miltiades Vaiden.

"Shore; I knowed I knowed ye, but yore connection with the Vaidens slipped my mind. Lemme see, yore mammy wuz . . ."

All this time the unknown was regarding, not Jerry, but the train. He was stooping and peering under the line of cars. Now he broke off his research into Jerry's genealogy to say quickly, "My name's Northrup. I'm debbity sheriff here. There's some damned niggers ridin' this train." He seemed wrought up over the idea and continued his search. "I b'lieve they's one under there," he said *sotto voce* to Jerry under cover of the hiss of the air brakes. "I'll git on the other side, an' if one crawls out, you nab him."

Jerry nodded.

"I made shore you was a Southern man before I ast you. A dern Yankee is jest as li'able to turn a nigger aloose as hold him."

Jerry nodded again. The officer climbed across the platform of the day coach and from the opposite side began yelling:

"Come out o' there, you black devils! I see you-all! This is the law! Come out or I'll shoot!"

A half minute later Jerry did hear the hard clap of a pistol shot followed by the sound of running feet, apparently with Northrup in pursuit.

Catlin himself stood beside the car on the alert while the chase was in hearing, but as it faded away he picked up once more his rather pensive hope that he would not see Mrs. Sydna Vaiden.

It was really an irrational feeling: he knew that. In the first place, there was no way permanently to avoid meeting her. And then what had come and gone between him and Sydna Crowninshield, before she had married his old uncle, was buried under a drift of years. No doubt she had changed, and certainly so had he. He had no present valid reason to avoid her; still, the thought that at any moment Sydna might appear in a car quickened his breathing and made him nervous. He thought how absurd it was to feel so about a girl . . . a woman now . . . his old uncle's wife whom he had not seen for sixteen . . . eighteen . . . twenty . . . What a long, long time it had been!

The sun, the spring sun, became disagreeably warm and brilliant. Jerry stepped up on the first step of the coach into the shade of the overhang of the roof. The fact that he was really getting into Florence again came over the man with its ancient charm. The place looked more like itself with the fortune seekers gone. It was quiet and sleepy, and across from the depot he saw a house with a live oak and a magnolia in its yard. They grew anywhere at all, these lovely aristocratic trees. The lacquered leaves of the magnolia made him think once more of Sydna Crowninshield before she married his uncle Miltiades. From that day to this the hue, the rustle, the smell of a magnolia induced in his thoughts a kind of complementary image of . . . A movement beneath his feet broke into his reverie. A little negro boy was squirming out from under the step on which he stood. The white man stooped silently and caught the child by the neck of his coat.

The little yellow boy twisted about, startled, looked up, and asked in a hurried voice to be let go before the policeman came back.

Jerry replied with the easy philosophy of the person who is not in trouble that he should have thought of policemen before he stole a ride on the train.

The boy stammered:

"I . . . I didn't weigh much, Mister, the . . . the train went just as fast with me."

Jerry was faintly amused at the argument.

"Even if you weighed nothing at all, you would have to pay your fare as a service charge."

The pickaninny stood silent with a screwed-up face. After a moment the assistant minister asked:

"Do you know what a service charge is?"

The light brown lad moistened his lips and answered in the monotone of a child before a teacher:

"It's what you pay at a restaurant to get to eat."

Catlin nodded with the humor fading out of the situation, "Yes, that's an example."

The two stood silent in the shadow of the overhang. The small captive finally asked:

"Is this Florence?"

"Yes. Have you never been here before?"

"No, sir . . . but this was where I was coming . . . . Won't you let me go, Mister?"

"No-o . . ." denied Jerry undecidedly.

"I won't steal any more rides now, I won't have to."

"Where did you come from?"

"Chicago."

"What did you come here for?"

"To see my folks."

The youngster's full lips twitched sidewise after the fashion of black folk in distress, and Jerry saw tears in his eyes.

The assistant minister was half minded to loose his captive. Had he been a white boy he would have done so. But in the South there rests upon white men a kind of racial obligation to correct and reform as best they can the missteps and short-comings of the colored people, so this impulse to liberate the child was overruled in the Reverend Jerry Catlin by his wider duty to his country. And indeed, at this point Jerry's inward discourse was brought to an end by Deputy Northrup appearing from the direction of the locomotive with another boy, blacker and larger than Jerry's, hobbling in front of him. Blood on the negro's bare leg gave Jerry a shock.

"You didn't shoot him, officer!" he ejaculated.

"I stopped him . . . he ain't much hurt. Now, boys, where are the rest of you young devils?"

"How many more are there?" asked Jerry.

"Four!" snapped the deputy. "They're hid around here some'rs! Out with it, you black idiots, if you know what's good for you!"

As the two boys simply stood, Northrup got down on his hands and knees and caught sight of another rod-rider. He whipped out his automatic and threatened the new refugee with instant destruction unless he came out.

A car approached from the direction of Florence driven by a negro man. This colored man stopped his machine and watched the deputy corral still another black boy from beneath the cars.

As soon as the chauffeur saw what was up he said in a corrective tone:

"You niggahs, hoppin' trains, that ain't no way to carry on!"

"Hush your gab," snapped Northrup, glancing at the negro man.

The chauffeur hushed at once. After a few moments he said in a careful voice:

"Ah come down heah fuh a white ministah, de Rev'unt Jer' Catlin. Colonel Milt Vaiden sont me to fetch him."

"There he is," said Northrup, pointing at Jerry, "take him and go."

"Yes suh; yes suh!" He got gingerly out of the sedan and came to Jerry with his cap off. "Ah'll take yo han' bags, Doctah Catlin; an' lemme have yo trunk checks; me an' de baggage smashah will ten' to 'em." He walked around the deputy and his prisoners, giving them a wide leeway as he went to the baggage room.

When the Reverend Jerry Catlin was ensconced in his uncle's car, gliding swiftly into Florence, he was sorry somewhat that he had committed the negro child to the obscenities of the county jail. He had been a likable sort of boy, and stealing a train ride was an offense enterprising youngsters were wont to commit.

As he thought about the little prisoner he asked the chauffeur his name.

"My name's Wilson," replied the negro in a gloomy voice.

"What ever became of Sam . . . my uncle had a man of all work called Sam?"

"Do' know, suh. . . ." Wilson waited for this question to evaporate from their conversation, then he said:

"That Mistuh No'thup sho shoot a niggah boy quick. . . ."

"It did seem uncalled for . . . merely hoboing."

"Yeh . . . if'n an' s'posin' . . ."

Jerry waited for the end of this sentence and finally asked:

"Supposing what?"

Wilson puckered his chocolate brow.

"S'posin' hit was a niggah, pullin' out his gun so quick to shoot a white man, 'nen whut?"

"Northrup is the deputy sheriff," pointed out Jerry, not relishing Wilson's tone.

"Yes suh, I'se makin' 'lowance fuh dat too," mumbled Wilson.

This whole conversation was really banned. It was a topic which white men and negroes did not discuss together in the South. Jerry Catlin was vaguely affronted that Wilson had done so. He thought of saying, "Now, now, Wilson," in a corrective tone, then he decided to let it pass with his silent disapproval. Wilson, who was quick to feel the reproof, also became silent.

The brown man's insubordination gradually faded from Catlin's mind, exorcised mainly by the billboards that flared in yellows, reds, and black along the boulevard entering Florence.

Nearly all of them bore real estate advertisements. Jerry did not so much read them as they stamped themselves blatantly upon his eyes.

CYRIL JONES
Houses, Lots, Mercantile and Industrial Building Sites

Coming & Tergune, Choice Suburban Property Bought and Sold. . . .

Buy Now in Beautiful Bonnybloom Park. Highly restricted. Convenient Terms. . . . Lerganthall and Barth. . . .

Build your Bungalow under the Flapjack Tree down by the Molasses Pond. See Bill Bradley, *President Northern Alabama Realtors' Association.* . . .

As an earnest of all this building activity, here and there along the boulevard stood small frame houses in various stages of construction. In front of most of these buildings were For Sale signs, giving the names of the agent and the building contractor. A few bore big cards,

SOLD BY
Coming and Tergune.

LET GO,
By Bill Bradley,
President of North Alabama Realtors' Association.

The only name that Jerry knew on these signs was Bill Bradley's. He remembered talking to Bill Bradley one night in front of Sydna Crowninshield's home. His uncle Miltiades had accompanied Bradley, for some reason or other, and Jerry realized now with a queer distant sort of shock that that night had been the first time his uncle ever really had seen and talked to Sydna.

Thus, by a somewhat circuitous route, he came back to his original aversion to seeing Sydna. He turned to his silent driver:

"Are we going to Uncle Milt's home?"

Wilson came out of his own absorption and answered with an apology in his voice:

"No suh, Doctah Blankenship in a hurry fuh you. He say if'n I take you up to Col'l Milt's you won't git loose fuh a long time. He say take you to de pahsonage an' let you fix yo'se'f up, 'nen bring you straight to him at the Flaunts Hotel."

"What's he doing there?"

"They're havin' a Motor meetin'."

"Motor meeting?"

"Yes suh, you know, de Motory Club."

"Rotary Club?"

"Yes suh, hit allus soun' kindah lak a automobile to me."

CHAPTER THREE

Pine street, with its ancient manors and time-crowned trees, its box rows, flower beds, and bird coverts, lay embalmed in years amid the stridor of the new Florence boom. The people on Pine Street neither sold their homes nor built. The only inroad made by the flare of the market on this quiet thoroughfare was a great raw excavation lying just beyond the parsonage and the Pine Street Methodist Church. The Reverend Jerry Catlin noticed this when Wilson stopped the car, got out, opened the door of the parsonage with a key, and let Jerry into the study.

The parsonage itself had a very low floor; lower, in fact, than the surrounding lawn, so that Jerry, when he entered, took a step down as if performing an act of humility.

Wilson spread the bags on a table ready for their keys, then entered a bathroom and turned on the water for Jerry's shave, which he had not been able to get on the day coach. As the black man bobbed himself out the door he repeated that he would be in the car ready to take Jerry to the Motor meeting and that if Jerry wanted anything else please to call. The brown man was so well trained and thoughtful that Jerry decided the *faux pas* he had made about Northrup shooting the black boy was a kind of verbal slip amid a life of otherwise upright conversation.

The topic faded from Jerry's mind as he busied himself with brush, safety razor, and clean linen. He turned off the bath and over the bowl turned on the spigot marked hot. This presently became a stream of faintly warmish water, and while he was waiting for it to become hot, it grew cold again.

Outside the birds were singing. From the near-by church Jerry heard the sound of an organ. Someone was practising over and over a difficult phrase from Bach. The notes rose and fell in repeated triplets; then at a certain point the player would stop and begin again.

Two linen towels hanging on the white glass rod in the bathroom were elaborately embroidered and marked with blue letters, "D. S. to Dr. B. Merry Christmas." On the wall hung a little cloth pocket offering small sheets of crêpe paper embroidered with

When shaving troubles gather
Wipe away the lather.

It was a feminine gift and quite as useful as the homespun couplet was clever.

These details gave the assistant minister the familiar but somewhat oppressive sensation of entering once more the contracted feminine world which makes up religious life in an American community. There had been a time, years ago, when he had sought in travail of soul for the vast roofless freedom of the realm of religion; a widening of spiritual and intellectual frontiers; and here he was now somewhere near the mid point of his churchly career, drying his cold-shaved face on the embroidery considered suitable for ministers by "D. S."—probably the Dorcas Society.

The organ practice in the church stopped. In the silence the assistant minister heard two negro voices talking in front of the parsonage:

"'At's whut dey say dey's done," said one of the voices in a troubled tone.

"Who says hit?"

"A telegram."

"My lawd, if'n a telegram say hit, hit mus' be so. . . . How come so many niggahs?"

"Don' ast me, black man. I got you told. I ain't got no

time to stan' here splanifyin'. I gwi' drap along up de street while de drappin's good."

This talk provoked in Jerry a momentary curiosity which immediately vanished with a white man's indifference toward the senseless conversation of negroes. He was drying his face when there came a tapping at the door of his bathroom and Wilson appeared. The brown man had a troubled look.

"Scuse me, Doctah Catlin, but you ain't 'bout ready to go, is you?"

"Any rush?"

"No-o suh. I thought maybe if you could drive a ca' yose'f I would mosey on."

"I'm ready to go now. . . . Anything wrong?"

"No-o suh . . . I reckon not. You know dem fool niggahs at de deepo made a whole lot o' folks mad at 'em; 'at's why Shurf Northrup was treatin' 'em boys so rough."

"What did they do?"

"Well, I do' know zactly. . . . Gimlet was tellin' me 'bout hit. . . . I thought maybe if you could drive a ca' . . ."

"I'm ready to go now," said Jerry, coming out of the bathroom.

Wilson moved more rapidly than usual and got into the driver's seat ahead of Jerry. As the motor purred toward town, Jerry observed again the wide excavation piled around with stone and bags of cement covered with sheet iron; vats for making mortar, timber for scaffolding. Jerry surveyed it with some curiosity.

"Who's putting up such a big house right next to the church?"

"Doctah Blankenship."

"What's it going to be?"

"'Nothah chu'ch."

"What does he want with another church?"

"'At's gwi' be a biggah chu'ch . . . de Doctah has responded to de boom."

Jerry looked back at the foundation as long as he could see it; then presently the matter was driven from his thought by the car entering the business section of Florence.

As Jerry had been away from Florence since his boyhood days, the shops and stores had the dwindled, shabby look which always surprises a man on such a return. This smallness was further stressed by the motors and crowds of pedestrians lining Market Street and overflowing into alleys and by-streets. The town had the look of a host bewildered by a multiplicity of guests.

When Jerry got out at the old Florence Hotel, Wilson pointed out a place behind a bootblack stand where he would park the car, and said if he were not there when Jerry got back for Jerry to drive it anywhere he wanted to.

A few minutes later, the assistant minister followed a crowd of gathering Rotarians into the lobby of the hotel. There were so many visiting members for this luncheon that not many of the guests knew each other. The lobby, however, was full of laughter and cigar smoke and the jovial intimate familiarity with which one perfectly strange Rotarian greets another. From the hotel dining room came the sound of vociferous but not unpleasant singing.

A doorkeeper at the entrance of the dining room asked Jerry for his ticket but a moment later inquired:

"Aren't you the man Dr. Blankenship is expecting?" Then pointing across the room said, "There's Jim sitting at the head of the table with Miltiades."

"Jim?" inquired Jerry, not understanding.

"Yes, Jim Blankenship, the Methodist minister."

At this moment a rough-looking man, distinctly not a Rotarian, tried to pass the ticket taker. That official touched his arm and inquired if he were a member, or did he happen to be a guest of anybody.

"I've got to see Colonel Milt Vaiden," said the man hurriedly.

"That's Milt at the head of the table," repeated the guard.

The man hurried on up the long double row of tables with the awkwardness of a laborer among a gathering of middle-class professional business men.

Jerry himself looked at his uncle and felt that faint shock of dismay which fills a man when after many years he meets someone whom he remembers as in the prime of life and sees in a glance that he is very, very old.

"Well," said Jerry in a flatted voice, "his hair is perfectly white, isn't it?"

"That's not Jim, that's Miltiades you're looking at," corrected the doorkeeper, "he's the president of the club."

"Yes, I know that. He's an uncle of mine. I haven't seen him for a long time."

"M—m . . . yes, Miltiades is getting along," agreed the ticket taker, sticking to Rotarian informality, "he must be up in the nineties, but he's still an old game cock. He still shows the boys how."

As Jerry noted the guard's admiration for the venerable white-crowned figure of his uncle a queer remembrance flickered through his mind of an hour he had stood one chill autumn night in an alley a block or two south of this very hotel, peering into a narrow barred window of the Lauderdale county jail in which his uncle Miltiades was confined.

Not irony, not satire, but a kind of penetrating joy and triumph filled Jerry that time had brought honorable amends to the brother of his mother.

This aged uncle at the head of the tables bore a family resemblance to Jerry's mother just before she had died. The old Colonel's face was tanned and time worn and spotted here and there with the darker blotches of extreme age.

The doorkeeper had escorted Jerry up the table behind Blankenship's chair. He touched the shoulder of the big powerful ecclesiast.

"Jim," he said, "a friend of yours."

The Doctor turned, divined who it was, for he got to his feet, displacing his chair with an effect of power and size.

"Young man, you've come! I was getting jumpy about you! There's a meeting of the Realtors' Association going on in Sheffield right now. How quick can you get to it?"

"I suppose in . . . oh, ten or fifteen minutes . . . in Uncle's car."

The aged man at the head of the table looked at the newcomer.

"Are you Jerry?"

Jerry acknowledged his identity.

"Jerry, my boy, I'm glad to see you. . . . Sydna was just saying this morning . . ."

"Miltiades, you won't mind me rushing him off?" inquired the minister in his hearty baritone. He explained to Jerry in a kind of aside, "Your uncle is just as wrapped up in making the cathedral the ornament and grace of Southern Methodism as you and I are, Jerry. He has been more than generous: he's been lavish."

"I'm interested in a . . . a crypt," said the Colonel, "and of course the whole idea of a classic, monumental . . ."

"You don't mind," interposed the Doctor rotundly, "if I whisk your nephew away and use your car again?"

"Not at all, if Marsan or Sydna doesn't need . . ."

"I telephoned both. Now, if you'll excuse us, Milt?"

"Certainly, Jim."

The Doctor and his assistant minister withdrew to the hat shelves in the hallway. The place had no attendant, as the Rotarians disliked tipping. As Jerry identified and recovered his hat the Doctor explained something about the Realtors' meeting in Sheffield.

"Sorry I haven't time to develop the whole idea, Jerry, but we want a contribution to the cathedral. Not a check down affair, you understand, but a drawing account."

"I see."

"Now, any minister can get a check, but to get a drawing account—I mean checks when you are not there to ask for them—you've got to sell them something they need and want."

The Doctor's manner hurried Jerry away and at the same moment detained him for necessary details.

"Look here," said Jerry, thinking over objections he might meet, "how am I going to approach Sheffield men for a subscription to a church in Florence?"

".First, of course, it's a Tri-City . . . really North Alabama cathedral . . . you know . . . reflect honor and dignity on the future metropolis of the South . . . that's the idea . . . merger . . . Tri-City . . . North Alabama . . . All Alabama . . . All South . . . step it up to metropolitan importance . . . building for hundreds of thousands yet to come . . . they'll get that, Jerry, a lot more quickly than you'll say it . . . they're real estate men."

Jerry nodded, put his hat on his head. The Doctor began moving with him to the door.

"And listen . . . don't forget this . . ." he paused an instant, "don't forget to point out that a great interdenominational church, such as All Souls Cathedral will be, would prevent so many smaller churches having to be built here and there . . . you know . . . in a dozen new developments."

The assistant minister had never before been in charge of an urban pastorate. He paused to ask:

"What objection could there be to smaller churches?"

The Doctor lifted a casual hand.

"That I really can't say, but be sure to mention it to the Realtors' Association. It is a fact. What influence this fact may have, no one can say. We perform our duty when we place it frankly before the Association."

Dr. Blankenship's earnestness and enthusiasm thrilled Jerry even after he had spent a night in a day coach.

"Now, about what should I try for?"

"Ten thousand . . . spread out, of course, monthly payments."

The amount surprised Jerry, but there was a "go," an attack about the Doctor that suggested to Jerry he would get the amount. As the two shook hands, Jerry thought how potent the Doctor would be in spiritual accomplishment, once he had finished the actual building of his church.

As the assistant minister went out of the door of the hotel he heard an uproar break out in the dining room. He thought some visiting Rotarian must have told a new joke; or that there were enough visitors to laugh loudly at one of the regular jokes told by a Florence Rotarian.

Still, the noise in the dining room of the old Florence Hotel did not sound quite like laughter.

CHAPTER FOUR

JERRY found his uncle's car where he had left it behind the bootblack stand, but Wilson was gone. The black man had left the key in the switch in mute invitation for Jerry to do his own driving. The Reverend Catlin got in the car with a wave of annoyance at the characteristic untrustworthiness of negroes, backed around, and set forth for Sheffield.

The crowded streets occupied his attention for a few minutes, but as soon as he reached thinner traffic, his thoughts came back, with some concern, to the technique of obtaining ten thousand dollars in subscriptions. He was trying to clarify the precise reason why one large church was so much to be preferred to a number of smaller churches when a girl, a blonde, well-set-up athletic girl, came running across the campus of a school building and waving her hand above her shining corn-silk hair.

"Hey, stop! Stop! Cousin Jerry, stop! I've got to see you!"

Jerry slowed up, looking with interest and speculation at the excited and extremely graceful creature in blue sweater and skirt.

She came running to his car and swung on the fender with something of the effect of a bird lighting.

"You don't know me. I'm Marsan." She shook Jerry's hand with a firm, delighted pressure; then, after a moment's appraisal, leaned in the car and kissed him.

"Of all odd things," she cried looking at him, "a first cousin of mine being a preacher!"

"Somebody has to be the preacher," said Jerry, admiring the girl's clear tingling cheeks, short nose, blue eyes, and round athletic neck. "How did you know this was I?"

"Oh, Dad's car . . . and we were expecting you. . . . Where's Wilson?"

"He deserted me."

"Deserted you!" Marsan stared in amazement. "Did he just walk off and leave the car?"

Some more girls were edging out from the campus toward the motor. Marsan began introducing them:

"Cousin Jerry, this is Lizzie Lanceford, this is Sarah May Tergune, this is Daisy Beckwith."

Lizzie gave a brilliant smile which showed a dimple and said she was glad to meet Marsan's cousin.

Marsan was a little annoyed at Lizzie's rusticity in saying "Glad to meet you," when their whole class had just been instructed to say, "How do ye do."

In the little pause Jerry said he had been dispatched in a great hurry to Sheffield.

Marsan, who had no intention of letting him go so soon, asked:

"What you going to do over there?"

"See about a contribution to All Souls Cathedral."

"When are you going to see Mamma and Drusilla?"

"Why-y . . . just as soon as I possibly can."

"Well . . . you'd better. Drusilla and I were talking this morning about how queer it was to have a minister in our family."

"You don't call Mrs. Crowninshield grandmother?"

"Oh no, she won't let me. She makes me call her Drusilla."

Jerry smiled at the vivid picture this drew in his mind of Sydna's mother.

"Well, tell Drusilla for me that it seems queer to me to have such a pretty, athletic young cousin in my family; and we'll let the minister and the beauty offset each other."

"Marsan!" cried Lizzie, "I can trade lasts with you!"

Lizzie was rapidly disgracing Marsan with her kiddishness.

"Cousin Jerry, maybe I'd better go to Sheffield with you and be your chauffeur," she suggested with quite a grown-up, thoughtful air. "Wilson shouldn't have run off like that."

"You do, and we'll go too, Marsan," declared Sarah May Tergune.

At this moment a youth about two sizes larger than an ordinary man came across the school grounds calling:

"Marsan, we're up in the lab. Come on now and help flay Frederick!"

Lizzie giggled and dimpled appreciatively at some concealed jest in the young man's words.

"That's Red McLaughlin," cried Marsan, with the necessity of introducing everybody to everybody else hard upon her. "We're up in the lab now. I'll see you right away, Cousin Jerry, and Mamma and Drusilla said to tell you . . ."

Jerry was stepping on the starter.

"Kiss him good-bye!" cried Lizzie, giggling.

"Kiss him yourself," wished Marsan in an undertone, disgusted at such repeated bad taste in a boon companion. Then, as Jerry looked back through his rear window at her, Marsan waved an adieu as enthusiastic as her first hailing had been.

Lizzie's dazzling smiles fell from her like a mask the moment the man was gone.

"Marsan," she said with dreamy speculation, "do you think you could ever marry a person like that?"

"He's my first cousin," said Marsan.

"I mean another man like that."

"Oh, I don't know . . . I don't think about that, every man I meet."

"Oh, neither do I!" cried Lizzie earnestly. "Marsan, now you know I don't!"

By this time Red McLaughlin, looking as casually hung together as a mastiff puppy, came down to the girls. He started at Marsan again to get her to go to the laboratory and broke off to ask suspiciously who that was driving Colonel Milt's car.

"That was a preacher," said Lizzie, beginning to giggle again.

"A preacher!" cried the hobbledehoy, looking at Marsan in bewilderment.

"What if he is a preacher?" asked Marsan defensively.

"What was you talking to a preacher for?" asked Red.

"Oh, he's her first cousin," put in Lizzie not caring to tease Red any longer.

"I declare," ejaculated Red, no longer jealous, "a preacher for a cousin!"

Marsan became annoyed.

"Well, you needn't talk like that . . . there has to be ministers. What would a town be like without churches?"

"Aw, toodle," ejaculated Red, "that's what preachers always ask. I say if you want to know what a town would be like without churches, just go to some part of town that hasn't got a church in it and look around . . . it would be like that."

Lizzie giggled.

"Red, you're a sight!"

Miss Marsan Vaiden compressed her lips together and started in the direction of the high school laboratory.

Red McLaughlin saw that he had gone too far and regretted it. He tried to edge his biological partner away from Lizzie so he could talk to her privately. Lizzie instantly sensed his trouble and moved away on her own account.

"Marsan, I didn't mean anything personal," said Red in an undertone.

"Well, you know that's the way you actually think about preachers."

"Why, no, it isn't."

"Yes, it is."

"Well, now, I'm not saying preachers ain't preachers," admitted Red reluctantly.

The blonde girl walked on with her pretty chin tilted..

"They do a lot of good in the world . . . they're a good influence."

"Sure, sure, that's so," agreed Red hurriedly, then he added out of an unfortunate habit of saying everything that passed through his mind, "Would you say all this, Sandy, if he wasn't your cousin?"

"Don't call me Sandy . . . of course I would . . . why, no, if he hadn't been my cousin I wouldn't have thought about it, but since I have thought about it, this would be exactly the way I would feel no matter if my cousin was a minister or not."

"You never talked this way about a preacher before."

"Why can't you say minister?"

"Well, minister then," snapped Red.

Both the adolescents were disturbed. Red had a contempt for preachers, but at the same time he reflected that Marsan's cousin Jerry was a scion of the Vaiden family, and that the Vaiden fortune was founded on a theft, that Colonel Milt Vaiden had stolen a whole steamboat full of cotton from a Mr. Handback who had committed suicide. He now thought with irony of a preacher, whom he misprized, coming from such a family as that. The two walked on in a bitter antiphony of thought.

The laboratory which the two entered had the acrid smell of chemicals and the mortuary odor of pickled cats. In the room were several other couples among the tables, boys and girls, who by pairing off had made the smelly work of dissecting at least pleasant and interesting if not fragrant.

Red McLaughlin rescued fragrant Frederick from a jar of brine, fastened the half-skinned body on the dissecting table, then took the forceps and opened up an old incision and waited for Marsan to trace the mesenteric artery. When the girl began her work the difficulty that had arisen about preachers passed out of Red's mind. By force of habit he watched mainly Marsan's hands, shapely, small, and tanned. He was much taller than she, and now and then, as she stooped and bent, he glanced through the yoke of her smock and glimpsed the beginning of her bosom, whose final rounded completion was always lost under the brown linen. There was an undergarment, something white, that always interfered, and Red at times wondered how his dissecting partner persuaded the cloth to lie so closely against her breast.

Across the laboratory he could hear a boy named Porter Lee pushing and slapping Lizzie Lanceford in a coltish courtship, and he could hear Lizzie's giggling laughter and her exhortations to Porter to behave.

Porter's success in putting his hands on Lizzie reflected in a way upon Red and made him envious. At times Red was sure Porter kissed Lizzie behind a screen of test tubes, bottles, and retorts. Red thought to himself that faint heart never won fair lady. This quotation, however, seemed to have no reference to Marsan, who was concentratedly following the artery with a lancet. However, the example of Porter Lee was at that moment being enacted on the other side of the chemistry shelves. Red shifted his pincers to his left hand, put his right around Marsan's cheek, drew her face about, and kissed her.

The girl twisted her head free, gave him an instant's amazed look, then swung open-handed at his face. The slap sounded all over the laboratory. Red was stung out of the usually masculine stoicism and flapped Marsan with the back of his hand. It struck her bosom, and a spasm of pain went through her. She began crying and gasped out:

"You mean, hateful beast! Talk about my cousin as you did, then do that . . . and hit me!"

Red McLaughlin was aghast at what he had done.

"Good Lord, Marsan, I didn't mean to do that, honest I didn't . . . and I wasn't thinking about your cousin!"

Porter and Lizzie began laughing at what they knew had happened when just at that moment the laboratory door opened, and Professor Petrie, the science teacher, entered the room.

McLaughlin stood taut with apprehension of what Marsan would do. Already Petrie didn't like him, and he didn't like Petrie. He whispered in a pleading undertone:

"Marsan . . ."

As he whispered this he thought if Marsan did tell on him he wouldn't take any of Professor Petrie's discipline; he would stop school first.

Petrie, in his turn, knew at once something was wrong, because the whole laboratory was silent and too busily at work. He walked around to Lizzie Lanceford's table and looked at what she was doing. He pointed out a mistake in her dissecting, paying more attention to her than to her work. Then he went over to Marsan.

"Did you find the artery, Marsan? . . ."

Then he saw her flushed face and brilliant angry eyes and was amazed to think that she had anything to do with the trouble. It was as if a lady suddenly had turned hoyden in her own parlor.

"I think this is it," said the girl, drawing an easier breath now that the bell-like pain in her chest was subsiding.

Petrie nodded.

"Now it divides a little further on."

Red McLaughlin stood by, big, awkward, and apprehensive. Petrie, who was a middle-sized man, seldom addressed Red in overlooking the work of the pair. He told what was necessary to Marsan, who understood quickly, and let her explain it to her slower partner. Now, as he was turning away, Marsan said gravely:

"I'd like to see you a moment when we get through here, Professor Petrie."

The instructor looked questioningly at the girl, nodded agreement, and turned to another couple. When he was out of the room McLaughlin said in an undertone:

"I hope you won't mention anything, Marsan."

"I won't," said the girl in a flat voice.

"Well . . . you said you wanted to see him when you get through here. . . ."

"It's not about you."

"Well . . . I appreciate that, Marsan. . . . I apologize for what I did . . . both of 'em."

"Well, that's all right. Now this is the artery here, it leads into the . . ."

"I sure don't know what made me do it. . . ."

"What I don't see," ejaculated Marsan with a brush of

renewed anger, "is why you tried to kiss me right after you had insulted my cousin. It looked like you were trying to show how . . . how insignificant you considered me!"

Red McLaughlin was aghast that such a construction should have been put on his act.

"Insignificant! You insignificant! Why, Marsan, when it comes to being significant, you've got it spread over all the other girls six ways for Sunday!"

Marsan looked at him, surprised at the earnestness of his compliment.

"Then what did you do it for . . . right after you had insulted my cousin?"

"Why, Marsan, I forgot all about your cousin."

"Forgot it!"

"I sure had."

"How could you?"

"Why, I got to thinking about . . . well . . . about . . ."

"What?"

"You."

"What were you thinking?" probed the girl with less irritation.

"Why . . . doggone it . . . I was thinking about how you looked . . . and . . . and about how ever'body else kissed ever'body . . . and I didn't."

"Why, they don't!"

"Blame near all."

"Lots of girls don't kiss boys."

"Who?"

"Well . . . my mother didn't kiss boys."

"Oh, sure, your mother never did. I was talking about modern times."

They talked on about kissing with a certain delicate satisfaction on both sides, and gradually it began to dawn on Mr. McLaughlin that he had improved his position with Marsan quite distinctly, and that the old adage, "faint heart never won fair lady," had its value even when its execution appeared most hazardous and ill-timed.

CHAPTER FIVE

Half an hour later Marsan Vaiden went up to Professor Petrie's room to speak to him while Red McLaughlin remained outside the school building waiting her return. Red himself was not the sort of student who appeared voluntarily before any teacher; when he went to an instructor's room after school hours it was under direst necessity.

Marsan climbed the flight of dusty stairs leading to the second story, revolving in considerable uncertainty the odd subject she had in mind. As she slowly mounted the steps she tried to think of some other person to whom she could turn with the peculiar problem before her, but there was none. Her mother's store of information could not even brush the question. Her grandmother Drusilla, whose wisdom embraced all her mother knew and went far beyond it in a sort of backward direction, had no authentic information about what she wanted to know. Her old father, Miltiades, whom she loved, probably would not believe that such a question honestly existed. The only person, Marsan felt, whose knowledge and philosophy could possibly cover the field in which her answer lay was her science teacher, Mr. Petrie.

Mr. Petrie, it seemed to Marsan, knew all things relative to human life and the physical universe. When she saw him in the classroom with his dark eyes, broad, rather low brow, and quiet, almost brooding demeanor, she was always somehow moved at the thought of his endless, coördinated, and minutely detailed information. And she wondered about him himself, why he was always thinking, musing, touched with a constant tinge of unhappiness.

When she stood in the empty upper hallway before the

science teacher's door, the impossibility of putting into words the trouble in her mind stopped her still. She hesitated a moment, then turned and moved silently toward the stairs again. She would explain to Mr. Petrie later that she had forgot to come up.

At that moment the science door opened and Mr. Petrie asked:

"Marsan, you wanted to see me?"

"Why, yes, I wanted to see you," said the girl in a negative tone.

"Will you come in?"

"Thank you."

He went back to his desk and stood beside it with his hands on an old brass-tubed microscope. Marsan became exquisitely uncomfortable before so young and so wise a professor. If he had been a very old man she felt she would have got along much better; as it was she stammered:

"Mr. Petrie, I—I don't hardly know . . ."

"Has McLaughlin been objectionable to you, Miss Marsan?"

"Oh, no," ejaculated the girl, surprised.

"I'm glad to hear that. In the laboratory today, I was afraid . . ."

"No . . . but it was something that Red said to me."

Petrie frowned and increased his attention.

"Something about a cousin of mine," hurried Marsan, to set him right. "We were talking about Cousin Jerry Catlin . . . he's a minister. . . ."

"About Dr. Catlin?"

"Yes."

"What could he have said about Dr. Catlin?" queried Petrie, his apprehension about Marsan's well-being giving way to curiosity.

Marsan drew a breath. The importance of her question now had suddenly dwindled, and it had become almost silly.

"Well . . . he said Cousin Jerry was unnecessary . . . that all preachers were unnecessary . . . and churches were unnecessary. . . ."

Petrie gave a faint, unusual smile.

"You disturbed about what Red McLaughlin thinks of such things?"

"Oh, no," denied the girl at once, "it's what I think, it's what people think . . . it . . . it's what really is. . . . What do you think about it?"

Marsan's fundamental disturbance transferred itself to Mr. Petrie in some degree.

"Certainly they are necessary; they perform wide and various functions in society."

Marsan regarded her oracle without satisfaction.

"But . . . but, Professor Petrie, that isn't quite the point, of course ministers do a lot of good, but . . . are they necessary?"

"Since they do good they must be necessary."

"Oh, no, that isn't right . . . a broom does good, but they aren't necessary, because there are vacuum sweepers. . . ." She stood with her embarrassment quite gone now, getting at her problem with her classroom technique. "I mean . . . is what they teach necessary?"

"Look here, Marsan, Red McLaughlin never asked any such question as that."

"He may not have . . . exactly that way, but that's what it finally amounts to."

"What you are doing," observed Petrie acutely, "is asking yourself the question about preachers because you have one in your own family, and you don't quite know whether you are . . . well, a little dampened by the fact or not."

This slight analysis created a stir of intimate surprise in Marsan, as if Petrie had stepped inside of her mind and read a truth which she herself did not know was there. It was a faintly embarrassing but a distinctly pleasant feeling.

"Even if it is my question, it doesn't make much difference where it comes from, how am I going to answer it?"

"We-ell . . . let me see . . . the doctrine of preachers is

necessary because there are hundreds of thousands of people in a stage of intellectual development that demands . . ."

"Look here . . . do you believe it?"

The scientist looked at her for several seconds.

"Marsan, I am a teacher of science here in the Florence High School, I am not supposed to spread my private religious opinions among the pupils."

The girl looked at him with a sense of helplessness.

"Then who can I go to . . . who has thought anything about things like this?"

"Why, the ministers . . . the preachers, of course!"

"Why, the idea of going to a minister to find out if what he preaches is true or not! Of course he would say it was."

"He'd give you his arguments."

"Yes, and he would convince me . . . any smart man can convince you. You are a smart man, too; you have nothing against the ministers and nothing for them . . . you are the only person I can think of to ask."

"Marsan, I can say this for you: you are the only sixteen-year-old girl in Florence who would come out and say such a thing as that. One or two others I know might possibly think it, but they wouldn't say it."

"I'm seventeen," corrected Marsan with a seventeen-year-old girl's stress on this important point.

"Very well . . . seventeen," agreed Petrie smiling with his dark eyes.

What he smiled at, Marsan did not know, but she suspected it was something else inside her mind which she did not know was there, and this renewed her former titivated feeling. The interview apparently was over. She picked up her books with her hands, and mentally she collected her odds and ends preparatory to going. Then it became clear to her that Mr. Petrie never had answered her question at all, he had talked around it. So with her books in her hands she said to him:

"You never did tell me."

"Marsan," said Petrie in an odd voice, "I make my living by teaching science in the South. I once lost a fairly good position in Tennessee. However, I'll break a rule of mine and say this much: I think it is unfortunate that the morals, laws, and manners of the modern world are supposed to hang upon a false-true test of some old Hebrew myths. I think that is one of the most grotesque and pathetic things I ever heard of."

The girl nodded slightly and thanked him. She had known what he thought all the time. His opinion lay implicit in the high-school atmosphere ever since her junior year.

She slowly descended the stairs again, and as she went out the front door, Red McLaughlin hurried toward her. She had forgotten he was waiting.

In the interim Red had not forgotten Marsan, however. He had been thinking of her with anticipations of dizzy delight. That Marsan, in the laboratory, had objected to his kiss on account of what he had said about her preacher cousin was an unbelievably happy augury. He could hardly credit it. As he had waited impatiently for her in the empty school yard, he had thought bumptiously to himself, "All skirts are alike, they all fall for somebody . . ." but he did not believe his own thoughts. He wondered if he could kiss Marsan again. He wondered if he could go further than that. His heart beat at the thought. He fancied himself overcoming her resistances, enjoying the luxury of her . . . there was a wood on the way home through which they might walk together, if they chose. Red meant to try to persuade Marsan to go with him through this wood.

As he moved restlessly before the door, he saw someone running along the street from the direction of Florence. When the runner saw Red, he waved a hand and called in a desperate voice. Then he saw it was Porter Lee come back from town. McLaughlin anticipated being drawn away from Marsan and shouted antagonistically:

"What in the hell do you want?"

Porter came panting across the campus.

"Downtown . . . they've caught six niggers . . . that raped a white girl."

Red was astounded.

"Six!"

"Yeh . . . six . . . they're getting up a crowd to . . ."

"Hell fire," cried Red, "six . . ." Visions of what could be done to six negroes flickered through his head in a lurid cinematoscope.

It was at that moment that Marsan had appeared in the doorway, and Red hurried toward her, calling:

"Marsan, I got to go to town!"

"Sure . . . I'm going too."

Porter explained:

"Yeh, but we kain't wait. They've got some niggers arrested down there . . . attacked a white girl . . . making up a crowd to take care of the black devils!"

"Oh, what a terrible thing!" cried Marsan.

She watched, with wide eyes, the two boys run toward town. The way Red McLaughlin, who was a football player, bore himself as he ran, the chivalric cause for which he was running, gave Marsan one of her rare thrills of admiration for her slow-witted dissecting partner. She recalled the kiss he had given her because she was pretty.

Then she began thinking what she should do. She had intended waiting on the school grounds for the return of her cousin Jerry, but with such excitement in town this became impossible.

She thought of Professor Petrie; she had half a mind to run back upstairs and tell him the news, but she did not want to appear before him twice in the same afternoon. She wished she could hear what he would think about the crowd gathering to wreak vengeance on the negroes. He might conceivably be opposed to it because he did not think popular thoughts. He doubted the rightness of religion, he might doubt the justice of lynching negro offenders against white women.

She began walking toward Florence. She walked slowly at first, looking back toward Sheffield to see if her cousin might not come in sight with the car. Presently she gave up this hope and hurried along toward the business part of town.

CHAPTER SIX

Marsan was deprived of her father's car because in Sheffield the Reverend Jerry Catlin required time. At the Realtors' meeting he found himself under the necessity of disregarding time and creating the impression of boundless leisure which is so useful psychologically to the higher type of salesmen.

The Reverend Catlin had had a number of years' experience in his line of endeavor. Every church he had occupied was not only a business enterprise within itself with the usual financial problem of making income meet outlay, but it was expected to return, over and above its running expense, a certain amount to the General Conference of the Methodist Church South. It was for this reason, the Reverend Catlin sometimes told himself, that the various congregations placed under the care of ministers throughout the country were called charges.

On this particular occasion some leeway in time was important, because Jerry had arrived late at the hotel where the Realtors were holding their luncheon. He regretted this. He liked to meet beforehand and make one or two humorous but dignified jests with the men whom he hoped to interest in his contributions.

When Jerry finally reached the Modler Hotel he entered the dining room, went up to the toastmaster, introduced himself in an undertone and apologized for being late.

The toastmaster, whose name was Brekker, had reserved for Jerry a chair beside his own, as this is a convenient station for a minister to ask grace on a luncheon, but as Jerry had not arrived in time the eating had proceeded without grace and had reached the ice cream. Jerry sat down and ate some of this, and a few minutes later the business part of the program began.

The object of the meeting was to bring about a closer cooperation between the realtors of Sheffield, Tuscumbia, and Florence in zoning the industrial, residential, and business properties in these three towns.

A small black-eyed man arose, produced a map, and argued that the real estate development of the Tri-Cities could best be considered as a whole, and that a permanent board of controllers be appointed for the three towns, with arrangements for any dispute between any two of these towns to be referred to those members of the board coming from the third, disinterested town.

Discussion immediately broke out. Bill Bradley, an old gray-headed Florentine member, suggested that the different towns be represented on the board in proportion to their population. A Sheffield member wanted representation based on the number of industrial enterprises in each city; while the Tuscumbia member wanted the board fashioned along the line of the American Senate allowing each town to appoint two members. The six should choose a seventh as chairman who would cast a deciding vote in the event of a tie.

Everyone knew that the source of future difficulties would lie between the two larger towns, Sheffield and Florence, and that the Tuscumbia members would always be in the position of arbiters. Someone at the table said in a hollow voice without exposing his identity by arising:

"How do we know these Tuscumbia boys won't sell out when it doesn't concern their town?"

A Tuscumbia man arose and began indignantly:

"Gentlemen, it is to be supposed that each of the three municipalities will select honest men . . ." when old Bill Bradley interrupted to say:

"Well, even if they do sell out, it will be an open market. Florence money will buy a Tuscumbia Solon just as quick as Sheffield money . . . what could be fairer than that?"

A Sheffield realtor got to his feet and retorted that he wasn't thinking of the fairness of the proposal, he was thinking of the expense.

Brekker, the toastmaster, hammered the laughter into silence and stopped the discussion, because now everyone understood the motion and that it could not come before the association for a vote for three meetings. He now had another matter of importance to bring before the meeting.

Dr. Blankenship had not been able to attend this luncheon himself, but he had sent a younger man, a man whose heart vibrated to the oncoming flood of prosperity and wealth which would be the sure result of the great Wilson Dam development in northern Alabama.

"Members of the Realtors' Association," he continued, "you who are the virtual directors of the expansion of the Tri-Cities; the health, happiness, and education of tens of thousands of future citizens depend upon the wisdom of your city planning today. May I ask you in this hour of your great responsibility to give a thought to that Hand which molded the Tennessee River Valley; which today marshals the argosies of the clouds and wafts them northward from the Gulf upon the wings of His goodness to refresh our thirsty hills and dales and to make possible the great governmental dam and all that men may hope to make and do with it? Gentlemen, I wish to introduce to you a representative of that great power this afternoon, the Reverend Jerry Catlin, assistant minister of the Pine Street Methodist Church of Florence."

Brekker bowed to Jerry and sat down.

Mr. Brekker himself did not care anything at all about Jerry's mission and did not mean to contribute a cent, but his father had once been speaker of the Senate in Montgomery, Alabama, and therefore the son on every possible occasion mounted Pegasus and rode as close to the empyrean as possible.

Jerry Catlin arose under the heavy handicap of following a speaker more florid than himself. He gripped the edge of the table in his determination not to lose his audience. He began his exegesis upon the ancient but somewhat shaky theme that money given to good works would be returned tenfold to the giver. He tried to put enough personal force into this to persuade the gentlemen before him to lay out a considerable sum upon his guaranty. The great drawback in this particular instance was that the realtors, by profession, trafficked in rosy promises themselves. So they sat at the long table, with eyes courteously fixed on Jerry. Some drew slowly at cigars and directed the smoke upward to avoid annoying their neighbors; others moved the pepper and salt stands here and there; others refolded their napkins.

With the certainty of failure upon him, Jerry wondered if he would not better wait for Dr. Blankenship to come and actually make the plea for money. He knew, if an appeal be once denied, it was very difficult to get it on its feet again. He also knew that for some reason Doctor Blankenship had high hopes of this Realtors' Association.

As Jerry floundered about there flickered through his head the memory of what his superior had said to him about the cathedral doing away with the necessities of so many smaller churches in the Tri-Cities. Now, in his conclusion, he touched on this idea.

"And finally, gentlemen," he said, "all of us must feel that the Tri-Cities needs a great cathedral in keeping with the future metropolis of the South.

"This is important to you real estate men, because one great magnificent church will not only make Florence the religious center of Alabama, but its spaciousness will accommodate the population of all of these three cities combined. Smaller churches, scattered here and there, will be unnecessary. You would not be asked or expected to set aside lots in your subdivisions for religious use, because that would be taken care of in the many-storied structure we contemplate. And it is from this point of view particularly that Dr. Blankenship asks your coöperation and financial support."

Jerry ended his talk with a little more heart than he had

begun, because the men had quit twiddling things and had listened to what he had said at the end.

The black-eyed realtor inquired:

"How could the people of Sheffield and Tuscumbia be persuaded to go to a Methodist church in Florence?"

"Well, nearly everybody has a motor, the buses are cheap. It is no greater distance than they go to churches in any other large city."

"No, I didn't mean that . . . I mean other denominations."

"That's Dr. Blankenship's point; it will be interdenominational. It will be called All Souls Cathedral, not in any sense that it is a bishop's church, but that it is catholic in its welcome to everyone. Dr. Blankenship feels it will be a great step toward church unity in the South."

Old Bill Bradley drawled:

"That idyah ort to work because the lay members of the ordinary churches don't know exactly what they believe anyway."

The black-eyed man arose with a practical remark:

"The Doctor's cathedral will be the biggest church in the Tri-Cities and will be the most fashionable. If it is, every family in the highly restricted subdivisions will go to it, no matter what its denomination may be—you men know that."

There came assents from up and down the tables.

"The point I'm getting at," said the black-eyed man, "is that the promoters of highly restricted subdivisions ought to contribute more than firms handling ordinary subdivisions."

"You must handle ordinary subdivisions," put in a voice.

"No, it just happens that I handle highly restricted lots. I simply want this business to go through. I think it solves a big problem in Tri-City real estate."

Mr. Brekker arose.

"As your chairman, I will now open the meeting to any sort of motion you gentlemen see fit to offer in regard to the Florence cathedral. I myself have no objections to smaller churches located in the subdivisions I have for sale."

"Neither have I," interrupted Bradley, "but the damned Yankees pouring into this town won't hardly buy a lot within five blocks of a church, especially if they're Yankees with money."

Brekker turned to Jerry.

"That's a fact, and I never could understand why people don't like to live close to churches . . . they're quiet most of the time."

"Mr. Chairman," proposed Mr. Sanborne, "I move that the North Alabama Realtors' Association make a contribution to Dr. Blankenship's cathedral payable in installments through the treasurer of our body. I think that the amount should be determined in a closed meeting of this body in order that the pros and cons may be discussed more thoroughly."

The motion was seconded and carried by acclamation, and Brekker asked for a motion to adjourn.

Jerry raised his voice:

"I wonder if I might have some intimation of actuality, gentlemen, to carry back to Dr. Blankenship?"

"Say five or six thousand," suggested someone.

"The realtors are the most numerous and prosperous group of business men in the Tri-Cities," said Sanborne, "why not make it ten thousand dollars?"

This amount was more than Jerry had hoped, but a ministerial quirk made him suggest that twelve thousand dollars would divide evenly into monthly installments, and it would be beautifully symbolic of the twelve apostles who followed the Master.

Old Bill Bradley called out:

"How about making it one thousand dollars, Jerry, to symbolize the jailer in Antioch who put the apostles in chains . . . that would come cheaper."

The luncheon broke up with everyone pleased with the idea Jerry had advanced. A number of members came to him and congratulated him on his address. As Jerry moved to the door a shabby little man hovered on the outskirts of the group around Jerry and at last caught his eye. The little man had such an urgent look on his face that Jerry veered toward him and extended his hand. Mr. Brekker hastened to introduce the small man as Mr. Marvin Petman.

"I—I was just hoping," stammered the little man, "that I would get a word with you, Dr. Catlin."

The other real estate men scarcely concealed their annoyance with Petman, but they turned Jerry over to him. So the minister parted with the group with many compliments and hat tippings.

Jerry walked with his new host a little way along the wooden piazza of the Modler Hotel.

"And now what can I do for you, Mr. Petman?"

The little man looked at Jerry in visible embarrassment.

"Have you . . . did you ever hear of . . . of Luggy?"

"Luggy?"

"Well," said the realtor apologetically, "I didn't know whether you had or not . . . it's been talked around a good deal."

"No, I haven't."

"Well . . ." Petman paused unhappily, "I'm troubled . . . my wife and I are both troubled about our boy. . . ."

Jerry thought over the troubles natural to a boy: drinking, gambling, women . . .

"How old is your boy?"

"Six."

Jerry revised his guesses to ill health.

"And what's wrong with your son?"

"Well . . . that's it . . . I don't know . . . I'm terrible worried."

"How is he affected?" asked Jerry, worried.

The man moistened his lips and drew a breath.

"Well . . . it's sort of hard to explain. . . . Marvin . . . he's named after me . . . plays in the yard all day long. . . ."

"Then his health's all right," said Jerry, stumped again.

"Oh yes . . . perfect . . . that is, his physical health."

"Oh . . . you mean his mental health," ejaculated Jerry in sympathetic comprehension.

"I don't know," admitted the father; "as I told you, Junior plays all day long in the yard quite contented by himself. One day I asked him why he didn't go over and play with Theodore, and he said he would rather play with Luggy."

"Luggy," repeated Jerry curiously, "who is Luggy?"

"Well," ejaculated Mr. Petman with a slight mechanical laugh, "that was what I didn't know, either. I asked Junior who was Luggy, and he was amazed. He said, 'Why, don't you know Luggy?' I said I didn't. He could hardly believe what I said. Finally he cried out, 'Why, Papa, can't you see him now . . . standing right there? . . . and of course I didn't and couldn't."

At last Jerry understood the trouble.

"He was playing with another child?"

"Yes, he was perfectly sure of it."

"And it was imaginary?"

"That's right, there was nothing at all where he pointed. It took some time before I could understand . . . before I was willing to admit that my little boy thought he could see things where there wasn't anything." Mr. Petman looked at the minister in distress.

"Have you called in your doctor?"

"Yes, he examined him and found nothing wrong. He gave him some sort of test for mental diseases."

"Had you thought of taking him to a psychiatrist?"

"Well, I'd thought of it. . . . I don't suppose there is one this side of Birmingham. The trip would cost money . . . then a specialist's fee on top of that . . . his mother and I tried to convince Junior he didn't see anything."

"But he clung to it?"

"I suppose he could hardly believe us . . . whatever it was seemed right before his eyes."

"Then what did you do?"

"We-ell . . . we finally forbade him to see Luggy or mention his name again."

"I see . . . that may have been the wise thing to do. . . . What happened?"

"The little chap turned white as a sheet. He said aloud, 'Luggy . . . Papa says for you to go away. . . .' Then he followed something off with his eyes, and a minute later he fell down and began to scream, and we couldn't hush him. He won't eat or play or anything . . . I'm afraid he will be really sick."

"Probably if you would give him some mild sedative . . ." suggested Jerry, troubled by the father's trouble.

"I wish you'd come over and see him, Brother Catlin. I want a minister to see him. Somehow I haven't got much confidence in doctors in a case like this."

The thought flickered through Jerry's head how superstitious were uneducated people. Aloud Jerry asked the man where he lived. Petman said in South Sheffield. The two men started for Jerry's borrowed car. A few minutes later Petman asked:

"Do you suppose there could possibly be anything to it, Brother Catlin?"

"No, certainly not," declared Jerry with assurance. "No, there have been a number of cases on record, children playing with imaginary companions . . . they get over it. . . . I don't see that my looking at him will do much good."

"I thought maybe you would pray with me and his mother over Junior; I thought maybe it might help."

"We can try it," agreed Jerry dubiously, "and it might be a good idea to let Junior hear our petitions . . . you know . . . for the psychological effect it would have directly on him."

CHAPTER SEVEN

JERRY CATLIN's visit to the home of Mr. Petman in South
Sheffield put him in an odd mood.

Petman lived in a poor street called Carver's Lane, and
this led onto Grey Mule Hill, which was one of the negro
quarters of the town. Grey Mule Hill was called "hill" not
because it arose in height but because it fell away into a
sluggish swampy creek. Down this decline huddled the negro
shacks. They were not in rows, but were dropped down here
and there, with footpaths winding among the coarse sparse
grass and Canadian thistle that blotched the desolate de-
scent.

The odd reaction which came to Jerry was caused by the
poor white houses along Carver's Lane just before it broke
away down the descent of Grey Mule Hill. It seemed to be
a place where he had been at some undated period of his
life; where he had gone up and down doing works of faith
among the poor. However, this did not give Jerry the usual
shadowy feeling of metempsychosis because he knew the
roots of his impression.

When he had been a schoolboy in Florence, he used to
fancy himself moving among the poor and humble, stopping
at just such houses and praying for and healing the afflicted.
Now, here he had come to Sheffield to ask contributions for
the cathedral and found himself on the salvatory mission
fancied by his adolescent longings.

Through some association of ideas he began telling the
real estate dealer how he came to join the ministry. It had
come upon him, he said, through a flock of crows.

Mr. Petman blinked at his prosperous companion.

"I was standing on a hill in the woods at sunset," explained Jerry, "and these crows came flying past me cawing at each other, and suddenly it seemed to me that the most important thing in all the world was the God who made it. It came upon me that I ought to spend my life making people feel the love and glory of God. . . ."

"But how could crows . . ." marveled Mr. Petman.

"Well, their calls were so lonely . . . flying into the night . . . that they reminded me of people . . . and yet I knew God would preserve the crows . . . and the people, too. I was never so moved by anything in all my life."

Mr. Petman became awed.

"It really must have been a call from God."

"I once thought so," said Jerry in an odd tone, "but it probably wasn't. In the seminary you study about conversions . . . it's a kind of accumulation of religious emotion and a sudden release. You take Paul's conversion. He wasn't an ordinary Jew. He had been subjected to Greek mysticism in Tarsus and the Greek cities in Asia Minor . . . it was a sudden outbreak and flooding of his subconscious . . ." Jerry broke off and drove for several moments in silence, then added, "It was the same with me, of course."

Mr. Petman removed his somewhat faded derby and rubbed his sleeve around it.

"I got in the real estate business in an odd way, too. I always believed I would be a prosperous, influential business man some day. It's really in the Petman blood, Dr. Catlin . . . my folks descended from royalty . . ." the little man hemmed slightly, "or so they always told me."

Jerry picked his motor's path along the nail and can strewn Carver's Lane.

"A number of Southern families think that," he explained gently. "You see the South was pretty well sprinkled with royalists right after the Revolution. The people said they were royalists. Their descendants gradually corrupted the word into 'royalty,' and nearly every Southern person you see nowadays will tell you he is descended from the 'royalty.' My own father held that idea about the Catlins."

"Well, I declare," blurted out Petman, quite taken aback, "maybe that is so . . . well, anyway, the thought that the Petmans were somebody gave me heart to go on with my Jericho idyah."

"What was that?"

"A subdivision for niggers . . . you know, the dependable sort of niggers. . . . I decided I would try to give 'em something really good."

Jerry winced at the idea that he was driving home with a dealer in negro real estate. The two remained silent until they reached the Petman home.

Two women were on the Petman veranda when the car drove up, Mrs. Petman and a Mrs. Swartout, who lived a little further down the lane. Mrs. Swartout was a small woman with a large head, inattentive washed-out eyes, and an expressionless mouth. She acknowledged her introduction to the minister in a complaining tone and immediately afterwards her eyes followed a dog that came sneaking along the lane.

"He's pastor in the Pine Street Methodist Church, Mrs. Swartout," explained Mr. Petman.

"Oh, is he!" exclaimed the little old woman taking interest in Jerry, "then you know my Minnie . . . I mean Aurelia."

"Law, Brother Catlin," interposed Mrs. Petman earnestly, "you ought to hear Aurelia play."

"I suppose he has," said Mrs. Swartout, "she works in his church." Here Mrs. Swartout laughed heartily.

Jerry explained that he really knew nothing of the church as yet, that he had just arrived in Florence.

Here Mr. Petman made it known why he had brought Jerry to his home, and Mrs. Petman went into the yard and called Junior in penetrating tones. When the child finally appeared, the grown-ups prepared themselves for united prayer. The preacher placed his hand on the little boy's motionless but unwilling head and prayed God to remove the hallucination from the child's vision; and he prayed that the little boy might grow up to be a strong, well-balanced, good, and useful man.

As the assistant minister prayed this prayer, a kind of sadness came to him at the contrast between the messiah he had dreamed of becoming back in his adolescent days and the kind of man he really was.

CHAPTER EIGHT

JERRY CATLIN had scarcely finished his odd and perhaps not fully considered prayer when two or three negroes came at a jog-trot along Carver's Lane toward Grey Mule Hill, turning now and then to look back toward Sheffield as they hurried along.

Mrs. Swartout watched them and finally called out:

"What's the matter with you-all, Ludus?"

Ludus turned his black face for a moment toward the porch.

"Nothin', nothin' a-tall, Miss Swartout."

The little woman watched the black men out of sight.

"That ain't so," she said, "something wrong with them niggers."

The Reverend Catlin arose from where he knelt, looked absently after the colored men, and hoped the little boy would recover from his affliction, then bade the family good-bye and went out to his motor. He got in, maneuvered the car around in the narrow lane, and started for Florence. As he drove along by himself, he presently forgot the little boy he had been praying for and began thinking of Sydna Vaiden again, because he had to deliver the car to her home. He wished now that Wilson had stayed with him so he could get out at the parsonage. He was once more passing the Modler Hotel with this in mind when he saw half a dozen men, the last of the luncheon guests, gesticulating urgently at him. He stopped, and one of the men called out tautly:

"Give us a lift, Jerry . . . not another bus for thirty minutes!"

The assistant minister opened his door, and all six crowded in and slammed the door shut after them.

"What's the matter?" asked Jerry, seeing something unusual was happening somewhere.

"Why, the whole Sheffield constabulary has gone over!" cried Sanborne.

"We tried to get 'em to take us," laughed another man, "but of course they were too wise."

"Who could have phoned for them to come over, anyway?" demanded Sanborne in an amazed and disapproving tone.

"The Florence police," said a man named Tergune.

"But they wouldn't really want to stop it!" cried Sanborne.

"No, but they got to put up a show so if this ever comes up before the court . . ."

This discussion snapped back and forth, to the complete bewilderment of Jerry who nevertheless had put on speed in response to their obvious haste. Finally, he asked them again what was happening.

Terhune stared, then gave a short laugh.

"I guess we sounded crazy . . . why, they got six nigger rapists in jail over in Florence."

"Eight," corrected a voice.

"Ten," snapped Sanborne.

A kind of horror trickled through Jerry's chest. He understood now why the negroes had come running out of Sheffield to their homes in Grey Mule Hill. He understood why Wilson, his chauffeur, had deserted him. If Wilson were with him now, the black man would be in the greatest peril. He would have to get out of the car and get home through an excited white population as best he could.

At these disquieting thoughts Jerry involuntarily slowed up his machine. Behind him came protests:

"Hurry up, Jerry!"

"Everything will be over before we get there!"

"Folks in Florence won't wait long, Dr. Catlin!"

Jerry was in a painful predicament. He had seen a lynching in Florence, a triple lynching, and he had no desire to witness a sextuple murder. However, to delay this handful of men for a few minutes would do no good at all. He wondered if he could dissuade them from their purpose.

"Look here, men, we must think twice about this. . . ."

"Watch your road there! Watch out, that damn fool's not going to slow up!"

A car was coming in from a side road at full speed. Jerry barely missed it. The man behind Jerry breathed a nervous apology:

"Excuse my back-seat driving, but I knew he wouldn't stop!"

The car that had cut in ahead of him raced, and Jerry raced too. In fact, a string of cars dashed down the dusty road toward the Florence bridge. Along the side of the road an increasing number of pedestrians held up desperate hands for a hitch into Florence. When Jerry disregarded them, they began running.

A quarter of a mile from the bridge traffic became so thick that everything was slowed down to a snail's pace. People on foot began to pass the motors. A distant din of horns announced to Jerry that he was approaching the bridge. When he finally came into sight of the long narrow bridge it was jammed with vehicles, and every motorist on the bank was honking his hurry. Jerry's car became a unit in the creeping procession.

The men saw the pedestrians were getting along faster than they were and began to talk about getting out and walking. Jerry encouraged them to go, but they remained in the car, hoping for an opening.

The machine now entered the narrow mouth of the covered bridge which sloped down in perspective to an exit about the size of a dime. Through this streamed the honking motors. About a fourth of the way across, Jerry found out what was holding up the traffic. A frightened little man was driving an ancient car against the stream of motors. As Jerry scraped past him the fellow wailed out:

"I didn't know ever'body wanted to get acrost at once!"

"Don't you know there's going to be a lynching in Florence?" yelled Sanborne.

"Yes," wailed the unfortunate driver, "but I kain't turn round on the bridge . . . I'll never git back in time!"

A still greater uproar broke out ahead. Suddenly the jam in front of Jerry performed the almost impossible feat of hurrying. Jerry speeded his own car up to about twelve miles an hour. Voices ahead of him bellowed:

"You-all kain't do this; it's aginst the law!"

"But, hell, they are doing it!" cried someone else.

"Why don't somebody stop 'em? . . . they ain't no steamboat in sight!"

Then ahead of him Jerry saw the draw of the bridge begin slowly to swing around. Everybody near Jerry's car rushed forward shrieking frantically:

"Stop that draw!" . . . "Stop it somebody!" . . . "You kain't open up a government bridge for nothing!" . . .

Every person, however, who succeeded in jumping on the draw dashed to the other end of the turntable and jumped off onto the far end of the bridge. Jerry's car was the last vehicle that made the crossing. He put on speed just behind a driver of a wagon who was lashing his mules. Both vehicles crossed onto the Florence end of the bridge and went on their way. The rest of the crowd had to stop. One man made a jump for it, caught on his belly, and hung on the edge of the draw high above the river until half a dozen hands pulled him to safety.

The crowd on the Sheffield side bellowed their protests:

"This is against the law, you damned bridge tender!" . . . "You kain't open a bridge with no steamboat in sight!" . . . "We'll have you up before the federal court for this, you damn law-breaking skunk!" . . .

The Reverend Jerry Catlin himself had no idea why the

draw in the river bridge had so illogically but so opportunely opened. He did not stop to inquire. The realtors in his car also forgot the incident as they peered forward, trying to see the lynching while still a mile away.

The block on the bridge had somewhat cleared the road of traffic, and now Jerry moved along at a moderate speed.

Amid the general uproar cries began to be heard. Men were shouting, "Boom! Don't stop the boom! Florence is on a boom!"

As Jerry got nearer the center of town these cries sounded all along the thoroughfare:

"Florence is on a boom!" . . . "Don't bust our boom!"

Somebody in the moving throng hallooed back,

"What the hell if it is on a boom?"

And the reply was shouted at once:

"Do you want to give it a black eye with a lynching?"

At that moment a man sprinted alongside of Jerry's car at the risk of his neck and leaped on the running board.

"You men from the Realtors' meeting in Sheffield?" he shouted.

The whole car full of men yelled that they were.

"Go to the fire station down the alley from Intelligence Row. There'll be a guard at the door of the fire house. Just say, 'The Colonel sent for me.'"

The passengers leaned toward the fellow.

"Colonel who?"

"What does the Colonel want?"

Sanborne caught on:

"It must be Colonel Vaiden organizing the lynching. . . . I swear he's an old game cock!"

The man on the running board swung off rather dangerously and leaped on another car.

CHAPTER NINE

A JAM of men poured through the alleyway from Intelligence Row to the county jail. A string of men standing along the sides of the buildings were strangers brought in by the boom, watching Florence move itself aright. Shouts from the crowd already gathered around the jail filled the alley with indistinguishable noises.

"The Colonel" was the goal of Jerry's group. That the Colonel meant to organize the lynching into something directed and effective nobody doubted.

Sure enough, in the alley at the side door of the fire station stood a uniformed fireman, which is to say that he wore his helmet to distinguish him, as that is as far as uniforms went in Florence. Somebody said that the Colonel had sent for them; the guard opened the door a little way, and they all filed inside. As Jerry went in he groped for an argument which he hoped might move his dictatorial old uncle from his purpose.

As Jerry climbed the steps to the upper story of the fire station, he heard a number of voices, and when he actually entered the room he saw a surprising number of business men, all carefully dressed as if for a banquet. Then he perceived that the whole Rotarian Club had been transferred almost to a man from the old Florence Hotel to the upper floor of the fire station.

When Jerry entered, the man nearest him ushered him automatically to his old uncle, who was giving directions in the sharp-edged voice of an old man when he is excited.

"We will all march out in strict ranks, four deep, put your heaviest men in front. Don't give an inch for anybody in your march to the jail . . . walk straight over them! You want them to realize you are iron . . ." he clenched a mottled fist, "nothing can stop you!"

Assents, quick nods, came from the men.

"March right up to the jail door?" asked an excited voice.

"You won't be in the front ranks . . . you just hold your place."

"Yes, sir . . . hold my place."

The talk became general in the selection of the biggest, heaviest men to form the front rank.

Dr. Blankenship offered himself, but Colonel Vaiden lifted a hand with the first suggestion of a smile that had been on his face.

"We'll have the clergy in the center, Doctor, the church in the heart of things."

One of the realtors drew Jerry over by the side of Dr. Blankenship.

"Wish you could have seen this man handle our meeting in Sheffield."

"Did he do well?"

"Well . . . I think he is going to get a thousand a month."

"He's the Colonel's nephew," said the Doctor.

Sanborne was moving around among the Rotarians, measuring himself.

"You stand there," directed the Colonel, pointing out a place for him.

Sanborne got in his position and turned to the next man.

"How did you get Dr. Blankenship into this?"

The man looked at the Bishop.

"Well, you see, he was there, and while he didn't want to go against the town, of course he was opposed to such a thing."

Sanborne looked at his companion sharply.

"Opposed to what?"

"Why, the lynching, of course!"

Sanborne stared, stepped a little away, and asked in a loud voice:

"Look here, is this an anti-lynching crowd?"

Two or three men answered, yes, of course.

Sanborne burst out excitedly:

"Hell and damnation! I thought you men were fixing to march to that jail, get them damned niggers, and swing 'em up!"

Half a dozen voices denied this.

"No, no, we're going to stop it!"

"It won't be popular away from here, Sanborne!"

"Popular, hell, what do we care if it's popular or not?"

"It'll ruin our boom!" cried somebody earnestly. "Hell, Sanborne, we don't get a boom like this but once every ten years!"

"Do you think I'd stand back and see Southern women outraged by niggers on account of a God-damned boom? To hell with the boom!"

Some of the Rotarians made a movement toward Sanborne; others begged:

"Sanborne, for God's sake, be reasonable!"

Old Colonel Vaiden pointed a skinny finger at the recalcitrant.

"Mr. Sanborne, this is a meeting of the Florence Rotary Club. We invited in a few gentlemen whom we hoped would assist us in creating a public sentiment against lynchings in Alabama. If you can't see your way to help us, we respect your decision, but be kind enough not to interrupt our proceedings." The old man made a stiff, courteous bow toward the head of the stairs.

Sanborne looked at the crowd, who stood mutely seconding his dismissal.

"By God, I'm going down and organize every man on the outside against your damned feather-legged bunch!"

"Mr. Sanborne," snapped the Colonel, "Williams and Sanborne has a drawing account at the Second National Bank. Drawing accounts take fright very easily, Mr. Sanborne, and are difficult to tame again."

Several of the Rotarians licked sudden smiles off their

lips. Sanborne went on down the stairs without looking back.

When the luncheon club finally flung open the red double doors of the fire station and marched into the street, the excited leaderless crowd at once misconstrued their purpose. Everyone in sight fell in with this phalanx of well dressed, purposeful business men. They surrounded the marchers, running ahead, waving their arms and shouting for everybody to come on. A number of voices yelled out, "Come on, the police won't shoot into us now!"

The whole street now moved against ten or twelve men wearing police stars who stood spaced before the jail. As the jam drew near, the rabble in front of the Rotarians fell aside and the phalanx marched up to the police, who fell smoothly aside and let them pass to the jail-house steps.

An enormous hurrahing and laughter broke out at this easy entrance past the officers. Miltiades directed his men in quick tones, placing the small men on top of the steps and the large men at the bottom. The crowd viewed this maneuver with growing curiosity. Somebody yelled:

"Have you-all got the keys? Are you goin' to bust in?"

The Colonel made a gesture to Dr. Blankenship who stood on the top step. The Bishop lifted a hand, and one of the mob yelled out:

"Hush! Hush, ever'body, they're goin' to open this lynchin' with prayer!"

The Northern visitors around the edges of the crowd sort of laughed and sort of did not, because they didn't know what they were getting into. The Doctor's voice boomed out:

"Friends, fellow citizens, in this surcharged hour I am going to ask you to act, not for law, not for justice, but in accordance with your own feelings!"

Approving shouts:

"Yeh, yeh, go to it, preacher!"

"What does your best self-interest tell you to do, gentlemen?"

"Hang the niggers!"

"String up the niggers!"

"I can't think so. Ponder this situation! You can summon a grand jury and hang these negroes just as efficiently and far less expensively than you can lynch them now. What will the ten thousand strangers in our gates think of us if we hang six men without legal sanction? Why, we will be the worst advertised town in America! You know that! Every outsider here will write home about it! People pay no attention to reports of lynchings in newspapers, but they certainly will pay attention when their own folks write home and say they saw one! They'll be shocked! America will be shocked! We can't afford to do this!"

An uproar broke out when the street really caught the speaker's drift:

"Hey, shut up! Cut it out! Move away and let good men up there!"

"Gentlemen! Gentlemen! You can't afford to sacrifice this wave of prosperity we are enjoying to snuff out the lives of six insignificant negroes!"

Hoots, catcalls.

"By God, preacher, are you willing to let our women be raped to keep up the price of your damned city lots?"

At this the whole crowd surged forward when there came the crash of pistol fire. The police had shot into the air. During the pause that followed, old Colonel Vaiden climbed to the second step and shook a thin fist in the air.

"Clear out of here, everybody! Get on home with you! I have men here taking the names of every man in this crowd! If you don't clear out at once, I'll have every man-jack here hauled up before the grand jury for mob violence! Get out! Be gone!"

The crowd nearest the jail wavered. A few men turned and began to sift back through the mob. Somebody yelled:

"We got a right to stand in a public street!" The old man pointed his finger at the speaker.

"I know you, Tom Stegall! Know your face, know your voice. Do you want me to indict you?"

"I'd be turned loose!"

"I know you would, but, by God, you'd pay a lawyer fifty dollars to get you loose. Have you got fifty dollars to spend on a lawyer?"

"No, by geemeny, I haven't," said Tom.

"Neither have we business men got hundreds of thousands of dollars to spend on six damned little niggers, especially when they are sure to be hung anyway! What's the idea, all of you men paying fifty dollars apiece; all of us business men paying thousands of dollars to hang six niggers who will be hung for nothing if we'll just wait! Now, go on back home, men! By the Eternal, you'll catch it if you don't! Your lawyers' bills will bust you!"

More men began backing away. Then from the outskirts of the crowd arose yells of:

"King Cotton! Who set you up to rule, King Cotton? Hey, towboat cotton! If you are so law-abidin', Milt Vaiden, why don't you pay the Handbacks for the cotton you stole from 'em, you damn doddering old cotton thief?"

One of these shouted insults snapped off suddenly. There came the sounds of blows and struggles. Over between the jail and the fire station the crowd began yelling, "Fight! Fight!" The attention of the mob swung to the fisticuffs, and the threat of jail delivery was off for that day.

CHAPTER TEN

THE street fight which had broken out among the hecklers of Colonel Miltiades Vaiden had been started by a big red-headed youth who had a girl in his care.

The phrase "in his care" is perhaps misleading because, precisely, she stood in the loop of his big arm. It was only thus that the red-headed lad could protect the girl from being shoved and mashed. The two stood against the red wall of the fire station, wrought up to a high pitch of excitement at what was about to take place, when suddenly Dr. Blankenship and the Colonel began to speak against the lynching just when it seemed on the verge of accomplishment. It was a most painful let-down. While neither Red McLaughlin nor Marsan Vaiden expected anything but horror, such an abrupt withdrawal of the spectacle filled them with frustration. Marsan was thoroughly exasperated by her father.

What filled Red McLaughlin with irony was for a doddering old rascal whose thievery virtually had murdered old man John Handback to come out like this and hypocritically defend six negro rapists who deserved death. Such hypocrisy! Such scapegracefulness!

Red was just drawing in his breath to shout scurrility at the two-faced old devil when quite near him a man bawled out,

"King Cotton! Towboat cotton!" Others took up the abuse: "You damned old thief, pay back what you stole from Lucius Handback!"

Then Red felt Marsan move in his arm. She twisted about, faced him, and pressed her face against his shoulder, cried out, "Red, make 'em hush!" and began sobbing.

On his football team, Red McLaughlin played center. Now he loosed himself from Marsan, made two or three swift yards through the crowd without the aid of interference, and swung at the jaw of a shouter. The fellow dropped as if he had been struck by a pile driver. Red swung on another man, and the fight had started.

The crowd turned on Red, hitting at him and demanding to know what in the hell he meant, when the big fellow flung an arm desperately toward the girl and shouted:

"Don't you see her, you damn fools! Yelling about her daddy to her face! Damn pups, haven't you got no respect for a lady?"

With this lack of courtesy pointed out, the fight quieted as swiftly as it had sprung up.

The man on the ground got up with his hand on his jaw and began slobbering out a kind of apology:

"I didn't see her . . . what she doing here?"

"She's got as much right on the street as you have!" flared Red, speaking the co-educational language of the high school.

The man with the cracked jaw did not continue the debate. Red made his way back to Marsan.

"You can stand here as long as you want to, and if any of these babies get fresh . . ."

"Oh, Red, I don't want to stay, I want to go home."

"Well . . . all right. . . ." He looked around him, at the crowd now scattering under the threats of the Colonel, then added, "I don't believe we're going to have any excitement here anyway . . . your dad put the skids under that."

Marsan and her escort made their way through the alley toward Intelligence Row, to the distinct relief of the crowd around them.

A number of other persons were also leaving the scene. They moved through the alley, giving voice to all sorts of opinions:

"Let 'em live to boost the price of real estate!" . . .

"Simply means turning the black skunks aloose to repeat their act!"

A sharp Northern voice asked:

"Why do you say that? Wouldn't a fair trial . . ."

"Fair trial?" snapped the Southerner. "What the hell are you talking about? . . . Some damn lawyer will string out their case for a year. . . . Is it any different where you come from?"

"No, no, it isn't," clicked the Northern voice. "In Ohio we say, 'Kill a cow and go to jail; kill a man and go free.'"

"How would you Ohioans feel if it wasn't killing a man, if it was an assault on your wives and sisters? . . . Would you-all risk that in the hands of the law?"

Red McLaughlin squeezed Marsan's arm, leaned down, and whispered:

"Say . . . look . . . I know that man talking to that Yankee . . . it's Bodine."

Marsan had composed herself sufficiently to ask:

"Who's he?"

"Jeerusalem, Marsan, not to know about Bodine, why, he's the high grand guyescutis of his association!"

At this point, however, the importance of Mr. Bodine was dismissed because Marsan caught sight of the Reverend Jerry Catlin in the crowd flowing into Intelligence Row. She seized Red's hand and began pulling him along, calling Jerry's name.

When she caught up with her cousin, Jerry was shocked that a girl should be in such a place. Marsan began defending herself. The family car was gone, and she had had to walk from school. She couldn't help it if people staged a lynching in her road. Besides that, she had found Red in the crowd, who had taken charge of her and kept her out of trouble.

"She's a game sport!" declared Red, his red-brown eyes glinting with admiration.

"She's been crying," said Jerry looking closely at his pretty cousin.

"Oh, there was a little rough talk," nodded Red casually, "but it passed off."

"Red knocked one of them down," said Marsan, determined to give honor where honor was due.

The Reverend Catlin was not so favorably impressed.

"That is what came of my taking your car!" he cried in self-reproach. "I should have sent Wilson home with the car. . . . Come on, it's right up yonder under the third mulberry, and, Marsan, you drive home at once and show yourself to your mother!"

"Shall I telephone?" asked the girl.

"No, we'll be there in four or five minutes."

The three hurried on and got into the car. Jerry surrendered the keys to Marsan and climbed into the back seat, while Marsan allowed Red to drive.

The car backed out with Red honking and shouting:

"Hey, step aside there, brother, let us out, will you?"

His voice was good-tempered, and he was more or less careless about hitting anyone who failed to heed his warning. When he started forward he immediately put on speed and shot northward, veering here and there to dodge the pedestrians who were swarming across Courthouse Square.

"Like running through a broken field," called the football star.

Marsan saw that Jerry was holding to the side of the car in exquisite discomfort at the rate they were going and the narrow squeaks they were having.

This amused her, because she knew that Red was a safe driver, and it made her feel a little sorry for her cousin, too. She called to Red and wanted to know what he was driving so fast for. Red shouted back quite seriously:

"Because all the speed cops are still down at the jail."

CHAPTER ELEVEN

ONCE out of Courthouse Square the powerful Vaiden car made a prolonged "wh-s-s-h" and arrived at the parsonage. When the Reverend Jerry Catlin got out at the low-placed house, Red McLaughlin and Marsan were far too excited to drive into the Vaiden garage and end their day. They continued by common consent along the street, the rush of the machine keeping pace with the leap of their nerves and soothing them with the balm of speed. Now that the minister was gone, they began talking excitedly about what had just happened:

"I'm surprised at the Rotarians, I thought they were going to take the niggers out and hang 'em. . . ."

"So did I, Red," agreed Marsan with a shiver.

"Everybody did."

"Still, I'm glad they didn't," said Marsan, "although I certainly would have had something to tell Lizzie and Sarah May."

"Pshaw . . . tell Lizzie and Sarah May . . . I don't tell anything to anybody."

"Well, that's right."

"And it's just like Bodine said, who knows how a trial will come out?"

"They guaranteed a swift trial and certain execution."

"Yes, but they're not the court. And if these niggers get off, why, all the niggers'll break loose, and what woman will be safe?"

Marsan thought of the quiet gentle Wilson who worked at her father's house, but following the trend of public sentiment at that moment said that she supposed they would.

"By jiggers," said the hobbledehoy, "Bodine's got the idyah. Bodine was sure putting it up to that Yankee. . . . I wonder what he's saying now?"

"Why . . . I don't know," said Marsan.

"Of course you don't," agreed Red. He slowed down the motor and turned to the girl, "By George, I'm a good mind to go and see."

"Go and see what?"

"What Bodine says."

"Where'll you go?"

"I know where to go."

"Red, what are you talking about?"

Red blinked his eyes.

"Maybe I oughtn't to have said anything before you."

Marsan was beside herself.

"Red McLaughlin, for heaven's sake, are you one of . . ."

A queer eerie feeling came over Marsan.

"Listen, Marsan, do you mind if we turn around and find Bodine and see if he wants anything?"

"What could he need?"

"Oh, there's no telling . . . a messenger maybe . . . let's go see!"

"A messenger to who-o-o?"

"Look here," the youth nodded his red head earnestly, "you know the real reason those fellows backed away from that jail . . . it was because ever'body knew 'em."

"Yes, I suppose it was."

"Well, suppose a big gang of men nobody knew should come to the jail and order the niggers out . . . nobody could skeer them, could they?"

Marsan caught her breath.

"You think Bodine will send you after these men?"

"Thought I'd see."

"Red McLaughlin, do you belong to his association?"

"Now, Marsan, you can't ask me questions like that. . . . Shall we go back and see what he says?"

"Oh, yes, le's do."

As the football star turned the car and started his return dash, it amazed Marsan to think that she had worked in the laboratory with a member of the mysterious and powerful secret society and had never once suspected it. What a chivalric fellow Red was. No wonder he had defended her when he belonged to a kind of knights of the round table sworn to protect Southern womanhood. Her whole chest and torso grew soft toward Red. He had fought for her; he was so big and strong; knocking her father's insulters down.

The car retraced its course to Courthouse Square and stopped in front of the old Florence Hotel once more. Red asked Marsan to wait for him, climbed out, and went in. Once inside, he went up to the clerk's desk with a scattering of other somewhat furtive men and asked could he be shown to room number twenty-seven.

Godfrey, the room clerk, nodded to old Andy, the porter, and indicated to him that here was another man wanting to visit number twenty-seven.

Old Andy motioned mysteriously for Red to follow him and tiptoed off on his flat canvas slippers, now and then rolling his eyes about to see if Red were following.

The old negro's pantomime was very secretive, because Mr. Bodine's visitors were very secretive, and incidentally the fat and ancient porter had discovered the more eye-rolling and tiptoeing he could throw into his ushering, the bigger the tip he could expect.

When the door of number twenty-seven closed on Mr. Red McLaughlin, what occurred could never be guessed, but some twenty minutes later that young man reappeared at the door of the Vaiden car in a high state of excitement.

"Listen, Marsan," he whispered, "I told somebody I had a car and could take a message. . . . I can, can't I, Marsan?"

"Take a message . . . where?"

"To Huntsville."

"When?"

"Right now."

"Why, Red!"

"We can get over there in two hours in your car . . . paved road . . . besides, Marsan, I promised."

"I didn't say we couldn't go, I'm just surprised."

"I say, Marsan, that's a sport."

"Oh, that's nothing, look at all you did for me."

"Oh, that's nothing, that isn't a tenth of what I'd do for you if I got the chance."

While he was saying this Red started the car around the Square at a moderate pace, because the speed cops had returned from the jail and could be seen in the last light of sunset.

When Red was outside the city limits, headed east, the drone of the Vaiden car mounted to a high querulous whine. A hurricane of wind clutched at but lost the smooth stream-lined body of the flying sedan.

Marsan held to the arm rest, watching blank walls of trees and flashes of field fly past. Occasional streaks of fire marked the windows of farmhouses.

"Didn't know you were such a good driver," she gasped.

"Oh, this isn't fast."

"Hope we don't have a blow-out."

"Be too bad, wouldn't it?"

"Isn't it thrilly, going like this on such an errand?"

"Ye-es . . . it is, the first time you go."

"Red, you don't mean you do this often!"

"Saying nothing, Marsan . . . saying nothing."

His secretiveness impressed her.

"Red, what does your society do, anyway . . . what's its object?"

"We're against niggers, Catholics, and Jews," catalogued Red with intensity, "and just anything un-American."

"What is something un-American?"

"Why, you know, Marsan . . . just anything that is not American."

"Well . . . aren't lynchings un-American?"

Red was surprised.

"Marsan, what's eating you? Don't you know lynchings don't occur anywhere except in America?"

The zooming car slowed down now and then to pass through villages. Once, where the highway paralleled a railroad, the speedster crept past the flame-spouting length of the Chattanooga Flyer. An hour later the motor drew up in the outskirts of Huntsville. Red left his car at a filling station and inquired an address Bodine had given him and set off for it alone.

As Marsan waited for him, filled with the tingle of her ride and Red's mysterious mission, she had the car refueled with her courtesy card. Presently Red appeared, coming back up the street at a run. He climbed into the driver's seat and panted out, "Is everything oke?" meaning had Marsan bought gasoline and oil.

"Sure, sure, get in . . . are we still in a hurry?"

"Want to get back by eleven forty-five . . . what time is it now?"

The garage man answered that it was nine-fifteen.

"Nine . . . ten . . . eleven," counted Red aloud, to see how much time they had.

For the next fifty minutes their return was as hurried as their coming. Marsan was wrought up now at what the rest of the night would hold for her . . . a gathering of strange men from all over North Alabama to reinforce the fumbling hands of the law. There could be no threat now of reporting anyone to the grand jury . . . a swirl of unknown men from everywhere accomplishing their duty as patriotic Alabamians and vanishing into space.

Marsan remembered that her father had formed one of the original secret societies right after the Civil War, and now here were she and Red, carrying on. Her cousin Jerry Catlin flickered into and out of her mind, then Red knocking down the man who had called her father a thief. . . .

A waving of lights ahead puzzled and disturbed the motorists. Red dashed toward the signals with a wailing brake. Then Marsan saw a truck standing across the road.

Red said to Marsan:

"Look here, if they try to take your rings, I'm going to paste em'!"

And Marsan cried:

"No, you don't, they might shoot you. Let my rings go!"

As the car halted, a speed cop came to the door.

"Where do you people live?" he asked in the unhurried drawl of the South.

"Florence," said Marsan.

"That's right," called a second man, "their car has a Lauderdale license number."

"We haven't been speeding," said Red a little apprehensively.

"Certainly not," agreed the officer good-humoredly, "the minute any car stops it hasn't been speeding, that's what makes 'em so hot."

The second man called out to the men on the truck:

"All right, fellows, let 'em by."

The truck chortled and moved aside a few feet.

"What's the big idea?" asked Red curiously, seeing that he was not to be picked up for speeding.

"Why, there's talk around town of a mob coming into Florence tonight. Guards have been put out on all the roads to stop all out-of-town cars and turn 'em back."

"I see," said Red with a sinking of the heart.

"Yeh," drawled the guard, "personally I'd go in with anybody who wanted to string up them six black devils in the Florence jail, but as I said to my wife at supper, 'I draw twenty-two a week from the state, and if I throwed up my job ever' time some nigger needed lynchin' I'd be out of work dang near all the time.'"

As the car eased past the truck the two motorists were dumbfounded.

"The idea of a Southern man saying what that guard said!" ejaculated Marsan.

"He's a man not trying to uphold what he knows is American and right," pointed out Red.

"That's right . . . still I'd hate to watch anything done to the niggers myself."

"Sure . . . you're a girl. I thought to myself this afternoon when they actually got the niggers out, I'd take you home."

"Why, Red, you wouldn't have done it!"

"I might not have done it, but I sure thought of it."

"Red, you certainly have got higher principles that I thought."

"Why, I belong to Bodine's society, I have to protect women, I swore to."

Marsan rode forward, much more slowly now, with a thrill of satisfaction in her escort. There was a chivalry about Red. . . . At that moment he turned to her.

"Say, I got an idyah, let's take the back track, get pretty close to that truck, and park!"

"What for?"

"So if any Huntsville fellows do come along and get stopped, I can tell 'em to walk around the truck, get into this car, and we'll drive 'em on into Florence."

"You could do that," agreed Marsan, beginning to see that Red was not so slow-witted as she had always thought.

Red turned the car once more, cut out his lights, and moved silently along the pale ribbon of the road. When he saw the light of the truck ahead, he drove to one side of the road and stopped.

"You suppose the other messengers will do this?" whispered Marsan.

"They will if they think of it."

"That's the point, thinking of it."

With the lights off and the engine motionless, the two sat in the cold spring-scented darkness of the surrounding woods. The only sound they heard was a faint regular clicking under the hood of the car as the metal cooled.

"I wonder when they'll come?" whispered Marsan.

"Soon, I imagine, they're supposed to be there by eleven forty-five."

They sat waiting, gazing at the lights of the truck.

"Hadn't you better go up there and be ready to tell them?"

"No, I'll have time enough . . . they'll chew the rag with the cops."

"Yes . . . I guess they will."

They sat in silence for a number of minutes. The clicking in the engine hushed. The silence, the darkness, and the chill green smells brought an odd feeling over Red. He moved restlessly, stretched his arm along the back of the seat; when it touched Marsan's shoulders he said:

"Excuse me."

"Oh, the idea . . . after all you've done."

The hobbledehoy sat silent a little longer. A faint internal trembling set up inside of him.

"Well . . . I made you mad, today, Marsan . . . in the biology class."

"Well . . . I didn't know then what kind of a man you were, Red . . . working with you two years . . . and . . . and didn't know you at all," explained the girl a little unsteadily.

Red felt his heart beating against his ribs. He swallowed with a dry feeling in his throat. His thick arm now lay on the girl's shoulder, his hand hung down, barely touching her arm.

At that moment Marsan said:

"Oh . . . look . . . is that a fire?"

Red looked, and automatically encircled her with his arm, as if that had been part of looking.

"Do you suppose it's the fiery cross?" he whispered, awestruck.

The girl shrank closer in his arms.

"Oh, Red, if it is?"

"I'd have to go to it," whispered Red.

"And leave me?"

"Well . . . I don't know . . . I . . . I'd have to protect you, too. . . ."

They stared at the growing illumination fixedly. A huge red arc defined itself behind the distant trees. It was the rising moon.

Profound relief flooded the two watchers that Red did not have to go. The overgrown youth leaned down and touched his lips to the girl's cheek. She did not move. His big fingers moved shakingly along her arms to the mounds he had so long and so tantalizingly glimpsed in the biology class. Marsan pushed faintly at the hairy hands upon her heavy bosom. She made an effort to stop her own voluptuous excitement. She pushed hard and tried to jerk away. Red lifted her from the seat, with a free arm shoved the cushions into a new position. Marsan pushed ineffectually at his chest. She gasped out:

"Red! Red! Please . . ." then suddenly stopped struggling.

With shaking hands Red sought his consummation with the animal innocence of a bear.

CHAPTER TWELVE

O<small>N THE</small> following morning newsboys flung onto the lawns of the well-to-do copies of the *Florence Index* flaunting the headlines:

LAW AND ORDER REIGN IN THE TRI-CITIES.

B<small>USINESS</small> M<small>EN</small> <small>OF</small> F<small>LORENCE</small> S<small>UPPRESS</small> V<small>IOLENCE</small> <small>AND</small> Q<small>UIET</small> C<small>OMMOTION</small>

Personal Bravery of Colonel Miltiades Vaiden Noteworthy.

T<small>HOUSANDS</small> <small>OF</small> <small>VISITORS</small> <small>DRAWN</small> <small>TO</small> <small>FLORENCE</small> <small>BY</small> <small>BOOM</small> <small>CONVINCED</small> <small>OF</small> <small>COMPLETE</small> <small>LAW-ABIDING</small> <small>CHARACTER</small> <small>OF</small> <small>COMING</small> <small>METROPOLIS</small> <small>OF</small> <small>THE</small> <small>SOUTH</small>

On the fourth page of the paper the leading editorial read:

"The *Florence Index* in no shape or form condones the crime charged against the six negroes now in the Lauderdale County jail. In advocating that these miscreants be brought to a formal trial, we are simply upholding the dignity of the law and the best sentiments of our community. The *Index* believes that a great forward step was taken by the citizens of Florence in law enforcement. To the thousands of visitors from the North who are in our city to build homes and establish industries, the *Index* wishes to point out that they have settled in a municipality where law and order are supreme and all attempts at violence are sternly suppressed."

The Birmingham and Memphis papers were also scattered along with the *Index*, and these metropolitan papers passed the matter off with a brief:

FLORENCE LYNCHING NARROWLY AVERTED
NIGHT RIDERS KEEP POLICE ON THE HOP
Situation Still Shaky.

Among the thousands of Florentines who read these accounts was Mr. J. Adlee Petrie, who boarded with a Miss Waner down on Tombigbee Street.

Mr. Petrie was interested in the account of Colonel Miltiades Vaiden's heroism for a peculiar reason. He was thinking that the old banker had once been a thief, and now he really was a law enforcer, and he wondered what part of the Colonel's character was discovered in Marsan. That, of course, was a very hazy point. Who knew anything about heredity? Still, there was a forthright intelligence about Marsan, a penetration about her which evidently she had inherited from her father. So now he looked at the papers and stood thinking of the girl in a pleasant kind of reverie.

After a while he stopped this line of thought and turned to the real estate news. After some search he found that a certain lot which he could have purchased a few days ago for three hundred dollars had sold for twelve hundred dollars. He lowered his paper with a faintly sick feeling at the nine hundred dollars he might have had. Then he looked through the advertisements and chose two more lots which he believed would advance. That was what the boom meant to Petrie, a forecasting of rises in real estate.

There was still another man scanning the papers, and this was the Reverend Jerry Catlin, at the parsonage. Jerry noted the paper was given over to the two topics, the boom and the attempted lynching, and it struck Jerry there was a peculiar similarity about the two; both were short cuts to powerfully desired ends, and both were questionable.

Another feature in common was that they disturbed Jerry's mind so that he could not properly attend to his morning devotions. His mind twitched away from his prayers, and from his meditation on God.

A negro's voice calling Jerry's name in a low tone caused the assistant minister to look around. A chocolate-colored man was standing inside the fence of the parsonage garden.

"Mistuh Catlin," he said, "I want to 'pologize fuh leavin' you yestiddy, but . . . but I got called away."

"That was all right," said Jerry.

"Yes suh . . . you foun' de ca' all right?"

"Oh yes, I found it all right."

"Yes suh . . . dat's good . . . you haven't seed Col'l Milt dis mawn'in', has you?"

"No, I haven't."

"I don't s'pose you know anything about Jericho?"

"You mean the one in the Bible?"

"No suh . . . Mistuh Petman's Jericho."

"What do you want to know about Petman's Jericho?"

"Well . . . would you think hit was a good inves'ment? . . . Mistuh Petman, he say evahthing boun' to go up."

Jerry smiled faintly.

"I don't think I would invest."

"Wouldn't you aftah you heard what Mr. Petman say?"

"Well, maybe I would, but I haven't heard it. There is another thing I never heard of, that is negro property going up. Did you ever know negro property to go up?"

"No suh, I nevah did. Nigger proputy go down, but Mistah Petman, he say she boun' to go up some day."

"It may do it . . . but it never has."

Wilson stood by the palings for a moment, finally he said:

"They's another reason fuh buyin' a lot in Jericho."

"What's that?"

"Mistuh Petman say he gwi' donate a great big lot right in the middle of Jericho fuh to build a colored chu'ch an' a Benevolent Hall. You could jes' step out o' yo' house right into de chu'ch. That sho' would save walkin'."

Jerry agreed to this and stood thinking of Wilson as he took himself off in the direction of the Vaiden manor.

When the negro was out of sight of the parsonage his cheerful expression dropped from him like a mask. He moved along with a gloomy face, thinking of the negroes who had so narrowly escaped lynching, and of the precarious position of all the other negroes in town.

"These white fo'ks don' know who dey is foolin' wid," he mumbled aloud to himself. "Dey sho' don' have no idee."

He was thinking of a meeting of the Princes and Potentates of Ethiopia which he had attended the preceding evening. This was an organization directed toward the upbuilding of negro morale. An educated negro had lectured to the Princes and Potentates of the great negro kingdoms in Africa, and his hearers, so the lecturer had said, were descended from these great black statesmen and warriors. That is why Wilson walked along muttering to himself that the white folks didn't know who they were fooling with.

When Wilson came in sight of the manor, he saw a white-headed old man walk out on the lawn and stoop for his morning papers.

The negro hallooed for the Colonel to wait a minute, he would come and pick up the papers.

The Colonel, however, picked up the papers himself and then called out:

"Do you know where Marsan was yesterday evening, Wilson?"

"No suh, I don' know. . . . Why, Col'l Milt?"

"Nothing. Take that dandelion to the kitchen range and burn it . . . don't let its seed float off here in the spring . . . you'll never quit digging dandelions!"

"No suh, I won't," said Wilson, cupping his hands.

A comely woman with handsome white hair and remarkable eyes came out on the veranda and stood near one of the stone columns.

"Good-morning, Milt, telephone for you."

"This time of day?"

"It's from Brekker . . . he says ask you what lawyer you would suggest."

"Lawyer," repeated the old Colonel thoughtfully, "lawyer . . . I've got to think that over . . . have Mary telephone him we'll talk that over in the bank."

The dark-eyed old lady went to the door and repeated the message to someone inside.

"When did Marsan come in last night, Drusilla?" asked Miltiades.

The old lady paused to look at the old man curiously.

"When did she come in? . . . Why, I haven't the faintest idea . . . why?"

Miltiades frowned and shook his head.

"I had a bad dream about her. . . . I don't know when I have dreamed about anyone before."

Drusilla laughed.

"Well . . . are you getting superstitious?"

"You can call it superstition, but my mother dreamed of my brother Polycarp's death at the very hour he was killed," answered the old man soberly.

"Yes, and just think how many dreams she dreamed without a speck of truth to them."

The Colonel did not continue the discussion with his mother-in-law, who was several years younger than he was. He did not feel that Drusilla was in a position to criticize the beliefs of the Vaidens. Before the war the Lacefields (that was Drusilla's maiden name) were a wealthy family, and the Vaidens were poor, but the Lacefields had gone down, and the Vaidens had gone up. This rise had an odd retroactive effect in the Colonel's mind. It made all the Vaidens of more consequence and worth than the Lacefields, because the Vaidens finally had outstripped Drusilla's family. It showed that the Vaiden family had "bottom" to them and the Lacefields had not. That was why it was improper for Drusilla to criticize a Vaiden belief.

The Colonel's wife, Sydna, came out on the porch and

asked if Miltiades had slept well; then she asked why Wilson had not been at his work yesterday afternoon. Finally she asked if Miltiades had seen Jerry Catlin yet and what he looked like.

As the old banker kissed his wife on the cheek he inquired if Marsan were up yet.

"She ought to be if she isn't. . . . Mary!" she called, "wake Marsan and tell her she just has time for school."

"Miltiades is uneasy about Marsan because he had a bad dream about her," smiled Drusilla.

"There she goes again," thought Miltiades, "a Lacefield laughing at the Vaidens . . . and look where we are now."

CHAPTER THIRTEEN

AFTER breakfast that morning Wilson took the larger car
to deliver Colonel Vaiden to the Second National Bank
and Marsan to the High School.

As the car sighed faintly in first gear and then moved
in silence down the driveway into Pine Street, the Colonel
looked covertly at his daughter's face, trying to read there
the explanation of his vivid and disquieting dream. The girl
rode along with her fingers plucking faintly at the cushioned
arm rests and her blue eyes fixed on nothing. What she was
thinking, the Colonel did not know and could not ask.
Marsan was a Vaiden, and the Vaidens were a talkative
lively folk up to the point where they were serious or hurt
or disappointed, and then they became silent, inaccessible
behind the curtains of their Vaiden souls.

Now Marsan recalled to the Colonel his sister Marcia,
Jerry's mother. On the eve of Marcia's proposed marriage
to A. Gray Lacefield, Drusilla's brother, she had come to him
troubled and overwrought, longing to place her difficulty
before him, but in the end she had said nothing. Now the old
Colonel wondered, almost to physical sickness, if Marsan
wanted to tell him some trouble in her heart.

Wilson slid back the glass panel and asked the Colonel
if he wanted to stop by the cathedral; the banker nodded
and continued his solicitous musing over Marsan.

The Colonel always drove by the cathedral. He had con-
tributed heavily to its building, and he meant eventually
to have his tomb in one of its chapels. He liked to pause
mornings as he drove to the bank, look at the deep yellow
excavation, and build up in fancy the domed and columned

beauty of the marble edifice that was eventually to house
his bones and illustrate his name. It would be, the Colonel
felt, a continuation of his position and prestige, a kind of
shadowy survival of himself, when finally he slept beneath
its stones.

On this particular morning, however, he did not mean to
indulge in the solemn pomp of his usual reverie; he hoped,
by keeping Marsan with him a few minutes longer, she
might decide to tell him what troubled her.

When the car stopped and the two sat looking at the ex-
cavation, a possible solution of his daughter's mood occurred
to Miltiades.

"By the way, Wilson wasn't in this car yesterday after-
noon, was he?"

"No, Cousin Jerry had it," said the girl absently.

"Did Jerry drive around to bring you home, Marsan?"

"No, I walked to town."

The Colonel waited a moment, then asked uneasily,

"When you came through town, had . . . had the crowd
collected around the jail?"

"Yes."

"You didn't stop, I hope, Marsan."

"Yes, I did, I never had seen a mob."

Miltiades shook his lean head regretfully and sadly. He
had now come by the explanation of his daughter's bleak, un-
happy mood. She had heard the crowd boo him and call him
a thief; she had heard the old libel of the Handback cotton
bandied about among the stinking riffraff of the mob.

A faint touch of impatience went through Miltiades that
Marsan should allow such scurrility to affect her. It had been
to him, for years, a kind of bitter tonic upon which he throve,
but of late years it had degenerated, so he told himself, into
a sweetish sickly admiration and respect of nincompoops
for a man they did not understand. He wished Marsan could
be like him, but of course she was a girl, a sweet innocent
flower, a bluebell, who, one distant day, would kneel by his

tomb in this cathedral and lift his name to God on the incense of her love and purity.

When the Colonel finally directed his chauffeur to proceed, Marsan added through the open panel:

"Take us around by Tombigbee Street, Wilson," and she added to her father, "I have some friends I thought I might pick up on the way to school."

As the colored man turned across town at the next corner, Marsan began thinking just how she would invite Mr. Petrie for a ride if she should find him. And, when she had invited him, and they were together in the car after her father got out at the bank, what would she say then? These nebulous conversational problems screened for Marsan the real reason why she was driving around by Tombigbee Street at all. In her heart she wanted to know just what Mr. Petrie would think of her intimacy with Red McLaughlin on the preceding evening. He would surely condemn it, but why would he condemn it? There were no religious grounds. Sexual desire was normal and unless gratified became an obsession and affected the mind . . . but it seemed to Marsan, after she had gratified it, it still was an obsession, because she thought about it constantly with doubtful, half-regretful thoughts. She had an almost hungry desire to spread all this before Mr. Petrie and see what he thought about it. . . . Still, there was no way whatever for her to get all this said.

She rode along, staring into the streets that grew poorer and shabbier the further they went across town.

She decided she could arrive at Mr. Petrie's opinion by making it general . . . what did he think of girls who "put out" to boys? . . . that was the school euphemism for the act. There were some girls who did and some who didn't. What did he think of the girls who did?

As long as Marsan had abstained, she had required no theorizing on the matter; the givings of sex seemed not to pertain to her, but now she did want to tell Mr. Petrie what she had done. She wanted to question the one person who she thought might understand and make rational the riddle of sexual conduct, with which, as far as she knew, every pupil in the High School struggled beneath the surface of convention.

Marsan kept a nervous lookout for Mr. Petrie all the way down Tombigbee Street but saw nothing of him. Either he had gone on to school or had not yet come out of his boarding house. If the latter, she was on no such terms of intimacy with her science teacher as to stop and call for him.

When Wilson finally turned north into Courthouse Square and delivered the Colonel at the door of the Second National Bank, Marsan drew a long breath and gave up hope of seeing Mr. Petrie. She thought momentarily of Jerry Catlin, her cousin, as a possible substitute for the scientist, but the notion died a-borning. She gave up the hope of moral peace and intelligence which she sought in her imagined confessor.

CHAPTER FOURTEEN

THE Reverend Jerry Catlin, who appeared and vanished on the surface of Marsan's thoughts in a manner somewhat ironic, if one considers his calling, was at the time sitting in the low-placed parsonage talking to Dr. Blankenship. They were discussing the financial possibilities of the cathedral fund, a topic close to Dr. Blankenship's heart. In this talk the Doctor was developing the idea of Sunday schools. He believed Jerry could organize all the Sunday schools in North Alabama to finance a "Children's Arch" in the nave of the cathedral. The precise point which interested the Doctor was this: Would it be better to have each Sunday school contribute as a whole, or contribute class by class?

"What difference would it make?" asked Jerry.

"I want your ideas on it, I already know my own," smiled the Doctor in his warm, pleasant baritone.

Jerry had no ideas, but as assistant minister it was incumbent upon him to start a sentence, so he began:

"To keep a record of each class would mean a lot of book work."

"Which plan do you think would bring the most money to the fund?"

"Classes, probably."

"Why?"

"Well, there would be emulation among the classes of the same school and among the same classes in different schools. We could send around reports to all the schools what each school was doing."

"Would we make enough extra money to pay for the bookkeeping and the notifications?"

"I believe Miss Chisem could arrange a card-index system to take care of the various classes almost as easily as she could take care of the schools as units."

"Thank you very much, Jerry, that agrees with my analysis. I wish you would work out the details with Miss Chisem."

The Doctor's study was filled in an orderly way with reminders of the projected cathedral. Over his desk was an architect's picture of the finished cathedral. What were called "cathedral cards" were stacked on the Doctor's table with plans of the different floors, showing the location of restaurants, kitchens, cold storage, game rooms, library, children's library, moving-picture room, basket-ball court, gymnasium, running track, laundry, billiard room, lecture rooms, and, of course, on the first floor, the main auditorium and chapels. On the second, third, and fourth floors, additional auditoriums equipped with loudspeakers were designed to accommodate overflow congregations.

"It is very fully equipped," observed Jerry, looking at one of the cards.

"It is designed to minister to the Body, Brain, and Soul," quoted the Doctor automatically.

"I wonder if that could possibly lead to any confusion of function?" pondered Jerry.

The Doctor smiled.

"That is precisely what your uncle said. The idea must run in your family, and oddly enough the cathedral obtained all these modern ramifications by trading on you."

"Me!"

"Yes, your uncle wanted the old-fashioned church, just a main auditorium and Sunday-school rooms, anterooms, and so on, but he also wanted you installed as assistant minister, so I compromised with him on a modern church with you as my assistant," the Doctor laughed again. "So you see you were really of great service to me even before you arrived."

Jerry was surprised.

"Is Uncle Milt much interested in the cathedral?"

"He's the nucleus of the project," said the Doctor; "if I hadn't had you as a set-off we would have been building a formal Greek basilica today."

The assistant minister stood looking curiously at his superior.

"I didn't know my uncle was a very religious man."

"Not only religious, Jerry, but of extraordinary breadth of religion. It was his idea as well as my own to make the cathedral non-sectarian. He is not at all bound down by a creed; in fact, his sympathies extend to . . ." Here the Doctor paused, straightened in his chair. "By the way, Jerry . . . the Arch of the Unconverted . . . what do you think of that for an idea?"

"What do you mean?"

"I mean the very first arch of the nave shall be erected by gifts from unconverted men and women . . . the entrance, you see, before you reached the altar . . . it would be symbolic . . . and think of the crowds and crowds of possible contributors."

"I wonder if it would be sufficiently dignified?" queried Jerry.

"Well, it's a minister's profession to lend dignity to . . . to ordinary things," returned the Doctor; "anyway, think it over."

He drew out his watch and snapped it shut.

"Good gracious, I should have been gone eight minutes ago to a meeting of the Physicians and Surgeons Association at the Planters' Rest Hotel!" and he hurried out into the street where his car awaited him.

The Reverend Jerry Catlin did not immediately set to work at the vast amount of detail the Doctor had outlined. He got up and walked to the door of the study moved by an impatience to be at the work a minister would do if the actual building of the cathedral were over and done. But it would not be done for probably several years. It occurred to Jerry that he easily could spend a large portion of his life in just this preparatory bustle. It was in little what Florence's boom was in large: a rattling disorganized hurrying and building for presumably future quiet and satisfaction. Jerry really had entered the ministry for spiritual ends of his own. These appeared more and more remote as his work progressed.

As he stood in the doorway he became aware of music in the brick church that adjoined the parsonage. How long he had been hearing it he did not know. It came to his ears in the full swing of a developed figure.

The assistant minister definitely gave up his thoughts and followed a brick walk around to the rear door of the church. As he entered, the interior of the Pine Street Methodist Church had the raw unfinished look common to Protestant churches in the South. Its builders, evidently, had enclosed the most space possible with the means they possessed and had left the decoration to the ingenuity of the women members, who did what they could with flower pots.

Jerry knew it so well, the whole decorative calendar of the church stood open before him. On important days the women brought in great banks of ferns and lilies, so that the minister might very well be delivering his sermon in a greenhouse. On ordinary days, when the pots were all gone, the interior gave a faint impression of a barn with its long benches supplying too many mangers, and its clerestory a hayloft without a floor.

There was something not only bare but hopeless about the appearance of the church, as if a group of journeyman carpenters, without any blueprints at all, had done all they could think to do and then had gone away and left it.

The pipes of an organ formed an arch above the centrally located pulpit and choir stalls, and even the almost inevitable beauty of the graduated pipes did not come off. It was frustrated by maroon designs painted on tarnished gilt.

The organist now playing the instrument was concealed by the screen of the stalls. All Jerry could see was a movement of the top of her head in the little mirror above the manuals.

The music itself was a Bach fugue, something like a curling silver filigree that wove into another and another until the whole dome above, in, and around Jerry was a maze of argent scrolls wrought in the strange fourth dimension of music.

Presently the music stopped, came a movement behind the stalls, and a girl stepped up on the dais which held the pulpit. She stopped on seeing Jerry.

"I didn't know anyone was here. . . . Are you Dr. Blankenship's assistant?"

"I am Jerry Catlin."

"My name's Aurelia Swartout. . . . Do you sing, Dr. Catlin?"

"I'm not a doctor yet, and I'm afraid I don't sing."

The girl's very fair complexion reddened a trifle.

"I know the minister doesn't sing. I didn't mean you weren't the minister, but I thought on the days when Dr. Blankenship preached you'd be free and . . . still, I suppose that wouldn't look right . . . a minister in the choir . . . I see it would be a kind of let-down."

The girl had the bluest of eyes, of pleasant Dresden china blue, which had the inconvenient charm of advertising every emotion that flitted through their owner's blonde head.

Jerry hastened to assist the organist out of the verbal impasse in which she had involved herself.

"I think the real reason ministers don't sing is because they can't, but of course it is more complimentary to say that they could but won't . . . on account of their dignity."

Miss Swartout laughed, and Jerry noted her mouth, small and well shaped, with lips that were as full of curves as a very young child's.

"I wonder what side you are going to take in music?" speculated the girl, looking seriously at the assistant minister.

"What kind of side?" asked Jerry beginning to smile.

"Why, classical, romantic, modern, or sentimental dish water?"

The organist plainly meant what she said and was concerned about it.

"I like classical . . ." said Jerry uncertainly, "I know I like Wagner. . . ."

Miss Swartout straightened.

"Why, he's not classical!"

"He isn't?"

"No, he's bombast in the brasses. . . . Who else do you like?"

Jerry became chary lest he be hewn down with another aphorism from so unexpected a source.

"Well . . . I . . . I sort of like Macdowell," he ventured, like an unsure chess player, ready to take his move back at the first sign that his man might be caught.

"M—m—m . . . Macdowell," pondered Miss Swartout with a slight narrowing of her Dresden blue eyes. "He's mainly fluff when he writes what's actually in him, but when he decides to do big serious things like his Fourth Symphony, then he becomes a kind of musical turtle . . ."

"A what?" interrupted Jerry, interested in the girl's tang of novelty.

"Turtle," repeated the organist, "you know they say when you eat a turtle you taste all sorts of meats: chicken, ham, beef, fish, what not. Well, when you listen to Macdowell's serious works you hear all sorts of music: Grieg, Liszt, Wagner, and once in a while you even get a little something from Macdowell."

Jerry stood laughing at Miss Swartout's turn of phrase.

"I think you ought to illustrate what you mean on the organ."

"I will," she agreed earnestly. "I think everyone ought to know good music, especially ministers."

"Why ministers?"

"Because a good sermon is like good music, it's not something to think about, it's something to feel . . ." She caught herself up and began correcting, "Not that sermons haven't got any reason to them. . . . I'm sure some of them have, but I do think the more reasonable they are lots of

times the worse they are as sermons . . . but . . . but I'm
sure yours wouldn't be like that. . . . Oh, I know I've hurt
your feelings!"

Miss Swartout seemed to be composed and piquant only
about music. Jerry assured her that his feelings had been
much more cruelly treated by what she said of Macdowell
than what she had said of sermons, and begged her to il-
lustrate Macdowell's fluffiness.

She disappeared behind the screen, set the electric motor
going, and presently began the queer delicate prelude of
"To a Water Lily." The notes spread, almost at once, be-
fore Jerry's eyes a red-tinted sun-pierced pool holding on its
surface a white corolla and its yellow-dusted center. Then
the music somehow melted into the lily itself and revealed
what veiled desire opened its snowy petals to the sun and
to the honeyed pandering of bees.

Presently, as is the wont of music, it began to retell to
the man the breviary of his own intimate and hushed un-
happinesses . . . his foolish, grotesque, and God-haunted
boyhood . . . Sydna, whom he had loved and from whom he
had received a kind of wistful, patient, non-understanding
pity . . . the theological seminary he had attended and in
which he, somehow, had substituted proof for awareness of
God . . . as if the water lily which floated in the music had
decided to open its white heart by the calendar and not to
the passion of the sun . . . he thought of his uncle's marriage
to Sydna . . ".

In the midst of this half-melancholy, half-sweet reverie
Jerry became aware that someone had entered the church
and was coming up the aisle behind him. He glanced around
and saw a woman, familiar, but whom for an instant he
did not know. The woman herself, however, came to him
with both hands extended and gave the kind of hushed cry
an excited person uses in a church.

"Jerry, how glad I am to see you! Marsan told me you
were here! Isn't it lovely for you to be in Florence again!"

In the next breath her voice, her face, everything except

the feel of her gloved and matronly hands within his own belonged to Sydna.

An irrational disconcert came over Jerry for not having gone to her sooner. However, he pressed her unremembered hands with a social automatism and told her how pleased he was to be back, and how charming it was to see her again; but his real amazed feelings were not of charm, but surprise, shock, almost disbelief . . . was this really Sydna? Was this she, this gracious, handsome, beautifully kept woman within whose ampler outlines he caught glimpses of the sweetheart he had known? . . . It did not occur to Jerry to wonder what Sydna saw.

Their conversation went on in the conventional questions and answers while they were really getting acquainted with each other again. It finally drifted around to Jerry's religious calling, and Sydna said she was glad the family had a representative in the ministry. "It does give a certain tone to one's clan," she went on lightly, "especially when we get the cathedral finished and it becomes an old building softened by time and full of memories."

This last pensive phrase Sydna based subconsciously on her knowledge that Colonel Miltiades Vaiden, her husband, meant to build his sarcophagus in the new cathedral, and this filled her mind with a poetic sadness, a kind of graceful sorrow and a premonition of black Parisian gowns.

She picked her conversation up, however, almost immediately:

"I was half expecting you to come over and have breakfast with us this morning, Jerry."

"I was half expecting a summons," smiled Jerry.

"Well . . . you almost came," laughed the woman. "I hope we'll both do better tomorrow morning. . . . I will, will you?"

Jerry promised he would.

"And I wanted to ask you about the Colonel," went on Sydna; "the Colonel is thinking about going to Shiloh on next Decoration Day . . ."

"A Confederate reunion?"

"Yes, the U.D.C. are sponsoring it. We have six veterans in this county and five in Colbert. The chapel in Athens reports eight in its district."

"If you have it, Sydna, I'm afraid it will go hard with some of those old men when they march."

"Oh they won't march, they'll sit in the grand stand and watch the young military organizations pass in review . . . you know . . . the New South holding the Old South in its heart sort of thing."

"Are you going to want me to help in any way?" asked Jerry gravely.

Sydna opened her dark eyes with an idea.

"Oh, Jerry . . ." then she obviously changed her sentence, for she ended with, "that is certainly sweet of you to offer your services."

She really had thought of asking Jerry to make the Decoration Day address, but a fear had struck her in the nick of time that perhaps her nephew by marriage might not be sufficiently eloquent. A U.D.C. Decoration Day speech demanded very great eloquence indeed and Sydna had chosen in her mind Mr. Brekker of Sheffield, who was a most eloquent orator.

The music had stopped, and Miss Swartout walked across the pulpit platform toward the door. Sydna lifted her voice:

"Aurelia, have you met Jerry Catlin, our new assistant minister?"

"Yes, we've met, thank you," said Miss Swartout self-consciously and went on out the door.

"A very deserving girl," said Sydna, looking after her. "She has given herself a very excellent musical education . . . worked her way through a Chicago conservatory . . . suffered real privation . . . I don't know her very well, she's a little hard to get acquainted with."

At that moment Miss Swartout reappeared at the door,

"Mr. Catlin," she called, "some men in the parsonage want to see you."

CHAPTER FIFTEEN

WHEN Jerry Catlin walked out of the Pine Street Church his thoughts were not at all on the men who were waiting for him in the parsonage. Instead he had an odd shaken feeling as if someone very dear and intimate to him had vanished. His sense of queer ironic loss penetrated even further than that. It questioned the validity of his long harbored feeling which had clung about the memory of Sydna. He had held a kind of pointless loyalty in his heart. There was but one kindly thing about it: he was no longer afraid that his emotion for Sydna would tear him again, or cause him to overstep the bounds of conventionality; which, after all, was something.

The three men who were waiting for him in the parsonage began talking about a lawyer and the force of the pulpit on public opinion. In the midst of this explanation, to which Jerry hardly attended, one of the men, quite old and gray-headed, laughed and said heartily:

"So we thought we'd try you, Jerry . . . figgerin' a preacher might be good for something and it might be this."

Here the assistant minister became entirely aware of the cocked black cigar, the half-shut left eye and humorous wrinkled face of old man Bill Bradley the real estate agent.

Jerry shook hands with Mr. Bradley with the bygone doings of the old man passing humorously but undefined through his thoughts.

"What am I to do about a lawyer?" inquired Jerry, puzzled.

"Help select one . . . a conscientious dependable attorney," said the first speaker gravely.

"A man who puts his conscience and the welfare of his country before anything else," added the second.

Old man Bill closed his left eye at Jerry.

"That's goin' to take a lot of selectors and a lot of selectin' to find a lawyer like that."

"What's the object of this conscientious attorney?" asked Jerry.

"Why, to defend them niggers, of course."

"But I don't know a thing in the world about the lawyers here in Florence, they've all been changed since I left here."

The first man held up a hand.

"We simply want a group of irreproachable men to recommend a lawyer on whom Judge Wilson can rely. If a number of our best business men and ministers recommend an attorney as fair, capable, and reliable, there can't be any public criticism about the matter. You see this trial is sure to be seen by thousands of Northern men here in town, and it will be spread over every newspaper in the country. And everybody will put the worst possible construction they can against Alabama and the South. We want to start in right at the beginning nipping criticism in the bud. That's why we want a preacher on the committee to help select a lawyer to defend these niggers."

Jerry saw this, and he went out with the men to ride down in town and pick out a reliable attorney. They had come up in Bradley's car, and now the old man half apologized for the look of his automobile.

"It's so an ordinary man will get in it and feel at home," he explained. "When I show a prospect a lot, he don't look at my car and think I'm cheating him. And I God, it helps me politically, too. I'm president of the North Alabama Realtors' Association simply because ever' man that voted for me owned a pore car, but it was jest a shade better than this 'un of mine."

Old man Bill cocked his cigar a notch higher and accelerated the motor he maligned.

The car stopped in front of the Second National Bank

and Mr. Tergune led the way through the lobby to the president's office. A number of men were seated about a long, handsome oak table, and one of them was saying,

"No, we couldn't possibly recommend Sandusky to Judge Wilson."

Another man replied:

"Sandusky is one of the ablest criminal lawyers at the Florence bar, and he would give the whole proceeding an appearance of the strictest and most impartial justice."

The thin yellow figure of old Colonel Vaiden seated at the head of the table shook a negative finger at the speaker.

"Sandusky would try to win."

A small black-eyed man named Sanborne ejaculated:

"You can't really believe, in a case like this, Sandusky would think of personal fame in assisting Alabama over the most critical point in her legal history since the Civil War!"

"I know Sandusky would try to win," said the Colonel. "I have had some experience with Sandusky."

The assistant minister asked naïvely why the negroes should not have a bona-fide defence.

Sanborne turned on the speaker.

"My God, Dr. Catlin, if we really don't want another lynching, those niggers have got to be hanged!"

"But won't any jury you pick in this county be sure to hang them?" asked Jerry.

"That's what the verdict will be, of course," explained Mr. Tergune more mildly, "but think of the bill of exceptions a lawyer like Sandusky would pile up. There wouldn't be any way to hang those niggers, if Sandusky really decided to block it."

Sanborne interrupted to say sharply:

"No, we've got to pick a lawyer who would rather see justice done than to make himself a big reputation by winning a case that has all the publicity this one is sure to get!"

"Look here," put in a voice, "why couldn't we recommend a real first-class criminal lawyer and compromise with him on half the niggers to be hung and the rest get life imprisonment? That would give a lawyer a thundering big rep.: to get half the niggers off with life imprisonment."

Old Colonel Vaiden got stiffly to his feet.

"No, no, gentlemen, this trial must end the excuse lynching parties always make—that the law is uncertain. A swift trial followed by immediate execution will consolidate public opinion here in the South against illegal violence. We have got to rescue the South from the stain of barbarism. These six negro miscreants must be hanged to protect the law-abiding colored population of Alabama from future outbreaks of mob law. I have worked with niggers all my life. I have nigger friends who are just as sincere and devoted to me as any man sitting at this table. Out of the affection I have for those niggers and the value I place upon the colored people as the economic foundation of Southern life, I must ask that every one of those six niggers in the Lauderdale county jail be hanged so as to make the lives and property of hundreds of thousands of colored citizens of the South free from the gusts of passion and of chance."

The Colonel spoke with the utmost earnestness and feeling, not, as the men thought, from emotion created by this particular situation. As a matter of fact, the Colonel had witnessed, years ago, the hanging of a negro to a mulberry tree in Courthouse Square for the bare offense of having brought suit against a white man to retain a pair of mules. The white man had been the Colonel himself, and the negro who had brought suit against him had been the Colonel's own son. Ever since that time the mere thought of a lynching sickened the Colonel. That was why he had organized the Rotarians against the mob a few days before.

A hand-clapping and ejaculations of "That's right! That's to the point!" greeted the Colonel's eloquence; and the question arose again, what lawyer in Florence could be entrusted with the delicate self-sacrificing task of losing the case of the six negroes in the county jail.

Finally old Bill Bradley shifted his cigar and ejaculated:

"I God, gentlemen, I got it!"

"What is it? What's your plan, Mr. Bradley?"

"Recommend some young lawyer and let him actually try to win. You see young lawyers depend on pleading and the justice of their cause. They expect the jury to make the final decision. Then they stop. They don't realize the decision of the first jury empaneled in a big case is, you might say, just an idle opinion expressed by twelve negligible onlookers. They don't know the real decision will be handed down decades later by the grandsons of these jurymen on the recommendation of the Supreme Court and with the advice of some criminal judge yet unborn, to throw the damn case out, as the defendants are all dead."

The table began laughing. The names of a number of young lawyers were mentioned, and finally Mr. Jefferson Ashton was selected as a lawyer not so young as to be ridiculous, and yet not so shrewd as to be dangerous to the future peace and dignity of the commonwealth of the state.

A delegation of five men was chosen to visit Attorney Ashton and persuade him to accept the case of the six negroes. Among the quintet went Jerry Catlin, to lend the dignity of the Church to the request.

When the five emerged from the bank they found quite a crowd had collected, awaiting the outcome of their proceedings. As the quintet picked their way along the pavement, someone caught Jerry's arm and whispered:

"Who'll defend 'em, Dr. Catlin? . . . I'm the local reporter for the Memphis and Birmingham papers."

Jerry neither glanced around nor answered, but walked on with a tightening of the nerves as he realized the publicity that would be given to the approaching trial.

Tergune grumbled in a lowered voice:

"Isn't it a damn shame, this breaking loose right here in the middle of the boom!"

"May draw bigger crowds than ever," said old man Bradley hopefully.

"Won't be the sort of crowds we can use," grumbled Tergune.

"Hell, I can use any sort of crowd it'll draw," said the old man, striking a match and lighting his cigar.

As for Jerry, he moved across Courthouse Square toward the mulberries along Intelligence Row with a disturbed feeling. He was uneasy about his own part in selecting a lawyer to hang the negroes.

Ashton was the kind of lawyer who collects notes and sues on accounts, and does the pick-and-shovel work of the courts. To allow six negroes to go on trial for their lives defended by Ashton, and for him, Jerry Catlin, to aid and abet such an arrangement . . . the assistant minister shook his head solemnly.

The five men walked two and three abreast across the northern edge of the Square. As they passed the old Florence Hotel, Sanborne asked aloud:

"Me? Did you want to see me?" A moment later he called, "It's you, Dr. Catlin . . . she wants to see you."

Jerry looked up out of his musings to see a brunet girl who was pretty but who was so frightened that for the moment her prettiness was quite lost. She was standing near the mouth of a little passageway between the hotel and the first of the low brick offices that made up the row.

She looked at Jerry with black eyes that were urgent, bitterly embarrassed, and uneasy. Jerry pointed at himself to see if he actually was the man wanted. The girl nodded with a breath of relief and put a hand against the brick wall, as if she were about to faint.

The assistant minister left his group and went to her.

"You wanted to see me?"

"Yes, sir," breathed the girl, with an almost colorless mouth.

"What can I do for you?"

The girl moistened her lips.

"Are . . . aren't you gentlemen . . . seeing about a lawyer . . . for those boys in jail?"

"Yes, we are," he said wonderingly.

"Would . . . would you mind talking to Dr. Sinton . . .

just for a little while . . . about five minutes . . . three min-
utes . . ."

"You mean about . . . what lawyer we shall engage?"

The girl nodded rapidly in sharp relief that he so quickly
understood her mission.

"Why, I don't mind at all," agreed Jerry earnestly, "if
Dr. Sinton has any ideas on the subject. . . . I wish he had
been at the meeting at the bank."

"Then you'll come with me?"

"Certainly."

Jerry lifted a hand at the other four men.

"You fellows go ahead . . . be with you in a minute."

The girl turned, and Jerry followed her up the alley and
presently entered the rear door of the hotel. They were
headed, Jerry thought, for the lobby by this unconventional
route when the girl turned into a hot little room adjoining
the main kitchen of the hotel. Three or four negroes were
talking in undertones. When Jerry entered all these negroes
went out but one, a heavy, grave-faced, very black man. This
black man began speaking in a careful nervous voice:

"Dr. Catlin, I have heard of you by reputation. May I
ask you to imagine, just for an instant, that you are in a
country of black people such as I am. Imagine six white
boys of your race were in danger of almost certain death.
Can you think how earnestly, how prayerfully you would
seek to help those unfortunate boys if every man's hand
was against them and they could not see in all the world
the face of a possible friend?"

Jerry stared blankly at this obviously studied and re-
hearsed speech. The girl interrupted to say:

"Dr. Catlin, may . . . may I introduce to you Dr. Sinton,
the bishop of our church?"

CHAPTER SIXTEEN

WHITE educated Southerners are completely cut off from black educated Southerners by the inherited attitudes of master and slave, and the one really does not know that the other exists. So now the Reverend Catlin looked at the heavy black man who used correct and moving if rather florid English with a feeling of surprise and grotesqueness, as if a bootblack should begin discussing the quantum theory.

The girl, too, whom he had taken for a white girl, now stood before him for what she was, a high cream, and was therefore not entitled to the courtesy he had shown her. And the thought that she had led him into the back entrance of the Florence Hotel and had introduced him to a negro angered the minister with its indignity. It obscured for Jerry the peril of the six black boys in the county jail. He was minded to turn and walk out of the hotel and proceed with the business men to Mr. Jefferson Ashton's office. He did say, however, in level unsympathy:

"Just what did you expect me to do, Sinton?"

The black minister stood watching the white minister's face.

"Is any white attorney going to represent the accused in court?"

"Certainly, the court is just about to appoint one."

The black man cleared his throat:

"Do you happen to know whom, Dr. Catlin?"

The correct use of the word "whom" gave the white man a further impression of distaste and absurdity.

"I understand the court will select Mr. Jefferson Ashton."

After a moment Jerry added, "He is a reputable lawyer and a very thorough Christian gentleman."

The black bishop repeated thoughtfully:

"Mr. Jefferson Ashton . . ." and then looked at the girl.

The high-cream girl with the apprehensive eyes shook her head faintly at a moment when Jerry was not watching. The black bishop gave a nervous frown.

"Mr. Ashton is a very good lawyer and an excellent man. We were just wondering, Dr. Catlin, and that is why I took the great liberty of stopping you on the street. Mr. Ashton may need help, because this is a very serious case; he may need help and advice, and we were wondering if we could get some other attorney to assist in the defense?"

"Who is 'we'?" asked Jerry.

"A society among us colored people," explained the bishop in a respectful voice.

"Why don't you just go to a lawyer and hire him?"

"Because, if a colored man was seen entering a lawyer's office on such an errand, it would be dangerous for him, it would be at the risk of his life. Besides that, no lawyer in town would accept the case if a colored man offered to retain him."

Jerry felt an impulse to deny this, then ignored it.

"Now, just what do you want to see me about?"

The black bishop cleared his throat and began with a troubled face:

"If we succeed in getting any lawyer at all to defend these boys, Dr. Catlin, some white man will have to engage him for us. And it won't be a simple retaining. He would have to show some white attorney that after all these black boys are human beings; that one of them is just a child, thirteen or fourteen years old. It is almost impossible for the child to have committed the offense charged against him. And they are all quite without friends, Dr. Catlin. They haven't seen a colored man since they were put in jail."

"Why did you choose me for such an undertaking, Sinton?"

"I didn't," stated the negro at once, "Rose there chose you. I told her to look at the faces of the men as they went past the alley and try to speak to the man with the kindest-looking eyes. She may not have known who you were herself."

"Yes, I knew," said the girl, "my grandmother cooked for Dr. Catlin's Aunt Rose Vaiden . . . I was named for her."

"You are Miss Tony's granddaughter?" queried Jerry, interested.

"Yes, sir."

"Who was your mother?"

"Jinny Lou Sparkman."

Jerry remembered Jinny Lou, a yellow child with dark eyes and black curls. This information that the girl's people had worked in his family formed a humanizing touch for Jerry. He felt more kindly toward her, and toward the negro man. He decided he would tell them the course determined upon at the bank.

"Look here, Sinton," he said in a gentler tone, "I don't know whether you have thought of it or not, but the trial and conviction and execution of these boys will have a deep bearing on the future of the colored people all over the South."

"Yes, we know that, too," agreed the black man, "that's why our society is stirred up about it."

"Yes, but had you ever asked yourselves if you were stirred up in the right way?"

"How do you mean?"

"I mean, if the boys are hanged, the next case of assault will probably be brought into court, too. It will set a precedent. The people of Alabama will have confidence in their courts. They can be persuaded to let such cases come to trial instead of taking violent and illegal action. You know very well such a precedent settled into custom would be a thousand times better for the colored race than the present state of things."

The heavy black man stood frowning at this.

"Then why should we not have the best lawyer in town?"

"Because you would lose the whole point of the trial. The best lawyer would certainly prolong the trial and might easily set the culprits free. The next mob would remember that and would certainly claim their victims while they were sure of them. No, the very point is for them to have an ordinary lawyer who will not abuse justice with every technicality the law provides."

The bulky black man stood on widely planted feet chewing this.

"In other words," he said slowly, "if a colored man is accused of attacking a white woman, no matter whether he is guilty or not, he must be lynched either by a white mob or by a white court."

"No," snapped the assistant minister, quite out of temper; "if these boys are proved innocent to the satisfaction of the jury, they will be liberated. The important thing is that no improper technicalities be used to drag out the trial and defeat justice."

"Dr. Catlin, why . . . why is it more improper to use technicalities to defend a negro than anyone else? Technicalities are used against negroes in Southern courts year in and year out; why not use them for them once?"

Jerry's patience gave out completely.

"Can't you see, Sinton, it is not a matter of justice, it is a matter of policy? Justice is defeated endlessly in American courts, North and South, but right at this moment it is good policy, it is the hope of the black people of Alabama, that justice be administered. It will make safe in the future hundreds of thousands of black lives . . . that's all I've got to say." And Jerry turned and walked angrily out of the anteroom door.

The assistant minister reëntered Courthouse Square more subtly irritated because there was a certain cogency in the black preacher's logic which he himself had glimpsed before he had gone into the hotel. Another disturbing point was that he had followed a negro girl into the back door of a hotel. He hoped none of the white men knew that Rose Sparkman was a negress.

Now, as Jerry hurried to rejoin his companions in Ashton's office, the thought came to him that all this turmoil about the six negroes was really an effort of the white race to protect their racial purity against negro blood, and this very cream-colored girl who had called him aside was a subtler and more uncontrollable threat against a purely Anglo-Saxon South than all the negro men the county jail would hold.

He turned into Ashton's office, which was the corner building on the alley which led to the jail. As he entered he heard Sanborne saying:

"Jefferson, we are asking you to do this out of patriotism for your country."

"But, listen," cried Ashton earnestly, "how would you men like to stand up and defend six black beasts . . ."

"Wait!" begged old man Bradley in a voice muffled by his cigar. "Jeff, my boy, how many doctors do you suppose have worked to save lives of patients they wished were dead and in hell, but their Hippocratic oath wouldn't let 'em flicker? Now, the oath you took to enter the Florence bar means the same thing. You swore to uphold justice, the laws of Alabama, and the Constitution of the United States. All right, the laws of Alabama guarantee every accused the right of counsel; a man skilled in the law and in the conduct of cases. . . . Jefferson, we're going to recommend to Judge Wilson to draft you."

Attorney Ashton stood nervously fingering a criminal code of Alabama that lay on a littered table:

"It'll disgrace me."

"Not a soul in the courthouse but what'll know the Judge appointed you, that your heart is on the other side and nothing but your integrity as a lawyer and a citizen causes you to defend niggers you know damn well deserve to be hung!"

"Besides that," added Sanborne, "your cross-examination

and your speech of defense will be printed in every big news-paper in the United States."

Mr. Jefferson Ashton wrinkled his brows, made a last clutch at the code, but visibly weakened. He had never in his life taken part in a trial of any prominence. Suits with notoriety, if not fame, passed him by with monotonous regularity. That was why he could never get any big cases to handle, because he had never had one. If he could just get one really dangerous case and get his rep up in the county, he'd be made. If he could contrive some extraordi-nary legal trick and set all six of the negroes scot free . . . he certainly would be made!

"Gentlemen," he said aloud, "although not for my right arm would I loose such criminals on the public, still, I'll go into their cases, spread the exact evidence before judge and jury without exaggeration, without false emphasis, with a plea that strict and accurate justice be done to my clients. If Judge Wilson will accept that assurance, you may tender my name as a tentative attorney for the defense."

The men assured him earnestly that he had taken a praiseworthy stand, and Bradley admonished him to write down what he had just said for his speech before the jury.

Jerry Catlin was on tenterhooks to get the other members of the committee out of Ashton's office. When he succeeded in herding them on the pavement he said:

"Look here, the niggers are about to hire Sandusky for the defense!"

"How do you know?"

"A nigger preacher named Sinton told me that moment; he wanted me to see Sandusky for him."

"He hasn't seen him yet?"

"I don't think so."

"Listen," said Sanborne to all the committee," we've got to telephone Sandusky and retain him for the prosecution!"

"How much will he cost, and who'll pay it?" asked an-other of the committee.

"Hell, it makes no difference what he'll cost!" ejaculated Bradley. "If he ever gits his pay he'll git it, and if he don't he won't. What we got to do is retain him!"

So the five men sought the nearest telephone and finished up their duty as keepers of the public morals by engaging one lawyer for the defense and retaining another for the prosecution.

WHEN the legal scouting party returned to the bank with their report, such a number of men were waiting to see Colonel Vaiden that even they could not go straight into his private office. Miss Katie, the telephone girl in the bank's house exchange, told the quintet that she couldn't disturb Colonel Milt not even for Miss Marsan, who at that moment was waiting outside in her car.

Old man Bradley and young Mr. Sanborne grew curious at once. The peril of the six negro rapists' obtaining competent counsel passed out of their minds, and they wondered who was closeted with the Colonel, and did it mean a new subdivision on the market, and who were the men behind it?

Old man Bradley asked in his artless countrified fashion:

"Who's old man Milt jawin' with in there, Miss Katie?"

The well trained exchange girl answered politely:

"I didn't say he was in a consultation, I said he was in a conference."

"That's diff'runt," nodded Bradley, taking the cigar from his lips and tapping the end. Miss Katie silently pushed him an ash tray.

"It's the damnedest thing," thought old man Bill to himself, moving about the waiting room and trying to get a glimpse through the door of the inner office, "It's the damnedest thing, old man Milt Vaiden keep me coolin' my heels in his waiting room when just a few years ago me and Frierson and old man John Han'back had him in jail for stealin'." And he thumped his ash on a rug.

The conference about which old man Bradley was so curious and Miss Katie so uncommunicative was composed

of the executive force of the bank: The cashier, the first and second vice presidents, the secretary and treasurer, a mere teller who was a bright young man who owned some stock, and two of the directors made up the consulting body.

The Colonel as president had on the table before him an application for a loan of forty-seven thousand, seven hundred and fifty dollars to be spent on a subdivision to be opened along Shoal Creek, west of Florence.

The Colonel, as chairman, sat slowly shaking his white head and jaundiced face.

"No, gentlemen, no . . . the land value isn't there."

"But the man himself is going to put in fifty thousand dollars cash," persisted the secretary and treasurer; "that will be ninety-seven thousand, seven hundred and fifty dollars in improvements . . . bound to be worth the forty-seven-thousand-dollar loan he wants."

"Forty-seven thousand, seven hundred and fifty," corrected the Colonel.

"All right . . . that's not half of the money he asks us to lay out."

"It's half of the money that can be got out of it when this boom breaks," said the Colonel dryly.

"You mean if the boom breaks," stressed the teller, who was young but very bright and owned some stock.

"I mean when it breaks," repeated the Colonel briefly.

Mr. Pingree, who was a grocer most of the time and a bank director at odd hours like this, arose to his feet.

"Mr. President and gentlemen of the executive committee, we know, of course, that this boom won't always remain at such a pitch as it is at present, BUT look how Birmingham went straight up from nothing to a hundred and forty thousand population."

"Birmingham is a place where iron and coal are found together," interrupted the Colonel.

"Well, haven't we got an endless mine of white coal in the government power plant?" demanded Mr. Pingree, "and iron right at us in Russellville?"

The first vice president said:

"Gentlemen, I think we can leave Birmingham out of this question. We want to know can we go into this deal and get out of it before anything happens to the boom. There is no way to finance a boom without taking a risk. But what is our risk? If the worst happens, it will be a wait. That Shoal Creek property with all the improvements they are going to put on it is worth forty-seven thousand dollars. . . ."

"Forty-seven, seven fifty," corrected the old Colonel impatiently.

The first vice president repeated the correction dutifully. The Colonel was getting old and had to be humored. He was with age losing his speculative nerve, that nerve which, a few decades ago, had caused him to seize another man's fortune, tell him about it, brazen it out through the courts with him, and finally keep it. He had been a wonderful man once.

The secretary and treasurer asked if the Colonel wanted to see the Second National just sit on its roll and see the other Tri-City banks gobble up the whole boom.

Mr. Ragsdale, the bank's lawyer, who was the other director of the bank, brought out a new point.

"If we turn down such a reasonable loan as this, it will certainly get abroad, and it will have a bad effect on the boom itself. When the people see this bank is skeptical, they'll get skeptical."

The old Colonel looked at the speaker.

"Mr. Ragsdale, if the boom has got that far along so soon, our bank had better get out from under the whole thing while we can."

"Well, that's my idea, Colonel," said Ragsdale with legal dryness. "I'm ready for the question."

"Send for Miss Katie," directed the Colonel, "I want her to make a record of the ayes and nays for our minutes."

When Miss Katie appeared Miltiades began dictating before she was fairly in her seat.

"A loan of forty-seven thousand, seven hundred and fifty

dollars, payable in semiannual installments, on the Shoal Creek property lying west of Florence in Range 16 Sections 8–9–10 to Lerganthall and Barth."

Miss Katie glanced up at the president with her pencil poised and asked the routine question:

"And who owns the property . . . who takes first mortgage over the bank's mortgage?"

"I do; I'm selling it," said the Colonel.

CHAPTER EIGHTEEN

WHEN Miss Katie had finished her work in the conference room she asked the Colonel if he would see Marsan, who was waiting in her car.

The old banker asked how many were before Marsan.

Miss Katie glanced at a list and read over a number of names ending with Mr. Jerry and Mr. Bradley and those men who went to see about the lawyer.

The Colonel nodded at this important committee, which he had half forgot.

"Oh yes . . . about the niggers . . . send them in ahead of the others."

The Colonel was very tired that day, not physically or mentally, but spiritually tired. He wanted to leave the bank and drive with Marsan along the river, seeing perhaps an anachronistic steamboat and going back home by way of the new cathedral, but on this afternoon he saw he was not going to get away at his usual hour.

So he said to Miss Katie:

"Tell Marsan not to wait, but to come back in an hour and a half. . . . If she has something else to do, let her send Wilson."

When Miss Katie went outside of the bank to deliver this message, she found Marsan waiting in her car talking to a middle-sized brunet man who stood with a hand on the car window.

"Miss Katie, how long before Papa can see Mr. Petrie?" asked the girl.

The information clerk referred to her list and counted up.

"There are seventeen ahead of him, Miss Marsan," said information, "that's counting five men as one."

"Do you mean there are eighty-five men waiting?" asked Petrie, out of hope.

"Oh no, that's just the last five that count one, all the rest of them are—are one apiece, you know."

The crowd around the door laughed at the information girl's mix-up. Marsan turned to her companion.

"Look here, if I can't see him for an hour and a half neither can you." She looked at him quizzically and smiled. "What do you want to know, anyway?".

"Well . . . I wanted to ask him about the advisability of making an investment."

There came a little pause. Mr. Petrie took his hand off the car to let it back out.

"Listen," suggested Marsan on the impulse, "if we both have to wait on Dad, you might as well drive around with me till the time's up . . . I mean, if you'd like to."

An apprehension flickered through Petrie's mind that if he became too friendly with Marsan she might scamp her work at school and rely on his favoritism to pull her through. Girls almost invariably did that. Aloud he said, "That's fine," and stepped into the car.

Marsan asked him where he wanted to drive, and as he had no preference she suggested the Sheffield road with its view of the dam from the bridge.

"Yes, we ought to look at the dam," agreed Petrie, "since it caused both the boom and the trial."

"Did it cause the trial?"

"Yes, the negroes were beating their way to the dam in a box car; they hoped to find work here. The dam was a contributory cause to the incident."

Marsan drove for several seconds in silence, and through her mind there moved a pensive, almost a mournful sequence of thoughts. The dam had brought the negroes and so had collected the mob which had insulted her father. This insult had led Red McLaughlin to protect her and had caused her to give to Red her first gift, as a woman, to a man. It had all flowed out of the dam.

Aloud she said:

"It's odd how circumstances twist people about. I suppose endless other things will be caused by that dam . . . endless."

"It's what the old Greeks called Fate," said Petrie. "We call it Chance and Luck, and Happen-so, because we are not so dignified as the Greeks."

"We don't believe in Luck and Chance," said Marsan.

"We are supposed not to, even when it happens all round us," said Petrie. "We are not as direct as the Greeks. They accepted Chance as Fate and elevated it to the will of the gods. We build up our gods and pray to them, trying to overcome Chance and Fate. But we've never really been able to do it, and so our gods have more or less ceased to function. That's why you came to me the other afternoon with your question: you were disturbed about your gods. For our deity we have installed Cause and Effect, that's what rules us. The trouble is we feel the Effect and then with much pain figure out the Cause, but it is all over by that time, and there is nothing we can do about it; so it returns to the Greek idea of Chance or Fate."

"Yes, but you say we figure out the Cause with much pain. We do that so the next time that thing comes up we'll know and we can avoid what's unpleasant."

"That sounds very practical," agreed Mr. Petrie; "the trouble is nothing ever happens twice alike, but assuming that things did and could happen twice alike, and their causes be determined, then men could prepare themselves; the catch is that the set of causes you have figured out are the effects of causes still more remote. You have shoved Chance back a notch or two, but you have made it more mysterious and inscrutable." The school teacher looked at the girl driving, "Do you know what I'm talking about, Marsan?"

Marsan drew a long breath.

"Oh yes, I know."

Petrie gave a deprecatory smile.

"I seem to grow indiscreet when I talk with you. You're a dangerous person for me to have around."

"What made you start thinking like that?" asked the girl intently. "What happened to you?"

"What makes you think anything happened to me?"

"Why, it would have to . . . you couldn't start just thinking like that without any reason at all."

Petrie laughed.

"There you are, doing exactly what I described, pursuing our Anglo-Saxon god of Cause. If I told you what happened to me, you would want to know how that came about, wouldn't you?"

The girl smiled.

"I suppose I would." After a moment she added, "I see you aren't going to tell me either one."

Mr. Petrie's sober face took on a funny expression, but he sat in silence, looking at the Florence bridge which they were approaching.

Marsan had an uncomfortable feeling that he was laughing at her; to recover herself she began talking about the affairs of the day; Ashton's appointment to defend the negroes, which she had overheard at the bank.

"He isn't much of a lawyer . . . I suppose that's the point," said Petrie.

Marsan was shocked.

"Do you mean Judge Wilson is going to appoint Mr. Ashton so the negroes will lose?"

"I suppose that's the idea."

Marsan looked at her companion with horror-struck eyes.

"Why, I think that's terrible!"

"Did you think the lynching they nearly pulled off was such a bad thing?"

"Not as bad as this."

"What difference does it make whether they lynch the negroes with a mob or a jury?"

"Why, a lot . . . a mob is at least honest."

"Huh . . ." said Petrie, "m—huh . . ." and he looked at the girl with a new intereest. "Now don't think I was defending the jury, Marsan . . . I wasn't."

"Couldn't somebody do something about it?" cried the girl.

"I don't suppose anybody is interested . . . at least, not here in the South."

"Is anybody interested anywhere?"

"Well . . . no-o . . . probably not . . . not away down here in Alabama. In the North they have an association to protect negroes from injustices. It's called the Association for the Betterment of Colored People."

"Where is it?"

"In New York."

"What's the street address?"

"I don't know . . . 'New York' would get it, I fancy."

Marsan pressed her foot on the accelerator, and the car shot down the river hill onto the bridge. As the machine hummed toward Sheffield the girl asked:

"How came you to know about this association?"

"Well . . . it attempted to do something for a college mate of mine once."

"What did it try to do?"

"Get him established in a prize position which he had won."

"Did it do it?"

"No."

"What was the position?"

"A fellowship in a big research laboratory in Schenectady."

"How did he win it?"

"In a competitive examination."

"What in?"

"Metallurgy."

"Lot of folks take it?"

"Oh yes, four from the Pittsburgh Tech, and I don't know how many other colleges."

Marsan suddenly remembered Mr. Petrie's microscope and his hobby of collecting pieces of iron.

"You know because you studied metallurgy?" she hazarded.

"Yes, I majored in metallurgy," he admitted uncomfortably.

A still more dramatic question leaped into Marsan's head, but she censored it as unaskable. But she wondered if he had . . . she wondered poignantly if he really had. And as she was thinking firmly to herself that she must never under any circumstances ask such a question, she said in an odd voice:

"Mr. . . . Mr. Petrie . . . d-did you take it too?"

"Yes, I took it," said Petrie.

"O-oh my goodness!" gasped the girl.

A nigger had beaten Mr. Petrie! A nigger in a metallurgical examination in Pittsburgh! Beaten Mr. Petrie, who knew all the things that were!

It sounded irrational . . . fantastic.

"But you say he didn't get it after all?"

"No," said Petrie gravely, "when Denison went up to go to work, they saw he was a negro and let him out somehow . . . I never learned the particulars."

"I declare! I just declare . . ." Marsan could hardly go on with her thinking. After a while she said:

"I suppose you were glad of it?"

"No-o . . . I wasn't . . . I was awfully sorry for Denison. While we were studying together in the Pittsburgh Tech. I never really thought of him as a negro. We had a Hindu and a Mexican there too, that helped the feeling along. I suppose that he was just a man, a brown man.

"The first time I realized that Denison was really a Georgia nigger was when he won. Marsan, it was the strangest feeling I ever had . . . a nigger . . . a Georgia nigger to win over all of us white men!"

"But you weren't glad when they kicked him out?"

"No, I wasn't. I was sorry. I was damn sorry. Somehow it seemed to me the most pathetic thing I ever heard of."

The big Vaiden car scorned the miles between Florence and Sheffield in a contemptuous murmur. Marsan spun up to and stopped before the railroad station. She slammed open the door, jumped out, and went running inside at a basket-ball gait.

Professor J. Adlee Petrie, scientist, but not so grand a scientist as he had been five minutes before, remained in the car wondering in distraction why he had ever told Marsan Vaiden such a chapter in his life history. If it got out, what would it do to him in the school! And she was sure to tell it . . . what seventeen-year-old girl could keep such a secret as that!

A small shabby old woman came walking past the car, glanced at it, paused, looked at it more closely, and finally came over and asked in a thin voice:

"Ain't that Brother Jerry Catlin's car?"

Petrie had no desire to waste words on her.

"No, it isn't."

"It's the same color . . . it's the same shape . . . it's the same size . . ." she walked around it, "it's the same license number . . . don't any two cars have the same license number, do they?"

Petrie recalled that Jerry Catlin was connected in some way or other with the Vaiden family.

"It may be the same, but it doesn't belong to Catlin, it belongs to the Vaidens."

"Will you be seeing Brother Catlin?"

"Not if I can help it."

"Lawzee, what you got against Brother Catlin?"

"Nothing . . . I just don't know him very well."

"Don't you want to see nobody you don't know very well?"

"Listen, I'll see him for you . . . what do you want me to say to him?"

"I've got a little message. . . ."

At that moment Marsan came out of the depot.

"Marsan," called Petrie, "here's a woman with a little message for your cousin Jerry."

"Who are you?" asked the girl.

"My name's Swartout."

"And what did you want me to tell Cousin Jerry?"

"Tell him Luggy told Junior Petman how many words they was in morningglory and nobody else knowed, not even the grown folks at the party, ast him how he explains that?"

"Wha-at?"

The old woman repeated what she had just said, word for word and accent for accent.

"What does it mean?"

"Your cousin'll know what it means."

"Who is Luggy?"

"Huh, you got me there, miss." The little old woman gave a kind of a grunt of a laugh of long-accustomed wonder.

"Well . . . who is Junior Petman?"

"Now I can tell you that. He's the little afflicted boy that lives across the lane."

As Marsan could get nothing more out of her than this, she wrote the message down exactly as Mrs. Swartout dictated, because it was impossible to remember such a string of words.

The shabby old woman gave brief dry thanks, as very poor people always try to show in their gratitude that they are just as good as the person whom they are thanking.

When Marsan and Petrie started back to Florence, Petrie asked if Jerry could make heads or tails out of the message for Marsan please to relay the interpretation to him.

The girl promised she would by telephone and took his number at the old house on Tombigbee Street.

"Marsan . . . don't mention what I told you," said Petrie.

She looked at him quizzically.

"Don't worry . . . folks don't get things out of me as easily as they do out of you."

On their return trip they drove slowly across the Florence

bridge to look at the dam, which had been their objective from the first. It lay far up the river like a low modern fortress stretched from shore to shore.

"What did you do in the Sheffield depot?" asked Petrie idly as he looked at the white blotch of cataracts at the foot of the dam.

"Oh, I telegraphed that society you told me about."

"What society?"

"Why, the one that protects niggers. . . . I told them they were hanging six niggers down here and they wouldn't allow 'em to have a lawyer."

"Marsan!" cried Petrie. "I hope you didn't do that!"

"Yes, I did."

"I hope you didn't get the address right!"

"I sent it to the Association for the Betterment of Colored People . . . New York."

"For God's sake, Marsan!" The teacher sat staring at the girl. After a moment he added:

"That's the right address."

CHAPTER NINETEEN

Mr. J. ADLEE PETRIE and Marsan reached the bank door somewhere near the hour and a half limit. Miss Katie's waiting list had been checked off, and the school teacher was admitted to the Colonel's private office.

The gayety which Petrie had felt with Marsan vanished abruptly in the presence of the old banker with his yellowed face and bright wrinkled old eyes. A certain faintly supercilious feeling of being broadly educated, of taking informed and scientific views of life fell away from the school teacher in the Colonel's presence. Petrie remembered, as who did not, that the Colonel had founded his fortune on theft, but the old man's adroit handling of his original fortune had somehow completely expunged his misstep. That long past offense certainly detracted nothing now from his aura of magistral wisdom and fortressed and inscrutable integrity.

Petrie moistened his lips and began by saying that he had been a depositor in the Second National Bank for four years. As he made his statement he produced from his pocket a number of newspaper clippings.

"I wanted to ask your advice," he began, "about the Anderson place. It has changed hands fourteen times within the last two months at irregular advances of from five hundred to two thousand dollars."

Miltiades nodded.

"Yes, I know, I sold the place, I owned it for a number of years."

This disconcerted the scientist, but he went ahead with his questions, although he had the grace to put his next in a negative form:

119

"Then you wouldn't advise me to—to buy it?"

"No, I sold it," repeated the old man courteously.

Petrie for some reason was oddly depressed. He felt as if the old banker were trying to cheat him out of something.

"Don't you think the Anderson place will go higher?"

"I don't know . . . what has it sold for lately?"

"The last quotation," supplied Petrie promptly, "was forty-seven hundred dollars. Do you think it will go higher than that?"

"It may do it."

"Don't you think it will if the boom lasts?"

"It probably will."

"Well, do you believe the boom will continue much longer?" inquired Petrie, more and more depressed and dissatisfied at the Colonel's answers.

"Uh . . . excuse me, Mr. Petrie, but . . . may I ask what is your profession?"

"Well, I . . . teach science in the High School," said Petrie, using the circumlocution to avoid coming out and stating flatly what he was.

"Then I . . . I really don't believe the boom is going to last much longer," said the Colonel in the kindliest of voices.

Petrie was honestly puzzled.

"Why do you say that?"

"Because I have noticed when prices get so high and so absurd that even school teachers begin to buy, any boom is about over."

Petrie flushed.

"Well I be damned!" he ejaculated. "I didn't mean to be . . ."

"Now, now," pacified Miltiades, a little sorry he had insulted his depositor, "I knew I ran a risk, Mr. Petrie, in saying that, but while I may lose a friend and the bank lose a customer, still I hope it will keep you from losing your money. A young man has to work a long time and live a very self-denying life to save six or seven thousand dollars, Mr. Petrie. I would like to see you keep yours."

The old man's correct guess at how much Petrie had in the bank ironed out much of the scientist's resentment.

"Look here," said Petrie, calm and sincere once more, "a man can't get on and do well off the salary I'm making. If I ever have anything I've got to invest in something . . . what do you advise, Colonel Vaiden?"

"What I would say may not have much application now," replied the Colonel.

"What would you say?" inquired Petrie.

"My rule is, my advice is, Mr. Petrie, always buy when other men want to sell, and sell when other men want to buy. So all the advice I could give you is to sell off what you've got."

"But I—I haven't anything," said Petrie, uncomfortable again.

"That's why I said I was afraid my advice wouldn't be applicable to you," explained the Colonel gently.

Petrie stood looking at him for five seconds longer.

"Thank you, Colonel, good-day."

And he put on his hat and went out the door.

The old Colonel himself sat at his desk pulling at his wrinkled mouth with a kind of smile on his lips and a touch of sympathy in his heart. He wondered if Petrie would now go buy the lot anyway? He probably would.

The reason the Colonel had given way to his rather nasty if honey-coated temper was that the third man before Mr. Petrie who was admitted to his private office had made the Colonel thoroughly angry.

The offender had been Bodine, organizer of the secret society to spread Americanism and stamp out Jews, negroes, and Catholics.

During his visit to the bank, however, Bodine was interested only secondarily in canvassing for his society. He really wanted to know the commercial rating of Lerganthall and Barth and obtain information as to their business ability and honesty.

Miltiades had recommended the firm with his accustomed

reservations; they were very good men, energetic, aggressive, honest in their dealings with the bank. "And as trustworthy as their business will allow."

Bodine was a heavy man with blue bulging eyes.

"What do you mean by as trustworthy as their business allows?" asked the organizer, with the frown of a blustery man who wishes to appear profound.

"I count the probability of success in a man's operations as part of his general trustworthiness," explained Miltiades.

Bodine nodded his big head slowly and with an air of wisdom.

"Yes . . . I see that . . . and do you think Lerganthall and Barth will probably succeed?"

Miltiades pulled at his chin.

"The bank has assisted them in one or two ventures . . . however, it has assisted nearly every other firm in town . . . and a certain percentage of them fail."

Bodine lifted his head up and down.

"I see you are a man of caution, Colonel Vaiden . . . so am I. By the way, Lerganthall and Barth's property along Cypress Creek, it's bound to be a big residential section one of these days, don't you think?"

"It's rather far out of town," pointed out Miltiades.

"Yes, but consider, Colonel Vaiden, the tendency in cities of today toward suburban development."

"That's true . . . in cities."

"Don't you think Cypress Creek would make marvelous sites for beautiful well wooded estates?"

"You do have the woods," agreed Miltiades with a touch of his tongue to his thin, faintly smiling lips.

"There you are," rolled Bodine with satisfaction, "we have the woods, the scenic creek, bathing, canoeing, horseback riding. . . . Mr. Barth even visions a flying field . . . what do you think of that, Colonel?"

"That's fine." The old banker paused, and after a moment added, "Barth's a Northern man, isn't he?"

"Yes, I believe he is. Why did you say that?"

"Because Northern people bathe and canoe and horseback ride."

"Why, they do it in Birmingham, in Atlanta, in New Orleans . . . all the big cities."

The Colonel nodded pacifyingly.

"All I did was to ask if Barth was from the North, and you said he was."

"Well . . . yes . . . that's correct," conceded Bodine, as if he had checked over a long bill of particulars and had found them substantially correct.

The Colonel decided to waste no more words on Bodine. The organizer was the sort of man who greatly impressed ordinary people and for whom an aristocratic person formed an instinctive dislike on first sight. So now Miltiades remained politely silent, waiting for the fellow to take his departure.

Mr. William Yancey Bodine, however, for that was his name, had arrived only at the second phase of his mission. He cleared his throat, changed his voice to a broadly flattering tone:

"Colonel Vaiden, I have been thinking about you."

"Yes?" queried the banker dryly.

"Yes, I have. You have great influence in Florence, Colonel; you're a force in your community."

Miltiades waited impassively.

"I know, Colonel, Florence knows, Alabama knows, that first, last, and always, you're an American citizen, sir, a citizen of the United States of America, sir." Bodine shook a heavy fist at these periods, as if defending the Colonel from a charge of treason.

"Where do you come in on my citizenship?" inquired the Colonel.

"I don't come in at all, sir, not personally, but I represent an organization, sir, of pure-blooded Americans upholding pure Americanism. It is an unselfish organization of patriots, sir, impelled by the highest motives that ever stirred the human heart to deed of heroism. I refer, sir, to the love of one's country . . . I know you love your country, Colonel Vaiden."

The Colonel looked straight at Bodine.

"My country was crushed, overrun, poisoned, and polluted years ago, Mr. Bodine."

The organizer stared at the old man.

"Why don't you consider this your country?"

"It's where I'm living. It's a place without leisure, without finesse. Look at those six negroes thrown in jail! Why were they ever permitted to run loose in the first place? It is as outrageous as it would be to allow a vicious stud horse to run loose. They should have been confined and set to work. Rapes wouldn't happen if the niggers had plenty of work, but a mawkish sentimentality brought down here by Yankees . . ."

Bodine considered the Colonel's kidney. He had handled old Confederate soldiers before.

"Colonel, nobody in the world has a greater respect for the ideals of the old South than I have. But I say we are not lost. The South is just as much the South today as it was before the Civil War. Only nowadays we are in the midst of another battle, more insidious, more subversive than an open appeal to arms.

"That is why I am asking you, Colonel Vaiden, to join our mystic brotherhood who are bound together by ties of loyalty, fraternity, equality, and help hurl back this second invader of our Southland."

"Who do you want to hurl back?" asked the Colonel, rather ashamed of ever expressing a sentiment to Bodine.

"The nigger, the Catholic, the Jew," quoted Bodine. "What a shame it is that those six niggers are still alive!"

"The shame reaches back to 'sixty-four, Bodine, when they were dumped into our commonwealth as citizens, but since they have been dumped, it is obligatory upon us to consider them as citizens and surround them with all the safeguards of the law."

"Well, they may not be hanged if they come to trial."

"That's the problem we are struggling with today, Bodine, and I feel we have this particular case arranged for."

Bodine was discomfited. He had thought the Colonel was about to come over on his side, but here he was settling back just where he had started.

"Well, look here," he demanded, "what do you think about the Catholics?"

"I don't think anything about them."

"Don't you believe the Pope's trying to run this country, just like he tried to run Mexico? Don't you believe the Protestant people ought to chase 'em out of America?"

"Well, I couldn't subscribe to that, Bodine," said Miltiades, becoming amused now that the topic had shifted from his personal sore; "we have a number of Catholic accounts here in the bank I'd hate to see withdrawn."

Bodine blew up.

"My God, I hope you wouldn't let a dollar stand between you and your duty as a citizen . . . and look at the Jews . . . don't you know they have a money trust that's turning the whole United States into a business organization run entirely for the benefit of the Jews?"

"Bodine," suggested Miltiades with a twinkle in his eyes, "are you aware that Mr. Lerganthall, your partner in the Cypress Creek development, is a Jew?"

Bodine's highly colored face grew redder than ever.

"Hell, while they're here, we might as well use 'em. You can't keep 'em from making money, and you might as well let 'em make some for you!"

"When your association quits dealing with the Jews and sticks up to its principles, I'll join you, Bodine," agreed Miltiades suavely.

"What a hell of a way for you to talk, throwing up a dollar to me!" boomed Bodine. "You'll let your country be ruled by Catholics so as to save their bank accounts, and you'll turn niggers aloose on the women in your own family because you're afraid, if you lynch 'em, the damn Yankees won't buy your land. . . ."

The old banker sprang to his feet and jerked shakily at the drawer of his desk.

"Bodine, get out of here before I blow your damned insolent brains out! You beefy, addle-headed wind-bag! Get out of here!"

And the Colonel brought a blue steel automatic above the level of his desk.

Bodine walked out silently and fairly quickly with what dignity he could muster at that gait. He thought, without looking back, "You damned yellow skeleton, I'll pay you off for this!" but he said nothing, and was careful to give the furious old man no further outward cause of offense.

CHAPTER TWENTY

I T WAS this unpleasantness with Bodine that had caused the old Colonel to deal so crustily with J. Adlee Petrie. When the school teacher finally left the bank, Miss Katie telephoned the Colonel that his list was cleared, and the old man arose, still shaky from his anger.

The waiting room was empty save for Miss Katie arranging her desk for the night. The Colonel went on out into the street where Marsan sat patiently awaiting him in the car. When she saw his face she called out anxiously:

"What's the matter, Daddy?"

The old man made a gesture.

"The fools I have to talk to!"

The girl opened the door for him.

"What makes you talk to them? . . . You don't have to."

That was an old debate that arose in the Vaiden manor at odd intervals: why the Colonel continued at the bank, why he still worked. He did not answer but held his wrinkled jaw to be pressed by Marsan's delicately rouged cheek.

"Where do you want to drive?" she asked.

"Up Pine Street."

"Not along the river today?"

"No, I don't want to see steamboats. I don't want to see anything men have bet their money on and lost. I never heard of anybody betting on a cathedral . . . so far, have you?"

Marsan drew in her lips to cover a smile.

"Would you like to go around and meet Dr. Blankenship?"

The old Colonel looked at his daughter.

"Why, Marsan!"

127

"I was joking, Daddy."

"Honey, you shouldn't joke about religious matters. We never did at home . . . Polycarp . . . Augustus . . . Cassandra . . . none of us."

Marsan thought of the long roll of her aunts and uncles with their clear-cut sins and virtues. It must have been comforting to know exactly the one from the other with no confusion about it.

It seemed to Marsan, back in the days of her father's youth, the very sins of the people were tonic experiences illustrating evil and promoting virtue, but nowadays who knew which was which?

As she drove along, her own experience with Red McLaughlin came to her mind. She recalled that they had used this very seat on which she and her father now sat, and it made her ashamed. And yet there was nothing to be ashamed of . . . it was a universal biological impulse. She knew unmarried girls developed neuroses if they persisted in abstention, and fell into moral degeneration if they indulged. It sifted down to a matter of taste as to what sort of catastrophe a girl would choose. However, now, Marsan wished she had continued virginal until she married, if she ever married, and her science teacher, Mr. Petrie, floated into and out of her mind.

This in turn recalled the negro who had beaten Mr. Petrie in the metallurgical examination, and this reminded her of the six negro boys in jail, and so her thoughts would probably have turned round and round like a squirrel in a cage, when her father rescued her from this unprofitable circle by ejaculating:

"Riding . . . canoeing . . . tchk!"

Marsan looked at him.

"What's the matter with them?"

"They are not done any more."

"I've ridden. . . . Mamma used to ride till she got too fat and lazy."

"I mean men. If a man rides he must do it in a motorcar

at not less than fifty miles an hour. If he makes an invest-
ment it must net him three hundred percent. per annum or
the investor will change to something else. There is no sense
of leisure in anything any more."

"How did folks get like that?" asked Marsan, looking at
her hands on the wheel and thinking they needed manicuring.

"Because the nigger has been set free. Slaves and planta-
tions brought a sense of leisure and a sense of responsibility
toward God which no turn of fortune or misfortune could
shake. Slavery not only preserved the original American
idea of a family, it enlarged and ennobled it into that of a
patriarchy. It produced leisure and culture and that deep
wide responsibility without which men drift into hedonism
and dilettantism. The Yankees not only set aside the or-
dained institution of slavery, they have set aside the ordi-
nance of marriage with universal divorce, and courtesy with
universal boorishness."

"Southern people get divorces too."

"That's because people mimic men with money, no matter
how sad an example they set."

Here the car stopped before the foundation of the new
cathedral. The old banker ceased his fulminations and sat
looking at it, but his thoughts ran on as mordantly as ever.

Presently Marsan cried out:

"There's Cousin Jerry in the door of the old church. I
have a message for him."

"Who from?"

"An old woman named Swartout."

"I want to see Jerry, too," said the old banker, and they
both climbed out and went slowly together into the old
church.

From the doorway of the old church Jerry waved at his
kinsfolk. He had come to the door because he had been
listening, half unconsciously, for a motorcar to stop at the
curb. The purring sound of the big Vaiden car which he had
heard was not the rattletrap which he had been expecting,
but still he was not absolutely sure, so finally he went out

to see. It was Marsan and her father. The daughter lifted a hand at him and called, in the gay inflections of a young girl:

"Got a message for you, Cousin Jerry."

"Yes, what is it?"

Marsan waggled her hands about her head to show complete bewilderment.

"That's what I've come to ask you about. I can't make heads or tails of it." Then she added that her father, too, wanted to see Jerry.

The old banker said:

"Take her first, find out what she wants. I'm in no rush but she's in a hurry, she has only about seventy-two more years to live."

"Daddy, you know I won't take up Cousin Jerry's time with you waiting."

As she said this she got out the note that Mrs. Swartout had dictated.

"Now, what does this mean?" she inquired in a puzzled tone. "The old woman said you would know."

It required a few seconds before Jerry could place the message, and then he explained to Marsan the old story about Junior Petman and Luggy.

The old banker interposed:

"Why do they come to you with such superstitions as that, Jerry?"

"Why, Daddy," put in Marsan reproachfully, "how can you call that superstition when you know in what a queer way you got your deed back!"

The old banker clicked, "Tchk! Tchk! This wouldn't be like that. Besides, this is a baby. It's too young for anything . . . real to happen to it. And my deed didn't come back to me through Polycarp: one of the clerks just happened to find it. If there had really been anything supernatural to it, why couldn't Polycarp have just brought me the deed?"

The old Colonel was talking about a very strange incident in his life, when something which he thought had been his dead brother Polycarp had appeared to Landers, who was now dead, and had told Landers where Miltiades would find the deed to some property which was in a lawsuit.

"There you are," said Jerry, "why couldn't he?"

"I don't think it was anything at all," said Miltiades. "Looking back at it, I have decided it was nothing at all."

The Colonel then said he would like to speak to Jerry a few minutes. Jerry said certainly and asked his uncle into the small anteroom where he worked.

When the two were by themselves the Colonel began tentatively:

"Jerry, are you very happy in your service here?"

"Do you mean in my immediate tasks? . . . Why no, I'm not."

"What are you doing?"

"At present I am organizing the Sunday Schools of North Alabama, getting up subscriptions to build what we call the Children's Arch . . . it isn't exactly the line I wanted to grow in. It wasn't my intention to become a financier."

"That isn't all you do?"

"No, I plan picnics for Sunday-school classes. I teach weekday religious school on Fridays. Once a month I mimeograph a bulletin of the cathedral's progress and send it out to everyone who has subscribed ten dollars, and to people we hope will subscribe . . . and so on."

"On the whole, it isn't what you want?"

"Well . . . when this scraping around for money lets up, I hope it will get to be what I want."

"Look here," interrupted Miltiades, "do you imagine this money drain will ever be over when you are starting a restaurant, a rooming house, a swimming pool, a bowling alley, and God knows what else . . . don't you know it will be always nip and tuck whether you can keep the church going or not?"

"It will do a lot of good," said Jerry beginning an uncertain defense of his work, "it will be a modern community center . . . and a church."

"Well, I don't know whether you are getting what you want or not; I don't think you are; but I do know I'm not getting what I want. Now the only reason I traded my idea of a church for Blankenship's idea of a church was for your benefit. And if it doesn't benefit you; if neither one of us is getting what he wants . . . I'm out. That's what I stopped by to tell you."

The nephew looked at his uncle with sharp concern.

"My goodness, Uncle Milt . . . don't think of such a thing. Why, the Doctor . . . what is it *you* are not getting?"

"Why, damn it, a church! A church to be buried in, a reverent place where there will be music and solemnity and beauty. I don't want to spend the first three hundred years after my death in a damned hotel and amusement hall. I don't like hotels; I don't like amusement halls. I don't want boys whooping and running over my grave! The more I think of it, the more outrageous it is in Blankenship to insist . . ."

"Wait! Wait!" begged Jerry. "Let me show you something. Dr. Blankenship said if you ever appeared dissatisfied with your donation, would I please show you this."

The Colonel watched Jerry as he went to the wall of the anteroom and pushed back a panel. It was a panel of some size, and as it slid back the Colonel saw a plaster of Paris model of a sarcophagus covered with a carved Confederate flag. Above it arose a segment of a blue vault set with four gold stars. The central panel of the sarcophagus bore the legend:

COLONEL MILTIADES VAIDEN, C.S.A.
COMMANDER OF
FOURTH ALABAMA VOLUNTEERS
SOLDIER * MERCHANT * BANKER * PATRIOT

"He told me to tell you this would give you an idea of the way it would look," explained Jerry in a lowered voice.

As he said this the two men heard a little gasp behind

them. They turned and saw Marsan apparently on the verge
of toppling over on the floor.

Jerry jumped for her.

"What's the matter? What's wrong, Marsan?"

The girl clung to Jerry's arm, still staring at the model
inside the wall. She quavered out:

"Oh! Oh! Daddy!" and suddenly began weeping.

The two men cuddled her, held her up, got her to a chair.
She appeared on the brink of fainting.

"Why, Marsan, darling . . . Jerry, get some water. . . .
What's the matter, honey?"

The girl drew a long breath and stretched her eyes open.

"How came such a horrible thing in here?"

"Marsan," explained Jerry with a dipper, "you know
your father expects finally to lie . . ."

"A long time off . . . a long time off," assured Miltiades,
patting and rubbing her hands.

"Ye-es . . . I knew that . . . I . . . I don't know why it
. . . it tears me up so. . . ."

And she tried to repress her weeping, swallowing her sobs
and wiping her eyes with a wisp of lace.

CHAPTER TWENTY-ONE

W<small>HEN</small> Jerry Catlin saw the Vaidens off in their automobile, another car, a small shabby rattling machine, came up the street from the direction of town. Through the dirt and flickering reflections on its windshield Jerry caught glimpses of the driver, a girl, whom he knew to be Aurelia Swartout.

The assistant minister felt a lift of spirits as he awaited her on the curb. He had hardly known it, but he had been uneasy lest she should not come and practise on the organ that afternoon.

Now, as she drove up, he smiled with pleasure and opened the door of her rickety car, but she remained motionless, looking at him with an odd whitened face.

"You were just seeing some friend off," she said with a faint smile.

"It was Marsan and the Colonel," said Jerry, "come on in and play for me."

"Didn't she play for you?"

"Who?"

"Why, Miss Marsan."

Jerry looked to see if she were jesting.

"Marsan play a pipe organ?" He began to laugh.

"Maybe she does," said Aurelia with prickles in her even voice. "Did you ask her to?"

"There was no use in asking her . . . I know she can't."

"What was she doing in the church?"

"Nothing at all . . . sitting down . . . she was with her father, who came to see me."

Miss Swartout smiled.

134

"I don't see how it could have been that when her father wasn't with her."

"Why, he was, he and I helped Marsan into the car."

"Just then?"

"Certainly . . . as you drove up."

Miss Swartout sat looking at Jerry with a faint odd smile on her blonde face.

"You're a funny man . . . just say Marsan's father was with her."

Jerry was bewildered.

"I don't see what you're driving at, Miss Swartout. Maybe you didn't see the Colonel, what difference would it make? If he really wasn't here, what object would I have in saying he was here?"

"You and Marsan were there together."

"What if we were? You and I are here together. Besides that, she's my first cousin."

The organist moved to get out of her car.

"I know that, of course, I was just teasing. I saw Colonel Vaiden."

"Well . . . come on in and play," invited Jerry, moving toward the door.

"No, I didn't mean to practise today. I just came by for some music. I was on my way to give a lesson to the Dodds girl."

"I'm sorry; I wanted to hear you play; I've had a mechanical day."

The two walked into the bleak dusty church with its depressing benches and stiff dark choir stalls. As Aurelia went around to get her music she said in a casual voice:

"Mrs. Sydna Vaiden is no kin to you, is she?"

"My aunt by marriage."

"No blood kin."

"No . . . just that."

There was a pause; then, as Aurelia picked up and arranged her music sheets, she said in a monotone:

"You are in love with her, aren't you . . . Sydna Vaiden?"

Jerry was shocked and offended.

"What is the matter with you, Miss Swartout? Why do you make such—such unwholesome suggestions?"

The organist turned and faced him.

"I'll tell you. The first time I ever played for you, Sydna Vaiden came in and began talking to you. Neither of you ever knew I was playing or when I quit playing. I could see you in the mirror. But that didn't surprise me. She never listens to music anyway. I thought maybe you were like her, since you belonged to the same family. But afterwards I found out that you do listen to music very closely . . . a certain sort of music . . . so then I knew you were in love with her."

Jerry stared at this remarkable deduction which had hit on the exact opposite of the truth.

"Such an amazing chain of reasoning, Miss Swartout!" He broke out laughing.

He was half minded to tell her the odd truth that he had been hurt and depressed in a way because he had discovered in that first meeting with Sydna that he no longer loved her. It really was a strange hurt, and yet it was a very fortunate one for him.

As for Miss Swartout, she had been piqued that he and Sydna had talked instead of listening to her practice. She had saved up her pique all these weeks and finally had brought it down on his head like this.

"Well, I haven't misbehaved myself any more, have I? Since then I've listened very nicely. You have no more complaints to make of my deportment, have you?"

"No-o," admitted the girl beginning to smile herself, "but I was right about Sydna Vaiden, wasn't I?"

"Not in the least."

"Oh, by the way, my mother said tell you Junior Petman got more words than all the grown-up persons put together . . . how do you explain that?"

"Listen . . . sit down . . . now, for pity's sake, tell me what you people are talking about . . . got more words . . . how got more words?"

"There was a party, and we had a contest to see who could make the most words out of the letters in the word 'morningglory.' Well, the rest of us studied and studied, but Junior wrote for four or five minutes and quit. His mother said, 'Junior, can't you think of any more?' and he said, 'I've got 'em all.'" Aurelia came to a little pause, looking oddly at the assistant minister in the bleak church.

"Had he?"

"Yes, he had. I suppose he had. There were some words we didn't know. We looked them up in the dictionary, and they were words all right. He had eight more than the next best list."

Jerry looked at the girl with astonished eyes.

"That didn't really happen?"

"It did. I was there. He beat me by thirteen."

"Did he say . . . how he did it?"

"Oh yes, he said Luggy called the words over to him."

"M—huh . . . so that's what happened . . . and your mother wants me to explain that?"

"She's very keen for you to."

"She has a lot of confidence in me?"

"She hasn't any at all. She's for Junior. She hopes he'll stump you." Miss Swartout began to laugh again.

"Well, there you are," said Jerry, enlightened, "so it is now my move. Tell her that Junior is telepathic. That he had telepathic access to the minds of all the persons at the party, so he just wrote out what everybody knew, right off, like that. Luggy, of course, is an illusion, it is merely the form which his telepathic insight assumes. By the way, that last is quite sensible. If a child received its communications in the form of words, it would almost automatically visualize a body to speak the words . . . that's really an idea, Aurelia."

"Yes, but it had words the rest of us never had heard of."

Jerry considered another moment.

"Tell her the Petman child is a psychic. That it had seen the words in newspapers, dictionaries, anywhere, and that it has a photographic and instantaneous memory."

Aurelia nodded, impressed.

"Why, that makes it very simple. He got his words just like the rest of us got ours, only he was better at it than we were."

"Why, yes, I suppose it does," admitted Jerry, a little disappointed himself that the marvel and his explanation of it had sifted down to anything so usual as that. "You can tell your mother that."

"I don't think she will like it much," said Aurelia.

"I'll go over and tell it to her myself," said Jerry.

"We-ell . . . that might help," agreed Aurelia reluctantly.

"You pick me up on your way back, after you give the Dodds girl her music lesson," planned Jerry. "I'd like the drive. I've been stuffy today."

"Now, look here, I'm not going to bring you back home," warned Aurelia.

"No, I'll take a bus."

"Well . . . all right . . . let's start."

"But you have to give the Dodds girl her music lesson?"

Aurelia glanced at her wrist watch.

"It's too late now. . . . I don't see why Mother bothers her head about such things, do you?"

"Well, it's a human frailty to seek after wonders," said Jerry more thoughtfully, "and if there should be a reality back of the little boy's illusions, it would exist outside the metaphysics of the church, and it would create a confusion and necessitate a certain rearrangement of orthodox religion."

Aurelia looked at her companion as they went to the car.

"The idea of Mother thinking of that!"

"No, she doesn't think of it, she feels it. It is my belief, Aurelia, that the subtlest and most glorified philosophies attainable by the human intellect lie nascent in the humblest minds. The bushman wondering at the Australian stars at night is an embryonic Kepler or Einstein. The savage father enduring the ordinary hardships of everyday life for his mate and children is a far-off Christ upon a cross."

The organist became quiet and directed her car through Courthouse Square and along the Sheffield road as the sun spread its silent conflagration in the West. From the brow of the river hill the two could see a long lane of the color repeated in the river with trees and the spindling bridge etched against it.

"I don't know what people will say about you driving home with me," said the girl, glancing at the sky and then back at the road.

"Nothing," opined Jerry.

"M—m, you don't know Florence women . . . if a man goes out and educates himself, people say that's fine; but if a girl does the same thing, people think she's a little queer . . . you know . . . not the sort of a girl that other girls chum with . . . or men go with."

Jerry looked at her.

"Are you lonely, Miss Swartout?"

"No-o . . . I play."

"Have you no men friends?"

"There's a boy named Tony Vicelli who wants to marry me," she said with brooding frankness.

"What does he do?"

"Work for Papa."

"What does your father do?"

"Builds houses."

"Contractor?"

"A kind of a contractor."

She spoke with reluctance and obvious distaste, and Jerry abandoned the point.

When the motor crossed the bridge, Aurelia asked if they should go through Mr. Tergune's subdivision, it was a very pretty drive.

Jerry agreed to the extended drive provided the girl would let him fill the car with gas in Sheffield.

Aurelia refused this; she said she often drove that way

by herself, and it was nice to have somebody in the car who understood what she was talking about if she wanted to say something.

"Are you going to want to say anything?" asked Jerry in an effort to lighten the conversation.

"Talk doesn't keep folks from being lonely," said Aurelia, "it's the feeling that you will be understood no matter whether you talk or not." She thought a moment then gave a brief laugh. "You know *they* don't know a motet from a pavane; *they* couldn't tell a Scottish snap from an Italian cadence."

Jerry gathered that she referred to the other women, who thought her a little queer.

Before the car had gone far, night fell, and the motorists moved along wide empty boulevards, passing through the ornamental and solitary entrances of the various subdivisions. These ornate entrances were symbols of the boom itself; newcomers hurrying to buy, hurrying to sell; every man proclaiming the mighty future of Florence and wondering uneasily and subconsciously how long he dared hold his belongings to squeeze the last cent out of them and yet not be caught in the catastrophe.

At the Southern end of their drive they moved along a narrower, but still a paved road sentineled with the black shapes of cottages. Aurelia broke her silence:

"This is Jericho."

The assistant minister looked around in the darkness with interest.

"Mr. Petman's subdivision for colored people?"

"Yes; my father is building these houses."

Jerry was surprised.

"Well, it's about the only subdivision under way . . . your father must be doing pretty well."

Aurelia drove a space and then said in a flat voice:

"My father's a fool."

Jerry opened his mouth to remonstrate when the girl gasped out:

"Look! Look! Oh, my goodness, it's one of Papa's houses on fire!"

The light she saw lay on their left. Jerry could see flames leaping up at some indeterminate distance. Aurelia veered her car and set out toward the light.

"Oh, if it's one of Papa's houses . . . the water isn't on yet . . . the main is laid but it isn't connected. We'll never put it out!"

"We can get back to town and send a chemical engine," hurried Jerry.

Miss Swartout drove faster when Jerry ejaculated:

"Why, that's not a house!"

The girl slowed down her motor.

"Why, it isn't, it's a cross!"

Through some caution she switched off her lights and moved at a slow pace toward the queer illumination. It defined itself as a tall cross with the angles somewhat blurred by the flames. Around it marched a line of white-sheeted figures. The girl looked at the scene fixedly.

"Do you suppose," she began, "that they mean they won't let the niggers move in here?"

"Why, no-o, they can't mean that," comforted Jerry in an uncertain voice; "the plans of this negro subdivision were approved by the building Committee of the Realtors' Association." He looked around the car. "Besides, we are out of Mr. Petman's subdivision. There are no houses anywhere around."

Aurelia was reassured. She sat watching the red-lighted sheets moving around the flaming cross.

"What are they doing that for?" she asked finally.

"Would you really like to know?"

"Yes . . . what?"

"Right at this moment it is on account of those six negroes. The boom almost killed Bodine's organization, because it gave people something to think about and gamble on. Before the boom men joined this society and marched around bonfires because their lives were humdrum and unimportant.

Doings such as these, masking themselves, riding up and down the countryside on secret political missions, provided an escape from, say, selling hardware all day long, or filling teeth. And then for them to think that somehow or other they were saving their country by such antics . . . it was a bargain at the price."

Miss Swartout broke out laughing.

"It's the South's remedy for an inferiority complex."

"I wouldn't say that," objected Jerry, "because the term is a bit out of date."

CHAPTER TWENTY-TWO

B Y A somewhat odd coincidence, just before Jerry Catlin
and Miss Swartout reached Carver's Lane they passed a
building known as Benevolence Hall. It was a structure
owned by the negroes. On this night it was lighted up, and
through its windows they could see figures wearing the cheap,
brightly colored regalia of the negro society of Princes and
Potentates of Ethiopia.

The two stopped and watched the performance for a while,
laughing at the way the black people imagined kings and
princes deported themselves; then they drove on to Aurelia's
home.

Jerry's actual visit in the Swartout cottage was not
particularly noteworthy save for his meeting with Tony
Vicelli, Aurelia's lover, and a completely unexpected dona-
tion to the cathedral from Mr. Swartout.

Mr. Swartout was a small man with a red lumpy face and
blue eyes that were always stretched wide. When Aurelia
introduced him to Jerry, Mr. Swartout was immensely im-
pressed at being presented to a minister. He began at once
talking about the foundations of the new cathedral, giving
details which Jerry himself had never observed. From this
topic he led, or rather leaped, for his conversation was dis-
connected, to the subject of Aurelia's piano.

"Come into the parlor," he invited, "and have a look at it
... wonderful cabinet work, Doctor ... you can't tell where the
joints are ... and Minnie paid for it with her music lessons."

"Minnie?"

"Aurely," corrected little old Mrs. Swartout quickly.

Jerry went in to see the workmanship of the piano.

The daughter stood helpless in the bare parlor while her father exhibited the undisputed workmanship on the piano. As a relief Jerry mentioned seeing the houses Mr. Swartout had built in Jericho.

"You did!" ejaculated the little man, very pleased, "and did you take the trouble to go in one of 'em and see how it was built?"

"No, I didn't," admitted Jerry.

"You should have," exclaimed the little man, with wide enthusiastic blue eyes, "every stick in them houses is clear lumber, not a foot of sap. The sash weights have guides, they don't hang loose and get caught. The hardware in them houses would do for your uncle's manor, Dr. Catlin . . . all the best, first class . . . and built right."

"I wonder you could afford to do it?"

"It's a pleasure to do it. I was a carpenter before the boom, Dr. Catlin, and I worked for other contractors, and the way they scamped their material and their work made me sick. I thought to myself, 'If I ever get a chance I'll turn out work that is work.' Then, as I say, along come the boom, and Marvin Petman, who is a kind of partner of mine, said to me, 'Swartout, why don't you go into the contracting game and make some sure enough money?' And I said, 'Who would contract with me?' And he said, 'Why, I would, you're a good workman and an honest man.' And I said, 'I haven't the money to start.' And Petman laughed and said, 'If nobody started till they had the money to start, they wouldn't be any startin' done. Go to the banks,' he said.

"Well, we talked it over about twice more, when I took him up. Petman introduced me to his bank, the Merchants and Planters, right over there in Sheffield, and here I am, a contractor. . . . That foundation you are putting under the cathedral, Dr. Catlin, sure is a pretty piece of stone work. . . . What do you do over there?"

"Oh, Papa, Dr. Catlin isn't interested in what he's doing," pleaded Aurelia a little irrationally.

"Bound to be, or he wouldn't do it, Minnie."

"Certainly I'm interested . . . I organize contributions from Sunday schools, mainly."

"Collecting money?"

"Yes, to build the church."

"I suppose you'd take it from just anywhere you could, wouldn't you? . . . It's a good cause."

"Naturally," laughed Jerry. "I don't believe I ever heard of a church turning down a contribution."

Mr. Swartout stood a moment longer with his hands in his pockets.

"Well . . . make yourself at home," he invited, turned, and went out into the hallway again and closed the parlor door softly behind him.

Aurelia looked at Jerry with a flushed face and bright embarrassed eyes. Suddenly she began laughing.

"You must excuse him . . . that's his technique."

"Technique?"

"To arrange privacy for me and my callers."

Jerry smiled, amused by the father and not displeased at the result of his efforts. He glanced at the closed door and then at an open window. Through it, he saw by the parlor light the blossom of a climbing rose with the glint of dew on its petals. The almost antiseptic cleanness of the bare room seemed to take on the odor of the rose, although it was improbable that he actually smelled it.

Jerry did, after all, take an interest in the piano. He wanted to know why Aurelia had installed a grand piano in the cottage.

"I thought at one time I was going to be a concert pianist . . . my teacher told me I could."

Jerry was surprised.

"You must be extremely good."

"I don't know. . . . He was a Southern teacher . . . Josefy, in Birmingham . . . he thought I would get a scholarship in Chicago, but I didn't. In fact, I didn't even get under Straussman . . . I had to study with his assistant, Mr. Mentierre."

Jerry divined then the cause of the continual flavor of pathos about Miss Swartout. She was one of those artists who are almost good. She had far more ability than was required at a casual musical in Florence. She had the nerves of an artist; talk disturbed her when she was playing. Indeed, her work was most worthy to be listened to . . . free. But in ordinary social gatherings no one listened to music. Her extra skill in her work was of little advantage to her in attracting pupils, because the children in Florence wanted to learn to play popular tunes at once, and Miss Swartout did not teach popular tunes, nor, indeed, any tune, at once.

Jerry wondered if Miss Swartout was so professional that he dare not ask her to play for him. He was about to risk the point when he heard Mr. Swartout in the hallway inviting someone to walk into the parlor, saying that Minnie and a doctor friend of hers would be glad to see the newcomer.

Whoever it was declined the invitation in a low voice. He had just come over, he said, to ask Mr. Swartout on what house he was to work next day.

"On the Meggs house," returned the contractor heartily. "Won't you set a while, Tony?"

"No—no," said Tony in a gray voice, "I'll be going back to my boarding place."

Jerry, recalling his own boyhood and Sydna, knew all the perturbations of Tony's heart, and he was very sorry he had disturbed the young man's call.

Twenty minutes later, when the assistant minister left the home in Carver's Lane, the knotty little contractor walked with him to the gate and in parting, put a package into his hands.

"Something to go on the cathedral," he said. "I'm not religious myself, but I believe in churches. I've thought I'd like to build a church myself, sometime, when I'm old, just spend my days working on a church."

In Jerry's astonished hands was a roll of bills of small denominations.

Aurelia, who was driving Jerry to the bus station in Sheffield, gasped out:

"Why . . . Papa . . ." and became silent.

When the two were in the car together, Jerry held the money irresolutely in his hands, disturbed at his companion's gasp. He was considering a diplomatic way to return it when an extraordinary sight arrested both their eyes.

A constellation of lanterns was moving down Carver's Lane from Benevolence Hall to Grey Mule Hill.

These lanterns lighted one of the most chromatic and tatterdemalion pageants that Jerry had ever seen. They were the Princes and Potentates of Ethiopia on their way home. They sang, swayed, and laughed. Black men and women shuffled along in pairs arrayed in tinsel and bright cheap rayon. When the procession passed the car they became dignified before the white onlookers. Those who knew the motorists called out in their mellow voices:

"Hidy, Miss Rellie! Hidy, Mistuh Je'y! Nice night we're havin'."

To which the white couple called back courteous replies, keeping their amusement out of their voices as best they could.

In the line of march waddled a large, shining, very black woman, wearing a yellow and green robe with a crimson stole arching out and over a vast bosom, and crowned with a gilt and glass tiara.

She stopped before the car and brought to a stand her escort, a short, stumpy black man.

"Well, Mist' Je'y, I heard you come home. I heard my niece say she seed you."

"Who is your niece?" asked Jerry with a Southerner's dislike for admitting that he does not remember his negro friends.

"Rose," said the huge woman, so mellowly that it was music, "that high yellow gal what took you in de hotel."

Miss Swartout saw Jerry's predicament and prompted in a low tone:

"That's Pammy Lee."

The bulky negress caught this and burst out:

"Shoo, Mist' Je'y knows me!"

"Of course I do," cried Jerry, amazed at such a bulk sub-
stituted for the leggy, corkscrew-headed Pammy Lee whom
he had known more than a decade before. "How're you
getting on?" inquired Jerry heartily.

"Oh, fine . . . jess fine . . . one o' my husban's got killed
in de wah, an' I jess come into my 'surance money."

"You don't mean it!" cried Jerry in a congratulatory tone.

"Yes suh, I means hit. De good Lawd let me come into
my own at las', and I says, 'Good-bye, pot, good-bye, fryin'
pan, Pammy Lee has come into huh own at las'.'"

"I certainly congratulate you," said Jerry very sincerely.

"Thank you, Mist' Je'y, thank you ve'y much. I come putty
neah puttin' in my claim fuh anothah one o' my husban's
who got killed in de wa', but Mistuh Jeffe'son Ashton, who
runs my insu'ance business fuh me, he say, 'No, I wouldn't
do hit, Pammy Lee. 'Vide up yo' husban's. Let some othah
cullud woman put in a claim on Kinchus' dat was my othah
husban's name, fo' he got killed; he say, 'You got mo'n you
can spen' all yo' life long already, Pammy Lee.'"

Miss Swartout began to laugh irresistibly.

"Get into the back seat, Pammy Lee, drive to the bus
station with me, and I'll take you back home. I don't like
to drive by myself after dark."

"All right, yessum . . . still, I dunno . . ." She turned to her
escort in a red calico surplice.

"What you say 'bout dat, Ludus?"

"Sho! Sho! Don' stan' back on me," urged Ludus good-
naturedly.

He took her great black arm and moved her with a droll
sort of bow toward the car.

Pammy Lee hung back.

"I sho' don' know whethuh to go aw not. Heah I is in muh
robe, runnin' off an' leavin' Ludus in his robe . . ."

"Toss a nickel," laughed Jerry, "that will decide it without prejudice."

Ludus produced a coin, called out, "Haids she stay, tails she go," and tossed it. He caught it in the palm of his hand and leaned toward the headlight of the car.

As he did so, Jerry saw the outline of a long slender something under his robe and at the bottom caught the glint of a gun barrel.

It was as shocking as if the genial Ludus had transformed himself into a werewolf. Jerry looked fixedly at Ludus, then began scrutinizing all the garish robes that passed him. Under most of the robes worn by the men, he thought he detected the stiffness of guns.

The assistant minister hardly knew what to think or do. If he reported this he might be doing the black folk a serious wrong. On the other hand, it might very well be that the negroes used the guns quite innocently in some of their ceremonies.

Ludus looked up in the light and showed the coin in his yellowish palm:

"Haids, she stay wid me."

CHAPTER TWENTY-THREE

THE guns which Jerry Catlin had glimpsed under the robes of the Princes and Potentates of Ethiopia were entirely real, although Jerry had been not absolutely certain about it. They had even caused a sharp division of opinion among the Princes and Potentates of Ethiopia. Bishop Sinton, Grand Exalted Potentate, with a triple crown on his head had spoken against the men of Grey Mule Hill arming themselves.

He said to his lodge, "You are trudging in a land of sorrow toward a goal which you yourselves cannot see and will never see. The black people of the South have a patience under calamity, an endurance of wrong and injustice such as no other race of men has ever known.

"That is your strength, brothers and sisters, endurance, patience, and love, not rifles. The white people have more rifles than you have. They encompass you about like a cloud; their spears shine on a thousand hills. Yea, Lord, they rise in their wickedness and strike down your children without cause or warrant. But the Lord will protect and comfort us, and the Lord will repay."

He went on in the same strain to point out how much better off were his hearers than their grandfathers who were in chains, and their fathers who could not enter a court to sue a white man but who could only be sued; how much better off they were than their older brothers, who were hanged and burned when certain charges were brought against them without a thought of truth or justice.

"Today," he concluded, "men and boys of our color are to have their trial. Be patient, my people, put away your guns. Today we have our trial; tomorrow we have justice."

There was a negro doctor who belonged to the society, a tall yellow man named Greenup. Not more than fifty or a hundred white persons in Florence knew Greenup existed. He remained as closely as possible in the negro settlement in East Florence, Grey Mule Hill in Sheffield, and Black Bottom in Tuscumbia. He bought his groceries from negro stores in East Florence, and purchased clothes for himself and family from negro tailors and modistes in Birmingham.

At all the meetings of the Princes and Potentates of Ethiopia he wore a green silk robe slashed with white and scarlet, and a double crown. He was a somber, serious man, continually in mind of the fact that he was barred from the County Medical Association; that no white doctor would administer ether when he operated on his patients, and that the Florence hospital was not open to him. He read his medical journals with great attention, trying to make up in this manner what he missed in the ordinary doctors' consultations. He had two friends, negro doctors in Birmingham, whom he went to see when he bought his clothing.

Greenup was highly influential among the negroes of the three adjoining towns, and he strongly favored the Princes and Potentates of Ethiopia possessing guns and ammunition.

The difference which thus broke out between Bishop Sinton and Dr. Greenup was unfortunate. In their absurd regalia both men were intensely in earnest. The two had always worked together. They had planned and introduced into the black settlements negro dolls with curly black hair to be given to little negro girls instead of the usual blonde dolls. They introduced especial books into the negro public schools with stories of negro social leaders, negro warriors, negro poets, negro scientists.

All their efforts were directed toward a building up of negro pride of race. The cheap absurd costumes all of them wore were a childish step in that direction, whose emptiness both the leaders understood. But the two men differed with each other on the matter of guns.

When the meeting had been dismissed and the members shuffled home in their brummagem, the debate between the two men persisted among their followers.

"Brothah Greenup sho' is a man," said Ludus.

"Brothah Sinton sho' has got de Lawd on his side," said Pammy Lee.

"Brothah Greenup, he quote scripture, too; he say, 'I come not to bring peace but a sword.'"

"Yeh, but Chris' let de chillun ob dis worl' crucify He."

The two fantastically clad negroes moved on, fetching up what bits of the scripture they could recall by way of argument. Presently Ludus said in a different tone:

"Pammy Lee, gimme ten dollahs out'n all dat money de guv'mint give you."

"Huh, how come dat?"

"Well, it jess lak you pick it up in de road."

"Yeh, pickin' up ain't layin' down."

It was at this moment that the two members of Ethiopian royalty saw the lights of a motor coming and a few moments later met Jerry Catlin and Miss Rellie Swartout.

The delight of Pammy Lee was great, not that she cared anything about Jerry himself, but he was a unit of the great white family which placed before her imagination an ideal world of grandeur, nobility, and power.

When Miss Rellie invited Pammy Lee to go with her to the bus station, Pammy Lee almost climbed into the car, but she did not quite do it, and at the toss of a nickel she went on with Ludus to her home.

But the bulky black woman paid little more attention to Ludus. She was absorbed in the past; she recalled her mother, Miss Tony, who once worked for Mr. Augustus Vaiden and Miss Sydna, who once had been Jerry's sweetheart and who had married Colonel Milt. The past of her pantheon moved before her.

And she remembered one night, how Jerry, after kissing Miss Sydna, had taken her, Pammy Lee, a leggy screw-haired black girl, among the box hedges. That young Jerry seemed to her to bear no relation whatever to the grave man she had just seen in the car, and that vanished, leggy Pammy Lee who was so awkwardly and incidentally seduced bore no relation whatever to herself. That misstep was lost in the pensive perspective of Time.

Ludus was saying:

"Looky heah, Pammy Lee, why don' you gimme a little o' dat money you picked up? My Lawd, Pammy Lee, how much money did you git, nohow?"

Pammy Lee did not want to be disturbed in her reverie.

"Hush, Ludus, hush yo' mouf."

"How much 'surance you git frum de guv'mint?"

"I nevah count hit."

"Co'se you didn't, you couldn't, but Mistah Ashton, he count hit."

"Oh, Ludus, my min's on othah things."

"Yeh, yo min' gits on othah things when dat 'surance money comes up," said Ludus bitterly.

Pammy Lee made no reply, and the two left the primary clay road that meandered down the hill and took the path to Pammy Lee's cabin.

Resentment filled Ludus at the way Pammy Lee was acting. To the negro man Pammy Lee's insurance money appeared a trove which she had stumbled upon by the sheerest accident. He had the annoyed feeling that comes over a person when his companion stoops and picks up a coin that both of them saw. That a mere stoop and picking up should win a fortune never seems fair to the person who does not stoop.

"Look here, Pammy Lee," said Ludus in a hard voice, "is you or ain't you gwi' give me some o' dat 'surance money?"

"You fool niggah, I ain't."

"Is you hit on you now?"

Pammy Lee tried to see his face in the lantern light.

"Ludus, I ain't sayin' nothin' 'tall 'bout dat money."

"Well, I see if you is got hit on you."

The queer parti-colored figure put down the lantern, caught Pammy Lee's great arm, and with the other hand began to feel her enormous thighs to see what she had hidden in her stockings.

Pammy Lee flung the negro from her.

"You fool man!" she cried, "quit feelin' o' my laigs!"

Ludus' gun dropped to the ground. He rushed back at her unencumbered, determined to have his share of her windfall.

Pammy Lee screamed. The grotesquely colored figures struggled in the lantern light. The huge negress was almost as strong as the man. She began sweating and became so slippery he could not hold her at all. She shrieked and flung him from her. He fell heavily to the ground, his hands full of bright rags torn from her regalia. Lying beside him, Ludus saw his gun in the lantern light. He seized it and leaped up again.

"You damn stingy black slut," he yelled, "gittin' money off'n daid men!"

The huge half-naked black woman threw up her ponderous arms and turned for her cabin, screaming:

"Ludus! Don't kill me, Ludus! Don't kill me!" when he fired both barrels.

From all over Grey Mule Hill came shouts and cries.

"Ludus shoot Pammy Lee!" "Oh God, Ludus done shoot Pammy Lee!" "Run fuh de doctah; Pammy Lee got de money to pay!"

Lanterns converged on Pammy Lee's cabin from all directions. Presently another voice called out in a gray tone:

"You-all neen sen' fuh no doctah. De Lawd drap a fo'chun in Pammy Lee's lap, but He don' 'low huh to spen' hit. . . . Pammy Lee's daid."

The Princes and Potentates of Ethiopia gathered around to stare at the tragedy. A woman started a high shrill chanting; others joined in. As they went, they composed lines on the deep irony of Pammy Lee's death.

Six negro men in the garb of antique jesters bore the body inside the cabin.

CHAPTER TWENTY-FOUR

THE shooting of Pammy Lee came to the ears of the
Reverend Jerry Catlin as he was going for private morning
prayers in the old Methodist Church. The assistant minister
was shocked. The thought of the black, the ponderous, the
comfortable Pammy Lee being dead distracted his devotions.

Jerry went to pray each morning by the choir stalls on
the left side of the church and at a point nearest the manuals
of the organ. He chose this position arbitrarily because there
was really no place set off for prayer in the old church. It
had a pulpit but no altar, a collection box but no chapels.
It had no definite place to keep the sacraments and no defi-
nite sacraments. Old Sarah, Dr. Blankenship's cook, baked
the little cakes out of flour and made the sacramental wine
out of blackberries until a meeting of the stewards decided
they would use grapejuice instead.

Amid this lack of focus for spiritual works, and disturbed
by the death of an old acquaintance, and excited about the
six negro criminals whose trial would begin that day, Jerry
really had difficulty in keeping his mind on his prayers.

In such moments of distraction Jerry had found it helpful
to reach in his pocket and finger a coin as a sort of digital
aid to prayer, but on this morning his hands touched a
strange roll of paper money. Then he remembered Mr. Swart-
out's surprising gift of the night before. He had not as yet
entered it in the church ledger as a donation.

This was really important, so he got up from the choir
stall, went into the anteroom which served as the church's
office, and attended to it. As he entered the item, he thought
of the six negro boys in jail.

155

As a matter of fact, all Florence buzzed with excitement over the imminent trial. A great number of Southern people did not believe the trial would ever come off. They thought the black boys would be taken from the officers between the jail and the courthouse. Others thought a mob would rise up spontaneously in the courtroom itself. The men who augured this outcome did so with a hidden pride in belonging to a country so fiery.

However, at about nine o'clock in the morning the negroes were transported to the place of their trial. Deputy Sheriff Northrup had old Dr. Southwick come to the jail in his car as if on a medical mission. He bundled the negroes into this and shot them up the alley and into the courtroom before anybody could say Jack Robinson.

As a final precaution against violence, Sheriff O'Brien stationed a constable at each door of the courtroom, and these guards searched everyone entering the place for fire-arms. There were twenty-seven automatics and revolvers removed from the spectators by eleven o'clock that morning. One of the guards finally declared that he believed the guns were tickets and he would refuse to admit anybody without one.

At twelve o'clock sharp, the clerk of the court called out, "Oh yes! Oh yes! The court is now open!" The jammed room leaned forward as the sheriff, five constables, and eight policemen entered the side door near the Judge's bench in a cordon around the six negro boys. All of them took seats inside the rail, the officers negligently scanning the crowd with their pistols ready at hand. After the manner of officers, they did not appear to expect trouble.

The clerk of the court arose and read each one of the six warrants, all identical except for the names in them. Each defendant and all the defendants were charged separately and jointly with misusing, criminally assaulting, raping, knowing by force and violence, assaulting with intent to rape, assault-ing with intent to misuse, assaulting with intent to criminally know by force and violence, one Mary Roe, a white girl, at a certain place on a certain day of a certain month of a certain year against the peace and dignity of the State of Alabama.

There came a buzzing, a kind of growling, over the courtroom at the endless repetition of these legal obscenities. Judge Wilson tapped with his gavel and called out in a sharp voice that the courtroom would be cleared instantly if all undue noises did not cease. A shushing arose from various parts of the room from people who wanted to hear the trial even if they had to listen quietly to such a wrath-provoking indictment.

In the silence which this created Judge Wilson asked:

"Are the prisoners ready for trial?"

As if in answer to this question, a small wizened, middle-aged man with a long nose arose and said:

"Your Honor, may I speak a word?"

Judge Wilson looked around, and a quiver of apprehension ran over the entire courtroom. Voices ejaculated audibly:

"My God, that's Sandusky!" . . . "Sandusky's for the defense!" . . . "Damn shyster will do anything for money!" . . . "Some big-hearted man ought to shoot Sandusky!"

The court tapped again, more strongly than ever, and again threatened expulsion unless the strictest order were preserved. Then the Judge recognized Mr. Sandusky.

"I was going to say, your Honor, that the present trial promises to be a long and arduous one. I myself am defending a client called Ludus, a colored man charged with murder. The warrant reads, 'One Ludus Meggs charged with shooting and killing a negro woman named Pammy Lee Sparkman in a street fight on Grey Mule Hill.'

"Now, your Honor, I am aware that in a grave cause such as the present one, the court cannot be annoyed with legal trifles. My client Ludus shot this woman in the midst of a fist fight between the two. That we admit. A gun happened to be lying on the ground near the scene of the scuffle. The woman, Pammy Lee Sparkman, was a huge powerful woman, your Honor, and she flung my client with great force on his head and shoulders. He even struck the gun itself and was badly bruised. He has black spots on him, your Honor, from the fall . . . in fact, he is black all over. [Unrestrained laughter in the courtroom which the Judge permitted.]

"Ludus, my client, then, in his pain and rage, seized the gun, leaped up, and shot the black woman who had assaulted him. When this case finally appears for trial, your Honor, it is my intention to enter a plea of self-defense. At the very worst, nothing more can be made out of it than a case of manslaughter, although in this instance the slaughtered person happens to be a woman. [More laughter.]

"As Ludus cannot make a bond of more than fifty dollars and as he made no effort whatever to escape, but remained in his cabin until the constable came for him this morning, and as the constable did not feel it was necessary or safe to bring him here in court today for reasons which are unnecessary to mention, I therefore suggest that you set the prisoner's bond at fifty dollars or release him on his own recognizance until he is indicted by the grand jury at the next term of court."

Mr. Sandusky sat down.

Judge Wilson directed the clerk of the court to release Ludus Meggs without bond and on his own recognizance, pending investigation of his case by the next grand jury, and for the order to be effective at once.

Mr. Sandusky then thanked the Judge and walked out of the side door, to the intense relief of the audience.

The court then returned to the case of the six rapists, and the trial continued.

The six negro boys in question sat in the dock lined up according to size, like the pipes of a syrinx. The smallest prisoner was almost white. He wore dirty knickerbockers, and he could just touch the floor with the toes of his shoes by bending down his feet.

The next boy was almost black, wore trousers that had been cut down from some man's garment, and they fitted him loosely like two sacks joined in the middle. The other four negroes ranged up to a big strapping black boy, as large as an ordinary man.

Four of the prisoners who were really black wore the gray pinched look of negroes who are sick or badly frightened.

The small light yellow boy was clayey, and he kept batting his black eyes and looking at the field of white faces which began close to him and stretched away in an upward incline until it reached the furthest walls. These innumerable pale faces gazed fixedly on him and his five companions.

The child heard a man on the second row whisper to a seat mate, "They'll have to tie weights to that little one's feet to break his neck."

The little yellow boy looked down at his feet with which he had been trying to reach the floor and hitched his heels self-consciously on the second round of his chair.

Mr. Ashton, the attorney appointed by the court to defend the negroes, arose and said the defendants were ready for trial. The state's attorney, a lawyer by the name of Cathey, asked the permission of the court to withhold the actual appearance of the principal witness on the stand, that is, Mary Roe, but to be allowed to introduce a transcript of the interrogatories put to her by Sheriff O'Brien and the girl's answers thereto.

Mr. Ashton objected at once on the score that such testimony was not the best evidence, also that written interrogations were not subject to the probe of cross-questions; also that it denied the defendants the right guaranteed them by law, of facing their accuser.

Mr. Cathey, for the state, looked at Mr. Ashton with a faint disparaging smile.

"Your Honor," he began, "I am aware of the right of the attorney of the defense to probe the truth of the accusations brought against his clients by cross-questioning the witnesses for the state. I am also aware of Mr. Greenleaf's rule requiring the best evidence, and also that the accused have a right to face their accuser in open court, not only to deny what has been charged against them, but so that the court itself, by the cast of their faces, by the expression of their eyes, your Honor, those windows of the soul, may determine which party is in the right and which in the wrong.

"But . . . but, your Honor, may I inquire of the honorable attorney for the defense if he proposes to invoke these historic rights in behalf of six slimy, lecherous, lustful, brutal black rake-hells; animal in form but devils in constitution, the foulest despoilers of the fairest flower that blooms in the hearts of men, a woman's virtue?

"And will the honorable attorney for the defense stoop to ask that the woman herself appear before the gaze of half the county and not only admit a cruel, repulsive, and obscene misuse, more terrible than death, but to describe it, go into the grisly, greasy, and unthinkable horror of its details merely for the formal fulfillment of a criminal code?

"There is another code, your Honor, I have heard old men say, another code in the South, higher than the criminal code, and that is the code of Honor, the code that requires the protection of the sensibilities of its women. Will the attorney for the defense appeal from that higher to that lower code?

"He says that under the rules of evidence the defendants have that right; I say that in the flames of their lust, which God, even among the lower animals, tempers to the use of love, I say they have burned up that right!

"At this moment there sit the six, in the prisoners' bar, on sufferance most fragile and most extreme. Your Honor, can you imagine what this crowded courtroom would do if the pale and bleeding victim of their attack were presented to their eyes as . . . the best evidence?

"Christ in heaven, do you imagine your gavel, your officers set about with ineffective pistols, yea, Sir, do you dream that the Angel with the Flaming Sword whom God set guarding Eden could withstand the impetuous fury of their wrath?"

Uproar from the audience drowned his last period; men howled, stamped their feet, leaned forward with clenched fists. The officers leaped up with drawn arms and formed a

line in front of the prisoners' box. All the officials of the
court began shouting for order. Judge Wilson hammered on
his desk. Finally a nasal shout penetrated the uproar:

"Hey . . . let the trial go on . . . let's hear the other lawyer's
oratory!"

Several voices yelled:

"Put that damned Yankee out!"

This diversion, however, eventually quieted the court-
room.

Mr. Ashton, with a very pale face, walked over and talked
in low tones to the judge. State's Attorney Cathey joined the
two, and they formed a little group of three talking earnestly
together, nodding now and then at the negroes and now and
then at a legal paper on the Judge's desk. Calls broke out to
know what they were saying. Mr. Cathey held up his hand
at them backward so that his palm faced the audience while
he continued talking to the Judge and Mr. Ashton. Silence
fell again, and the crowd watched the trio intently. Finally
Judge Wilson rapped his gavel and said:

"Mr. Ashton withdraws his objection to the absence of
the state's principal witness, but insists on the right to cross-
examine by writing, as if this were a case in chancery. I have
upheld his objection thus modified, and the case will be sus-
pended awaiting the filing of the cross-examination for the
defense."

At that moment a Western Union boy entered the side
door of the courtroom and went to the nearest officer. The
bailiff pointed out to him Judge Wilson. The youngster
took off his blue cap and went up to the bench with his en-
velope but kept his eyes fixed on the six black boys in the
dock. Two of them were not so old as he.

Judge Wilson opened and read the telegram. He frowned,
removed his eyeglasses, polished them, and read again.
Then he beckoned Cathey with a nervous finger, and the
two men read the telegram together.

A reporter for one of the papers arose from the press table,
walked up and looked over the shoulders of the lawyers.

Amazement filled his face, then delight. He made a full-arm gesture at the other reporters at his desk.

"My God, boys," he called in a tone so tense it carried all over the audience, "Ponniman, the great Phineas Delfase Ponniman, has taken this case! He'll defend the coons! He's been retained by the A. B. C. P.! This—is—going—to—be —good!"

CHAPTER TWENTY-FIVE

WHEN the news rolled out of the courthouse and got abroad it seemed hardly credible to the people of Florence that Ponniman would come away down into Alabama merely to defend six little negroes.

Phineas Delfase Ponniman, the great Ponniman, knight errant of justice; war eagle of human rights; ethical paladin of such deep and world-embracing sympathies that he defended all human actions against all human laws, be either what they may . . . such a colossus of the law coming to appear in the cause of six little negroes!

From the day this information appeared in the newspapers, the criminal assault case of the six negro boys leaped from merely Southern into national and even international publicity.

It was made. It had arrived.

Great Northern journals that were published normally every hour, under this heavy break of Ponniman news, appeared at ten- and fifteen-minute intervals, with flaming electric letters traveling around and around their buildings to keep the public informed what was happening to Ponniman and the six little negroes during those dark and unenlightened ten-minute intervals between editions.

These journals dispatched crack reporters and press photographers to the scene of the trial. There they interviewed and photographed, and telegraphed said interviews and photographs to Chicago and New York of the following persons and things, to wit:

The six negro boys; the girl Mary Roe; Judge Wilson; Sheriff O'Brien; Deputy Sheriff Northrup; the constables;

the policemen; the courthouse janitor; wives of the judge, the sheriff, the deputy sheriff, the constables, the policemen, and the janitor. They reproduced recipes given by Judge Wilson's cook for baking Southern biscuit and frying Southern batter cakes, and told how many the Judge ate of each at a sitting.

In these interviews, by the aid and artifice of phonetic spelling they contrived a Southern dialect such as is retailed by Loew's circuit and manufactured in powerful concentrates in the theater district along Forty-second Street in New York City.

In other words, thanks to the impulsive telegram dispatched by Miss Marsan Vaiden, the Florence rape case had broken into big-time publicity.

There was all sorts of talk in Florence as to what would happen to Ponniman when he arrived there. He would be ridden on a rail, tarred and feathered, horsewhipped; they would make it clear how welcome in Southern courts was a Northern defender of negro rapists.

This, however, was a kind of public and collective anger; individually and privately, everybody in Florence was impatient to see the great Phineas Ponniman. Also collectively, the Florence people resented what the Northern papers printed about them, but individually they cared very little, because, after all, nobody read the Northern papers except Northerners.

However, the North did not understand this peculiar dual way the South has of regarding them, and all this Southern talk finally invoked a telegram. The telegram originated with the Mayor of New York and was directed to the Mayor of Florence. It read:

THE MAYOR OF NEW YORK WISHES TO INFORM HIS HONOR THE MAYOR OF FLORENCE THAT MR. PHINEAS DELFASE PONNIMAN AND HIS ASSOCIATES ARE EN ROUTE TO FLORENCE AND WILL INVESTIGATE THE CHARGES MADE AGAINST THE SIX NEGRO PRISONERS NOW IN CUSTODY AT FLORENCE IN THE IN-

TEREST OF JUSTICE, LAW, AND ORDER; AND DESIRES THAT
YOUR HONOR WILL EXTEND TO MR. PONNIMAN AND HIS AS-
SOCIATES EVERY PROTECTION OFFERED BY THE POLICE DE-
PARTMENT OF YOUR CITY. (SIGNED) MAYOR OF NEW YORK.

On the following day this telegram was reproduced in the
Florence Index, and immediately below it in black-faced
type appeared a transcript of the telegraphic answer which
the Mayor of Florence had returned to the Mayor of New
York. It read:

THE MAYOR OF FLORENCE WISHES TO INFORM HIS HONOR THE
MAYOR OF NEW YORK THAT MR. JAMES SANDUSKY AND HIS
ASSOCIATES ARE EN ROUTE TO NEW YORK, AND IN THE INTER-
EST OF JUSTICE, LAW, AND ORDER, WILL INVESTIGATE THE
GANGS OF RACKETEERS, WHO, IN CONNIVANCE WITH YOUR
HONOR'S POLICE, EXTORT MILLIONS FROM THE CITIZENS OF
NEW YORK; THE KIDNAPPING OF INNOCENT MEN AND WOMEN
AND HOLDING THE SAME FOR RANSOM; THE SHOOTING DOWN OF
MEN, WOMEN, AND CHILDREN ON THE STREETS OF NEW YORK
BY GUNMEN ENGAGED, NOT EVEN IN LUCRATIVE ROBBERY,
BUT IN CASUAL TARGET PRACTICE; AND THE MAYOR OF
FLORENCE DESIRES THAT HIS HONOR THE MAYOR OF NEW
YORK WILL EXTEND TO MR. SANDUSKY AND HIS ASSOCIATES
EVERY PROTECTION AND ASSISTANCE AFFORDED BY THE POLICE
DEPARTMENT AND THE CONSTABULARY OF YOUR CITY. (SIGNED)
MAYOR OF FLORENCE.

Perhaps in all Florence only Mr. Jefferson Ashton was
genuinely disturbed and gloomy over this turn taken by the
trial of the six negro boys.

Mr. Ashton sat in his office, which was equipped with a
code, a notarial seal, and a shirt tail full of Alabama Reports.
The lively hopes that he had entertained of improving his
fortunes and surroundings had vanished utterly. With
Phineas Ponniman as a colleague in the rape case, he, Jeffer-
son Ashton, would disappear from the picture. His speech of

defense, which he had been working on for three nights, would be heard by nobody, much less printed in the papers, because everybody would be waiting for the closing plea of Mr. Ponniman.

And presently the defense which Mr. Ashton had been appointed by the court to conduct took on a distinctly reprehensible aspect. He doubted the integrity of a man who would appear in such a cause. He had been seduced by the too insidious arguments of his fellow townsmen. He tapped the ashes of his cheroot onto a piece of dirty cardboard. He was considering resigning from the case.

In the midst of his quandary, the heavy plausible figure of Bodine entered his door. The organizer stood with legs apart, nodding his big head at the lawyer with a kind of slow satire.

"Well," he said in his portentous voice, "this comes of turning the law loose on a case like this, Ashton . . . anything's li'ble to happen . . . any God damn thing."

"What has happened?"

"You ask me? Huh! If Ponniman ever gets here, don't you know that girl's going to be questioned and cross-questioned? Do you think Ponniman would ease up on a single rule of evidence to spare anybody?"

"Sure I know that . . . what about it?"

"I come in here to ask you what about it."

Ashton bit off the end of his cheroot, worked his lips back and forth, got the shred on the tip of his tongue, leaned over, and spat it on his cardboard.

"You're not going to do anything to Ponniman, I hope."

"Hell, no, now that would give a black eye to real estate prices . . . manhandle a big lawyer like Ponniman . . . why, investors from the North wouldn't feel safe down here any more. No sir, we've got to make it clear to the world that a man with money is safe down here in Alabama, Ashton . . . and the more money he's got, the safer he is. By God, that's not only good business, it's justice, it's a man's reward for accumulating something."

"They were talking about doing something to him," said the lawyer.

"Yes, and that's a mighty good sign they ain't going to do anything at all to him," returned Bodine.

"What was your idyah?" asked Ashton.

"I think we better drop back on our original plan and finish up the work we started out to do a coupla weeks ago. You see, when Ponniman gets here and doesn't find any clients to defend, if they've just vanished while he was riding the train, that ought to be pretty convincing to the Yankee nation that they can't dictate to the Southern people how they're to manage their niggers."

Ashton sat for a few moments in silence and began to shake his head slowly.

"I couldn't have any part in that."

"I don't want you or anybody in Florence to have any part in it. All I ask is for you to stay at home and don't go around organizing a damned illegal mob of Rotarians and Lions and what not to oppose the perfectly regular application of the unwritten law here in the South. Now, there's Colonel Vaiden, the damned old . . ."

"Now look out . . . he's got money!"

"He stole it!"

"But he's got it."

"Hell, I'm not saying anything against him."

"I thought you were going to."

"No, I just believe he's wrong when he says stringing up half a dozen niggers will hurt the boom. I think it'll help it."

"How?"

"Why, Ashton, a big lynching like that would make the Yankees down here realize that their wives and daughters are safe. Why, hell, we'd go after a nigger that had ravished a Northern lady just as quick as we would a Southern lady . . . quicker, a strange lady in a strange land needs protection more."

Ashton had not realized that there could be a touch of

gallantry in lynchings; he had considered them stereotyped; short cuts to avoid the law's delay and uncertainty.

"So what I'm asking of you Florence business men," repeated Bodine, "is . . . hands off."

"I have no personal interest in a bunch of negro brutes," assured Ashton earnestly. "If their case ever comes up before the court, I'll do what I can to clear them, because it's my sworn duty; but I hope you understand, and every man in the country understands, that I wouldn't lift a finger to protect 'em . . . I mean outside of my duty as a lawyer."

"Ashton, people believe lawyers haven't got any consciences . . . they little know . . . they little realize . . . Well, good-day, Brother."

Bodine opened a silver cigarette case, tapped one, put it in his mouth, lit it with a silver lighter, and went out the door.

CHAPTER TWENTY-SIX

Rumors that Bodine would renew his attempt at jail delivery and lynching went about Florence through swift and devious channels.

Miss Marsan Vaiden heard it through Red McLaughlin, who had every reason to know what he was talking about. Red came to the table where Marsan was working in the laboratory and told her the news that another lynching was due that night, but veiled it in clumsy innuendo.

Marsan replied sharply that she was not interested in the recurrence of the melodrama. Red was no longer her dissecting partner. She had had him transferred to another table. The girl now detested Red, but Red did not detest her. Instead of that, he thought about her more continuously than he had ever done before. She was the most puzzling girl he had ever met.

In the one or two sexual affairs into which Red had blundered with good-natured animality, the girl had never before dropped Red instantly and completely after their first contact. They usually ended through jealousy or parental discovery or parental suspicion. Marsan had none of these reasons, she simply had cut him off. She had even gone beyond the usual verbal cattishness of the normal angry girl and had asked Professor Petrie to give her another bench mate in biology. This had been done.

Red was furious when Petrie called him upstairs and informed him of the change. Something violent must have happened, for a few minutes later Red came down with shining excited eyes and told Marsan that from now on Petrie would not be butting into their business.

The girl, instead of siding with Red, cried out:

"What have you done, Red McLaughlin?" and ran past him up the broad dusty stairs.

She found Petrie bathing a puffed cut lip in a carbolic solution. His shoulders were dusty and a sleeve was ripped. Marsan rushed to him and wanted to take the sponge to dab on the solution herself. She was trembling with fury at Red and with pity for Mr. Petrie.

"You can turn him out of school," she quivered, "the beefy, butt-headed, thick-skulled bull!"

She brushed the dust from his coat and used a pin on the rip in his sleeve. Marsan's heart melted for Petrie. She recalled the Goths entering the Roman Senate and standing in awe until one of their number pulled a venerable Senator's beard.

When Petrie was ready to go, Marsan drove him home in her car.

"How came you and Red to get into a fight?" she asked as she motored toward Tombigbee Street.

"Oh . . . he said something. . . ."

"What?"

"It . . . makes no difference."

The concealed thoughts of men appear very clumsy and obvious to women. Marsan immediately knew just about what had taken place between the two. Petrie had asked Red to move his bench. Red had asked why, Petrie had replied that the reason was not to be discussed. Red had said it was because Petrie was jealous of Marsan . . . or something like that. Whatever it was, it had caused a fight.

The whole affair had placed Marsan in an uncomfortable and embarrassing position. Petrie was evidently more or less in love with her, or he would not have changed her desk so promptly or fought Red. She saw this clearly enough, or thought she did.

"You are going to expel Red from school, aren't you?" she asked tensely.

"No-o," said Petrie, "I don't think I'll do anything about it."

This let Marsan in for another long anxious cycle of analyses. The reason Petrie was going to let it go was because he was putting Red on an equal footing with himself as far as Marsan was concerned. It was the same as saying they were both her sweethearts and he would take no advantage of his being a professor in the school.

Then a completely new idea came to Marsan. Red had told of their intimacy, and Petrie had knocked him down for it. This was dismissed as soon as imagined, but it gave the girl a sudden painful wrench . . . if Mr. Petrie really felt that way about her . . . if something came up about her sufficiently serious to cause him to endure a knock-down and a cut lip and let it go . . . Marsan drove on with a kind of dizzy, painful imperative in her head.

"Mr. Petrie," she said, "did Red say anything about me?"

"Why . . . yes . . . he did, Marsan."

"Something . . . against me?"

"Why, no, not against you," Petrie gave a wry swollen-lipped smile, "for you, in a way."

The girl slowed down the car, she was growing so shaky it was hard to guide it.

"Mr. Petrie . . . did . . . did you know that . . . that there were girls in school who . . . well . . . who . . ." she moistened her lips, ". . . well . . . don't act just as they ought to act with . . . with boys?"

Petrie looked hard at her.

"It has come up once or twice in school."

"It . . . happens maybe oftener than it comes up."

"I suppose it does . . . naturally."

A little pulse began beating painfully in Marsan's temple.

"I . . . Red was with me the night they tried to lynch the nigger boys. When . . . when everybody was . . . was yelling at Papa . . . Red knocked one of the men down and . . . and stopped them. . . . I was awfully grateful to him."

"Yes?"

"Then . . . then we went on car riding together, and . . . and he wanted me . . . to do something for him. . . ."

"I knew he had insulted you," said Petrie tensely. "I accused him of it, he denied it, and I struck him before I thought."

Marsan drew a long breath and clung to the steering wheel.

"He . . . he didn't insult me . . . he . . . I . . . but, afterwards, I wanted to get rid of him. . . ."

Petrie remained silent for a full minute staring at the white-faced girl; he asked in a strange voice:

"Why did you tell me?"

"Because . . . you . . . taking rides with me . . . like you do . . ." the road made little shakes before her eyes at each beat of her heart, "I wanted you to know . . . that's all."

CHAPTER TWENTY-SEVEN

Mr. J. Adlee Petrie got out of the motor at his boarding house on Tombigbee Street, and Marsan Vaiden drove home alone. On her way back Marsan reflected that all of her speculations about Mr. Petrie had been wrong. He had not been in love with her. He had taken it for granted that she was a virtuous girl, and this assumption had caused his fight with Red McLaughlin. Her confession to him had been entirely without point.

Dusk was gathering when she reached the manor, and the dinner gong sounded as she turned the car over to Wilson under the porte-cochère. When she entered the dining room she marked the somewhat unusual circumstance that Sydna had no guests that evening and the table had been shortened to a square. The fourth side was waiting for Marsan. As she went around and kissed her father, whom she had not seen that day, the dark eyes of her grandmother, Drusilla, followed the girl. Finally the pretty white-haired old lady asked what was the matter.

Marsan placed a smile on her face, said nothing was wrong, and slipped into her chair.

"There's no use my asking her," observed Sydna looking at Marsan, "she never tells anything to me."

"She's a Vaiden," said Drusilla, "you can always tell when anything has happened to a Vaiden, but you never can find out what it is. Now, when anything happened to a Lacefield the family was never allowed to forget what it was."

Her elders always got at Marsan obliquely. Now the girl sat with a faint smile on her face, thinking, "Suppose I should tell them about Red McLaughlin and then that I had

173

actually told that to Mr. Petrie because I thought he loved me . . . what would they do?" Aloud she said:

"Well, if you must know, Red McLaughlin told me that the men were going to make another try at hanging those negroes in the jail tonight."

Old Colonel Vaiden laid down his fork.

"Do you suppose that's true, Marsan?"

"Oh yes, Red never thinks up things; he hasn't enough imagination to lie."

"Fib, darling, fib," corrected Sydna.

Her mother's Victorianism always amused the girl.

"All right . . . f-i-b . . . 'for insuring belief' . . . that's what it stands for . . . well, Red doesn't."

The table then began talking what really ought to be done to the "niggers" now that Ponniman had taken a hand in it. Ponniman should be shown, the North should be shown. The only trouble about this conversation was that it was broken on account of Mary, the maid. When Mary was in the dining room, none of them could use the term "nigger" lest they hurt Mary's feelings, and they could not call the six criminals in jail "colored boys," as that was far too complimentary a term, so they were forced to shift topics each time Mary reappeared with a dish.

"I wonder who sent for that outrageous Ponniman, anyway," ejaculated Sydna. "The person who did it ought to be spanked."

Marsan straightened up.

"Why ought he?"

Sydna was surprised.

"For bringing him down here, of course; why, likely as not he'll set those negroes free!"

"He'd do it legally, wouldn't he?"

"That's the danger," said Sydna, never knowing how far Marsan's eccentric opinion would go.

"It's in the constitution of the United States and Alabama too that everybody has a right to be tried by a jury in court."

"You know very well, Marsan, constitutions weren't made to be applied to negroes."

"They don't teach that in the High School."

"Of course, your teachers can't come out in plain English and say it, Marsan, but at least they ought to give their pupils enough of a hint so when they come to study the constitution they can read between the lines."

As Marsan continued eating and talking, she wondered what her mother would think if she told her that a negro had won a prize in college over Mr. Petrie. Her mother would just go up in the air, she would expire if she knew that. It would be as cataclysmic to Sydna, but set in a different key, as a knowledge of her own and Red McLaughlin's affair.

When dinner was over, old Colonel Vaiden went up to his own private study on the upper floor. Drusilla followed him a little way, asking him would he remain and listen to the radio. The older women knew what disturbed her long ago suitor who had become the husband of her daughter. She thought if Miltiades would stay below and listen to the grotesque noises of some jazz orchestra he would forget that which troubled him, the phantom of a negro boy who was hanged.

The old man, however, thanked her and followed the wide turn of the steps into the upper hallway with its solemn row of dark doors and polished knobs. He walked through the hall and entered his study, a wooden room which he had added to the main brick building over his porte-cochère. He went inside, closed the door after him, walked across and stood by a window looking out into the last of the evening light.

The Colonel was turning in his mind whether or not he should drive downtown and attempt once more to organize the business men of Florence against Bodine's repeated threat. The trouble was, with Phineas Ponniman about to defend the prisoners, not many men would oppose Bodine. The Colonel himself was shaken in his own resolution against lynchings. A kind of debate in pictures moved through his imagination like rival cinemas: a Yankee lawyer taking it

on himself to set a Southern court right in its handling of
negroes; and the opposing picture of an almost white negro,
the Colonel's own son, who was named Toussaint Vaiden,
strung up to one of the mulberries in Courthouse Square.

This boy, of his own flesh, had come to his death because
he had had the temerity to enter suit against the Colonel for
the possession of a pair of mules. The effrontery of a negro
offering to appear in a court of law against a white man had
encompassed his hanging.

During the events that led up to this lynching, Colonel
Vaiden had been unaware that the negro boy opposing him
was his son. Then it had happened, just on the hour of the
tragedy—the octoroon mother of the boy had come to the
Colonel and told him Toussaint Vaiden was their son and
pleaded with him to come and face down the mob and save
the octoroon's life.

The two had got into an old wagon together from the gate
of this very manor in which he now stood and had loped the
mules to Courthouse Square in time for the cream-colored
woman to cut down the dead body of their son.

All this went through the old banker's head with mournful
iteration. He had not known Toussaint Vaiden was his son.
He had known, of course, that he had had congress with
Gracie, the quadroon girl who had been his father's slave,
and whose body, on one single ill-starred night, he had taken
by force.

From somewhere in the grove surrounding the manor the
Colonel heard the high quavering call of an owl. This re-
minded him again of his father's log cabin, of fox hunting,
of the rides of the original Ku Klux Klan of which he was an
organizer. He thought how, after the war, everyone had ex-
pected him to become a great man, and how for twenty
years he did nothing at all, lived a most penurious hand-to-
mouth existence, and then, abruptly, the collection of an old
debt had started him on the road to the wealth he now
possessed. And as he had climbed that road to power, his
octoroon son, who had inherited something of his own tenac-

ity and pride, had come into conflict with him, his father, over a mule . . . and this had led to his violent death.

The Colonel thought how strange all this private history would seem when he lay in his sarcophagus in All Souls Cathedral, where Honor and Fame would sentinel his name.

A discreet tapping at the side door of his study caused the Colonel to switch on a light and call for his visitor to come in. It was his chauffeur, Wilson, who had climbed up a narrow blind stairway that led down between the walls to the porte-cochère below. The Colonel asked what he wanted, and Wilson said there was a lady to see him.

"In the porte-cochère?"

"Yes suh."

"Doesn't she want to see Sydna . . . or Drusilla?"

"No suh, she wants to see you."

"What made you climb up the back stairs to announce her?"

"She said she wanted to see jest you, suh; I clum' up to see if jest you wuz in."

The Colonel divined that the woman had come to ask about the wisdom of an investment. He told Wilson to show her up, then sat down and awaited her coming with resignation.

The woman would want to ask very privately whether he thought lots would go still higher, and would the boom last much longer. The distrust in the permanence of the boom which lay implicit in these questions had long since lost their humor for the Colonel. The pertinacity of people in getting more money when he himself was thinking of life and fate disgusted the banker. Here the side door of his study opened again and Wilson ushered in a white-haired old woman who, for a second or two, Miltiades thought was Drusilla. But this woman was stooped, her face was thinner and more worn than Drusilla's. On this old woman's face was an expression of habitual sadness, instead of the satirical tolerance with which Drusilla smiled on the world.

The old banker arose and indicated a chair.

"We're having fine weather," he began conventionally. "I was just sitting here waiting for the moon to come up. I had a landscape gardener from Baltimore come and do my grounds particularly for moonlight effects, because I'm at home mostly at night. The different quarters of the moon make quite different effects." The old gentleman paused, looking out of his window onto the still dark landscape.

"And now, madam, I trust I can be of some service to you?"

"My great-grandson is in jail," said the visitor.

"In jail?"

"Yes, and he is just a little boy, as you can see he would have to be."

Miltiades looked at the old woman closely.

"What jail?"

"The jail here in Florence."

"But . . . there isn't anybody in the Florence jail except six negro boys. . . ."

The caller nodded. Her old face twitched, but she composed it by force to its habitually sad expression, then sat outwardly calm again.

"James is a negro," she said in a low voice.

The Colonel frowned; he regretted that he had given this old negro woman a chair. It made him uncomfortable for a negro to be seated in his presence. His caller must have sensed this, because she put her thin hands on the arms of the chair and with an effort got up. The old white man came away from the window and sat down.

"What do you want me to do?"

"Couldn't you bail him out, Colonel Milt?"

"Not with the charge against him, he—he's one of the—of the six, isn't he?"

"Yes sir."

"Look here," interjected the Colonel at the slight mystery that had developed in his mind, "I thought all those boys were taken off a train; I didn't know any of them lived around here?"

"My great-grandson doesn't."

"Where does he live?"

"In Chicago."

"A Northern negro!" ejaculated the banker. "Why in the devil did he come South? . . . You are not Northern."

"I used to live here in Florence, and . . . a long time ago . . . in Montgomery."

The Colonel did not observe this bit from the old negro woman's private history.

"Why didn't you tell him to stay where he was? Didn't you know there is no place for a Northern negro except the North?"

The old woman drew a long breath.

"He wanted to see his folks."

"Your folks?"

"Yes sir, I'd been telling him about them all his life; so he ran away, beat his way down here on a train to see them . . . he is only fourteen years old."

Miltiades sat frowning at the old woman.

"Of course," he said harshly, "his own people down here, the ones he came to see, are in no position to help him . . . but there is no way to bail him out under any condition."

The old quadroon stood looking at the Colonel.

"Yes . . . his people could help him, Colonel Milt."

"You . . . you don't mean his . . . white people?"

"Yes sir."

"M—m . . . well, they couldn't possibly acknowledge . . . especially considering the crime he's charged with. . . ."

"But, Colonel Milt," pleaded the old woman, "that's impossible . . . he's only a little boy. . . ."

"Well . . . why don't you ask some of his . . . white kin?"

"I am."

The Colonel stared at the thin weak old woman before him.

"Me? Me? You're not asking me?"

"Yes sir."

"Who in the hell are you?"

"I'm Gracie, Colonel Milt."

The old banker and dictator of Florence was inexpressibly repelled by the identity of the old slave woman his father once had owned; by the fact that long ago he had taken this old woman's body by force and she had borne a son. She had not borne him a son, she had simply borne a son, unclaimed by anyone save herself.

"Why in God's name did you let your damned grandson come down here, Gracie?" cried the old white man in extreme exasperation.

"I didn't . . . he ran away . . . he wanted to see . . . I had told him so much about you-all."

"Why didn't you tell him about his colored relations? . . . My God, are the white Vaidens . . ."

The withered old quadroon pointed a scornful finger at the man.

"Colored relations! What colored relations? I was born to my mother, old Hannah, long after Old Pap sold off her husband Jericho! I'm not white for nothing! Aunt Creasy told me long ago that my father was Old Pap, the same as yours! Toussaint, the son I had by you, was nothing but a Vaiden on both sides. The child Lucy had by Toussaint, the son you hanged, I named Marcia; and Marcia's boy you're holding in jail this minute is named James Vaiden Hodige. Who would my grandchild come back to see except white people, Miltiades?"

The tone of the old woman's voice, the look about her eyes made it seem to the old banker as if his domineering older sister Cassandra had arisen from her grave and was bemeaning him.

There was almost nothing for him to say. He did ask why Gracie had not sent her grandson somewhere to see the Hodges, whoever they were. And the quadroon answered:

"Because I, Gracie Vaiden, his grandmother, told him about the Vaidens; because I came from the white Vaidens of Alabama, and not from the white Hodges of Georgia."

The old Colonel stared, made a peremptory gesture toward the side door.

"Shame on you, Gracie, coming here and talking disrespectfully like this! If you weren't so old ... y-o-u ... Get out! Take yourself off! Go!"

CHAPTER TWENTY-EIGHT

THE moon and the landscape gardener from Baltimore conspired together against old Colonel Vaiden's wrath.

At first the moon set forth the Vaiden trees in solemn silhouette, then rising higher, it spread over their dark masses a silvern veil. The moon pleaded the cause of the Hodige negro in the Florence jail more subtly than did the great-grandmother's bitter tongue.

The prisoner was not only the great-grandson of old Gracie, but of the Colonel himself. Through what obscure channels his blood had flowed since that distant hour in his father's barn when he had taken by force . . . half sister . . . daughter of a slave called Old Hannah . . . his father. . . .

It was like strangling a python at night. He fought, but out of utter darkness looped another coil; another and another.

The old banker stood at the window, trembling at the chain of wrongs and violences around which his life had been molded. . . . Gracie's rape . . . his theft of the Handback estate . . . the lynching of his boy Toussaint . . . now this great-grandson lodged in jail under the shadow of violence.

Any or all of these catastrophes the old Colonel could have borne with fortitude, but tonight, standing in the moonlit window, he seemed to discern in his life the cold maleficent direction of Nemesis. And a sudden dismaying conviction seized on the old man that his future lay under the shadow of the same unseen power which had shaped the mien and horror of his past.

By an effort of will the old Colonel put such empty thoughts out of his mind, crossed his study, and pressed a button. He stood waiting with the patient belligerence of an

182

old man when Wilson appeared. The Colonel ordered his big car.

"And, Wilson," he continued, "I want a driver . . . somebody who . . ." He broke off, pondering.

"I won't do?" asked the colored man in surprise.

"No, you won't do."

He stood casting about in his mind for a possible driver for his undertaking when he thought of his nephew, the Reverend Jerry Catlin. So he continued to Wilson:

"You go get Jerry and get back here by the time I get my hat and coat."

Wilson was immediately concerned to make precise connections. From the head of the stairs he turned and asked his master not to get into his hat and overcoat too fast.

Fifteen minutes later Wilson was back under the porte-cochère with the assistant minister in his car. Miltiades had just come down the blind stairway. He stepped out under the dome light, a trim, sedate old figure, adjusting a soft beaver hat. He hoped he hadn't disturbed his nephew from important work.

It was nothing important; Jerry had been working out a sermon for children on the text in Samuel, "Lord, here am I," illustrating the sacrificial spirit.

"Wilson said you wanted me to drive you tonight."

"Jerry, I wish you would."

Wilson got out of the car, and the old banker stepped in. As the sedan moved out into Pine Street the Colonel began in a serious tone:

"Jerry, are you willing to help stave off the trouble everybody is expecting at the jail tonight?"

The assistant minister glanced at his uncle.

"I knew that was what you wanted."

"And it's all right . . . you're willing?"

"Why, of course. . . . What are we going to do? . . . I—I'm not a pistol shot."

"Drive me to Judge Wilson's home on Laurel Street."

"Think he'll help you?"

"I believe so."

"Don't you think he will resent Ponniman coming into this case the same as everyone else?"

"Naturally, but I have a plan that may appeal to the Judge . . ." He broke off. "That's his house, yonder."

The car stopped before a dark low bungalow. Jerry got out and went up to the door. After knocking and later finding and ringing a bell, a porch light came on above his head. A little later the door opened, and Judge Wilson appeared. When the jurist saw it was Jerry, he asked with excitement:

"Dr. Catlin, has anything happened . . . downtown?"

Jerry explained that his uncle Milt was in the car.

"Tell him to come on in. . . ."

Here the Colonel himself called in a low voice for the Judge to come out. Judge Wilson stepped back inside, switched off the porch light, then went with Jerry to the motor.

"It's a damned shame," observed the Judge when the three men were in the car, "when citizens like us who have legal intentions here in Florence find it advisable to hold their councils in the dark."

"Then you know what we've come for?" suggested Miltiades.

"In a general way. I don't know exactly what you want me to do."

"Listen, Henry . . . I don't want those niggers lynched."

"Neither do I, but Ponniman's come into court. He'll object to every scrap of evidence we've got. I'll quash his objections, he'll appeal, and the Supreme Court will sustain him. . . ."

"Listen, Henry," interrupted Miltiades impatiently, "I've thought of a solution to all our difficulties, personal and civic."

"What do you mean by civic?"

"Oh, I mean our financial objection to lynchings."

"Well, what's your idea?"

"Change of venue."

Both Jerry and the Judge were surprised. They tried to look at each other in the dark car.

"Oh what grounds?" inquired the Judge curiously.

"Why, those niggers can't get justice before any jury you could select in Lauderdale County, and you know it."

Judge Wilson hemmed slightly.

"To just what Southern court would you suggest that I transfer this case, where they would get justice?" he inquired dryly.

"I don't care a damn about that. It makes no difference where they go or what happens to them when they get there, I want 'em out of Florence. That's my real grounds for asking a change of venue. What may break out any minute now will be the worst possible publicity for our town. So I'm asking you for a change of venue."

Judge Wilson pondered, shook his head slowly, and said in a regretful voice:

"Milt . . . I can't grant it."

"Why not?"

"You're not the defendant's lawyer. You are no relation to any of the accused. You have no position in the case the law can recognize."

The old Colonel began with a sharp, "I'm the . . ." then broke off, cleared his throat, sat in silence for upward of half a minute, then began again in a strained voice:

"Listen, Henry, all my holdings, all the bank's holdings, and I suppose most of your holdings are wrapped up somehow or other in the boom. There is not a citizen in town who will not be disastrously affected if a great blow should be dealt Florence real estate. In my opinion, if Bodine's gang commits any violence tonight; if Ponniman brings about the farcical sort of trial that Northern lawyers have succeeded in imposing upon Southern courts: any of those things will do great and irremediable damage to Florence just at this moment."

"Well . . . what about it?"

"Just this: I'm asking you, as an interested citizen of Florence, for a change of venue on the ground that the trial is a public nuisance."

The three men remained in silence for three or four seconds; then both Jerry and the Judge broke into roars of laughter.

"Colonel! My God, of all pleas! Oust a trial because it's a public nuisance!"

"Hell . . . isn't it?"

"Well . . . yes . . . in a way . . . but, my God, Milt, what will the Northern papers say if I abate my court as a public nuisance?"

"You needn't put it in those words, Henry. Grant a change of venue, the public welfare requiring it. For it certainly does, there's no question about that."

Judge Wilson sat pondering this extraordinary request. Finally he began:

"Do you know, Milt, I believe your plea would hold. If a trial held in a certain place would work great harm to the community, I see no reason why it shouldn't be held somewhere else. I'm going to grant you your change of venue."

"All right . . . I'd like to take the prisoners to Athens tonight."

"You'll take them . . . personally?"

"Yes, Jerry and I, nobody will suspect us of trying to get away with them."

"I would have to send an officer with you."

"Send Deputy Northrup. I know his family. I stood up when Heck Northrup, this boy's granddaddy, married Susie Ham in Waterloo at the outbreak of the war. Write me out a habeas corpus, and I'll have Northrup serve it."

All this was spoken very rapidly. Judge Wilson responded to the Colonel's urgency and hurried back into his house with the assistant minister on his heels. In his study the jurist produced some blank forms and began to fill them in. Jerry looked at his watch. It was fifteen minutes after ten. He listened to see if he could hear any commotion downtown.

Although the Judge scratched away at a great rate, he seemed to write slowly. Finally he handed Jerry two papers, a habeas corpus and a mittimus with which to lodge the prisoners in the Athens jail.

Jerry took them and ran to the car. Before he got in, he listened intently in the silent streets.

"Get in, get in," hurried the Colonel, "if anything is happening, it's happening; all we can do is start."

"Where does Northrup live?" asked Jerry starting the car.

"Now, damn it, where does he live?" repeated the Colonel.

Neither of them knew. Northrup was one of those poor men who live in houses nobody except other poor men can locate.

"He's not a Methodist," twitched Jerry impatiently, "or I'd know where he lived."

"His granddaddy was a Baptist," supplied Miltiades.

"Let me see . . . I know where the Baptist minister lives," said Jerry.

He veered the car into a side street and presently stopped at a house. He honked, and the minister came out and asked if anybody wanted to get married.

"We want to know where Deputy Sheriff Northrup lives," called Jerry.

"Let me see, I have a Mr. Ham Northrup . . ."

"That's the man," hurried Miltiades, "he's named for his grandmammy's family."

The Baptist minister gave an address, and the car sped across town to East Florence. The Reverend Catlin stopped before a small dark house, blew his horn and honked. He continued this disturbance until a voice shouted:

"What do you want with me?"

"Come out, Northrup . . . this is Colonel Miltiades Vaiden."

"The hell it is . . . be out in a minute." When he came up to the car he asked, "What in the world do you fellows want?"

"We have a habeas corpus from Judge Wilson to take those six niggers to the jail in Athens."

"Well, we better get a move on us. . . . How did you get such a writ?"

"The Colonel here got the writ on the ground that the trial is a public nuisance."

Northrup exploded into laughter.

"Public nuisance! By the gray goats! Well, the damn thing is . . . But, looky here, I don't want to run into trouble trying to serve these writs."

"Well, if you're any kin to old man Erasmus Ham," stated the Colonel roundly, "you don't particularly give a damn whether you get into trouble or not, as long as you are doing your duty."

Northrup cleared his throat.

"Now, that's so, too." He nodded firmly. "Gimme your papers an' le's git to Courthouse Square quick as we can. While I ain't shunnin' trouble, I ain't looking for it, either. I ain't that kind of a fool."

Jerry got to Courthouse Square at high speed.

The Square itself seemed deserted. The big car crossed to Intelligence Row, passed through the alley leading by the fire station, and stopped before the jail. Jerry and Northrup got out nervously and went to the door. Northrup climbed the steps and knocked, while Jerry waited on the ground. At the third knock they heard the jailer inside ask in a tense voice what was wanted.

Northrup whispered through the keyhole:

"Jim . . . for God's sake, lemme in . . . this is Ham."

"Ham!"

"Lemme in quick. I got a habeas corpus for the niggers!"

"What you goin' to do with 'em?"

"Take 'em to jail in Athens."

The key turned inside; the jail door opened a small space to verify Ham's words, then swung wider. Northrup went inside.

Jerry stood listening and looking all about the street as he waited for the prisoners. In the midst of this watching and waiting he was startled to see a man step out of the shadow of the jail almost beside him. The fellow looked at Jerry intently for a moment, then made a grotesque gesture and whispered:

"Hello, old peckerwood, what's up?"

"Who are you?" asked Jerry.

"Eighty-two," whispered the newcomer, "eighty-two of seventeen. . . . Is the head knocker out there?" He pointed to the car.

"What's your name?" asked Jerry.

"Of course, that's q.t., but it's Rutledge, Willie Rutledge," said the man in a low tone. "Who's in that car?"

"Colonel Milt Vaiden."

"The Colonel . . . what the hell's he doing here? I thought he was aginst . . ."

"Go talk to him," suggested Jerry.

"What's he waitin' for?"

"He'll tell you . . . talk to him."

Rutledge turned toward the alley and gave a soft whistle; another figure came around the corner of the jail. Rutledge whispered to the newcomer:

"It's Colonel Milt Vaiden in the car."

"What does he want?" asked the new man.

"I suppose he's going to stay here and make another speech," surmised Rutledge.

The newcomer laughed in an undertone.

"His speech will have a hell of a chanst tonight."

At that moment a clanking came from inside the jail. The door opened, and six bedraggled negro boys came out, handcuffed and chained together. The smallest boy asked, "Where's the car?" then saw it and started to run toward it, but was jerked back with a sharp rattling of the chain. The next boy started to run and was jerked. Then the next and the next until the whole line gathered headway and the six scuttled to the car jangling their chain.

Rutledge and his fellow guard watched the negroes dash for the automobile in the utmost amazement.

The door of the car swung open. As the six scrambled in the old Colonel said:

"I am Miltiades Vaiden. Hodige, stand behind me. The rest of you niggers pack yourselves in the best you can!"

"Yes suh! Yes suh!"

Northrup and the jailer climbed in after the prisoners. Jerry hurried around to the other side and slid into the driver's seat.

Rutledge and his companion ran up alongside.

"Hey, who's running this?" cried the strange man.

"I am," said the Colonel. "Drive on, Jerry!"

The car began to move away. The two men stepped on the running board:

"Did you-all get 'em out for the association?"

"We've got them out on a habeas corpus," stated the Colonel crisply.

"Who for?"

"For the citizens of Florence."

"Where you taking them?"

"There's no telling . . . faster, Jerry."

As the car gathered speed the two men jumped off the running board, struck the street, took two preternaturally long steps, and dived headlong into the pavement. They jumped up again and began yelling something. Men here and there began appearing along the seemingly empty street.

"Step on it," said Northrup to Jerry; "them men have got cars!"

Jerry shoved down the accelerator, but he was no expert driver. The powerful car began weaving from side to side.

"Hell fire, hold her in the road!" yelled the jailer. Everybody except Jerry began looking back. Sure enough, headlights were following them. They gained upon the sedan.

"Can you go faster and keep her wheels under her?" cried the jailer.

The miles were now whirling past with the minutes.

"Jerry," called Miltiades above the whistling wind, "slow down . . . we're coming to Shoal Creek bridge!"

"Hell, Colonel, they'll ketch us right now," cried the deputy sheriff.

"They'll catch us anyway. . . . Northrup, get out your keys!"

"To what?"

"The handcuffs."

"What for?"

"We've got to jetsam a nigger!"

"What's that?"

"Heave some overboard to save the others!"

"Will it do it?"

"Hell, yes, the mob will stop for one or two!"

"Which ones?"

"Why, the least ones. You know these little niggers didn't do anything wrong . . . they couldn't."

Northrup reached for the child behind Miltiades' seat.

"Here, boy, hold up your wrists!"

"Wh-whut you going to do?"

"Two of you are going to jump over that bridge into the creek," snapped Miltiades. "Can you boys swim?"

"Yes suh! Yes suh!"

"Take it slow, Jerry."

The headlights of the pursuing motors were now all over the fugitive car. Ahead the Shoal Creek bridge seemed to rush toward Jerry. The assistant minister slackened his speed as he took the approach. The cars behind rushed upon him. In the throat of the bridge the old Colonel shoved open the car door.

"Jump clear of the bridge!" he ordered.

The next instant the two smaller negro boys went out of the car like monkeys. One cleared the planking like a dark arrow shooting through the beating light; the other touched the side and fell whirling over and over.

"Jerry, you and Northrup get out and try to catch them!" cried the Colonel.

"When we catch them, won't the niggers get killed?"

"Yes . . . when . . . and if . . ."

Jerry halted at the end of the bridge. He and Northrup leaped out. The jailer took the wheel and started forward.

Jerry and Northrup stood in the oncoming headlights waving their arms, pointing at the side of the bridge, and shouting frantically:

"They got away! Men, they jumped out of the car! They're in the creek!"

CHAPTER TWENTY-NINE

The mob in the onrushing cars did not know how many negroes or how many white men there were in the escaping automobile. Every pursuer knew that some or all the negroes had escaped.

Jerry furthered the idea by rushing to the rail where the negro boys had jumped, hanging over, peering down and shouting:

"They're in the creek! They got loose in the car!" He flung up a hand at the slowing cars, "Get out and help catch these niggers . . . they got out of the car!"

The notion of an escaped negro flings a Southern mob into the same sort of hysteria that a terrier has over a rat.

The cars stopped, the men boiled out with guns and pistols and dashed to the point where the two children had leaped off the bridge.

"Where are they . . . where'd they go to?"

Sharp self-reproach filled Jerry that he had lacked the wit to run to some other place than precisely where the little negro boys had dived. He pointed at an angle:

"Down there! Right down there!"

A dozen men came and pointed their firearms over the rail. In the sudden chase they had not had time to put on their sheets and masks, and now they stood in the beat of the headlights with the simple, good-natured, but excited faces of carpenters, dentists, grocers, clerks, small storekeepers, male stenographers, who had gathered from neighboring towns into Florence for the excitement of the night. Now, to have two little black boys in the creek to hunt for and shoot at was a satisfying set-up for these men in this particular mood.

A man close to Jerry suddenly leveled his revolver and shot at something in the shimmer beneath the bridge.

Jerry's heart beat as he stared below to see if one of the boys had been struck. Fellow members of the association rushed to the shooter, shouting:

"Did you see one? What ye shoot at?"

"Trying to skeer 'em," explained the man in sharp tones. "Here, ever'body shoot! Scatter 'em around!"

A fusillade broke out from the bridge. Bullets flicked all over the surface of the creek. The men stopped firing to peer down again to see if anything below was struggling or floating.

Jerry himself scanned the surface of the water with such apprehension that it gave him a nauseated feeling. If one or both of the little negroes had been struck, they had sunk without a sound. He saw only the water, rippled by a slight wind.

"Get down below," somebody ordered; "look for 'em along the bank."

At this a number of men ran back to the end of the bridge, climbed down, and deployed along the edge of the water. Some of the more cautious shouted to those above:

"Don't shoot while we're down here!"

Voices above shouted down:

"Go ahead . . . hell . . . we're watching you!"

Jerry could see dim forms of men scrambling along the edge of the creek. Some had flashlights and directed their circles of light here and there.

Suddenly pistol shots broke out in one place. There were shouts:

"Here one is! We got him!"

Just then came a heavy splash. A voice hallooed:

"Don't shoot no more, fellows! A man fell in! Where is he? He went under right here. Can he swim? I don't know, he ain't up yet. Maybe he's hung in the weeds?"

"Look here, somebody, git him out . . . who can swim?"

"He may be foolin', tryin' to skeer us!"

"Hell fire, he ain't big enough fool to drown himself, trying to skeer us!"

"Don't know, brother, some mighty big fools in this here crowd!"

At that moment, some yards below the group, water was broken, a voice choked, gasped, and gurgled into silence again.

Voices of the cautious bellowed again:

"Don't anybody up there shoot! That's not the niggers! That's a man drownin'!"

"Somebody that can swim, go get him!"

"Hell, you'll get caught in the weeds . . . reach a stick to him!"

From the bridge in the shimmering light Jerry half saw men thrusting improvised poles into the water. Then a man jumped in to the drowning man. The swimmer shouted something and was dragged ashore with the victim in his arms.

Everybody legged it down to the scene of the near tragedy.

When Jerry reached the place, they had the drowned man out jouncing him over a log. Water gushed out of his nose and mouth.

A man, evidently a doctor, ordered the figure laid on its back. He knelt astride him and started artificial respiration. The doctor worked and worked. He grew tired and asked if anyone else in the crowd knew the technique. Jerry did, and took the physician's place.

"Don't go too fast," warned the medico, "that's the danger."

Jerry counted out his rhythm in one-two-three time to preserve his tempo.

The drowned man's ribs felt cold under Jerry's palms. The minister swung backwards and forwards. Then, under the rays of a flashlight, he saw it was Rutledge who had been drowned.

A queer thought came to Jerry that this had befallen Rutledge so he could not tell who had been in the fugitive car.

At that moment the passive form under his hands moved, groaned, moved again.

"Keep on, he's coming round!" cried the doctor in great relief. "I was afraid he wasn't going to."

Rutledge himself gave a choking gurgle and moaned:

"Stop! Oh . . . oh . . . stop!"

"Keep on," directed the physician.

"Lemme go back . . . lemme go . . . " blubbered the half-conscious man. Jerry continued his kneading. He was very tired.

Presently the doctor said:

"All right . . . that's enough . . . he's O. K."

Rutledge lay breathing with his mouth open. The ground around him was wet from his clothes. He lifted his head painfully, looked about, and whispered something.

"What?" asked Jerry, with a fear the reviving man would tell something about him.

He whispered again, and Jerry put an ear down to his lips. The prostrate man was saying:

"I . . . saw . . . God."

"You . . . saw God?" repeated Jerry believing he had heard wrong.

"What . . . you bring me back . . . for . . . I . . . was up . . . up in the moonlight . . . I didn't want to be . . . dragged back to . . . to this . . . carrion."

Rutledge turned over with an effort, put his head in his wet arms, and began sobbing in the mud because Jerry had brought him back to life.

CHAPTER THIRTY

No MATTER what had been the exact phraseology of the writ Judge Wilson had issued in changing the venue of the notorious assault case to Athens, Alabama, on the following morning every metropolitan paper brought out the droll story of an Alabama court that had abated itself as a public nuisance.

The Northern papers were, of course, especially cutting. One editorial said that Southern courts, over a long period of years, had been public nuisances *de facto*, and that it was high time that some clear, analytical, penetrating jurist should convert that standing to *de jure*. The Southern papers averred that Judge Wilson's action sounded the death knell of lynch law and mob violence in the South, and that henceforth the only uncontrolled criminal classes in America would be the New York and Chicago gangsters and bankers.

So the press of the two sections continued to fling their ancient and reciprocal mud.

But if the six negroes had been spirited away from Florence, the invasion of Phineas Delfase Ponniman was still imminent. Everybody wondered what would happen. The town was still full of imported members of Bodine's secret society. These strangers stood, if not above, at least outside of and on equality with the law. Nobody knew who they were. They were armed and organized and were irresponsible for anything they did except to keep their oaths as members of the association never to deviate in the smallest degree from a course of action which everyone would be forced to agree was thoroughly and fundamentally American.

Therefore speculation ran high as to what sort of American

thing would happen to Mr. Ponniman when he arrived in Florence.

Mr. Ragsdale, who was attorney for the Second National Bank, and who was a very prudent man, suggested to Colonel Vaiden that the Rotary Club telegraph to the famous lawyer, warn him of his danger, and advise him to return to New York, as his clients had vanished and there was nothing for him to do.

It just happened, however, that Dr. Blankenship was in the Colonel's office when Ragsdale came in, and the Doctor objected to the telegram. He said he meant to ask Ponniman for a donation to the cathedral, and that his idea was for Florence reverently to leave Ponniman's safety in the hands of Providence. Here the Doctor turned to Colonel Vaiden to bring to his attention some little financial details in regard to the cathedral.

As the hour drew near for the Ponniman train to arrive, a current of motors and pedestrians set through the streets toward the railroad station. As usual, the two hotel buses jockeyed for the best position to yodel their respective attractions.

Today, however, the buses could not get into their regular parking space because it was occupied by out-of-town cars. A policeman came and asked one of these obstructive cars to move, but the men in the car were not even interested in his request. They immediately began talking about something else. They said to the officer:

"Do you know who ordered Ponniman to come to Florence anyway?"

The silver badge said he did not.

"Wasn't there a nigger man trying to hire a lawyer to defend them niggers that got away?"

The policeman said he believed he had heard as much.

"Who was it?"

"Well . . . it was a nigger preacher," answered the silver badge cautiously.

"What's his name?"

"I don't know."

"The hell you don't . . . you know damn well you know. Look here, just because you are in the service of the law doesn't keep you from being a man and an American, does it?"

The policeman hastened to assure the car full of men as to his sex and nationality.

"Now, we're asking you for the second time, Brother, who was that nigger preacher that telegraphed for a damned Northern lawyer to come down and run a Southern court, and where does he live?"

"The lawyer?" asked the officer confused.

"Hell, no, the nigger preacher . . . what's his name and where does he live?"

"His name's Sinton, and I don't know where he lives."

"You don't!"

"No, I really don't. I don't much think he even lives here . . . he's a Bishop."

The men laughed at the idea of a nigger being a Bishop.

"Oh, well," said one of the men, "you're a good fellow, run along and move somebody else out of their place."

"Look here," said the officer, "you boys stay parked right where you are, but, lissen, if I was you-all I wouldn't get rough with Ponniman. After all, he may be honest in his beliefs. He don't understand niggers, he don't understand the Southern people. If he did, he wouldn't try to give no advice. He'd realize they ain't no advice to give."

At that moment from down the track came the far-off scream of a locomotive. The whole crowd moved closer. The policeman hurried through the press to get between them and the train.

"Men, fellows, lissen!" he begged, "no crowdin', no pushin' . . ." He was lost in the movement of the crowd.

As the express came to a stop with its bell ringing and engine hissing, a big rough-looking man in a baggy gray suit came out on the front platform of his Pullman and with his mere presence immediately took possession of the crowd.

Everybody began yelling, "Ponniman! Ponniman!"

The out-of-town men in the parked car boiled out and shoved their way toward the platform from which Ponniman was descending.

"Ponniman!" they shouted. "Speech! Speech!"

The negro porter dusted Mr. Ponniman from the top of the steps to the train platform, received a dollar, and expressed his thanks with a row of white teeth.

Women parked in their cars stared at him with the intentness of women for a great man. They thought of him variously: as defending them, as a husband, as an ideal for their sons, as a lover. They said to one another:

"Did you ever see such a rough-looking man!"

They meant by that that in the South all intellectual leaders wear a scholarly, aristocratic air, whereas in the North they are likely to come unkempt and coarse featured.

The Rotarians really gathered Mr. Ponniman unto themselves. He gravitated by affinity into the car of Colonel Vaiden, the Rotarian president. He was taken immediately to the dam and shown that. He was driven over the endless empty subdivisions of the future metropolis of the South. He was shown the four-story apartment house built out in a vacant cotton field so that the promoters could advertise that an apartment house had been built already on their subdivision.

That evening they gave Ponniman a banquet, an enormous blow-out at the old Florence Hotel at five dollars a plate. The public was invited . . . Bodine's association and all.

It was at the banquet, before Florence assembled en masse, that Dr. Blankenship suggested to the town's distinguished guest that the community was bending all of its spiritual and temporal energies in the construction of a great non-sectarian cathedral dedicated to the fatherhood of God and the brotherhood of man.

"And, Mr. Ponniman," proceeded the Doctor with a slight bow, "while it is nationally known that you find intellectual difficulties in subscribing to the first article in that creed, no one can doubt that your whole life has been dedicated to the service of the brotherhood of man." Here applause interrupted the speaker. The Doctor took a sip of water, then continued: "Mr. President of the Rotary Club, this applause convinces me that I need ask for no other proof as to the character of our distinguished guest. I will say, however, that Mr. Ponniman has come to Florence on an errand of brotherhood, and I feel encouraged to say to Mr. Ponniman, that not only the grown people, but even the little children, are bending body and soul in an effort to raise a great monument to the brotherhood of man. I refer Mr. Ponniman to our cathedral, whose foundations you saw this afternoon. If you could find it in your heart to forward the spiritual and temporal resources of our community, you would place, not only these people assembled here this evening, but generations yet to come, under obligations to you, sir."

The Doctor made another bow after this eloquent appeal for money and sat down. The whole dining room applauded. Everyone admired the stately self-respecting way the Doctor asked for a donation. The crowd realized as never before how perfectly Dr. Blankenship was fitted to be the great spiritual leader of the wealthiest congregation in Florence.

Mr. Ponniman arose to respond to the invitation. He began by saying that he was proud of the compliment the Doctor had just paid him, and since he had always found compliments from the clergy very expensive luxuries, he supposed the time had now come for him to pay the Doctor. [Laughter here in which Dr. Blankenship joined heartily.]

"I have been greatly interested in the fact that both grown-ups and children are bending body and soul to help build the Doctor's cathedral," went on the visitor. "I am not surprised at the grown-ups, but it does seem to me that modern children ought to know better. [Hearty laughter here in which Dr. Blankenship joined.]

"However, to be serious, or that is, as serious as one can very well be about so essentially humorous a thing as a cathedral: I have spent my morning in Florence in contact with the realtors of Florence. I learned from these gentlemen that the Doctor's underlying motive in building the cathedral is to erect a great church with the avowed object of ending all future churches. [General bewilderment here, with repressed laughter from the realtors, who understood the allusion.]

"Dr. Blankenship, in abolishing churches, is only following Judge Wilson's lead in abolishing the courts of Alabama. Judge Wilson, I have been given to understand, frankly admitted that his court was a nuisance and abolished it. I can only trust that Dr. Blankenship will not allow a lawyer and a judge to outdo a divine in sincerity of statement. [Shouts of laughter from everyone but the Doctor.]

"In regard to my position on the fatherhood of God, Dr. Blankenship has stated my position correctly. I will say here what I have said in numberless addresses and debates. I believe religion is the child of fear. It is man's dread of the dark, it is his shudder at the tomb.

"I have discovered, Dr. Blankenship, that those persons are most religious whose lives are cast in the most uncertain places. During the World War epidemics of religion broke out. Sailors in peril by sea are both superstitious and religious. I am using tautology here for the benefit of those who do not recognize those words as synonyms. Coal miners, trapeze performers, knife swallowers, people who take patent medicines, in fact, all persons whose lives are continually in great peril are, by the very texture of their days, religious people." [Loud laughter.]

Mr. Ponniman cleared his throat, looked about the banquet hall, lowered his voice to a solemn tone:

"The negroes here in the South, I have been told, are a profoundly religious people. [Laughter reduced to uncertain chuckles here and there.]

"Therefore, Dr. Blankenship, in your movement to abolish churches I join you heart and soul. But I disapprove your method. I think the surest way to abolish churches is not to build a huger church than ever, but to build schools and arrange human society so it is equally safe for both blacks and whites; otherwise you are going to have in your midst forever a black world incurably religious."

Mr. Ponniman sat down.

A silence fell over the dining room. The older women who had come to see and hear the almost legendary Northern lawyer and agnostic smiled mechanically with shocked faces. Some younger women and girls pulled down their faces to keep from laughing outright.

At this point, a plainly dressed diner with the simple face of a mechanic arose from his seat away over in the corner and called in a voice shaking with stage fright, "Mr. Toastmaster . . . Mr. Toastmaster . . ."

Bill Bradley, who was near the man, called out:

"Hey, Milt, recognize this gentleman!"

"I recognize the gentleman," called the Colonel from the distant speaker's table.

The new speaker stood up, twisting his paper napkin.

"Mr. Toastmaster, I—I wish to p-protest against Mr. P-Ponniman's speech. It—it isn't just fear—fear of death as—as he says. I—I was dead last night [sensation] I was drowned, and they brought me back to life. . . . Dr. Pratt did . . . and Mr. Catlin. But now, I, who died once, don't fear death at all. I am looking forward to it with all my heart. Oh, my friends, my brothers, you have no idea of what happiness, what bliss. I was up in the moonlight, free . . . freer than I have ever been in all my life . . . and I was dead. . . ."

Here Ponniman's Northern twang interrupted the man's ecstasy:

"My friend, your experience is not unusual. For some reason extreme weakness sometimes tends to produce beatific hallucinations in the human brain. You surely are not asking us to accept this vision you saw as verity?"

The man stood staring at the lawyer.

"But—but it's the truth, Mr. Ponniman. I—I was conscious every minute of the time. I could see up through a hole in the water . . . about four inches across . . . suddenly

I floated up through this hole out of the water high in the moonlight. . . . Oh it was wonderful. Then I felt something pulling me back. I hated to go worse than anything in my whole life. Nothing has ever been so horrible as to come back and enter my body again."

Ponniman said:

"My friend, you know there was no hole in the water."

"Oh yes—yes, sir, there was, Mr. Ponniman."

Someone pulled the fellow from behind.

"Rutledge, sit down," said a voice.

Everyone was pleased that the drowned man had been hushed. He made the diners uncomfortable. Everyone felt that his maunderings bordered on sacrilege.

CHAPTER THIRTY-ONE

EVERYBODY in Florence who was anybody had attended the luncheon given in honor of Phineas Ponniman. They had, indeed, under the spell of the man, laughed at his speech, but no sooner were they out of the hotel than they began to grow angry at what he had said, and the more they thought about it the angrier they got.

Colonel Vaiden said he could not understand how a man of Ponniman's brains could possibly be an atheist.

Marsan opened the door of the car where it stood parked in front of the hotel.

As Sydna entered, she said that she supposed Yankees always paid off courtesy with discourtesy. Her grandfather, during the war, had been the host of a Yankee colonel, and the last thing he did before he marched his regiment away was to burn down her grandfather's house.

As Sydna said this a queer thing happened to Jerry Catlin. The graceful woman seemed to embody all that men meant by the qualitatives charming and aristocratic. The very historicity of her resentment cast a glamour over her whole person. The change was like that which comes over a lamp when it is lighted. What had been casual and inconspicuous suddenly becomes a warm radiant center which reveals and gives meaning to every other thing. An extraordinary physical reaction set up in Jerry, a sudden stricture in his chest, a sensation as if his viscera had been lowered in his body. It was dismaying to Jerry to be so shocked and moved by the wife of his uncle. Why it happened, how it happened, he did not know . . . here on the crowded street with people pouring out from the luncheon. His psychical lunge toward her would go away as abruptly as it had rushed over him, he supposed, and hoped.

A man in the outpouring throng touched Jerry's sleeve. When Jerry turned, the stranger removed his hat in deference to the ladies in the car.

"This is Dr. Catlin?"

"Yes."

"You are the minister who invited the Realtors' Association to give a thousand dollars a month to the cathedral?"

"I requested the donation . . . yes."

"I was sitting beside Mr. Sanborne when Mr. Ponniman alluded to it. He pointed you out to me. I've been elbowing the crowd for the last five minutes trying to get to you. I wanted to express my compliments on your work."

Jerry thanked him.

"My name is Atkins. I'm connected with the steel mills in Birmingham. What is the nature of your position here under Dr. Blankenship . . . is it permanent?"

"I . . . suppose it is," said Jerry.

"You wouldn't be open to wider . . . more intensive religious opportunities?" inquired the steel man, choosing his words carefully so they would have an uncommercial sound.

Jerry gathered Mr. Atkins' drift, and the thought of leaving the quaint charm of Florence for the smoke and dirt and bustle of Birmingham was distasteful to him.

"Colonel Vaiden, my uncle, is very desirous that I remain here in the cathedral. . . ."

"Naturally, naturally, but the width of a minister's field, the possibility of good that lies before him, must influence him in his decision about his work."

"That's true, of course."

"Well, good-bye, Dr. Catlin. I won't hold you any longer. If I should drop you a line in care of the cathedral it would reach you, I suppose?"

"The cathedral or the Methodist parsonage."

The man drew out a little book and made a note.

"I'm a steward in the New Methodist Church in Birmingham. Good-bye." He touched his hat with a faint bow that included the ladies in the car, turned, and was lost in the crowd.

As Jerry entered the car, the thought came to him, if Sydna's charms made life too unhappy for him, the New Methodist Church in Birmingham might be a refuge.

Sydna herself widened her eyes at her nephew-in-law and asked in concern:

"Jerry, he's not trying to get you away from Florence, is he?"

And Jerry said:

"Oh, these vague suggestions from lay members seldom come to anything."

At this point Marsan broke into the conversation by ejaculating:

"Oh, there's Mr. Petrie ... Mr. Petrie, will you ride ..." Here she bit off her impulsive offer with a reddened face.

The school teacher turned, and Sydna called pleasantly:

"Marsan's offering you a lift, Mr. Petrie ... what did you think of the speech?"

"You mean Ponniman's?"

"Yes, of course, that last man's speech ... or stammerings ... was dreadful."

"Well, I didn't think much of it," said Petrie incisively. "To disbelieve in religion because its use is founded on fear is just about as sensible as to disbelieve in antiseptics because their use is founded on fear."

"Why, that is true," ejaculated Sydna, surprised at this reasoning, "you should have got up and said that: it would have been a hundred times better than what that crazy man said."

"As a matter of fact, I ... wasn't where I could," answered Petrie, in some embarrassment; "I was at the door, seeing him from there."

"Why, that's a shame!" cried Sydna. "The invitation committee were very stupid to keep the most intelligent listener on the outside."

"They had to draw a line somewhere," laughed Petrie ruefully, "and they naturally began on school teachers."

"To my way of thinking," said Sydna, punching Miltiades with her gloved hand and moving him in the seat with her and Jerry so Mr. Petrie could sit by the side of Marsan, "to my way of thinking school teachers are the very designers of our society. What they believe, the next generation are going to believe."

Sydna gave to this hackneyed observation the charm of freshness, and it moved Mr. Petrie in an intimate and reproachful manner. He recalled Marsan's visit to his office and her embarrassed inquiry about religion, and then later her confession to him of her relations with Red McLaughlin. What connection with each other had these two moments in Marsan's life?

Petrie had tried within the last week to put the girl and her impudicity out of his thoughts, but her confession to him "because he was going with her" repeated itself over and over to him with its frankness and pathos.

He knew very well why she had shouted out to him and then checked her sentence and sat silent and blushing. He himself had waked in his bed at the Waner boarding house in Tombigbee Street with a hope in his heart that Marsan would pick him up that morning, and then he would remember that she could not, and the day would go gray again. Marsan's chopped-off call to him had been like that.

When the car moved onward, Sydna, who saw that her daughter was not in a talkative mood, assumed the burden of the conversation.

"Wasn't it outrageous of that Mr. Rutledge to get up and talk as he did?"

"I think he believed it," said Petrie gravely.

"Yes, he did, but Mr. Ponniman took him down when he told him that drowning men very often had illusions like that."

"Yes, and that's a very lawyeresque proof," said Petrie.

"You know lawyers never use logical demonstrations: their proof is psychological. They say whatever they think will convince their hearers, even if it hasn't a particle of sense to it. They fall into this habit before juries."

"Why do you say that, Mr. Petrie?" asked Sydna, really interested.

"Why, look at Ponniman's implication. He said other drowning men had seen the same thing, therefore it was not true. That's about as sensible as to say if one man goes to China and comes back and reports it, China exists, but if a dozen men go to China and they all come back and report the same thing, China does not exist."

Sydna was amazed.

"Well, I declare, that's a fact . . . but you don't believe Mr. Rutledge went anywhere or really saw anything, do you?"

"No, I don't, but I certainly don't say he is mistaken because other men have seen the same thing."

Sydna had it on the tip of her tongue to say:

"Mr. Petrie, I'm surprised that a brilliant young man like you would teach in a high school," but being a tactful, well-bred woman, Sydna had long since formed the habit of censoring, suppressing, and changing whatever she really thought. She was a lady of charm.

Jerry Catlin sat by Sydna, half listening to her conversation with Petrie and distinctly aware of the slight touch of her hip against his own. He glanced at her from time to time, thinking that she was physically and facially what she had been in her youth. She was a luxurious woman, the fulfillment of the promise of her girlhood. Marsan might have been her younger sister; or rather, since Marsan was blonde and mental instead of being brunet and physical, as Sydna was, they might have been no kin to each other at all. Jerry tried to take his mind off his seat mate. If Atkins offered him that pastorate in Birmingham, he would take it. A faint suggestion of Sydna's perfume came to him now and then in the windy car.

Old Colonel Vaiden sat on the other side of his wife, thinking of Rutledge, who was almost drowned in Shoal Creek. He was wondering if the volley of shots fired into the water had struck a little yellow child who had been hiding below.

A few minutes later, when Marsan drove up Pine Street, Jerry Catlin asked to be delivered at the parsonage. Sydna insisted that he ride on to the manor, but Jerry pleaded work and got out.

Marsan then drove to the manor and delivered her father and mother. She asked Mary, the maid, for Wilson, with an unworded plan of having the chauffeur drive Mr. Petrie home.

The maid said that Wilson had gone over to Jericho.

"Confound that nigger!" cried the Colonel, "I told him not to buy that lot!"

"Yes suh, Wilson tol' me you tol' him not to buy that lot," declared Mary. "What do you want with Wilson, Miss Marsan?"

"To take Mr. Petrie home."

The school teacher offered at once and very firmly to walk home, but Sydna was shocked at such a suggestion . . . pick a man up, take him a mile further away from his home than where she found him and let him walk back . . . "that's as bad as Mr. Ponniman's logic, Mr. Petrie." The mother smiled at Marsan, made a sharp private motion with her gloved fingers that told Marsan that she was amazed and embarrassed at such discourtesy in a daughter of hers. Then, with extra sweetness, she reinstated Mr. Petrie in the car and started Marsan around the loop for Pine Street.

As soon as the two were behind the boxes that screened the drive, Petrie offered again in a formal voice to walk home. Marsan replied with equal formality of voice, if not of words, that she would have to drive around long enough to take him home, anyway, so she might as well actually take him home, unless he objected to riding with her.

"Of course I don't," said the school teacher, and he almost added, "What is it to me how you comport yourself?" but

the last question was so ridiculous and untrue that he did not
say it.

"I can get you home in three minutes," said Marsan, and
she speeded up the car, south . . . west . . . and was in Tom-
bigbee Street.

A kind of physical heaviness came over Mr. Petrie as his
boarding house was whisked into sight. In a minute or two
he would step out of the car, and then he would never be
alone with this girl again.

Within the last week, in the privacy of his own imagina-
tion, he had conducted endless conversations with Marsan.
He would ask:

"Marsan, why did you surrender your virtue to a creature
like Red McLaughlin? What moved you to do it?"

He felt now, unless he could get some of these unhappy
queries asked while he was with the girl, that they would go
on revolving in his head endlessly.

Her mere presence somehow allayed his feeling of pro-
longed suspense and privation but substituted for it a feeling
of despair.

He thought of saying to her frankly:

"Marsan, if I hadn't told you that I did not believe in
preachers and their cant, would you have done what you
did?"

He knew that if he were one tenth as frank and straight-
forward as the girl he would say that . . . if he possessed
just a touch of her honesty, that had come about, he sup-
posed, because she had always been wealthy, pampered,
protected, and spoiled. Only the spoiled were unreflectingly
sincere. He himself was born in the lower middle class. He
was still there.

The car stopped in front of the old Waner place on Tom-
bigbee Street.

"Thank you for bringing me home, Marsan."

"You're welcome, Mr. Petrie."

That was the only voice given to the surging questions,
denials, explanations that stormed through their two brains.

As Marsan turned her car, she blinked her eyes in order to see the street at all, and she cried out in her mind in a kind of spasm of anger and heartbreak:

"If it had been *him*, neither of us would have thought a single thing about it!"

CHAPTER THIRTY-TWO

O<small>N HER</small> way home Marsan stopped by the parsonage in order that she apparently would have consumed a reasonable amount of time in driving Mr. Petrie to his boarding house.

The parsonage was empty, and Marsan followed a walk to the rear door of the old church and looked into its great bare auditorium. She thought her cousin was in the office but did not go in because of the shock she had received from seeing the model of her father's tomb. She did not call Jerry because in reality she had nothing to say to him. In the office she could hear a typewriter going. The dark benches in the auditorium looked so uncomfortable that she did not sit down, but continued standing near the door.

The girl had read of women going into churches and praying when they were in trouble. She was not in trouble, and such a place as this offered neither the incentive nor the surroundings for prayer. She felt abysmally depressed. She thought how shameful it had been for Mr. Petrie to stand in the door of the dining room when he was the only man in the crowd who had the intelligence to pick that rough, shaggy coconut grater of a Yankee, Ponniman's, speech to pieces. The only man in town with the brains to do it, and him slighted by the committee and kept outside!

Tears stung Marsan's eyes; her lips trembled . . . she hated Mr. Petrie . . . she wanted to take his head in her hands and . . . shake it . . . and . . . press it between the mounds of her breast and kiss away the wounds and slights that these damned ignorant uppety Florence society people put upon him for being a school teacher!

Still, he really didn't have any sense! Broad-minded on

religion, narrow as a string on sex . . . not many girls would have had the decency that she had and told him what had happened . . . what difference did it make whether a preacher mumbled a few words over a couple or not? Still . . . they should love.

Marriage was just a social safeguard, like speed laws and iodine in the water works . . . but people should love each other, and she and Red hadn't done that . . . they hadn't even thought about it. She was weeping again, holding her face motionless but disconsolate, with the tears running down the side of her short straight nose. She felt faintly sick, nauseated, as if further looking at this drab depressing interior might cause her to throw up.

A wing of the double front door opened, and a woman entered the auditorium. It was Miss Swartout. Marsan watched her with the automatic curiosity which one woman always feels for the actions of another when there is a man close about.

Miss Swartout remained near the entrance for a moment, then moved uncertainly toward the door of the inner office. When almost there she happened to see Marsan. She gave a slight start.

"I didn't know you were there," she ejaculated, smiling and coming down the aisle to the girl. "That's a very pretty dress you've got on."

Marsan thanked her and began a lively speculation on what Miss Swartout had meant to do in the office and why she had started when she saw someone. Aloud she asked:

"Did you hear Mr. Ponniman's speech?"

"No-o . . . I didn't go . . . Father is not a Rotarian." This last seemed dragged out of the organist. She looked at Marsan with an odd expression in her clear blue eyes.

"You . . . are waiting for someone, aren't you?" she asked solicitously, as if she would go quickly out of the building and leave it to Marsan.

"No, I'm not waiting for anybody . . . I meant to see Jerry, but I heard his typewriter running and knew he was busy. I'm going myself this very moment."

With this elaborate explanation Marsan was really putting a feminine question to Miss Swartout as to what she was doing here.

The organist began at once with very close connection in what seemed to be a disjointed conversation:

"I thought I had left some music in the choir stalls on this side of the church . . ." She passed Marsan a little way and looked into the choir stalls.

"The song books aren't ever kept on this side, are they?" said Marsan.

"Well . . . a person couldn't see them over here, anyway, if she were crying," said Miss Swartout.

Having declared a war of suspicion on each other's motives and actions, they separated, with neither army able to wrest an indisputable victory on the field of battle. Marsan's parting salvo was:

"Well, good-bye, sorry I can't stay to hear you practise, Miss Swartout. I know you play lovely, because everybody says you do. I wish I could understand some of the things you select."

"Unless a person has a natural ear, they have to hear a lot of music," said Miss Swartout.

Marsan went out to her car and drove home. She was unreasonably angry about Miss Swartout's insults, forgetting that she herself had started the fray.

What the two girls had really been saying to each other was:

"You are trying to catch Cousin Jerry and you are not good enough for our family."

And Miss Swartout was replying:

"My family is as good as yours, you musical ignoramus!"

At home Marsan went to her mother at once and told her with incense that that Miss Swartout was setting her cap for Cousin Jerry.

Sydna had Marsan tell precisely what she had seen and said. A sharp and completely unexpected pain entered Sydna's heart.

"She may have had some ordinary business with Jerry, honey . . . hymns to select . . . Dr. Blankenship can't carry a tune, and Jerry is quite musical."

"Then what made her jump if she's not setting her cap?"

To Sydna, the suggestion that Jerry might be in love with somebody besides herself filled her with incredulity and at the same time distress. Her life and Jerry's, she had told herself, had reached a calm, comfortable tableland. He came to her home, ate many of his meals with her and the family; his was a warm masculine affection which gave a kind of body to her life. She was interested, of course, with social work and patriotic societies. She had been regent of the Florence chapter of the United Daughters of the Confederacy and of the Daughters of the American Revolution, but these honors were like the candles on a birthday cake, inedible and told how old one was getting.

Jerry Catlin really was the only intimate friend Sydna possessed. Drusilla, her mother, was the owner of a faintly satirical wisdom which always kept Sydna at a slight distance from her. Miltiades had settled into a middle course somewhere between a father and a husband once removed. Marsan she had never understood at all. Now and then Sydna gave her daughter a little random advice, and Marsan, in turn, gave Sydna advice not at all random in the form of opinions gleaned from her teachers, her father, with whom she was intimate, but who was not intimate with her, and ideas out of her own original head.

When Jerry entered the parsonage he had installed himself at once as the only thoroughly comprehensible human being in Sydna's world.

Now, the mere suggestion that he might marry any woman at all filled Sydna with a desperate feeling, as if she were clinging to a life buoy in deep water and some other woman were about to snatch it from her grasp.

Mr. Jerry Catlin, the object of Sydna Vaiden's disturbed meditation, sat in the office of the old church checking off a list of names by placing a number after each one. At another table Miss Chisem typed form letters which corresponded to the numbers Jerry placed on his index. Most of them were begging letters, a few acknowledged the receipt of checks. Miss Chisem had a pile of such letters awaiting Jerry's signature. All these form letters sounded very intimate and yet dignified, as if Jerry himself were personally grateful for the contributions in question.

As Jerry absently signed these communications he pondered the wisdom of his staying on any longer at the parsonage. The shock he had received from Sydna in the Vaiden motor suggested that he give up his work with the cathedral. He did not want to complicate his life and his mind with an unworded and impossible passion for his aunt by marriage. He would resign his position at the conference of the Southern Methodist Church which would be held in the fall and ask reappointment somewhere else. The steel man in Birmingham, whose name had got away from Jerry, might help him.

It seemed ironic to Jerry that this emotional stress should rise up in him in regard to Sydna, just when the annoyance and distraction of the rape case had cleared away and left the moral atmosphere of Florence free for sane and spiritual thinking.

Now, if the distraction of Sydna could be cleared away, the distraction of the boom cleared away, and the distraction of the actual building of the new cathedral could be ended, then he might reach up to that inner spiritual life which had been his goal ever since his adolescent days. But what could he do if he were always to be secretly tweaked by his longing for Sydna? How could he pray? How could he approach God?

Here the troubled circling of his thoughts was interrupted by the solemn prefatory chords of one of Bach's chorales.

The assistant minister arose from his desk, handed Miss

Chisem what he already had signed, and entered the auditorium.

For ten or fifteen minutes he sat out of sight of the organist, listening to the turbulent music of the pipes.

The chords somehow spread a vast stately architecture and noble demesnes before Jerry's mind, and the voices in the music were the action taking place amid the scene. And while the organ created a great superhuman drama before Jerry's fancy, at the same time, and by a strange double effectiveness, it was an idealized recountal of Jerry's own past life and a glorified vision of what he hoped he would yet become.

It was as if the music had unchained Time's feet upon his fatal path and allowed him to wander to and fro in unaccustomed freedom.

In the midst of a chord, the playing stopped, and the bare auditorium rearranged itself and slowly cut off the vistas the music had revealed.

Miss Swartout came out and looked at Jerry with a rapt expression on her face.

"I didn't know you were listening."

"You knew I was, if I was anywhere in the church."

"No, I didn't know it, because I wasn't thinking of you."

Jerry was delicately amused at Miss Swartout. The idea of a woman saying a thing like that to a man . . . admit she wasn't thinking of him . . . when she wasn't.

"What were you thinking?"

"I was thinking how sad it was that people can't live in the world of sound as they do in the world of light. You can hear wonderful romantic things in sound; they are all around you, in your very heart, but how far away it all is, how inaccessible; but in the world of light you can see a scene in the extreme distance, and you feel you can go there and become a part of it; yet they are both waves, one air waves, one ether waves." She looked at him musingly for a moment. "I am sure you don't know what you were doing in the world of sound?"

"Was I in it?"

"Yes, you were building a cathedral, not by gathering money, but by lifting the stones yourself, lifting huge stones and shoving them into place. . . ." She broke off again, continuing her regard of Jerry, and presently asked in a queer voice, "Are you in love with Marsan?"

Jerry was disconcerted.

"Why, no . . . of course not . . . she's my first cousin."

"Yes . . . I knew that. I was thinking of her too. When I came in she was standing over there by the choir stall, crying. . . ."

"Marsan was?"

"Yes, and as I sat there playing, I thought, 'There was Marsan, just crying and nothing more,' but if that were in music she could die of the wounds of her love, and a musician could play the same piece over, and she would be reborn, love again, and die again, over and over. Tragic deaths in music are a kind of sweet pain because they may always be played again and are a kind of eternal life. But out in the real world of light, if you die, that ends it; nobody will ever play again the symphony that made up you." She became quiet, looking at Jerry out of her Dresden china eyes, then said in apparent disconnection:

"I'm engaged . . . I told Tony Vicelli I would marry him."

Jerry was somewhat taken aback.

"Well, that's lovely . . . does he understand music?"

"Oh no, of course not. As far as I know, you are the only person in town who really understands music. I dreamed music last night. I had a very strange dream."

"What was it?"

"I dreamed I was about to be thrown from a great height, and a sad melancholy music was being played. And I thought the music really was my death, and I listened to it in terror, and when it ended, I thought in despair, 'Now I'm dead.'"

"What a strange dream."

"It was, wasn't it? When I woke up I couldn't quit thinking about it, the music stayed in my head."

Jerry stood pondering what she had told him.

"Do you ever read Freud?" he asked.

"Well, no, I don't read him, but I know about him . . . a little bit, at least."

"I was wondering, do you suppose there could be any possible connection between your dream and Tony Vicelli?"

"Why, no, I hadn't thought of that at all."

"Well . . . if I were you, Miss Swartout, I don't believe I would marry Tony Vicelli unless I was sure I loved him."

"Well, I . . . I don't think anybody else will ever want me, Dr. Catlin."

"You still can't marry for mere convenience. If there wasn't some profound necessity for love, why did it ever grow up in the human race?"

"So people would have children," said the organist.

"Then why is it so selective?" argued Jerry. "If just any man can fertilize your body, why can't any man fertilize your heart? And why does your heart cry out so against . . . just any man?"

"Does it cry out?" asked Miss Swartout, frowning in thought.

"I am sure so . . . what else can your dream mean?"

"I didn't know it meant anything," said the girl, "until you said so." She broke off suddenly to ask:

"Did you put that money Papa gave you in the collection?"

"Why, yes, of course, why?"

"Nothing . . . I just wanted to know."

"Is there anything wrong about it?"

"Well, he thought he was going to get paid some more right away, but he didn't."

"By whom?"

"The niggers who contracted for houses in Jericho."

Jerry nodded with gravity.

"Niggers are uncertain . . . as a rule, they don't pay."

"I told Father that," exclaimed Miss Swartout; "I told

him nobody trusted niggers down here in the South. He said this time it wasn't their fault, they had all been run away from their work, and they didn't have anything to pay with."

"Why did they lose their work?"

"Oh, you know, the trouble they had about the boys in jail, for one thing. Then the nigger carpenters and bricklayers and plumbers wouldn't join the union, so the white men wouldn't work with 'em. Now they are grumbling on Grey Mule Hill that my father and everybody else is trying to rob them."

"Well, niggers grumble to themselves and grin to white people," characterized Jerry. "Is the fifty dollars your father gave to the cathedral going to throw him seriously behind?"

Miss Swartout drew a long breath.

"Well . . . I don't know. He gets mad when Mamma or I ask him about his business. He owes the Sheffield bank for the lumber and stuff that went into the houses."

Jerry ruminated a moment and finally said:

"Suppose we step into the parsonage and see Dr. Blankenship about your father's fifty dollars."

Miss Swartout agreed to this gratefully, and the two went together out the side door around to the parsonage.

They walked in silence. About half of Jerry's thought was on the fifty dollars; he was also comparing almost involuntarily Miss Swartout with Sydna. Jerry wondered if Miss Swartout was a musical genius. She was the most emotional woman he had ever seen, not only in her music but in her everyday life. Then Miss Swartout not only had ideas on all manner of subjects, but she was amazingly frank and transparent in her expression. Sydna, on the other hand, was a woman whose intellectual effort was mainly to make herself agreeable to other people. Nearly all of her information was disconnected and picked up here and there, without system and purely to entertain herself and others. Some years ago she had been a member of "study" clubs whose study programs skipped around from fortifications of the American coast to the hoof-and-mouth disease in cattle. Of late she had turned almost exclusively to patriotic societies. If she could not cultivate her intellect, she would her heart.

This quality of lifelong agreeableness, adaptability, and solicitousness for others somehow had been transposed from her mind to her body, and she moved about, an unconscious suggestion of tenderness, sweetness, and luxury.

A tingling sensation went through Jerry at the mere thought of Sydna. He told himself now, that in comparison with Miss Swartout, Sydna was surfacy, but the fancy of possessing that surface quickened his breath.

Dr. Blankenship listened with sympathy to the story of the fifty dollars.

"I have sent it in," he said, "to the building fund, and I don't know whether it can be got back or not. The Methodist Church is an ecclesiastical corporation, and I don't know of any precedent for returning a gift. I can report to the board that this gift has worked a great and unexpected hardship . . ."

"Oh, let it alone," begged Miss Swartout.

"Suppose Jerry make a report on it to the board and I'll write a letter of recommendation," proposed the Doctor.

"I don't think we'll get it back," said Miss Swartout unhappily.

"We can hope for the best," comforted the Doctor, patting the girl's plump shoulder. "Jerry, you look into this. We can't have our organist in trouble. . . . Ah, Jerry, did Miss Chisem call your attention to Waterloo?"

"No, what about Waterloo?"

"It seems the Methodist Church has just about lost a Sunday school in Waterloo. It's been taken over by a fly-by-night sect called the Drownders."

"Drownders?"

"Yes, ever hear of them before?"

"Never did."

"Well, there's a Drownder preacher over there holding a revival. It is one of those revivals that doesn't stop, it goes on and on and on. We haven't received a cent from the Waterloo Sunday school for three consecutive Sundays."

"You don't know the preacher's name?"

"Two syllables, sounds something like Patridge . . . some kind of an 'idge' . . . idge . . . idge . . . Rutledge . . . Willie Rutledge . . . when a preacher calls himself 'Willie' or 'Jimmy' or 'Charley,' you already know the kind of sermon he will preach."

CHAPTER THIRTY-THREE

THE assistant minister and the organist of the old Pine Street Methodist Church set forth to Sheffield on the dubious mission of making such a report to the General Board of the M. E. Church South that it would O. K. a return of fifty dollars to its late and repentant owner, Mr. Swartout.

The two drove over in Miss Swartout's car, and as they rattled along it occurred to Jerry that if he should marry Aurelia Swartout it would be such a typical thing for a poor Methodist preacher to marry a poor music teacher and organist, and for the two to clatter around in the wife's poor car, until in some far distant future some shamed congregation would present them with another. And it was amazing how much shame a small town congregation will endure before it produces a second car.

"What are you smiling at?" inquired Miss Swartout.

"I didn't know I was smiling."

"A sort of disgusted smile."

Jerry was glad that he had not said straightaway that he was thinking of her car: there would have been ahead of him such an involved and personal explanation.

"It couldn't have been a disgusted smile when I am motoring with you, Miss Swartout."

"Do you like to motor with me?"

"Of course."

"And do you like the way I play?" She looked at him with concerned eyes.

The minister patted her hand in assurance.

"Why, Miss Swartout, how could it be otherwise?"

At the pat an odd tingle traveled up Jerry's arm, as if the

organist had been charged with some sort of sweet electricity.

Color came into Miss Swartout's face, then flowed out again and left it quite pale. Jerry observed these physical signals in himself and the organist with a touch of surprise and self-interrogation when a newsboy came running along the downtown street of Florence shouting:

"The niggers are caught! The niggers that got away here in Florence are caught! Read all about ketching the two niggers in New Jersey. . . ."

Jerry was not averse to the interruption. He reached in his pocket and said, "Let's get one."

Miss Swartout stopped her car, and Jerry beckoned the boy to him. A two-column headline announced:

NEGRO RAPIST ESCAPED FROM FLORENCE ARRESTED IN PLAINFIELD, NEW JERSEY.

ALAMABA GOVERNOR FORWARDS REQUISITION PAPERS.

The Four Accomplices of the Escaped Negro at Athens, Alabama, Sentenced to Death.

Jerry did not read the article after he had bought it.

Miss Swartout had stopped her car near the Second National Bank, and Jerry's attention was caught by a queue of men reaching out of its door and halfway down the block.

Jerry asked a man standing near if they were depositors waiting to put their money in the bank or were they men who wanted advice from Colonel Vaiden?

The man gave a short laugh and answered:

"No, they are depositors waiting to get their money out of the bank, and I suppose they are men who took advice from Colonel Vaiden."

"Why, what's the matter?" cried Jerry, alarmed at the fellow's irony.

The man nodded at the queue.

"You see for yourself . . . a run on the bank."

A shock went through the assistant minister.

"Aurelia," he said, "I've got to go in and see what's the matter. Do you mind waiting a minute?"

She nodded her consent, and Jerry stepped out of the car.

At the door a policeman told Jerry he would have to go to the end of the line and await his turn.

Jerry explained he was not a depositor, that he was going in to see his uncle. The officer moved aside and let him pass.

Inside the bank all the desks in the lobby were filled with men writing checks. They were copying amounts from their passbooks. All the paying windows were open, and the tellers were receiving checks and pushing forth piles of bills capped by a few coins of small change. At one of the windows a man was saying:

"I hate to damage the bank I've been doing business with for years, but, my God, I don't want to lose ever'thing I got."

Jerry went in through the lobby, nodded at Miss Katie, and passed into his uncle's private office.

As Jerry entered, the Colonel was talking over the telephone. He was saying in an affectionate tone:

"Darling, I don't see how I'm going to get off. . . . No . . . yes . . . I know I haven't been to Shiloh since the battle, and my personal feeling then was and still is that I never wanted to see the damned place again."

He listened a few moments longer, then said:

"Listen, darling, here's Jerry . . . let him go in my place." He put his hand over the receiver and said, "You talk to her, Jerry, she'll keep me here for the next half hour . . . make up reasons why I can't go to Shiloh," and he handed the telephone to his nephew, who put it to his ear with no very definite object.

"Jerry," said Sydna's voice, "persuade Colonel Milt to go to the reunion at Shiloh. I'm making out the list of the U.D.C. honorees. . . ."

"Sydna, he's terribly busy, and now, since there's a run on the bank . . ."

"A what?"

"Oh, didn't you know that?"

"Tell her it's a little run . . . it doesn't amount to anything," interposed the Colonel.

"Uncle Milt says it doesn't amount to anything."

"What caused it?"

Jerry relayed the question to the Colonel, who said:

"Fundamentally because everybody in Florence knows that real estate has been badly oversold; they're nervous, and when a pin drops it makes a very startling crash."

"Tell me something she'll understand," said Jerry.

"Tell her the Farmers' and Mechanics' Bank in Sheffield closed its doors this morning, and this is a sympathetic run, and it is really about a month behind the date I set for it."

Jerry transmitted this with considerable relief to himself. Sydna then talked the predicted thirty minutes and wound up by asking Jerry to go to Shiloh. He said he would go.

"I should think so," said the voice over the wire; "to leave you out would be like leaving Desdemona out of *Hamlet* . . . or is she in *Hamlet*? . . . who is it I'm thinking about, anyway?"

"Sydna," reconsidered Jerry, "I don't know whether I can go or not."

"What, *you* not go!"

Her voice enveloped him and took him perforce. His remaining in Florence when the U.D.C.'s were holding a function at Shiloh under Sydna's management was inconceivable. Her warmth aroused something of the tremulous intimacy which he had felt in the car on the day of the banquet. He agreed to attend and put up the telephone. He had an impulse to go up at once and see Sydna. His uncle was talking to him.

"That paper you've got says one of those niggers that we turned loose has been caught again."

"Yes."

"Which one?"

Jerry looked over his paper.

"Lascome."

"Wasn't Hodige?"

"No sir."

"And the governor is going to bring this Lascome back?"

"That's what the paper says."

"Mm—mm . . . I wonder whatever happened to the little yellow nigger?"

"That I couldn't say," said Jerry, not thinking very much about the matter.

"I don't believe anything happened to him . . . he made a clean dive over the bridge for such a young boy. . . ."

"By the way," remembered Jerry, "I'm the one who caught that yellow boy at the depot and held him till Northrup came back and arrested him."

The old banker stared at his nephew.

"You did?"

"Yes, I did . . . in a way, I started the whole hullabaloo about these niggers. . . ."

The old Colonel shook his head.

"Imagine a nephew of mine doing a thing like that . . . mhuh . . . and you did something else at the same time. . . ."

"What?"

"You started the run on this bank."

"How?"

"The niggers here in jail threw the niggers in Sheffield out of work and broke the Farmers' and Mechanics' Bank. It was caught on that damn fool Jericho subdivision idea. Imagine a banker with little enough sense to try to do business in any extended way with niggers!"

CHAPTER THIRTY-FOUR

As the Reverend Jerry Catlin walked out of the bank he was simultaneously disturbed and titivated over the feeling Sydna's voice had brought him. It was not the moonlit, bodiless yearning he had felt for her as an adolescent, it was a man's possessive desire for her. It titivated his body and deeply disturbed his loyalty to his uncle, and to the church, and his profession, and everything that he was or hoped to be.

A little later he climbed into Miss Swartout's shabby car with a sense of sharp relief. The organist's golden-silvery hair, her blue eyes, the lift of her full bosom beneath her blouse, the turn of her white neck, might have been a blonde anodyne against the brunet fever of Sydna in his veins.

"What did you find out?" asked Miss Swartout, with interest.

"It's a sympathetic run. The Farmers' and Mechanics' Bank in Sheffield closed its doors, and when any bank closes it always causes a little flurry among the others."

After a little driving Miss Swartout exclaimed:

"The Farmers' and Mechanics' is the bank my father deals with!"

Jerry was disturbed and sympathetic.

"That will have its bearings on what we find out about his gift to the cathedral. His donation may turn out better than depositing his money in the bank . . . if he gets it back."

"Wouldn't that be poetic . . . what . . . poetic finance?"

"It would have a fairy-tale sound," agreed Jerry thinking how effectively he could use such an incident in a sermon on "Giving to God."

The motor was out of Florence now, approaching the

bridge. Jerry's thoughts left the question of Swartout's contribution and came back to the girl at his side. She had the antiseptically clean look of a carefully groomed blonde. Her hands on the wheel were white and symmetrical with the muscular development of a pianist. The thought of what they could evoke gave Jerry the feeling as if the hands themselves were music. The girl was so sensitive and so emotionally responsive.

The dream Miss Swartout had told him in the church recurred to him and produced in Jerry a sense of pathos and incipient tragedy. He wondered whether he ought to mention the subject again, whether he ought not to tell her that her dream was a signal to her that she did not really love Tony Vicelli. Eventually he did say this to her.

Miss Swartout gave her attention to the long river bridge which was so narrow it required careful driving. On the other side she said, in a gray voice:

"I know I don't love Tony in any real sense, I mean in the sort of way you hear in some of Wagner's things, or Tschaikowski's."

"Do you think love is ever so idealized as that, Miss Swartout?"

The girl glanced at him.

"I think you know."

"Why do you say that?" asked Jerry interested in himself.

"Your face shows it. When I see you in the pulpit, it seems to me all the serious lovely things you are saying didn't come out of the Bible at all, but out of your own life."

"Or out of the lives of people around me," said Jerry. "I can imagine the unhappiness, the silent wasting away of a girl as sensitive as you are, as emotional . . ." He left his half finished sentence directed against any person who would marry for any other reason than a great overwhelming passion.

"Dr. Catlin," asked the organist earnestly, "why do you suppose people almost never marry for love? And yet think how sweet, how divine it would be to be in the arms of a person you really, truly loved. Everybody knows that; everybody feels it; it sets your heart beating and stops your breath even to think of it; but almost nobody at all lives it. The world is full of men and women who have just given up what they hoped for all their lives . . . I don't see why things are as they are."

Jerry sat for a few moments.

"The trouble is money," he said.

"Why, that isn't true, people don't marry for money, as a rule."

"I know that; money is the indirect cause. You see, our period of human mating has remained where it was in the Stone Age, from seventeen to twenty years old. That is the period of the greatest biological intensity and efficiency. But our technical civilization has advanced the age of efficient productivity to about thirty or forty years old. Adolescent boys and girls want to marry intensely. They want to marry just one person, and the thought of anyone else fills them with repulsion. But they have to repress these lovely monogamistic desires, because at that age the boys simply can't make a living.

"The girls, on the contrary, do not have to earn livings so they marry older men who are productively efficient. The boy, when he becomes able to support a family, chooses some younger girl of an age that corresponds to the girl he once loved. In the process both men and women have been taught to love polygamously, because they have been forced to change desire from one person to another and another. That's why divorces increase with the advancing technological complexity of our modern life. It will continue until the family is pulled completely apart and our civilization dies; then some other race of men will rise up and repeat the performance."

Miss Swartout's face took on a shocked pity.

"Isn't that pathetic?"

"It's the price people pay for doctors, lawyers, scientists, inventors, and musicians. They pay what they call their morals for it. And there is no way in the world for them to avoid the payment, for a really moral life can only be lived in a world where the biological and industrial ages of efficiency coincide. There is no such world in existence today."

Miss Swartout drove on in silence. Finally she said in an awed voice:

"That's why you told me not to marry for any reason except love?"

"No, I told you that out of instinct. It is what everybody's heart tells him to do. What I have just said was an effort to analyze the advice which I had just given you. Everybody knows what to do, Miss Swartout, but not many understand why they ought to do it."

Miss Swartout looked intently at her companion; she moistened her molded lips.

"Must I try to get the man I . . . would love to marry?"

"Why . . . yes-es . . ." said Jerry with an odd feeling.

"Knowing that he must have cared for someone else?"

"I couldn't decide so personal a thing as that," said the assistant minister slowly.

Miss Swartout said no more but speeded up her rattling car, passed through Sheffield to Carver's Lane and to her own home. She walked into the cottage calling her father's name, but the little house was empty.

"I think he'll be home soon," she said continuing her air of excitement. "We might sit here in the hall . . . or I could play for you until somebody comes."

The girl led the way to her beautiful piano, which must have taken her a long time to earn. She pulled the bench back, stepped inside, and sat down. She drew off a ring, laid it down, rubbed her fingers together.

"This is the Liebestod from *Tristan and Isolde*," she told him. "What you say about technology parting men and women is true of all the things that ever parted lovers. This is Isolde, waiting and watching and weeping."

She struck the first fateful, broken chord of the Liebestod with its premonition of pathos and tragedy. Then came the

clanging dissonances of uncertainty, of trepidation, of the
thousand fears and hopes and portents of delayed passion.
Then out of this tempest of doubt arose Isolde's love song,
climbing, flung back, climbing again in sobbing heartbreaks,
the passionate aching, hopeless music of the love death.

Jerry's own throat was pierced with the needle of tears.
His chest, hands, arms tingled with emptiness. He saw tears
running down Miss Swartout's face. He leaned over her, put
his arms around her. She lifted her childish lips to his, put
her arms about his neck, and sobbed out of her convulsed
and swelling bosom:

"Oh, Jerry, Jerry, please love only me, please never to
have loved before!"

CHAPTER THIRTY-FIVE

It seemed to Jerry Catlin that at last the long anchoritish emptiness of his life was over. When he had gone North to spend his undergraduate years in a theological seminary he had nursed a dreamy design of leading a life of celibacy in the service of God. This passing notion had been made permanent, quite unconsciously to himself, by Sydna's marriage to his uncle. Now, in his middle age, when his religious yearnings had become mechanized in the service of the Methodist Church, Sydna's reappearance had suddenly stabbed him with the long emptiness of his life. This was over at last.

Miss Swartout in his arms did not fill him with rapture, but with passion and a forecast of satisfaction. She was not a rainbow: she was a summer shower on a bank of dying passion flowers.

Miss Swartout herself almost fainted in Jerry's arms. She felt as she had felt when a child, when swooping out in the wide swift arc of a great swing over a high hillside: as if a strong sweet wind were blowing through her chest and loins. She wanted to pull away the hand on her breast to relieve for a moment its intolerable sweetness . . . she wanted to press it more deeply into her bosom.

She murmured over and over amidst their kisses:

"You love me! Is it possible you really love me?"

They moved from the awkwardness of the piano bench to a chair. She walked unsteadily with his arm about her waist, and presently he drew her down in his lap. Her legs and hips and back were exquisitely sensitive to the masculine hardness of his form.

To Jerry, Miss Swartout was a warm, comfortable, yield-

ing, faintly perfumed girl who could make passionate music.
She had the most kissable of lips. The length of her body
pressed against his own filled him with comfort and with a
feeling of having at last reached a resting place.

She was the frankest human being he had ever known.
She always interested him mentally. As many times as they
had been together, she had not grown dull. No matter to
what church he was assigned after Conference met, Miss
Swartout's music would help him in his ministry. It seemed
to Jerry they had more than a fair chance of happiness
together.

"Can they see us through the window?" she whispered,
looking out with heavy eyes along the stretch of Carver's
Lane to where it declined into Grey Mule Hill.

"When you can see outdoors, the outdoors can't see you,"
said Jerry.

"Will you always love me?"

"You know I will . . ." He hesitated for a second; he had
almost said "Sydna"; her given name slipped him for the
moment because he had almost never used it; then he added,
"Aurelia."

The girl lay against him, drawing long breaths, her bosom
rising and falling.

"I used to hope I would fall in love with some man who
was pure and good, like Parsifal, only I didn't believe there
were any. In Chicago, a girl by herself has all sorts of things
happen to her. . . . Jerry, my name used to be Minnie . . .
I changed it to Aurelia myself, to put on the billboards . . .
you may call me Minnie if you want to."

"Why should I do that?"

"I really am Minnie Swartout . . . you could never love
Minnie Swartout, could you?"

He pinched her cheek.

"The idea of you being so grave about it, sweetheart."

"You don't care?"

"Not at all."

Miss Swartout gave Jerry a queer look.

"You don't really love me."

"Why do you say that?"

"Why, if you had changed your name, Jerry, I would care more than anything. Oh, it would just hurt my heart."

"Why, darling, how silly, why would it hurt your heart?" She got up from his lap.

"It just would."

"Honey, sit back down, you know I love you."

"We must go see about Papa's fifty dollars . . . that's what we started out to do."

"And found out that we loved each other and became engaged to be married," smiled Jerry.

He got up and kissed Miss Swartout in a pleased mood. She accepted the caress gravely, lifting her lips to his.

As the newly engaged pair walked out of the house in a vague search for Aurelia's father, a motorcar came down the lane loaded with several men and two or three negroes on the running board. As they drew near it turned out to be Aurelia's father and two white men from the Farmers' and Mechanics' Bank in Sheffield.

The motor stopped, and Mr. Swartout asked if Jerry and Aurelia did not want to come along. They were on their way, he said, to look over some property in Jericho.

The two accepted and entered the car, where they were introduced to a Mr. Dykes of the Farmers' and Mechanics' Bank, and a Mr. Lindsay, a real estate appraiser, and Mr. Petman, the promoter of Jericho.

As Jerry found a seat he asked Mr. Petman how his little son was getting along. The realtor replied the child was getting on fine and gave Jerry a faint shake of the head to warn him not to carry the talk too far about his little son's infirmity.

Everyone in the car seemed absorbed in his own thoughts, and the black men hanging on the outside wore the frowning brows and protruding lips of negroes who are angry or in trouble.

"What did you say was the basic amount this property owed the bank?" asked the appraiser.

"Eight thousand," returned Mr. Dykes.

"With Swartout's material and labor on top of that?" asked the appraiser.

"No, the bank has been furnishing Mr. Swartout, too."

"I see," nodded Lindsay. "What length of time has this paper to run?"

"It's demand paper," said Dykes.

"Demand . . . on real estate?"

"Well, yes, you see Jericho was a real estate development for colored people, and there was no way at all to forecast how its value would fluctuate; whether the houses would be kept up or not, whether the tenants would be able to find work, whether they would be able to keep in work if they found it. The bank, to protect itself from all these hazards, wrote the paper on demand, with the understanding, of course, that full payment would not be demanded if everything got along all right."

"And now the negroes, I understand, have lost their work on account of that trial, and because they won't join the union, and the white men wouldn't work with them if they did join the union?"

"That's the layout for you to make your estimate upon," nodded Mr. Dykes.

Mr. Lindsay had the drooped mustache, dark eyes, thin lips, and smooth hatchet face that seem to go with appraisers.

The car presently entered Jericho, a series of neat pretty cottages grouped around a large unfinished wooden building. Behind this partly constructed pile lay a large enclosure. In the middle of this enclosure stood a small, very white, and very new marble slab over a new mound of red clay.

"There you are," said Mr. Swartout, climbing out of the car and waving a hand, "as solid a bunch of cottages as you ever saw, Mr. Lindsay, worth every cent that went into them."

The appraiser walked up to a cottage, looked at the ground

around it, at its foundation, its walls, its cornice. He went inside and tapped the dado, tried the planks with his thumb nail.

After a long inspection he said to the men who were following him around:

"These aren't nigger cabins at all, Mr. Swartout; why did you build them like this for niggers?"

"I wanted to build good houses," said Swartout with satisfaction; "made no difference who was going to live in 'em."

"What did you put so much money in 'em for?" demanded Lindsay.

"That's the minimum specifications under the general contract of the Realtors' Association," said Petman.

Mr. Dykes of the bank looked at Petman in amazement.

"Why, my God, man, the minimum specification clause is what you *show* to the man you are building for, it isn't what you read yourself!"

"Dykes, what did the bank let him sink so much money in nigger cottages for?"

"Why, hell, the boom was on, and there was such a rush of work . . . nobody dreamed he was following the minimum specifications in the nigger houses . . . didn't anywhere else."

The appraiser shook his head.

"This won't do . . . this won't do at all . . . not for niggers!"

"Aren't they worth the money?" demanded Swartout.

"That's the trouble," explained Lindsay, "they are far too good. You've got too much invested here to expect to get it back out of niggers. You know you only collect about three fifths of the nominal indebtedness contracted by a group of colored people. A man has to make allowance for that in his building and in his prices."

"What are we going to do about it?" asked Dykes, with a worried face.

"There is only one thing I can suggest," said Lindsay, "let the receivers of the bank take the property over at once and try to convert it into a white settlement."

"Can't do that," said Dykes, "as two or three of these houses are bought and paid for outright. They belong to colored people, and no white person would come out here."

Lindsay stood pondering.

"Then all I can suggest is for the receivers of the bank to sell the cottages to some white man who is starting a subdivision and let him roll these cottages to where they can be used and paid for. They are built strong enough to stand the rolling; that's the only good feature I see about them."

The negroes who had been listening to all this now asked apprehensively:

"Boss, you ain't gwi' roll all ouah houses away, is you?"

"Not those that are paid for," said Dykes.

"You mean we got to pay right now?"

"That's it."

"Ain't you gwi' give us a li'l' time to pay in?"

"When you default on your first payment, all the others fall due," explained Dykes, "and besides, in Petman's contract the amount due on the houses can be called for at any time."

"But we was to pay Mistuh Petman, boss."

"If the title Petman makes to you is not good and valid, you have a right to sue him personally for damages," explained Dykes. "You should have looked and found out what sort of contract Petman had with the bank."

"Well, now, fo' God," mumbled the negroes to each other, "spectin' us to read a contrack what we don't even see, when we kain't undahstan' a contrack what we do see."

Jerry went over to Dykes.

"Will Mr. Swartout lose his interest in the subdivision?"

"Oh, certainly, certainly, he ate up his profits in his material and labor. You know the labor bill has to be paid."

Jerry and Aurelia walked away from the men. Aurelia was saying hopelessly that her father was not a business man. The two walked on into the big central enclosure while the appraiser inspected the other cottages.

The slab of marble in the center of the space was a tombstone. On one side of the new raw grave lay a bedraggled tricolor of cotton cloth in red, black, and orange; worked in gilt letters on it was the legend, "Princes and Potentates of Ethiopia."

Carved so shallowly on the marble that it seemed a mere scratching was the name:

PAMMY LEE SPARKMAN
EXALTED QUEEN P. & P. OF E.
LADY IN WAITING, KNIGHTS OF BENEVOLENCE.
PAST PRESIDENT, SONS AND DAUGHTERS
OF THE HELPING HAND.
AGED FORTY-ONE YEARS, SIX MONTHS, THREE DAYS.

The big unfinished building and the enclosure squarely in the middle of Jericho were a negro church and cemetery.

CHAPTER THIRTY-SIX

On the bus going back to the parsonage the Reverend Jerry Catlin received his first dividend on his emotional investment in Miss Swartout. He was able to look at the women and girls on the bus with almost as much detachment as he viewed the men. They were now just women, not possibilities. Some of the prettier ones he compared to Aurelia. There was one girl, a brunet, whom he considered too tall, and he would really have given her no more thought except for the fact that she and her companion, a gangling hobblede-hoy, seemed very perturbed and excited about something. The two kept glancing at each other, asking mute questions with their eyebrows and answering with almost imperceptible nods. When their messages became too complicated, they whispered and giggled more or less.

Here a man sitting next to Jerry tapped the paper he was reading and said that he personally didn't care what became of that damn nigger in New Jersey, and he wasn't worth the fuss they were making over him.

Jerry asked the trouble and continued to think of Miss Swartout . . . how talented she was, what a musician.

"That damned nigger society in the North are raising a fight against Lascome's extradition," explained Jerry's companion.

"They have no grounds for such a fight," observed Jerry.

"Course not, but you'll find when you hear the details they are trying to keep the nigger up there on some sort of technicality. That's the great idyah these days, smother the law in technicalities."

Jerry agreed to this.

"If the people had just hung them niggers the day they started to, all this would have been over with. The labor union never would 'a' had to drove out the nigger bricklayers and carpenters, the Farmers' and Mechanics' Bank would 'a' stood up, and ever'thing would 'a' been hunkydory."

"The negroes who bought in Jericho wouldn't have lost their property," said Jerry.

"An' there's no tellin' where this'll end," said the passenger. "The other banks ain't propped up any too firm. The whole damn boom may bust any minute, all because six damn black skunks wasn't lynched in time . . . damnedest worst managed business I ever heard of in my life."

Here Jerry's conversation with the man was interrupted by the hobbledehoy getting up from beside the girl and coming back to Jerry's seat. The youth moistened his thick puffed lips.

"Aren't you Dr. Catlin?" he asked in an embarrassed manner.

Jerry said he was.

"Er . . . uh . . . thank you . . . I . . . I'll just keep my eye on you," stammered the boy. His face flushed, he turned and went back to the girl and communicated Jerry's identity with a faint nod.

Jerry's companion opened his eyes.

"What's he going to do to you?"

"Have no idea."

The boy and girl grew very red in the face, because they knew the two men were talking about them.

The bus rattled across the bridge into Florence. Passengers got out along the way, and when the conveyance had passed through the business part of town, only Jerry and the boy and girl remained in the car.

The assistant minister now saw that the boy really was keeping an eye on him. Before the bus reached the college where it turns for East Florence, the youth approached Jerry again, this time even more embarrassed than he was before.

"Uh . . . Dr. Catlin," he began, "Lizzie and I would like

. . . uh . . . for you to perform a . . . a little ceremony for
us."

"Ceremony?"

"Yes . . . uh . . . we . . . we want to get married."

Illumination broke over Jerry.

"Oh, that was why you were keeping an eye on me?" He
broke out laughing.

The boy was relieved that the worst was over.

"Yes sir . . . how much will it cost?"

"How much do you consider your girl will be worth to
you?"

"Oh, my goodness . . . I don't know," stammered the boy.

"Anything you want to give me," said Jerry.

"Would two dollars and a half do?"

"Certainly . . . do your parents know you are going to
be married?"

"Well . . . no-o. . . ."

"Yes, they do," put in the girl.

"That's right, they do," nodded the boy.

"Have you got a license to marry?"

"Who from . . ."

"Yes, we've got one," prompted the girl. "Porter, he's
talking about a marriage license. We've got a marriage
license."

"Oh yes, we've got a marriage license," seconded Porter,
"we just got it in Tuscumbia."

"Oh, then you can't marry in Lauderdale County at all,
you'll have to go back to Tuscumbia or Sheffield, somewhere
in Colbert County."

"Oh, Porter, we should have known that!" cried the girl.
"Go to the bus driver quick and see if we have to pay a re-
turn fare to Sheffield if we don't get off in Florence, go
quick!"

Porter rushed forward to inquire about the fare. The bus
stopped, and Jerry stepped off. As it started forward again,
the girl leaned out of the window and called excitedly:

"Don't tell anybody, Dr. Catlin, except Marsan!"

Jerry was surprised at this.

"You want me to tell Marsan?"

"Please," cried the girl and drew her head back inside the window.

The assistant minister walked from the station to the parsonage, amused at the boy and girl. He also wondered a little at the bride-to-be's message to Marsan. They were friends of Marsan's, no doubt, and she in turn would be excited when she heard of the runaway match, which it undoubtedly was.

The childishness, the haphazardness of the elopers contrasted in Jerry's mind with his own involved affair with Miss Swartout. How simply these children went about their mating . . . they loved each other so they ran away and married without scrip or purse . . . Jerry thought, if he and Sydna, years ago, had followed their example of innocence! He shook his shoulders a bit and put the notion out of his mind as a faint unfaithfulness to Miss Swartout.

He was very happy; then he reflected that presently he would have to tell Sydna his good news . . . and his thoughts came to a pause.

He did not believe Sydna would be hurt, but she would be pensive. She would not be, thank God, crushed as he himself had been at her marriage with his uncle. Even now, as he thought of that distant day, the assistant minister drew a short breath, and his heart sank.

At the new cathedral Jerry stopped for a while to watch the workmen. He wondered if the workmen felt any joy in putting up the white marble columns that stood in front of the rising walls. He wondered if they felt the poetry and the sanctity of raising a fane in the quiet park-like street.

As Jerry stood watching, Dr. Blankenship came out of the old church, went to the head carpenter, drew him aside, and began consulting with him. Presently the Doctor saw Jerry and beckoned him to him.

"Jerry," he said in a grave tone, "I have just received a

note from the Realtors' Association saying they won't be able to make their payment this month."

Jerry became concerned at once.

"Do you suppose it would do any good for me to go around and see Sanborne?"

"Probably wouldn't. They won't be able to do as much in the future as they have done in the past." The Doctor clenched his fist. "I knew we ought to have pressed on all sail while times were flourishing!"

"Well . . . we did."

"We should have done more . . . more. I think Florence has seen the high noon of this boom, Jerry."

The assistant minister tried to cheer his principal.

"I was speaking to the foreman here," said the Doctor, "wondering if the men would work on for some agreed percent of their wages in cash and the rest on time as a debt on the church. . . ."

When the Doctor said this the foreman began shaking his head.

"We'd have to take that up with the union, Dr. Blankenship. It's never been done, it's never even been suggested before. Labor gets paid for its work . . . that's why it works."

"But the church," pressed the Doctor earnestly.

The foreman shook his head and rubbed a smudge of mortar from the back of his hand.

"I'm afraid the men aren't much on the church, Doctor. Two or three of them have joined the Drownders, but they've quit work and gone to preachin' and singin', so they're not masons any more."

Jerry turned to his superior.

"Have you seen Uncle Milt about this?"

"Not yet, but I'm going to."

"He's a lot more interested than you seem to think, Dr. Blankenship."

The first preacher walked aside with his assistant.

"I believe your uncle will do a lot for us, Jerry, but he . . ."

Blankenship hesitated, then visibly changed his sentence: "Isn't it queer that our church never really gets the laboring classes?"

"It's a middle-class church," said Jerry with a dim, nascent feeling that heaven, when finally reached, would be found populated mainly by middle-class people.

The Doctor stood looking at the unsupported columns of white marble.

"The Catholic Church somehow embraces the rich and the poor, the proud and the humble . . ." He broke off with a pang at the spread of the Catholic Church. Then he recurred to his original topic:

"I would really rather not call on your uncle for more than is absolutely necessary, Jerry. Colonel Milt is a very old man and of course has old-fashioned notions about churches . . . which he certainly has a right to have."

"Yes, I know that," said Jerry, thinking a little uncomfortably of his uncle's trade with the Doctor.

"So I wouldn't want him to invest any great sum of money in anything he wasn't in full and complete accord with," amplified the Doctor.

"That's considerate of you." Jerry was really surprised at this new quality in his principal. "By the way, the fifty dollars that Swartout contributed, he really couldn't afford it. In fact, I think he's a bankrupt now."

The Doctor looked his interest.

"You don't mean it!"

"Yes, he built houses that cost more than they should. He was doing it all on a credit . . . on a string, and now the receivers of the bank he was doing business with have taken them all over."

"Well, that does look like a case for a refund. This contribution he gave you, was it before or after his bankruptcy?"

"Before, of course."

"Well, that puts it in a different light. His available funds would have been absorbed by his bankruptcy anyway, wouldn't they?"

"I suppose so."

"In that case, it seems to me he didn't lose anything personally in his donation, after all. His creditor, the bank, undoubtedly lost it, but the bank isn't applying for a refund, as I understand it, and they couldn't get it if they did apply, because the donation was certainly not given with fraudulent intent."

"Oh no, certainly not," agreed Jerry, with a dampening of his hope that Mr. Swartout would find his contribution to the church like bread cast upon the water, returning to him after many days in the hour of his need.

Jerry went on into the parsonage, thinking uneasily about Dr. Blankenship's tacitly expressed opinion about the approaching end of the boom.

Jerry believed that he, like the Doctor, was primarily concerned about the cathedral, but his thoughts continually hovered about his uncle Miltiades' fortune. His uncle was very old, and Jerry knew that he was widely involved in Florence real estate. Jerry thought how tragic it would be for his uncle, at his age, to be robbed of his life's accumulation. Such a tragedy would be a sort of retribution for the questionable manner in which his uncle had laid the foundation of his wealth.

"Heaven forbid such a thing to happen," he thought, "the day when my uncle did that is long past. He is a changed man. He has built for himself the most honored position among the business men of North Alabama. He has given generously to the church and to every charity. . . ."

Jerry walked to the parsonage anxious, apprehensive, silently enumerating to God the many virtues of his uncle Miltiades.

CHAPTER THIRTY-SEVEN

AT THE parsonage a telephone message from Sydna asked Jerry to come at once to the manor. The assistant minister hesitated about going. He had meant to tell his uncle's wife about his betrothal to Miss Swartout, but he wanted the matter first to settle in his own mind. He almost unconsciously had planned to stay away from Sydna for a few days, until he had been with Miss Swartout for a number of times, until he had kissed and fondled her, and the visual and tactile image of the girl thoroughly possessed his senses. Then he would tell Sydna the plans of his marriage.

So now Jerry thought he would better telephone Sydna and make the excuse that he was very tired. Then the notion struck him to tell her of his engagement over the telephone. But he rejected this plan. He would wait until he was with her so he could see her face. He did not believe she would be hurt, because their relation, since his return to Florence, had been of the simplest and friendliest. In fact, a little glow of hope went through Jerry that Sydna would be glad for him.

Her voice on the wire interrupted his thoughts. She sounded rather excited, and when he began his excuse about being tired, she swept it away at once and told him to hurry on over, that she was finishing her plans for the U.D.C. convocation. They were going to unveil a monument to the Fourth Alabama regiment on the battlefield, and she must go over the details with him. As that sort of planning was the natural by-product of preachers, male musicians, Y. M. C. A. secretaries and members of Congress, Jerry felt it was in the line of his duty, even if he was tired.

Fifteen minutes later he found Sydna in her own private study which she had created on the north side of the manor, further east and across the hall from that of the Colonel's. It was also much larger and more feminine than the Colonel's. She had sunk in the wall and hidden by a panel a deep steel vault which she believed to be fireproof on the word of the man who had installed it. In this she kept the genealogy of the Vaidens, the Lacefields, and the Crowninshields. To accumulate this she had hired the services of a professional genealogist in Washington, D.C., who knew nothing whatever about North Alabama families. She had paid this genealogist five hundred dollars for the three scrolls, and when she had received them she was forced to change the names about to some extent so that her own family would fit into them. The idea back of all this was to give Marsan an unassailable right to wear three stars in the Florence chapter of the D.A.R.'s, and Sydna was now in correspondence for a fourth star.

For a number of years Sydna had kept these precious documents in the safety vault of the Second National, but finally they grew so bulky the bank could no longer house them, so Sydna built this fireproof vault in her own study to safeguard her treasures.

Besides the genealogies of herself and her husband, Sydna was permanent custodian of the U.D.C. records, which were not small in bulk, also files containing her accounts as treasurer of two charitable organizations, a bridge club, a flower show, a dog show, and a half a dozen now antiquated study and culture clubs.

None of these activities had absorbed much of Sydna's time. She had taken them on one after another in the course of her social leadership in Florence. Now, for her to call in Jerry to help her plan the U.D.C. unveiling at Shiloh was nothing new.

When her nephew-in-law rang the bell and was shown up by the maid, Sydna turned from a little mahogany writing table inlaid with figures of sandalwood.

"Jerry, I'm making out a list of persons to invite to the unveiling."

"Well, you know I'm a stranger in Florence . . . just arrived here . . . whom do you want to consult me about?"

Sydna paused with an uplifted imitation quill pen made with a pearl shaft and silver feathers.

"I was thinking about asking . . . Lucius," she said, looking at Jerry with a soft intent gaze.

A kind of shock traveled through the assistant minister.

"Lucius Handback?" he asked in a queer tone.

Sydna shook her head and lowered her silver quill.

"No, I won't do it . . . I didn't know how you'd feel, Jerry."

"Oh, it isn't me!"

"I know it, dear . . . there's no use having Lucius, anyway."

"I really think it would be very generous of you."

"No, I won't ask him, it was just a notion that passed through my head . . . still, I hate for him to hold against me all that trouble that sprang up between our two families so long ago . . . I thought a formal invitation, sent out with hundreds of others . . ."

"How would Uncle Milt feel?"

"I'm not going to do it . . . that's why I wanted to ask you."

"But look here," protested Jerry, "I'm not saying I'm against it. In fact, I think it's a beautiful gesture, Sydna, I really do. The question is, would Lucius understand the conciliatory spirit in which you sent it?"

"Lucius is really brighter and more generous than you have ever given him credit for, Jerry. I don't believe ministers as a rule give their congregation credit for the intelligence they really possess."

"He's not in my congregation."

"Oh no, I was speaking generally."

"Sydna . . . I say invite him."

"Oh, no, I wouldn't think of doing such a thing."

Jerry went over to a window seat and looked out on the park which the Baltimore landscapist had designed.

"Is that all you wanted, Sydna?" he inquired, looking at a beech whose green was touched with the bronze of autumn. "Is that all you wanted to see me about?"

"Look here, Jerry, you're not trying to get away, are you?"

"Oh no, not at all."

"I feel as if I were just swinging onto you by the coat-tail." She got up and came down the long room to him. "No, there's a lot of things . . . Jerry, I was thinking of you making the introductory speech at the unveiling . . . presenting the speaker of the day . . . would you be willing to do that?"

Jerry was surprised.

"Oh, Sydna . . . I couldn't do that."

"Well . . . all right . . . I didn't quite think you would." She drew a long breath, "I wish I hadn't asked Mr. Brekker to make the principal speech. . . ."

"I don't mean I wouldn't introduce Brekker, I mean I wouldn't want to make any speech at all."

She looked at him in surprise.

"No?"

"Why, no, when your father died there, Sydna, and my father was captured there and imprisoned and starved into scurvy, when my uncle Milt and my uncle Augustus and Uncle Polycarp were all in the battle . . . why, Sydna, do you imagine I could utter a single word?"

"Oh, Jerry . . . no," she exclaimed, and took his hand, looking earnestly into his face.

"Let some eloquent man like Brekker, who has felt only the general loss of the South, speak at Shiloh."

"Jerry darling, pardon me. I hadn't thought of it that way at all."

She sat pressing his hand in her two palms with tears in her eyes. They continued thus, filled with tenderness for each other, tenderness for the soldiers who had gone out of the families of Catlins and Crowninshields and Vaidens in the tragic intertwined histories of their houses.

There came a knock on the door of the study. The mistress of the manor took her hands away and wiped her dark eyes on a film of lace.

"Come in, dear," she called.

The door opened, and Marsan entered. As she came to them Jerry noticed an unusual translucent delicacy to her complexion.

"What were you two crying about?" she asked simply.

"About Shiloh," said Sydna.

"Mother," warned Marsan, "be careful you don't start something like that at the unveiling!"

"Oh, I won't. . . . I asked Jerry to speak, and . . ."

"And I said I wouldn't, that too many of my people were in the battle."

"If you should cry . . . just a little bit, Mother," suggested Marsan thoughtfully, "not enough to get your eyes red, it might make a hit with the men."

"Marsan! You don't think I'd cry to make a hit, as you call it!"

"Why, no, if you really tried to do it . . . you wouldn't make one, it's got to . . . you know . . . just happen."

Sydna looked at Jerry hopelessly.

"Did you ever hear of such a daughter? Darling, how can you stand off like that and see me as if I were somebody else?"

"Marsan takes after her grandfather, Major Crowninshield . . . he was a politician . . . by the way, Marsan, a funny thing happened to me a while ago."

"Yes, what was it, Uncle Jerry?"

"A couple with a Colbert County license came and asked me to marry them. I couldn't do it, I was on the wrong side of the river. They went back by the same bus they came on. Before they left, they practically admitted they were runaways and asked me to tell nobody but you."

Marsan became visibly agitated.

"Who were they?"

"The boy's name was Porter."

"Of all things," ejaculated Marsan, "that must have been Porter Lee and Lizzie Lanceford."

"Must I telephone the families?" inquired Jerry.

"No-o . . . they are in my biology class. They are the second couple who has run away and married. They seem to come out all right, or, at least, the other couple did. The boy has a job now as a bookkeeper in the fertilizer factory. . . . Oh, Mamma, I came up here to tell you the Second National Bank has closed. . . ."

"What, Marsan!"

Marsan nodded.

"Yes, it closed an hour ago. I got a telephone call. You and Uncle Jerry crying like that when I came in made me forget it."

CHAPTER THIRTY-EIGHT

THE casualness, the seeming indifference with which Marsan Vaiden broke to her mother the failure of the Second National Bank was really not so devoid of natural feeling as Sydna and Jerry imagined. The young girl had been much more excited by the identity of the person who had telephoned the news of the disaster than she had been by the message itself. This person was Mr. Petrie. He had said to her:

"Marsan, have you heard about your father's bank?"

And the girl was so moved by the science teacher's voice that she had replied automatically, without paying any attention to his import:

"No, what is it, Mr. Petrie?"

"The doors of the Second National Bank were closed about an hour ago."

"Oh, isn't that terrible," she had continued with her automatism as she thought swiftly, "This is a new beginning; now he'll call me up again for other things."

"I thought maybe you hadn't heard it."

"Oh, I hadn't, Mr. Petrie, I do thank you for calling and telling me." Her voice sounded as if she could never possibly have found out the catastrophe had it not been for him. There came a silence over the wire. Marsan waited with every nerve tingling, mutely asking him to go on talking about any subject under the sun but not to leave her again in the desolate silence of weeks.

After a few moments he did say formally:

"I hope this won't affect you and your family adversely, Marsan. You certainly have my sympathy . . . Good-bye."

"Good-bye, and thank you for calling me," said Marsan.

She put up the receiver and stood in a kind of trance beside the telephone. She could see Mr. Petrie walking out of some telephone booth somewhere . . . he was probably downtown going about his unguessable business, and he had found out the bank's disaster and telephoned her. And now this momentary brightness amid weeks of darkness had closed. She had nothing better left than to think of him intently while his voice was still in her ears. She wondered why he had gone downtown. His affairs always seemed more momentous, more moving to the girl than those of anyone else. She wished she could know what they were. She wished she could help him somehow . . . or persuade her father to help him . . . she would gladly be his stenographer, sitting mute and humble at his desk, shamed because of her sin with Red McLaughlin, but loving Mr. Petrie far more than the pure girl whom he was about to marry . . . she made a crooked and highly modern little romance out of it based on the movies and the leftovers of the Victorian code.

After all these fancies and wistfulnesses had passed through Marsan's head, she recalled the relatively unimportant detail that her father's bank had closed, so she had gone upstairs to tell her mother and Jerry.

But upstairs another force had swung Marsan out of her calculated orbit: that was Jerry's report of the runaway match between Porter Lee and Lizzie Lanceford. These twain were near and important figures in Marsan's world, and their runaway match concerned her closely; whereas the bank failure was remote and of small personal concern. Therefore, for Marsan to mention at all the bankruptcy of the Second National was quite a feat of detached and impersonal thought.

Now, as she went out of the study to restore to her mother and her uncle Jerry the privacy they so obviously desired, her own thoughts returned gravitationally to Mr. Petrie.

Did his message mean anything more than that he was disturbed about her father's fortune? What had he almost

said in the silence just before he told her good-bye? Oh, if
only he had said it . . . said it . . . said it! And what was he
doing now?

The facts about the mysterious doings of Mr. Petrie were:
he had walked downtown amid the depressing excitement
that the boom was over. The closing of the Second National
had been the end of the boom. The street was full of desper-
ate men whose fortunes had vanished with the closing of
the bank's doors and who had town lots for sale. They would
sell them for anything they could get: a half, a third, a
fourth. And the school teacher had been filled with happi-
ness that he had had the foresight not to fling away his
savings on boom property. He felt superior to the poor dupes
who had trusted so unstable a thing as the boom. He rein-
forced his present triumph of financial prognostication with
an ironclad decision that never, under any circumstances in
the future, would he dabble in real estate.

Here, as Petrie walked down the crowded street, a hand
was laid on his shoulder. The hand belonged to old man
Bill Bradley. The old man's face was leathery and drawn,
and he offered Petrie for three hundred and fifty dollars in
cash the lot which the school teacher had been watching and
pricing for the last five months.

The president of the Realtors' Association explained
that he was giving away the lot because he knew Petrie was
interested in it and that he needed a little pocket change,
then he held his cheroot with his thumb and forefinger as
if his yellow teeth were no longer able to cock it up, and drew
a feeble puff.

The school teacher laughed and held up a negative hand.

"Thanks, Mr. Bradley, thanks, but I'm not in the mar-
ket."

The old man seemed hardly able to believe his ears.

"But, listen, I'm saying three hundred and fifty dollars;
that's the lot you've been offering me seventeen hundred
for when it was two thousand, that you offered me two
thousand for when it was twenty-five hundred, and one day,

don't you remember, you offered me thirty-two hundred dollars for?" He stood chewing the end of his cheroot, staring at the inexplicable Mr. Petrie. "You ought to jump at this, Petrie, if you've got any money!"

"I'm out of the market," repeated the school teacher, fortified by the crash against all buying whatever.

Mr. Bradley stood looking at this prospect who had shifted so annoyingly into a retrospect.

"Look here, I offered it to you first because me and you had dickered over it and I felt like you had a kind of right to the first chance at it. I'm going to let it go to somebody else, Petrie, this lot's got to be sold. . . ." As the old man stood watching the effect of these words, he asked by way of information, "By the way, what bank do you keep your money in, anyway?"

"Second National," said Petrie.

A change of expression came over old man Bill's face. He drew at his cheroot, took it out of his mouth, and looked at it as he let the smoke drift up past his nose.

"I God, you were right when you said you were out of the market."

When the school teacher inquired into this dark saying and found out that the Second National was closed, a profound shock went through him. Strangely enough, it was not for his own savings which had been swept away. It was for Marsan Vaiden. The thought of the original, straightforward Marsan losing her fortune and reduced to penury filled Petrie with the greatest anxiety. He knew the Vaiden fortune was more to Marsan than simple money: it was Marsan herself. It was the basis of her independence, her attack on life, her honesty, her impulsiveness, her odd, almost boylike charm. Marsan never paused to take a second thought because her first thoughts were all underwritten. If they went wrong on usual grounds, they functioned as being right on the unusual grounds of her father's position and fortune. If the Vaiden wealth were gone, so was Marsan . . . utterly.

The analytic Mr. Petrie stood trembling at this danger that threatened something very dear to him. He wanted to go to Marsan and take her in his arms and tell her that he would try to do something if her father failed her . . . he cursed the fact that all human beings did not have wealth enough to bloom out into what they really were instead of having to seep into forms already prepared for them like pseudomorphic rock. He had almost reached her home now, when he realized he could not perform any part of the gesture he had in his heart: a school teacher, such as he. Why he was nothing, he couldn't help himself!

Then it was that he had stopped in a home within a block of the Vaiden manor and had telephoned Marsan of her misfortune. He had wanted to continue the conversation with her, but being a man of great unity of purpose and fixity of design, a scientist, in fact, he had said good-bye and hung up the receiver.

It was only then that it dawned on him in full force that his own savings had been swept away, and that he himself, barring his next month's salary, was penniless.

And Marsan, shivering at her empty telephone, wondering where Mr. Petrie was, and what he almost had said to her; if she had walked out on the wide piazza of the manor, she would have seen the object of her obsession passing her gate along Pine Street on his way back to town.

CHAPTER THIRTY-NINE

Mrs. Sydna Vaiden's U.D.C. convocation at Shiloh was greatly disorganized by the failure of the Second National Bank, or, at least, her part of it was disorganized.

In the first place, she did not now know where the money was coming from. Reunions were expensive. The old Confederate soldiers had to be notified; then a certain number of railroad fares had to be furnished. A corps of nurses and doctors had to be employed at each reunion to look after the old men as they marched under their resurrected battle flags. The strain of marching slowly in review on the field where as boys they had double quicked, fixed bayonets, and charged was too much for their vanished strength.

Mrs. Sydna Vaiden always had furnished the greater part of this money for the Florence chapter. Now, before she contracted so heavy an expense, she felt that she ought to consult her husband and ask his advice, in fact, his consent. This was very embarrassing, because she never discussed money with the Colonel. She drew checks, and the bank honored them. Now there was no bank on which to draw.

In this predicament she asked Marsan's advice, because Marsan kept in touch with her father, driving him to and from the bank and talking to him endlessly, while she, Sydna, seldom saw Miltiades except at mealtime and talked to him only in the general conversation of the family.

When Sydna placed her financial troubles before Marsan, the daughter considered a moment, then advised her mother to go ahead and take care of the U.D.C. expenses as usual.

"Why do you say that?" asked Sydna, well pleased with the advice.

"Well, if Daddy has crashed, he has crashed for millions, and what you spend won't make any difference one way or the other."

Sydna was delighted at such a happy augury, but unfortunately it did not take care of her immediate needs.

"I can't go ahead," she pointed out; "the bank's closed, and there's nothing for me to draw on."

Marsan pondered a space.

"That's a fact . . . still, I hate for you to bother Daddy right in the middle of the bankruptcy . . . he must be busy."

"What else can I do, Marsan? "

"Couldn't you put it off till he comes home?"

"Marsan, the U.D.C. program is behind time right now."

"Mamma, your programs are always behind time, and they come out all right."

"Yes, I know, but if they get any further behind time they won't come out all right."

Marsan considered this, too, and finally she said:

"Well, if you're in that big a hurry, call him up, but, Mamma, don't talk forever, just ask him where you are to draw money from now, and then hush."

"Why, Marsan!" ejaculated Sydna, surprised and piqued, "I never talk much anyway!"

"Well . . . what I suggested isn't much."

With her telephone conversation countersigned by her daughter, Sydna called up Miltiades and asked him what bank she could now draw on, if any.

The Colonel hesitated for several seconds, finally he said:

"Darling, I had intended for you to use currency for a while . . . would it be too much trouble, carrying around bills?"

"Well, honey . . . it would seem awfully dirty . . . you know . . . everybody handling them."

"I think I can get you some very new, clean, nice bills, darling, green and yellow . . . I think yellow would be stylish for autumn wear, don't you?"

"Mamma, you're keeping him too long," whispered Marsan, on tenterhooks.

"Sweetheart, he's talking, not me . . . all right, honey, send some up, and I'll keep them in my vault."

"How much will you need?"

"It's for Shiloh. I imagine I'll spend six or eight hundred dollars."

"Your imagination is in the red; it will be nearer twelve hundred . . . I'll send you up twelve hundred."

"Thank you, darling, and you are going with us, aren't you . . . now you are, aren't you?"

"Mamma!" cried Marsan in despair, "you're not even talking about money."

"No, darling, that's settled."

"Then why don't you hang up?"

"Marsan, you talk so foolish . . . I've got to arrange my plans for the U.D.C.!"

"Sydna," said Miltiades, "I hate to miss it, but how can I possibly get off in the middle of these receivership proceedings?"

"Colonel Milt, the idea of you not going to Shiloh!"

"Mamma, how can he?"

"Hush, Marsan. . . . Honey, I haven't teased at you about this because I thought of course you were going."

"But I simply can't get off, Sydna . . . not this time."

"Listen, dearest," pleaded Sydna over the wire, "Marsan is going, of course, and what will she do down there on the battlefield . . ."

"Mamma, I'm not going, I won't go a step!"

"Do hush, Marsan . . . down there on the battlefield without you to take her around and show her everything, honey?"

"Well, of all things!" cried Marsan hopelessly.

Sydna waved her daughter into silence.

"Hush, you know he won't go without you, and he will if you do."

The voice of Miltiades interrupted to say:

"Listen, Sydna, I have thought of a way around that currency business."

"Yes, what is it, dear?"

"Go up in my study, look in the right-hand small drawer on top of the desk, not in the lower part, and you'll find some checks on the Fifth National Bank of Louisville, Kentucky . . . you may use them."

"Why, thank you, dear, so much, I certainly didn't like the idea of using bills."

"Sign my name to them and then write in brackets under my name, 'Mrs. Miltiades Vaiden.' I'll arrange for that signature to be honored."

"That's sweet of you, darling . . . and you are going, are you?"

"Is Marsan going?"

"Why, of course she's going; why, she wouldn't miss it for the world!"

"Mamma, I'm not going!" cried Marsan.

"Good-bye, and thank you again, honey," and Sydna hung up. "Why in the world do you say you're not going, Marsan?"

"Oh, Mamma, I don't want to go . . . all those things are just alike . . . walking and milling around and speeches . . ."

"But, honey, you have to go, you know your father is depending on you . . . he'll want to show you where his regiment was and where he charged and—and where my father was when he died, Marsan."

Sydna could never think of her father dying on the field of Shiloh in Colonel Miltiades Vaiden's arms without being inexpressibly touched. Marsan knew this and respected her mother's feelings but was bored by them.

"I don't want to go to Shiloh," she repeated.

"Honey, the trip will do you good . . . you don't look so well lately."

"I don't need a trip, I need a vacation," said Marsan.

"A what?"

"A vacation."

"What do you want to do?"

"Well, now, you'll think this is silly, Mother, but I'd like to go to Mobile for a while this winter . . . it'll be warm down there. They say you can swim down there in the winter time; they have oranges . . ."

Sydna stared in amazement.

"Marsan, what in the world are you talking about?"

"Mobile."

"You mean stay away from home . . . from your father all winter long?"

"Why, Mother, there's no use pulling a long face over that. Girls have gone away from home before. Look at Amalie Lawrence and Maybelle Sanderson and Sarah . . ." Her list evidently could be extended indefinitely.

"Darling, I couldn't give my consent to such a wild-goose chase!"

"Well . . . I came to you fair and square first, Mamma . . . now I'm going to ask Daddy."

The mother drew a hopeless breath; then of a sudden she grabbed up the receiver again. Marsan leaped at her, pushed the receiver down. She leaned across and kissed her mother vehemently, crying:

"No! No! No! It's not fair for you to get to him first! We'll see him together, Mamma! Be a sport! Be a sport! We'll see him together!"

"Marsan!" cried the mother indignantly, "this is rebellion!"

"No, honey, Mother, darling, sweetheart," pleaded Marsan white-faced, "you know if there is a court of appeal both sides ought to go up at the same time . . . why, Mamma, your civics tells you that . . . you know you ought to let me see Daddy when you do . . . before he has made any promises."

It grew fairly clear to Sydna, through some amazing freak, Marsan was determined to spend some time in Mobile. What reason she could have for such a caprice, Sydna could not imagine.

"Who'll you stay with down there?" she asked in distress.

"Well . . . Lizzie Lanceford and Porter Lee are going to move down there."

"How do you know they are?"

"They told me so."

"Oh, you knew they were going to run away and marry?"

"Oh, yes'm, I knew that."

"But, Marsan, Lizzie Lanceford and Porter Lee are not in your circle at all . . . I don't even know them."

"They're in my circle in High School."

"I mean outside of High School."

"Well . . . I don't know," said Marsan thoughtfully, "when I strike up with friends in one place, I feel as if . . ."

"Listen," interrupted Sydna, seeing that Marsan really was going to Mobile and deciding the best thing she could do was to trade on that fact, "listen, I'll tell you what I'll do. I won't say one word either way about your Mobile trip if you'll persuade your father to go to Shiloh with us."

"Listen, I'll get him to go, Mother, but not with me. I don't want to go."

"Why, Marsan, that's selfish, you want everything."

They talked on for some time, half arguing, half persuading, until Marsan promised to go to Shiloh and drive the Colonel.

Sydna and Jerry were going down on an excursion steamer which was carrying the Florence, the Decatur, and the Birmingham delegations.

Later in the day Jerry Catlin left the manor and went to Sheffield to see Aurelia. But somehow, the musician sensed he had been with Sydna and was not at home to him. Jerry was forced to plead with her, argue, kiss her, hold her in his lap for a full three quarters of an hour before she finally consented to talk with him.

CHAPTER FORTY

At the Shiloh National Park the American flag rises surprisingly on a staff high above the wild and continuous forest that lines the river.

To a foreigner, unmoved by memories of the national struggle and tragedy which haunt the spot, that high waving flag might mark some military outpost in the midst of primeval wilderness. To the Southern people, coming to decorate the graves of their remembered dead, it was elegy.

On this field, where Sydna and Jerry walked, their fathers had fought, years and years before. The two men had been on opposite sides. Jerry Catlin, Senior, had been in Prentice's division of the Union Army. Sydna's father had served under General Albert Sydney Johnston, for whom she was named.

The man and woman had come ashore with the other passengers, and Sydna had made shift to escape her ladies and maids of honor to go with Jerry out on the battlefield.

Everywhere on the wooded terrain stood bronze tablets giving the positions of this brigade and that regiment; such cavalry and such artillery.

Looking at the markers it was as if an astral army were maneuvering in a world where time stood charmed, and each division of the two contending forces occupied for eternity every successive position which it had won, or lost, on that fateful Sunday and Monday in 'sixty-two.

As the two companions moved from point to point they came presently to a marker bearing the simple legend, "The Hornet's Nest." Sydna stopped and stood looking at the scene. Here the grass-grown indentation of an ancient road overlooked a slope. In this scarcely visible sunken trail Jerry's father, in Prentice's division, had lain all Sunday long under Grant's orders not to retreat, but to hold this position at all cost, to the end.

Up that gentle incline charged the Confederates, all morning long, brigade after brigade, sowing the slope with their dead. They lay so thick that the last of the gray regiments double-quicked on the bodies of their own comrades.

On that fatal terrain Sydna's father, Major Emory Crowninshield, had died whispering to Miltiades Vaiden to take good care of his little baby girl. And now here was Sydna herself, bejeweled, honored, courted, loved, through Miltiades' faithfulness to that ancient pledge.

Jerry's father, who had been captured at the turn of the day, was sent to a military prison in the deep South. Today, Jerry, Senior, was dead, but the Union flag still floated high over Shiloh Landing, where he once had acted as a sacrificial screen, while behind him Grant reformed his shattered lines.

Jerry spread his handkerchief for Sydna, and the two sat down above the slope on the lip of the almost obliterated road. This common focusing of national history and their own dramatic family annals upon the scene gave it an overpowering sense of pathos and tragedy.

The queer thought trickled through Jerry's head that if Major Crowninshield had not been killed on this slope the whole drift of Sydna's life would have been changed. She would have known no girlish idealism of Miltiades Vaiden; she would doubtless have married some man of her age, Slim Bivins, Alfred Thorndyke, Lucius Handback, or, possibly . . . himself. Marsan Vaiden would never have existed. In her stead, it might have been his own children would have come, and yet all this normal probable development was changed by a bullet from a Union rifle in 'sixty-two . . . the most complicated fate imaginable making a single swift leap on a minie ball, accomplishing itself in the hundredth part of a second.

Jerry told his fancy to Sydna. She held out her hand to him.

"You have the gift of fantasy, Jerry," she said sadly; "you had when you were a boy. With you life might follow any path and reach any end. With me there is just one road it could have gone. I can't imagine a world without Marsan. If it took all those sorrows to create her, they were right to be endured for so sweet an end. If something should happen to her, if she should die, this would be a world where Marsan had lived and nothing else."

"I had no idea she meant all that to you?"

"She comes nearer being my life than anything else. I wonder what my father, Major Crowninshield, would think . . . I do wonder what he would think if he could know how all this has worked out."

"You mean about Marsan?"

"I mean all of it, the South belonging to the North, I belonging to Miltiades, you, the son of a Yankee who fought him and the nephew of the comrade who held him in his arms when he died, you sitting here talking to me like this . . . feeling like this."

"Most people miss the miracle of their lives, Sydna, because they can't realize upon how many thousands of the sheerest accidents their fate has walked."

"I know you are the most understandable thing in my life, Jerry. I could never have said any of that to anyone else. With your gift for getting inside people, I wonder you've never married. You must have known scores of nice women in your life. I think you were once a little in love with Sarah Crowe."

"No, Sarah coached me in algebra once . . . that was all."

The thought of Sarah brought up the reason why he had needed coaching. It had been Sydna's marriage with his uncle. This had brought upon him a kind of sickness. When he started to college again, Sarah Crowe had helped him in the work he had missed and had fallen in love with him.

Out of this meandering reverie he remembered:

"Sydna, I have something to tell you."

"Yes, what is it, Jerry?" she asked expectantly.

"Well . . . I . . . Miss Swartout and I are going to be married."

The woman sat perfectly still on the edge of the old road where Jerry's father had fought and been captured. Her only movement was a flutter of the lids of her brown eyes and a momentary moistening of her lips.

"Miss Swartout?"

"Yes."

"Married?"

"Yes."

The woman loosed his hand, reached to a little bush, and pulled herself up unsteadily. She stood looking at him with dazed eyes.

"Jerry . . ."

"Yes, Sydna," he cried in alarm, taking her arm.

"That—that's all right . . . I'm all right . . . a little dizzy . . . getting up. The speaking will begin . . ." She looked at her jeweled wrist watch but could not center her thoughts on it steadily enough to see it. "We'd better be going back."

And she led the way down the slope where, years before, her father had been slain in battle.

CHAPTER FORTY-ONE

W̲ᴴᴱN Sydna and Jerry reached the steamboat landing again they heard a band playing "Maryland" and saw soldiers marching. It was a regiment of Tennessee state troops assembled for the occasion. The main part of the crowd went hurrying ahead from the steamboat landing to form a long double string of spectators along the line of march to where the monument would be unveiled.

Behind the soldiers came thirty or forty very old men, some of them wearing faded gray uniforms, and those who were strong enough shouldering long antique muskets, whose rust had been scraped and darkened with recent oil. These old veterans formed in twos and under a torn and brittle stars and bars moved behind the band and the troopers across the field where they had fought and lost decades ago.

Behind the veterans came doctors and nurses in new white ambulances marked with the red cross.

Sydna ran forward toward the little company, anxious lest Miltiades and Marsan had not arrived from Florence in time for this parade of the veterans.

Ahead the band was now playing "My Old Kentucky Home," but only snatches of the music could be heard through the cheering of the throng. Sydna clutched Jerry's arm.

"Do you see him? Is he in the line?"

To Sydna, Colonel Miltiades had become once more the selfless savior of her father, the protector of her own penurious girlhood, the bestower of all good things upon her golden present. She reverenced and loved Miltiades with all her soul.

When Jerry caught her arm and pointed out his uncle walking straight and erect under the ancient battle flag, Sydna put an arm over Jerry's shoulder, pulled herself up; he caught her trim waist and held her at tiptoe. And as they looked and cheered, wrapped thus in each other's arms, a softness and sweetness and tenderness swept over them again as it had done years before, when they had watched Miltiades thus from a hammock in the old Crowninshield manor on Pine Street.

Almost automatically, out of some psychic mechanism, they clung to each other, and the parade and music and crowd vanished in the intensity of their feeling. With Sydna in his arms, Jerry received a dizzy impression of the complete ripened symmetry of the Venus in the Louvre. With a pressure of her palm against his face, Sydna whispered:

"Jerry . . . honey . . . good-bye."

In the solitude of the cheering throng he kissed her. Sydna strained him to her breast, loosed him; then, with tears in her eyes, ran through the jostling crowd, holding his hand to another point of vantage to watch the old soldiers march by.

Some ten or fifteen minutes later Jerry handed Sydna up on the speakers' stand, where the regents of the various chapters were gathered. He stood on the ground, near her chair, watching the ceremony of the unveiling.

A minister began the invocation. He asked God's blessing on the nation, the South, on these old veterans of a vanished but never a forgotten cause. As the preacher's voice rose and fell in the gray tones men use in prayer, Jerry stood thinking of the strange fatality of the Lacefield and the Vaiden blood. Here was he, an offshoot of the Vaiden stirps named Catlin, and Sydna, born a Crowninshield, but who was really a Lacefield, with hearts still turbulent at the ancient and persistent call.

As he stood beside her chair, he knew how she felt, the physical heaviness of her breasts, the languorousness of her body, and her heart torn between tenderness and daughterliness for Miltiades and this swift and saddening passion for himself.

He glanced up at her again and again. There seemed to be nowhere else to look. It was almost as if he had never seen her before. She was a perfectly kept woman who might have been any age . . . or none. She was a statue of Love to whom Time did not apply. She was standing in the autumn sunshine in the midst of a woman's last brief moment of eternal beauty. Jerry watched her dark eyes, liquid with tears, fixed on the minister. Not once did she glance down at him. Jerry divined that the moment that had just rushed upon them on the wings of their feeling for the sorrows and tragedies and heroism of the old South would be their last.

The minister gave way to Brekker, the speaker of the day. He came to the front of the stand, a grave, graceful figure. He bowed with the customary salutation to the chairwoman and the Daughters of the Southern Confederacy.

"For any speaker, no matter how eloquent an orator," he began slowly, "to approach this occasion on this sacred field without a studied address and with any wanton thought of uttering improvised words would be a sacrilege and a profanation.

"Nevertheless, I am moved to break away from the poor matter I have prepared for this occasion and to express my sorrow, to stand in tears for the South when that melancholy day arrives, as come it must, when the final remnant of Johnston's, Lee's, and Forrest's men shall foregather here no more.

"Then will the Holy Grail be broken.

"Then will the South no longer possess the Veronica to wipe away her historic tears.

"When we honor, when we reverence, when we bow our hearts before these old and fading men, we are lifting to our lips a Last Sacrament.

"No matter to what heights the future genius of the South may soar, it will never again reach those mountain ranges of chivalry and generosity; those sun-kissed peaks of

Pride which we behold today only through the blue mists of Time.

"Too truly has a Southern poet sang, 'Time, the tomb builder.'

"O Time, Time, Time, if in thy garnering thou canst not spare heroes, spare us their deeds.

"Spare us their constancy, their devotion, their patriotism, their selfless service for the healing of our nation.

"Daughters of the Confederacy, the monuments you have erected upon the battlefields of the South are chalices for the preservation of that rich heritage.

"We have the honor, Ladies and Gentlemen, of gathering with these Daughters today at the unveiling of their tribute to the Fourth Alabama Regiment, whose old commander, Colonel Miltiades Vaiden, will appear upon this platform."

Sydna wept. She had known that Miltiades would be asked to appear: that was why she had been so insistent upon his coming to Shiloh, but she had had no idea how the music, the speeches, and the crowd would affect her.

The women in the group were now handing her forward to the side of the Colonel. The throng cheered and shouted. The band played "Dixie," an air which is quick and should be gay and light, but which Time has remolded into the most poignant and moving of melodies.

As the old Colonel lifted and kissed his wife's fingers, Sydna felt a rush of gratitude for the apposition of his gallantry, and she had the quivering pleasure of knowing that she was beautiful.

Beside the stand someone caught Jerry's arm. It was Marsan.

"Oh, I've looked for you everywhere . . . I couldn't find you," she gasped.

"Anything the matter?" asked Jerry, looking into her face.

"No . . . nothing . . . I'm all right."

At that moment she swayed, she caught at Jerry and would have fallen.

The assistant minister picked the girl up in his arms and

went walking through the crowd toward one of the ambulances. In the big white motor several women and two of the old veterans were already under the doctors' care.

When a physician examined Marsan he looked at Jerry.

"She has badly overexerted herself."

"Yes, she drove a car from Florence, and then I think ran on the field."

Jerry turned and saw Sydna hurrying up. She had seen him carrying Marsan from the platform. The physician stood up from his examination and shook his head gravely at Jerry.

"You must be more careful with her, not only her exercise, but her diet and rest, first babies are dangerous."

"First babies!"

"Certainly, you know, of course, that she is about to become a mother."

CHAPTER FORTY-TWO

SYDNA and Jerry, of course, had to get the family back to Florence at once. The throng, the battlefield, the new tall monument to the Fourth Alabama Regiment, lost the unity of mood which they had possessed and became meaningless and disconnected obstacles to Sydna's homeward flight with Marsan.

The mother was so shaken she could hardly stand, but she searched Marsan's purse for the car keys and sent Jerry hurrying to get it.

On his way to the parking space Jerry could hardly believe what he had been told. It was most irrational . . . his cousin, his sweet little cousin, seduced, enceinte, with all her gay dancing girlhood broken and shamed.

As he found the Vaiden car and got in it, he thought maybe the physician had made a mistake.

When Jerry got back, Marsan had recovered consciousness and was sitting on her cot with her hand in Sydna's. She was saying she could not imagine what had happened to her.

"You can get in the car, Marsan?" asked Sydna. "You feel all right, quite comfortable?"

"Mother, what a fuss you're making," she protested shakily.

"Get Colonel Milt," said Sydna to Jerry.

"Not on my account," protested Marsan in distress. "Why he doesn't take a day off once in ten years!"

But Sydna got up and started with Jerry to find her husband. Before they were out of sight of the car she began in a voice that quivered against tears:

"What must I do? Jerry, what can I do?"

"Don't cry . . . not before Uncle Milt."

"He'll have to know it sometime."

"Yes . . . I wonder what he'll do . . . at his age?"

She looked at him with startled wet eyes.

"What do you mean?"

Jerry drew a breath.

"I mean . . ." he changed his words, "it will be such a blow at his age."

Sydna stopped and caught her companion's hand.

"Jerry, what's really in your mind?"

"Sydna, when Uncle Milt finds this out . . . what will he do?"

The woman pressed her lips with her slender jeweled fingers.

"Oh, Jerry . . . if he does some terrible thing . . . his position . . . the publicity . . . our name . . ."

"Sydna, he mustn't know . . . not right away . . . we'll keep it as long as possible."

"Yes, yes."

Jerry looked at Sydna.

"Do you know . . . who?"

The woman tried to swallow the ache in her throat.

"There is only one man. . . ."

Jerry nodded in a kind of furious despair.

"What a shame! What an outrage! To pose as an instructor of the young and innocent! You know I met him as I came into Florence on the train. In our talk I found he was atheistic, but I didn't dream he lacked ordinary moral standards."

"What little I saw of him, he seemed a quiet, rather brilliant man. . . . I—I don't care if Miltiades does k——"

"Sydna, please don't say that! For Miltiades to commit murder can't help Marsan!"

At this point both hushed abruptly, because they saw the tall gaunt figure of the Colonel coming toward them. He was evidently greatly excited; his stiff quick walk betrayed it.

The greatest dismay filled the woman's heart. She now did not want Miltiades to kill anyone. She gasped out:

"Jerry, who could have told him?"

"That doctor!"

"But he didn't know any of us!"

"He must have seen you and Uncle standing together on the platform."

"Oh, me . . . well . . . he would have had to learn it sometime, anyway."

Miltiades came up so bristling that Jerry felt as if he should fling his body against his uncle in an effort to save Petrie's life.

The Colonel's splotched yellow face was tense with anger.

"Have you heard the shame? Have you heard the outrage?" he demanded in shaken tones.

Jerry wetted his lips.

"Uncle Milt, you must control yourself. . . ."

Sydna seemed ready to fall.

"How—how did you hear it, honey?"

Miltiades shook a newspaper in his hand.

"Through this damned sheet, this villainous . . ."

Other voices in the crowd took it up:

"Yes, Mrs. Vaiden, the afternoon papers are full of it . . . they've just come up from Corinth!"

"Full of what?" cried Sydna, wondering if it were possible Marsan's condition had got into some vile sensational paper.

"Of the action of the New Jersey court, Mrs. Vaiden," explained a strange man who had admired Sydna from the crowd; "they refuse to grant requisition papers to the Governor of Alabama!"

Half a dozen papers were produced among the crowd; different persons began reading the headlines.

"Grounds for refusal was that the damned niggers wouldn't get a fair trial in the South. . . ."

"New Jersey judge says he would consider his court as an accomplice in judicial murder if he returned Lascome to Florence, Alabama."

Miltiades held up his hand.

"Gentlemen," he stated with a clayey face, "in my day, such an insult from one state to another would have been held not only as cause for secession, but grounds for an appeal to arms!"

Sydna went up to him with such relief in her heart that she only half followed what they were saying.

"Don't take it so personally, darling."

"Sydna, it is personal. . . ."

"Are you ready to go home?"

"Yes, I am, where's Marsan?"

"She is not feeling well. The strain has told on her."

"You are going back on the boat, aren't you?"

"No, we're all going back in the car."

"Well, all right . . . that decision can be counted as nothing more than an assault upon the purity of Southern women, Sydna . . . to harbor the venomous serpents that pollute the innocence . . ."

CHAPTER FORTY-THREE

Dᴜʀɪɴɢ the chill melancholy return of the Vaiden car to Florence, Alabama, one or two small incidents occurred which really were not explained until the family reached home.

One of these was the extraordinary number of automobiles they met coming out of Florence. The road was full of them. Nearly all of them bore Alabama licenses, and what particularly puzzled the Vaidens, one of the motorists thrust his head out of his car and yelled imprecations at Miltiades as the two machines whirled past each other.

Sydna, who rode in stunned incredulity at her daughter's condition, did not even hear the passing shout. The poor lady wanted to whisper to her daughter who sat beside her, "Marsan, can it be true, the terrible thing the doctor said?"

Marsan thought her mother was wounded on account of the action of the New Jersey court, and she kept patting Sydna's hand and telling her that it made no difference.

Jerry Catlin had no idea why a passing traveler should insult the family; he did feel a hazy premonition that it might be caused by another of his uncle's irregularities, which, although justifiable from Miltiades' point of view, served to offend people at large to a remarkable degree. Jerry wondered what his uncle had done this time.

It was not until he had arrived in Florence and had sped over to Sheffield to see his fiancée that he received any inkling of what had happened.

When he reached the little house in Carver's Lane, he saw Mrs. Swartout in the yard among her flowers and asked if Aurelia were in.

The little old woman shook her head.

"I doubt it, I doubt it after what you've done!"

Jerry came to an uneasy halt at the gate.

"She won't see me?"

"I don't guess she will. I don't blame Minnie a speck. Nobody could do me like that and come soft-soaping around afterwards."

The man at the gate wondered if Aurelia could possibly have heard of, or, on a wilder chance, could have seen him as he sympathized with Sydna at Shiloh. He remembered putting his arm around Sydna and kissing her; whether that was before or after they had learned about Marsan, he was not sure.

"Did she go to Shiloh today?" asked Jerry gingerly.

"No, but you did," exclaimed the little old woman.

"M—yes, I did," admitted Jerry, seeing that he and Sydna had been observed by someone from Florence, and gossip, of course, had made the incident much worse than it was. He went inside and tapped on the door, calling:

"Aurelia! Aurelia, are you in, Aurelia?"

As there was no reply, he opened the door slowly and went inside. The clean, bare little house seemed quite empty. He moved tentatively about through the family room, the kitchen, tapping as he went. Then he realized she must be in the parlor with her piano. She had been playing off her wrath when his arrival stopped her. He opened this door a little way, and Aurelia asked from the piano bench:

"What are you blundering into every room in the house for without being asked?"

"Listen, Aurelia . . ."

"I'll not listen to a word . . . that stuck-up Sydna Vaiden, she never did like me! She is trying to undermine me!"

Jerry made a gesture.

"Hush . . . she hasn't . . . she never said a word against you."

"Well, she caused you not to love me any more . . . if you ever did . . . you never did . . . you never loved anybody but her. . . ." Miss Swartout leaned over her music board and began sobbing convulsively.

Jerry went over and put his arms around her. A sobbing woman always seems warm, soft, and vibrant with an intimate attraction so long as a man is not married to her.

"Aurelia, let me explain about Sydna," begged Jerry, hugging her against his breast.

The girl shook herself free.

"There is nothing to explain . . . how can you explain anything?"

"Darling, there is. . . ."

"What?"

"Sydna had just suffered the deepest sorrow and loss that a woman can suffer."

Miss Swartout looked at him out of her sobs.

"What's that got to do with it?"

"Y—Darling . . . it explains why I . . . was trying to comfort her. . . ."

The girl sat up and stared.

"You've been kissing and hugging her?" she trembled.

"Darling . . . because she was so stricken over Marsan!"

Miss Swartout broke into uncontrollable weeping, then began laughing, then wept, then laughed.

Jerry grew genuinely frightened; he held her hard against his body, notwithstanding her struggles.

"Darling, do have some consideration, Sydna has suffered a pain and a shock in Marsan. . . ."

Miss Swartout controlled her hysteria.

"What about Marsan?"

"You must never breathe a word of this, Aurelia. . . ."

"No, I won't." She drew a long breath, stopped sobbing completely. "What did Marsan do?"

"Well, I shouldn't mention it . . . besides, it's not positive yet."

"Something not positive about Marsan?"

"Aurelia, you must never under any circumstances breathe this to anyone!"

"She didn't . . . *steal?*"

"Aurelia!" cried Jerry, scandalized.

The organist did not think Marsan had stolen, she was gauging her real suspicion by the vehemence and manner of Jerry's denials.

"Is she in trouble . . . you know . . . serious trouble . . . Marsan, I mean?"

Jerry drew a long hopeless breath. Soon, he knew, the news would be abroad anyway. He stood by the piano in silent assent.

Aurelia sat in a bewildered revengeful ecstasy that this amazing, shameful misfortune had happened to Marsan Vaiden. Like most women, she would have been secretly titivated for it to have happened to any of her girl acquaintances, but . . . Marsan Vaiden!

"How did you find it out?"

Jerry told his story.

"Well, darling," said Aurelia, grave and calm, "even that, dreadful as it is, shouldn't cause you to give kisses to anybody but me. . . . Oh, Jerry, the mere thought of you caring deeply for anybody but me . . ." She held up her white rounded pianist arms to him.

He took her again, kissing and fondling her.

"What a pity the pangs and yearnings of our flesh can lead anyone astray . . . it holds the possibility of such bliss, such happiness . . . just to have you . . . to assuage my desire upon the snowy mounds of your bosom. Oh, my sweet goddess of Love . . ."

He talked on and on, turning his passion into rhetoric with the art of a middle-aged man who is sufficiently detached to do it.

Aurelia lay in his arms filled with a woman's gratification over caresses and words without fulfillment. What completed her pleasure was the thought that Marsan Vaiden was in trouble . . . she had fallen into the ancient pitfall of women.

After awhile it occurred to Jerry that all this was new

to Aurelia. She had not been angry originally because he had caressed Sydna. He asked her what had been the cause of her first irritation.

The organist reflected.

"Oh, I was mad at your uncle Miltiades," said the girl; she straightened up and began to grow angry again.

"What did he do?" inquired Jerry in astonishment.

"Why, you know his bank hasn't got any money!"

"Yes . . . it's closed."

"Do you know why it's closed?"

"Why, no-o . . . it's just bankrupt."

"It's because he's stole all the money, that's why!" cried the girl, furious again.

"Aurelia, what are you saying?" cried Jerry with a great fear leaping into his heart.

"It's the truth!" she cried shrilly; "those Vaidens in their big house, living on other people's money that they stole!"

"Why do you say such a thing?"

"Because Sydna Vaiden paid out a big check, a perfectly huge check, to settle off the U.D.C., and she drew it on a Louisville bank on her husband's account!"

"If she did, I don't believe there's anything wrong about it!"

"Well, you're the only person in town who doesn't believe there's anything wrong about it. The woman whose child I was giving music lessons to today told me she was contributing her part."

"Her part of what?"

"Why, a fund to sue the Colonel and make him give up the money he stole!"

"Nobody's really making up such a fund!"

"Oh yes, they are," nodded Aurelia warmly.

Jerry sat for several moments digesting this extraordinary and unbelievable story. His uncle, here in his late days, Jerry knew, was one of the most careful of men from an ethical standpoint. He was not only a member of the Methodist Church, but he was the most generous and constructive lay member in the organization. Jerry knew Miltiades had not taken a cent that was not his own, but he also knew that Aurelia was telling the truth about a fund being made up to enter suit against him. As he wondered about this he said:

"While ago, when I came in, it wasn't I at all whom you were angry at."

"No, it wasn't you," said Aurelia, putting an arm about his neck and kissing him again, "I was just mad. It's enough to make a person mad, Jerry, losing all your money like that. And the house we are in is going to be sold to pay Papa's debt to the Farmers' and Mechanics' Bank. If your uncle Milt hadn't taken all my money I could at least have saved our home."

Here Aurelia began to weep again, not angrily but pitifully, and Jerry comforted her the best he could.

CHAPTER FORTY-FOUR

Jerry Catlin's marriage with Aurelia Swartout was of course quite lost in the scandal stirred up by Miltiades Vaiden's appropriation of the funds of the Second National Bank of Florence.

The wedding was very quiet and, in a negative way, very expensive to Jerry, as he could not circularize the event among the many churches where he had been a pastor, and therefore he was deprived of a shower of presents which he believed he would have received.

There had been a time in Jerry's early ministry when he would have welcomed a wedding without presents, but a series of pastorates in small Southern towns where the Methodist ministers are kept alive by irregular "showers" of goods in kind, instead of a salary, had numbed his natural independence, and incidentally his sense of gratitude. He therefore regretted the wedding presents which he might have received with the callousness of practising preachers.

This particular regret, however, was more or less dissipated by a munificent wedding present from the Colonel immediately after the ceremony.

The ceremony itself was conducted in the old Pine Street Church in the presence of the Swartouts and the Vaidens.

What Sydna thought, Jerry did not know. He himself was conscious of Aurelia's youth, for she was not much older than Marsan. She was a very desirable bride with her antiseptic cleanliness, her Dresden china prettiness, and her musical erudition.

When Dr. Blankenship repeated the phrase, "If any man has any objection to this marriage let him speak now or forever hold his peace," the pause filled the old church. The stillness seemed to mark the close of one life and the beginning of another for Jerry and Aurelia.

Marsan glanced at her mother. Sydna looked at the little black book in Dr. Blankenship's hand. It contained the offices of the church. Then he continued:

"I now pronounce you man and wife, what God hath joined together let no man put asunder."

There came a stir in the little group, as if some sort of strain were over. There were hand shakings and wishes of joy and happiness. Sydna kissed Aurelia with the sad automatic hypocrisy of women. Miltiades drew Jerry aside and handed him his wedding present in a long envelope.

By a queer coincidence, just as Jerry thanked his uncle for the check, a Western Union boy entered the church with a telegram. It was for Miltiades and proved to be from the Fifth National Bank in Louisville, informing him that the bank had been made party to a suit against Miltiades to recover certain funds held by the bank, and that therefore the bank would not be able to honor any future checks drawn by Colonel Vaiden until the adjudication of the cause.

All the wedding party, with the exception of the old Colonel, were sharply disturbed by the telegram.

Sydna said:

"What an omen on Jerry's wedding day," and a moment later asked Colonel Milt if it would be necessary for her to put off a meeting of the D.A.R.'s at the manor.

The old banker scouted the idea and said, "Certainly not."

Dr. Blankenship, however, was greatly concerned. After the ceremony he called Miltiades into his office and asked what effect the suit would have on the building of the cathedral.

"I don't believe this suit will have anything to do with it, Doctor," said the Colonel, "but if you ask about the whole situation, then, frankly, I think it will."

When Dr. Blankenship asked him uneasily what he meant, the old financier explained:

"I will be able to take care of the pay roll of the cathedral for the short time these Louisville funds are tied up, but the boom which Florence has enjoyed for a year now is finished. There won't be another for the next ten or fifteen years."

The Doctor nodded reservedly, like an experienced debater who concedes as little as possible.

"It may possibly be over," said the Doctor.

"It certainly is. The trains going North are just as crowded leaving Florence as they used to be coming in."

"Just exactly what point do you make there?" asked the Doctor uneasily.

"Simply this, the influx we received was just a boom, after all, and not a permanent addition. Florence will not leap to metropolitan proportions instantly, as everyone expected it would do. Now, Doctor, if it doesn't do that, we won't need such a large cathedral as we are building. It's a waste of money. The church has overexpanded in the same spirit and degree that the real estate business was overexpanded . . . now the real estate men are retrenching."

The Doctor stood tapping his fingers faintly on his desk.

"I hope that will not affect your support of God's cause, Colonel. Remember man's extremity is God's opportunity."

"My idea in asking you to see me," said the Colonel, involuntarily taking over the interview as his own, "was to revise our program in keeping with our new perspective.

"Now, Florence is Florence. It isn't going to change much. Our manufactories will probably shift from steam to electric power. So will those in Huntsville, Russellville, Athens, Decatur. You see, the current generated at the dam doesn't have to be used here at all and won't be. In fact, it may very well have a decentralizing influence, if there was much here to decentralize."

"What changes are you suggesting?" asked the Doctor nervously.

The Colonel made a brushing gesture with his fingers,

"Why, all that restaurant, library, gymnasium, and poolroom idea, Doctor. The population here in Florence is not going to be so great that the pool-room addicts will have to hold overflow meetings in the church houses."

The minister did not laugh.

"Colonel Vaiden, the object of these innovations is to attract young men and women into the church and help make them better citizens."

"I have never understood why the inherent dignity and sanctity of the church of God needs the reinforcements of frivolity and levity," said the Colonel. "To me, Dr. Blankenship, the church is a place were I can lay down the cares and pleasures of the flesh and consider the condition of my immortal soul."

The old man's confession of faith softened the Doctor.

"I wish the new generation had your feeling, Colonel, but there is no use deceiving ourselves. Unless our churches are turned into communal centers, we will lose our congregations. There was a time when religion was the product of the churches; it is now a by-product. Once the church fed its members on the word of God; now it attempts a very discreet inoculation."

Miltiades was shocked.

"What is the reason for such a defection?"

"Because people are not interested."

"Have they no regard for God and His eternity?"

The Doctor picked up a paper weight and laid it down.

"Their feeling toward God and eternity oscillates between a myth, a rumor, a loneliness, and a poem. The new generation are a curiously frank set, Colonel. I have had boys come and ask me what they could do to believe in God. Where ordinary people used to find it impossible to disbelieve in God, today they find it impossible to believe."

"What did you say to such boys?"

"I told them to pray. If I had answered as frankly as they questioned, I would have told them to change their generation."

Colonel Vaiden stood for several moments looking at a large drawing of the new cathedral that hung in the office.

"I don't see how it is possible for a human being to doubt his Maker. I remember when Jerry was a boy he was almost expelled from the college here on account of his nonconformist beliefs. When I questioned him about it, the real trouble was the prayers in the college chapel were not sincere enough to satisfy him. You know, ever since then that boy has owned my heart."

"He's a spiritual man, if there ever was one," admired the Doctor.

The Colonel paused again.

"What do you think of Marsan, Doctor?"

"Marsan?"

"Yes, has she ever spoken to you about her religion?"

"No, she hasn't."

"You know nothing of her condition?"

"Yes . . . I do know something of her condition. . . ."

"What is it?"

"Her mother told me about it. She is dreadfully concerned about Marsan; she doesn't know what to do."

The Colonel looked at the Doctor intently.

"Do you mean religiously?"

"In general, not specifically religiously."

"Just what do you mean?"

"Mrs. Vaiden and I were discussing how we could tell you. We wondered how we could persuade you to remain controlled and avoid any violence."

A terrible feeling came over the Colonel. He breathed through his open mouth.

"You mean . . . about Marsan?"

The Doctor nodded with the slightest of nods.

"Yes . . . she has been misused."

The tips of the old Colonel's fingers twitched a little.

"By whom?"

"We don't know; she wouldn't tell us."

And only then did Miltiades perceive that this was why the Doctor had called him into the office for consultation.

CHAPTER FORTY-FIVE

As COLONEL VAIDEN walked out of the old Pine Street Methodist Church, the thought that rankled in his head was that Jerry Catlin was a preacher. The boy could not, by his very profession, kill the man who had dishonored Marsan. It was a fantastic position for a nephew of his, an offshoot of the Vaiden blood, to fall into. He himself, an old, old man, without a son, was the only Vaiden left to defend his daughter's honor.

As the aged banker hurried stiffly to the manor, his mind slipped, and he thought for a moment that he was rushing to avenge an insult to Marcia, his dead sister, who was young and lovely and living again; then Time rearranged itself and it was Marsan once more. How it could have happened, through what flaw in heredity such a lapse in the blood of a Vaiden woman was possible, the old Colonel could not imagine.

He entered his postern gate and followed the box-lined path to the solemn Colonial portico. The very magnificence of his home seemed a kind of sham fortification for his daughter's honor; some enemy had scaled these walls . . . his thoughts moved in a kind of trembling, stately rhetoric.

In the hall he met Sydna and asked for Marsan. The wife's apprehension was extreme. She went up to Miltiades and caught his arm.

"Listen, honey, don't do anything you'll be sorry for!"

"Is Marsan in her room?"

"I think so . . . she was telephoning in there a moment ago. . . . Darling, please think . . . consider . . ."

"To whom?"

"To . . . to a man named . . ." The wife stopped with a white face.

"Petrie?" supplied the Colonel.

"No . . . I think it was Porter."

"Porter . . . what's Petrie's first name?"

"I don't know."

The Colonel tried to recall Petrie's given name from his dealings with him in the bank as he went on upstairs to his study over the porte-cochère.

In this room he opened a drawer in a chest, took out a small blue pistol, broke it open and looked at the circle of cartridges, snapped the hammer twice, then closed the arm and dropped it in his pocket. Then he went down the blind stairs to Marsan's room.

It was a gay room with dance favors on her vanity table and college pennants on her walls.

"Marsan," said the old man in an unsteady tone, "Dr. Blankenship tells me . . ." the old father lowered his voice to a husky whisper, "you're in trouble."

Marsan jumped up from the telephone, rushed to him, put her arms around him and her cheek to his.

"Damn! Damn! Damn such a preacher!" she cried vehemently, beginning to weep. "Stir you up about me! Make you miserable! I wish every preacher . . ."

Even through the Colonel's fury at the despoiler of his home, Marsan's outburst struck him as extraordinary and entirely unforeseen.

"Who was it, Marsan?"

"Oh, a kid," cried the girl in disgust, "nothing but a kid. . . . I swear I don't see what I was thinking about. . . . Honey, don't worry your poor old head . . . it's all right." She squeezed her father, kissed him, turned, and walked irresolutely back to the telephone.

"Are you phoning him now?"

"Listen, Daddy," she pleaded with the receiver in her hand, "are you and Mother and Uncle Jerry going to keep this quiet, or are you going to talk it? I want to know . . . I

got to make my plans. . . . Oh, my God, what did I go to
Shiloh for! I knew I felt woozy . . ." Here she turned quite
pale, hurried into her private bath, and Miltiades could
hear her retching and vomiting. After a while she came out
with a greenish tint in her face and a faint smile, half in
apology and half in disgust.

"Isn't it a mess!" she said.

Sydna entered from the hall, where she evidently had been
listening.

"Marsan," she reproached, "I hoped you wouldn't talk
so unfilial to your father as you did to me . . . I thought you
loved him, Marsan."

"Mamma, I'm not talking unfilial."

"You seem so unrepentant."

"Well, I want the baby to be healthy!" cried Marsan in
surprise.

"Darling! Darling!" cried Sydna in a shocked tone.
"Think of the disgrace!"

"There'll be talk, of course, especially if you folks make a
great stir about, but disgrace . . . hadn't you noticed, Mother,
wealthy people don't get in disgrace no matter what they
do?"

"Marsan!"

"Now, you just watch it, Mamma, watch it for your-
self."

"Marsan," said the Colonel trying to get at his part in
this strange conversation, "who is this Porter person you
were trying to get on the telephone?"

"A boy named Porter Lee," said the girl simply.

"Was he the . . ." The Colonel made a gesture.

"Goodness, no! He's married. He married Lizzie Lanceford
two weeks ago."

"Did—did he . . ." the Colonel made a wild surmise,
"did he marry Lizzie to escape . . . marriage with you?"

"Dad, of course not. Porter and Lizzie are friends of mine,
that's all. They . . . they married because I asked them to,
if you must know."

The two parents stared at their daughter at this irrational sequence.

"Marsan . . . what do you mean?"

"Oh, they were going to marry anyway, they just hurried it up on my account."

"What were you trying to telephone them for?"

"Oh," cried Marsan, out of patience, "I was going to tell them they could go ahead and have a baby if they wanted to, that you folks had messed it up at this end."

Sydna felt as if she were walking among a lot of jack-in-the-boxes, and heaven only knew what would pop out next.

"What in the world . . . what earthly connection has Porter and Lizzie's baby . . ."

Marsan hesitated.

"Well, it's all over now . . . I just as soon tell you as not . . . and it certainly speaks well for Porter and Lizzie, even you will have to admit that, Mamma."

"Go ahead, go on, tell me."

"Why, it's just this: They were going to live in Mobile, and I was going down there and pretend I was Porter's wife and that Lizzie was my sister, or the maid or something. When I had my baby, they would keep it, and I'd come back home; then they could move somewhere else with Lizzie for Porter's wife, as they would be all along, don't you see. Then, after a while, I was going to adopt my baby."

At the prolonged silence of her parents, Marsan seemed to feel that she should add something to this . . . itinerary, or whatever it might be called. "Of course, I was going to pay them for their trouble, but Lizzie vowed she wouldn't take a cent, that she would just be thrilled to have my baby and keep it and love it . . . and she would."

Sydna started to say something, then didn't.

She started again:

"Marsan . . . how in the world . . . where did you ever get such a wild, harebrained, moonstruck . . ."

"Why, it isn't wild. . . ."

"Most fantastic thing I ever heard of. . . ."

"Why, darling," expostulated Marsan, "it's an old plan!"

"Old plan . . . you mean you high-school girls . . . is that why so many of you get married?"

"Oh, Mamma, no, no, no. We got the idea from our English class. That's the plot of Tom Jones. All of us believed it would work because Fielding was a realist . . . he was the first English realist."

Miltiades stood listening with the most mixed reactions. A question which no Southern gentleman had ever before asked his erring daughter besieged his mind; finally he did say:

"Marsan, if you have such practical, unemotional ideas afterwards, I simply don't see how it happened."

"I don't mind telling you at all," said Marsan. "You know the day of the lynching . . . I mean the near-lynching."

"Yes."

"Well, you made a speech, Daddy, and tried to stop it. Some men began to yell . . . mean things at you."

"I remember that," said the Colonel with an odd feeling.

"This boy was with me. He told the men I was your daughter and for them to shut up. They didn't do it, so he broke one man's jaw, and then they all shut up. . . . I guess you heard the fight, it was there by the fire station."

"Yes, I did."

"It was that boy making the people quit insulting me and you . . . now . . . that's why."

"You mean . . . that . . . that is why . . ."

"Why, yes, I was awfully grateful . . . just awfully, Mother . . . and when he wanted me to do . . . something for him . . ." Marsan drew a long breath.

"After he had protected you!" cried Sydna.

"Oh, Mother, his protecting me was a reaction and—and what he wanted was a reaction . . . they didn't have anything to do with each other."

"Marsan," cried Sydna, horrified, "do you think this boy . . . that everybody is just a machine . . . is that the way you look on people? Don't you believe there's a God?"

Marsan stood looking at her mother with a greenish solemn face.

"Well . . . some of the girls do . . . and some don't . . . most of us just don't think about that at all."

After this indeterminate interview with his daughter, Colonel Miltiades Vaiden returned to his study. He drew his pistol from his pocket and stood fingering it uncertainly.

Marsan's world into which he had dipped for the first time in his life was not a world wherein fathers shot the seducers of their daughters. It was as if the symmetrical, well formed world which he had given into Marsan's care when she and her generation came into existence had shivered to pieces in his daughter's hands. Nothing at all held together. And it required a very strong, solid, resistant world as a foundation for murdering a boy for loving a girl.

Marsan's plot to keep her baby struck him as ingenious beneath its fantasy . . . it might possibly have worked if she hadn't gone to Shiloh.

But glimpses of such new worlds are hard to get and impossible to keep. Even while Miltiades pondered, Marsan's whole scheme of things dissolved in the Colonel's mind. The old man's own unimpugnable realities gathered around him again. That trinity, the Southern code, the seducer, and the innocent daughter, reëstablished itself in his pantheon. He did not, as he had at first intended, restore the pistol to its drawer; he dropped it in his pocket again and walked once more down the blind stairs.

CHAPTER FORTY-SIX

In the porte-cochère the old banker lifted a shaken call for Wilson. He looked about in all directions, but Wilson with his glum face did not appear. The Colonel stood nervously fingering the revolver in his pocket. As a left-over from his soldiering days, the weapon felt too small, toy-like: it was a thirty-two-caliber pistol.

He called again, automatically, as he thought of the trouble he would bring on himself when he shot the school teacher seducer of his daughter. It was almost unthinkable for him to give so much time to Petrie's murder and the trial that would follow when his bank was in such a bad way, and when he had endless foreclosures to make on property which he had sold to speculators on a margin. It was outrageous to be forced to shoot Petrie in a press of work like this.

He called Wilson again, and this time the negro appeared, coming up the carriage drive at a hurried shuffle.

"You heard me," accused the Colonel.

"No suh, I don' heah you," denied the chocolate man sheepishly.

"What are you running for, then?"

"I thought I hurry up an' tell you Ludus want to see you."

"Well, I don't want to see Ludus."

"Ludus . . . de Col'l kain't see you," called Wilson in the general direction of the carriage gate.

At this another black man shuffled out from behind a clump of crêpe myrtle and looked at the Colonel with blood-shot eyes.

"You kain't see me, Col'l, fuh jess a li'l while?"

"No, not for a minute . . . what do you want?"

"Col'l Milt, dem white men rollin' away my house in Jericho."

"Your house deserves to be rolled away in Jericho," snapped the Colonel, "and you ought to be horsewhipped in the bargain . . . shooting Pammy Lee like you did! Why aren't you in jail?"

Ludus was abashed that he was not in jail.

"Muh—muh trile ain't come off yit," he apologized.

"Yes, and it won't!"

"Maybe hit will, Col'l," answered Ludus in a hopeful appealing tone.

"No, that damned shyster Sandusky will keep having it put off and off until it's thrown out of court."

"Maybe he won't," said Ludus.

"What is it you want?"

"Col'l Milt, if I had five dollahs to pay dis week's 'stalmint, they couldn't roll my house out o' Jericho so quick. I was jess wond'rin' if you could 'vance me a li'l' money."

"I wouldn't advance you a cent on anything except your funeral. I don't want you, and I'm not hiring you."

"Yes suh . . . if'n you did want me, I could he'p Wilson polish de ca' an' cut de grass tull I wuck out my five dollahs. I sho' hates to see 'em roll my house out o' Jericho. Hit was right next to de Meetin' House an' Benevolent Hall wid de graveya'd right behin' me."

For a black man to be so well placed and then dispossessed must have touched the Colonel. He reached into his pocket.

"Damn you, Ludus, I oughtn't to advance you a damn cent . . . shooting Pammy Lee like you did . . . now, remember the grass and the car . . . don't forget them. . . . I'll allow you fifty cents each time . . . and here's three dollars."

Ludus received the bills gratefully. The three dollars were not enough to keep his house in Jericho, but the Colonel never gave a black man all he asked for. Nor had Ludus expected the whole amount. He had thought the Colonel would give him about a dollar and he would have to beg from four other white men to make up his installment.

The banker got stiffly into his car and set forth down Pine Street. When he was well away with his chauffeur he asked:

"Where does that man live that Marsan used to pick up in the mornings, Wilson?"

The odd monotone which the Colonel used caused the colored driver to give a start.

"Ah . . . do' know, suh."

"Don't know . . . you know you know! That dark-complected, black-eyed man, the teacher Marsan used to pick up on the way to school!"

Wilson slowed down the car and pulled at his jaw.

"Now, where 'bout do dat white man live at?" he asked, rolling his eyes apprehensively at his master.

"Wilson," snapped the Colonel, suddenly angry, "if you don't get me to that man's house in three minutes, I'll attend to you!"

"Yes suh, yessuh . . . I 'members now. Hit—hit's on Tombigbee Street, Col'l Milt!"

"Get me there," ordered the Colonel.

Wilson turned a corner and speeded the car with a feeling as if a chill wind were blowing through his bones. Anything could happen to him in the swiftly approaching fracas. He could be struck by a bullet. In the trial he could be indicted as the Colonel's accomplice, and in the judgment he would certainly be hanged for helping kill a white man. He felt as if he were driving the car over a cliff to certain destruction.

"Now y-y-yondah's d-de place," he stuttered, stopping his car two houses distant from the Waner home and wetting the thin carmine line that marked the closure of his thick brown lips.

A minute or so later Miss Claribel Waner, looking through her sitting-room window, saw, with the utmost astonishment, the archaic figure of Colonel Miltiades Vaiden enter her gate.

Miss Claribel was the second cousin and heir of old Mrs. Waner, and the legacy she had received from her ancient cousin was this boarding house and the manuscript sermons

of old Parson Benjamin Mulry. And as a final item in the
legacy, Miss Claribel had inherited from old Mrs. Waner a
thoroughgoing detestation of all Vaidens of whatsoever rank,
age, sex, or color.

Now, to Miss Claribel there was something diabolical in
the very mien and carriage of the old banker. His mottled
scorched complexion gave the boarding-house keeper an
impression that he had risen up at her gate out of the chim-
neys of hell. At the same time the liveliest curiosity mixed
with the repulsion the woman felt.

Then suddenly she solved the riddle to her own satis-
faction. The Colonel was coming to see about publishing a
book which she was writing called, *Life, Letters, and Sermons
of the Reverend Benjamin Mulry.* She was writing this book
under the auspices of the Ladies' Historical and Literary
Society of North Alabama of which she was a member. Now
she surmised that the banker had heard of her opus through
his wife, "Miss" Sydna Vaiden, who once had been a kind
of bellwether for Florence's literary flock, but who was no
longer, and that he, the husband, had come to make her an
offer for the manuscript.

However, when she went to the door and the Colonel called
for Mr. Petrie, the school teacher, she was so amazed at this
new tack of the banker's visit that all thought of the *Life,
Letters, and Sermons of the Reverend Benjamin Mulry* van-
ished completely from her head.

"Don't mention my name," directed the Colonel urbanely,
"just tell Mr. Petrie a visitor wants to see him."

"All right, all right, I won't," agreed Miss Claribel, and
when she hurried up the wooden steps to her boarder's room,
she tapped the door and called in an excited undertone,

"Professor Petrie! Professor Petrie! Colonel Milt Vaiden
is in the sitting room to see you! What in the world do you
suppose he wants?"

Professor Petrie appeared at the door holding a rusty bar of
iron about twelve inches long, one end of which he had filed
and polished. The scientist made swift conjectures himself.

"I wonder if he is refunding me my money?"

"No, no, he ain't doing that," whispered the literary aspirant.

"That's all I can think of," said the school teacher.

"Then you'll haff to go down and see."

Mr. Petrie really did not think Miltiades had come with his money, either. This had been something to tell Miss Claribel while he really revolved the puzzle in his head. He thought at once of Marsan. At a further guess, he divined that Marsan was in trouble, and one more throw brought the pedagogue his solution. The Colonel had come to ask him who had seduced his daughter. A serious mood came over Petrie. The blood went out of his face.

"All right," he said, "I'll go down and see. If it isn't money, I'm sure I don't know what it can be."

His conjecture that Marsan was enceinte gave the teacher a stunned feeling, as if someone had struck him with a club. The girl's misconduct vanished utterly from Petrie's mind in the face of her misfortune. He went down the steps with the iron bar still in his hand. From the top of the steps, Miss Claribel watched his progress. She had already opened her mouth to listen more intently.

As Petrie entered the door a kind of contempt went through the Colonel for the bar of iron in the schoolmaster's hands.

"I see you have an idea what I came to see you about," said the old man in a metallic tone.

Petrie nodded, closed the door behind him.

"I don't think you could have come here but for one thing, Colonel Vaiden."

The Colonel's hand was resting in his pocket.

"Will you place that piece of iron on the table?" asked the Colonel with his old eyes hard on the young man.

Petrie glanced down at the specimen he unconsciously had brought with him.

"Certainly." He stepped across and laid it on the table, wondering what that had to do with the Colonel.

Up until Petrie laid it down, the old banker expected the fellow to turn and throw it. When it was harmless on the table, Miltiades thought what a poltroon the teacher really was. No wonder he seduced the pupils placed under his care. He was on the edge of drawing and firing without another word when he recalled that the man's name was Petrie. He remembered it from the interview at the bank.

"Are you aware that my daughter, Marsan, is in a very deplorable condition, Mr. Petrie?" he asked in a hard tone.

Petrie nodded.

"I guessed it when Miss Waner told me you were down here to see me."

The banker looked at the man. He was plainly disturbed, but he had better control of himself than the Colonel had given him credit for.

"What can you tell me? What can you say to this?" asked the old man brittly.

Petrie made a gesture and answered in a deeply moved tone:

"Colonel Vaiden, I am a Southern man. I know the feeling and practice of the South, but do you think it best to handle this unfortunate affair in the way you have in mind? Would it be best for Marsan? And what is still more important, although I do not expect you at this moment to share my sentiment, would it be best for society at large . . . for the race?"

The banker looked steadily at the school teacher.

"I'm afraid I don't follow you."

"I am not surprised. But your daughter is a very remarkable girl, Colonel Vaiden. I have been teaching her for six years. She has qualities of mind and heart which I have never met before. Do you think it would be a service to the race or fair to Marsan as an individual to waste such a splendid girl on an unruly, shiftless, unreliable lout?"

The Colonel was bewildered at Petrie's strange plea.

"That's an extraordinary description you are giving."

"It's a true one, and I have wondered until I was half sick

how Marsan could ever have permitted such a thing . . . it's inconceivable . . . it's irrational."

Colonel Vaiden began to suspect either that his suspicions were wrong or that Petrie was enacting one of the oddest of lies in the hope that Marsan had not divulged his name.

"I'll tell you why she said she permitted it," nodded the banker, watching the young man keenly to see how he would take the information: "she said this young man had defended my good name and in gratitude for this, she . . . ah . . . the thing happened."

A look of extraordinary relief came over Petrie's face.

"I can understand that, she would do that . . . impulsive, without any fear of conventionality . . . yes, that's what she might do."

"That's what she did do," said the Colonel with a sudden letting down in his voice, convinced that Petrie could not possibly have simulated the emotions he expressed.

"What are her plans now?" asked the science teacher with concern.

"Oh . . . she was thinking about going to Mobile . . . she can hardly stay in Florence."

Petrie shook his head sadly.

"Poor child. . . . Colonel Vaiden, Marsan and I have been very good friends. I wish I might be allowed to visit her in her trouble . . . before she goes away . . . as a teacher interested in and attached to a pupil for whom he has the deepest sympathy . . . and respect."

The old banker's last doubt vanished.

"You are very welcome as far as I am concerned, Mr. Petrie . . . if you will drop a note to Sydna and Marsan."

The old man did not inquire as to who did actually mistreat his daughter . . . the whole affair had edged over into a world where the Colonel began to feel that he could not adjudicate the matter with a six-shooter.

CHAPTER FORTY-SEVEN

WHEN old Colonel Vaiden drove away from the boarding house his faith in the school teacher's story wavered to some extent, but he was very glad he had not destroyed the fellow. His guilt had become too uncertain for that.

Now, as he drove through the street to the bank, some of his friends along the sidewalk who were due to call salutations to him did not do it.

Such slights, of course, were really a service to the old banker. They were a counter irritant to his heartbreak and despair about his daughter.

At least half the substantial citizens of Florence were infuriated at the Colonel for having milked the Second National Bank of its money and deposited it to his private account in Louisville. As the old man got out of his car to enter the bank someone on the sidewalk said:

"Same damned old thief that he has been all his life!"

In his mail that morning the Colonel received a letter from the Rotary Club requesting that he resign the office of president.

The Colonel called in Miss Katie, dictated his resignation, and mailed it to the secretary of the club.

He did this with a queer latent feeling of satisfaction that he was returning once more to his normal self. His days of passive make-believe were over. The praise, the toasts, the admiration and eulogies which he had received as a philanthropist and public-spirited citizen always held a certain metaphorical ring in the Colonel's ironic old ears. But this abuse was sincere. It went through his veins like the whip of strychnine after the dullness of morphine. Had it not been for Marsan, the Colonel could have given his heart to the situation. He would have known again the solitary happiness of a hawk.

A tall well dressed negro with weary eyes and a heavy melancholy mouth was admitted to his private office. He wanted to ask the Colonel if he thought the Second National Bank would eventually pay off its depositors.

"I don't think so," said the Colonel colorlessly.

"I noticed in the *Index*," quoted the negro, "that the bank examiner, in his report, said that the paper the bank held was more than enough to cover its debts."

"The examiner was using the recent inflated prices in his estimate," explained the Colonel with a distaste for his questioner.

"You don't expect those prices to return . . . not with the full development of the dam?"

"I haven't time to go into that with you," said the Colonel, irritated at the air and correct English of the negro.

The colored man hesitated a moment.

"I was a depositor in your bank. I chose your bank because I knew you were at the head of it and I believed in your judgment. I am about to lose a house which I built over in Sheffield in a subdivision called Jericho. I need a small amount of money as a present payment to hold the house. I will make you over my claim to my deposit in your bank, or I will give you my note for a personal debt on me. I know I can take care of the other payments, and your note, out of my fees as a physician . . . if you would be willing to accommodate me?"

The Colonel's irritation turned to repulsion and anger at the negro's reproduction of a white man's speech, familiarity with business, and manner of approach.

"What's your name?"

"Greenup."

"Greenup, you'll have to take your chances with the other depositors. I'm not investing in bankrupt accounts. That's all you wanted to see me about, isn't it?"

Greenup bowed slightly and went out of the office.

"A doctor," thought Miltiades disgusted. "Tchk!"

Not many persons came to the bank since the break seeking Miltiades' advice on how to become wealthy. His methods were too drastic.

Presently Jerry Catlin arrived to see his uncle. Miltiades began by reproaching Jerry for not coming to the manor oftener. He said he hoped Jerry's marriage was not going to keep him away. His nephew assured him this was not the case.

"I thought you and Aurelia were going to keep house in the parsonage?"

Jerry said they had planned it, but Aurelia didn't like the lowness of the house . . . it was too damp for her piano.

A crinkle of mirth went through the old banker's mind at the choice of residences being determined by a musical instrument. In his heart he had always considered his nephew's bride a peculiar girl, and this was an amusing quirk in her general peculiarity.

"And now, what did you want to see me about, Jerry?" asked the old man.

"The General Methodist Conference is called at Wetumpka this fall," explained the assistant minister, "and the Doctor and I were talking about a possible location for me. There isn't much work for me to do here. Our organization in Florence has fallen through. In Waterloo a new sect has completely taken over the Methodist Church . . . can you guess who they are?"

"Haven't the slightest idea."

"They are called the 'Drownders.' That man Rutledge who fell in Shoal Creek on the night of the negroes' get-a-way to Athens, he's the guiding spirit of the sect."

Miltiades shook his yellow head at the quirks of life.

"And you helped resuscitate him?"

"Yes, I did."

"A man ought to be careful whom he resuscitates . . . especially preachers."

There came a knock at the door, and the bank examiner entered the Colonel's private office.

"I believe, Colonel, that we can reconstruct the bank so it will be in a position to receive and pay out new deposits, and there will be some monies coming in that can be prorated out among the old depositors."

Miltiades nodded comfortably.

"You have found everything perfectly regular?"

"Yes indeed."

"I'm glad to know we can open up for new business again."

When the examiner had gone out, the old Colonel said in a low voice, glancing at the door:

"Sydna asked me to ask you, did you know a discreet doctor we could get for Marsan."

"A doctor?"

The old man nodded in troubled reflection.

"Sydna thought Marsan would be better with an operation. . . ."

"No, no," protested Jerry, "that is strictly against the rules of the church. . . ."

"It's Sydna's idea," repeated the Colonel in a gray voice. "When I was young, Jerry, in a case like this we operated on the man, not the woman. . . . Sydna said, if you could spare the time, would you please come up to the manor for a few minutes?"

CHAPTER FORTY-EIGHT

THE Vaiden household did stand in need of advice and consolation. Sydna, with her idea of doctors, did not know which one to engage, or in what city to have the operation. Then, too, it was dangerous, and Sydna thought of going anonymously to some Northern city and there accomplishing her daughter's deliverance.

She said she could not possibly understand how Marsan, brought up in the Lacefield and Vaiden traditions, could have been so wayward.

Drusilla, with white hair and troubled, faintly ironic eyes, thought of a day in the old Lacefield manor down in the Reserve, when Sydna was a baby. She remembered a moment between Miltiades and herself, and now their distant uncandled giving had come home to both of them in Marsan.

It seemed to the old grandmother that Time did not go on, but that it was a vast wheel that turned slowly round and round, and now her almost forgotten sin had reappeared in her sweet granddaughter.

In the midst of these vague plannings and consolations the doorbell clanged in the hall below. It was not an electric buzzer; it was the same brass lion's foot which had served the old house before Miltiades had built so many additions to it. Its single clang seemed more in keeping with the portico and grand hallway and ornamental iron balcony at the second-story level than an electric bell would have been.

The two women upstairs stopped talking and listened to hear who had called. Presently they heard Mary the maid say, "I don't know whether Miss Marsan is at home or not, I'll go see."

Later they heard Marsan calling that she was in, and a young girl's voice replying:

"It's me, Marsan, Sarah May."

Sydna looked at her mother gratefully.

"It's Sarah May Tergune . . . well, nobody knows it yet. When it finally gets out . . ." she gave a great sigh, "there won't be any more Sarah May to see Marsan . . . friendship is such a fickle thing . . . and Marsan wasn't really to blame . . . if it hadn't been for those miserable niggers the Colonel was trying to save . . ." But what was the use in railing against coincidence?

Miss Sarah May Tergune passed through the lower hall filled with a kind of excited double envy of Marsan: that her friend should live in such a house as this and have so dramatic a thing happen to her. It seemed incredible to Sarah May that two such theatrical things could have happened together. The very breath of romance blowing through a stately old mansion . . . usually girls in trouble lived in such mean houses. She tapped on Marsan's door and opened it.

"Oh, Marsan!" crooned Sarah May, rushing to and embracing Marsan with the passion of girls who are not yet sure whether they love other girls or boys.

"Have you heard anything, darling?"

"Not later than this morning," said Marsan anxiously. "Lizzie called me up."

"Is Elroy going to get in touch with Porter Lee? . . . He said he would."

"That's nice, Sarah May."

"How do you feel, honey?"

"Oh, sort of sickish, on and off."

"Oh, I do wish I could be that way for you. . . . Where are you sick?"

"Oh . . . all over . . . at my stomach."

"Think of it . . . a baby . . . all your own!" Sarah May writhed with yearning.

"Mamma's against it."

"Of course, she would be."

"She wants an operation."

Sarah May opened her eyes.

"My goodness, Marsan . . . is your mother that antiquated? I know my mother is, but your mother is such an intellectual woman . . . doesn't she know that when you get married and come to want a baby regularly this operation will be a terrible drawback?"

"Mother is intellectual about things that don't amount to anything . . . she knows how many forts there are on the Atlantic coast."

"Well . . . that would be good to know in time of war," said Sarah May, trying to put Marsan's mother in the best light possible.

"Yes, a person could stay away from those places and not get hurt," said Marsan.

The subject of forts on the Atlantic which had occupied the attention of Sydna's study club for three months faded from the interest of the two girls in three minutes.

"Marsan, I've just been thinking and thinking about your baby, do you believe it's got the right . . . you know . . . what you call 'em?"

"Hormones," supplied Marsan, "well, I don't know, Sarah May, what do you think?"

"I think Red has the hormones for a strong body, and you have the hormones for a strong mind, Marsan."

"Yes, but suppose it inherits the other way round?"

"My goodness!" ejaculated Sarah May, "you'll wish you had your operation," and they both began laughing uncontrollably.

After a while they stifled their mirth and began going over a new plan by which Marsan was to be taken out of the manor by Leroy, Sarah May's friend, who would deliver Marsan to Porter Lee and Lizzie Lee regardless of adult interference. In the midst of this Marsan said:

"Sarah May . . . I don't know whether I can run off like that or not?"

"Why, why?"

"Well . . . Mr. Petrie has asked Mamma can he come to see me . . . he asked Papa, and then he asked Mamma."

Sarah May stared at her friend with rapture dawning in her eyes.

"And you don't want to be gone if he calls?"

"Of course not."

"Oh, isn't that sweet!"

She rushed at her friend and kissed her again.

"And for him to ask your father and mother could he call . . . oh, I do think that's the spiffiest thing. . . . Oh, I wish somebody would ask my father and mother could they call, but of course they wouldn't let 'em . . . they try to stop all they can. . . . Now, I hope this isn't just a teacher call because you're sick."

"That's what he told Father . . . but . . . it won't be."

"Oh, Marsan, you're the sweetest thing! Marsan, everything just breaks your way!"

"Still, I don't know for sure," cried the invalid, "it may be nothing but a teacher call. . . . Oh, he's treated me terribly . . . when the bank broke he called me up and that was all he said . . . just the bank's broke and rung off."

"Then he doesn't love you?"

"Well, how can I tell . . . what did he want to tell me the bank was broke for?"

"Why . . . maybe he thought you would be interested in it . . . it was your daddy's bank, wasn't it?"

"Yes."

"The one he got all the—er—does Mr. Petrie know about . . . you know . . . everything?"

"I sort of think he does. I told him about . . . you know . . . Red."

Sarah May dropped her hands.

"Marsan . . . why did you do it?"

"Well . . . I don't know . . . we were riding in the car a lot."

"Wasn't you afraid he'd expel you?"

"No."

Sarah May looked at Marsan and shook her head in hopeless envy.

"Oh, I wish I could fall in love with some man older than Leroy . . . a sure enough man . . . and tell him some terrible thing like that . . . and not know exactly what he was going to do. . . . Oh, Marsan!"

"You will, probably, Sarah May," said Marsan hopefully.

"Now, speaking of Leroy, when is he to come for you?"

"Tell him he can't possibly come until Professor Petrie calls."

"All right, that's settled, and I think it's extremely sensible . . . and I do hope it gets your hormones in its head."

The girls began laughing again.

As they laughed, the lion's-foot door bell clanged again. Both girls became quiet instantly and listened intently. Sarah May whispered:

"Do you suppose it's him?"

"Hush, don't suggest such a thing," whispered Marsan with her heart beginning to beat.

Then they heard the maid say:

"Miss Sydna and Miss Drusilla are upstairs, Mistuh Jerry."

Marsan drew a long sigh of actual relief from this sudden strain of hope.

"It's nobody but Cousin Jerry," she said shakenly.

Sarah May kissed her again.

"That's all right, little honey baby . . . he will come."

CHAPTER FORTY-NINE

Mr. JERRY CATLIN entered the Vaiden manor in considerable moral uncertainty.

To begin with, before he left Sheffield for Florence, he had told Aurelia that he was going to the bank to see his uncle Miltiades about the Methodist Conference but that he was not going to the manor. Whereupon Aurelia went off into a wild agony of jealousy and said she knew he was either going straight to the manor or that somehow he would wind up there.

Jerry grew annoyed and said, very well, he would go straight to the manor.

Aurelia then went into her parlor and played several of Chopin's nocturnes and presently came out and kissed Jerry and told him that she knew he was going to the manor, but for him to go if he wanted to, that she loved him and wanted to make him happy, and if going with another woman made him happy she wanted him to do that, because she loved him utterly and everlastingly.

Whereupon Jerry had kissed Aurelia and had told her positively that he would not go to the manor under any consideration.

As Jerry had passed out of his gate to go to the bus station, old Mrs. Swartout had told him that little Junior Petman had been prophesying again. Junior's prophecy had been, the old woman said, that all the white people had better get out of Carver's Lane.

The two had spent considerable time talking about this at the gate, Jerry explaining it away as best he could in a churchmanly manner, and the old lady clinging to her wonder as best she could in a paganly manner.

This matter would have floated out of Jerry's mind completely, as the old woman's remarks about Junior usually did, but they were impressed upon him by a slight coincidence.

Old Mr. Swartout was at that moment coming up the lane with a negro, and the two were on the verge of quarreling. The negro was saying that he had paid Mr. Swartout and didn't get any credit at the bank.

Swartout said:

"You have credit on my books."

And the negro returned:

"White man, that ain't at the bank."

When a negro says "white man" in that manner he is always angry. When Jerry inquired into it he found that the negro was referring to ten dollars which was in Mr. Swartout's contribution to the cathedral and which really never had gone to the bank.

Jerry made a note of that to bring it to the attention of Dr. Blankenship.

These two things, the Petman child's oracular utterance and the quarrelsome negro, did hitch themselves together, vaguely, it is true, when it just happened that Jerry had a chance to investigate the child's version of the matter himself. As he walked past the Petman home he saw Junior playing in the small bare yard by the side of the house. He called the little fellow up and began to question him.

At first Junior wouldn't answer at all. He said resentfully:

"You put your hand on my head."

"I'm sorry I did if you didn't like it."

"I don't like you."

"Well, now, that's the difference between us," said Jerry. "I do like you . . . heaps and heaps . . . didn't you get more words the other day out of some letters than anybody else?"

"M-m-m," assented the child.

"And did you say something about somebody had better move away from Carver's Lane?" asked Jerry cheerfully.

"Uh uh," denied Junior.

"You didn't?"

"Uh uh."

"Well . . . did—did anybody?"

"Uh huh."

"Who did?"

"Luggy."

"That's good . . . now, exactly what did Luggy say?" probed Jerry with precision.

"The white folks had better move away," quoted the child, leaving off all introductory material.

"The white folks?" repeated Jerry analytically.

"Uh huh."

"But you are one of the white folks yourself," pointed out Jerry.

"I know it."

"Well . . . 'the white folks had better move away' . . ." Jerry turned the sentence over in his thoughts. There was something odd about it . . . it was really a very queer sentence . . . in fact, it was a sentence that nobody would use except . . .

"Look here, Junior, this Luggy you play with . . . you can see him, can you?"

"Uh huh."

"Well, is he . . . is he . . . white?"

"Uh uh, he's a nigger boy."

Jerry pressed his lips together to keep from laughing and insulting his small neighbor.

"Thank you, Junior."

And he walked on, deeply amused at such a fantastic discovery . . . Junior's invisible companion and mentor was a little negro ghost . . . spirit . . . illusion . . . whatever it was. He would certainly tell Mrs. Swartout what he had found out. It would effectually spike her pagan artillery.

He broke out laughing as he walked on to the bus station.

When Jerry Catlin finished these minor adventures and was directed by the maid to Sydna's study, just as Aurelia predicted that he would be, he found Sydna and Drusilla in a painful state of indecision.

Sydna asked at once, in a troubled voice:

"Did Miltiades tell you, Jerry?"

"Tell me what, Sydna?"

"Oh . . . about Marsan . . . he told you, didn't he?"

Jerry then understood this referred to the projected operation.

"Yes . . . he told me," said Jerry in a disapproving monotone.

"I see you're against it."

"Certainly, certainly, Sydna!"

"That's right," said Drusilla, "the only operation I ever heard of when I was a girl was to place the baby safe and sound in its mother's arms."

"Well, then, it can't be," said Sydna dolefully. "If everybody's against me and anything should happen to Marsan," she gave a long sigh, "I can't think of anything else to do. . . . I could go off with Marsan . . . travel until the baby was big enough to . . . Listen to that . . . just listen to those innocent children. . . ." She was speaking of laughter from Sarah May Tergune and Marsan which came upstairs from below. "It doesn't seem possible that one of those innocent girls could even know what—what life is."

"Sydna, darling, don't torture yourself," begged Jerry.

"To think the day will soon come when Sarah May will pass Marsan by, when no more visits such as this will . . ."

"Hush, Sydna . . . don't . . . don't climb mountains. . . ."

"Well . . . it'll come," flung out Sydna in a high, quick, uneven voice, on the verge of tears.

Jerry strode across and put his arms around her.

"Honey, if you get her away in time, nobody need know it except the family and Dr. Blankenship. . . . Of course Sarah May doesn't suspect . . ."

"It's just like Marsan to tell it to her!"

"Oh, Sydna, Marsan is one of the most sensible girls. . . ."

"Well, the question is, who will go off with Marsan?" said

Sydna pathetically. "I would go, but everybody knows me almost everywhere, I've attended so many conventions . . . someone in the family will have to go with her."

Drusilla gathered that Sydna was casting her net gently in her direction and shook her white head.

"No, if anything should happen to Marsan I would never be forgiven; and I wouldn't forgive myself. I couldn't take the responsibility. Marsan is your child."

Tears came into Sydna's eyes.

"Mother, Marsan is so healthy . . . it's such a little risk."

"No . . . no . . ." said the grandmother.

Sydna wiped her eyes and looked at Jerry.

The assistant minister grew exquisitely uncomfortable. He thought of Aurelia and what a tantrum she would have if such a thing were even mentioned. If he were footloose he would gladly sacrifice himself for Sydna. The glance of her dark tearful eyes filled him with a trembling anxiety for her. He understood now why she was so anxious to have him come to this family consultation at the manor.

"The only way we could possibly do it," said Jerry, answering Sydna's silence, "would be for me and Aurelia to take Marsan. . . ."

"I don't believe Aurelia would want to do it," said Sydna.

Drusilla gave an odd smile.

"I don't believe all of us put together have thought of so sensible a plan as Marsan got up for herself."

"Why, Mamma, hers was utterly wild."

"It's wild because we're old and because we can't understand the unselfishness of young people . . . that's what sounded so wild about it . . . what that Lizzie and Porter offered to do."

At this point the discussion was interrupted by another clang at the door bell. The group in the study quieted to hear who was this newcomer. Presently they heard a man's voice saying:

"Will you please announce Mr. Petrie. I am one of Marsan's teachers. I was informed she is ill."

CHAPTER FIFTY

AT THE announcement of Mr. J. Adlee Petrie an extraordinary excitement filled both the upper and lower floors of the Vaiden manor. Sydna had talked to Miltiades about Petrie, and they were balanced in their opinion as to whether he really was Marsan's seducer or not. Now Sydna decided that if Petrie came to Marsan with a proposal of marriage, then there was nothing to think except that he had been her lover.

On the lower floor Miss Sarah May Tergune hastily prepared Marsan to receive her caller, and both girls wondered with painful anxiety whether Mr. Petrie had come as a teacher or a suitor.

Sarah May repeated over and over that she hoped he had, meaning come as a suitor, and embraced Marsan rapturously as an earnest of the fondling which she hoped Mr. Petrie would presently bestow upon her friend. Then she and Marsan came together out in the great hall to meet the caller.

Mr. Petrie was as unsure of his mission as anyone else in the manor. He felt very, very teacheresque. The sunlight falling across the deep piazza into the great hall formed exactly the sort of home which a concerned teacher would visit to inquire after the health of a pupil. Mr. Petrie decided that that must be what he was doing.

Miss Sarah May Tergune expressed her surprise to see Professor Petrie, who in turn begged Sarah May not to run off merely because he had come, but Miss Tergune was just on her way out . . . she had to be going . . . she had just started when Mr. Petrie rang the bell. And she took herself off.

Marsan stood looking at the man with a kind of shaky

questioning happiness in her heart. She was smiling faintly.

"Shall we go out on the lawn?" she asked, "or is it too chilly for you?"

The temperature was quite right for Mr. Petrie, and he followed her out a side door toward some wicker chairs on a reach of lawn. This grassy space itself was bordered by flowers, screened from the street by box and guarded by colored elms and beeches with here and there the somber polished green of a magnolia.

With the queer, habitual paradox of art, this subtly and temporarily arranged scene and color, with the sunlight slanting through the trees and falling on the old manor, even with Marsan straightening the pillows in the wicker chairs, gave Petrie an impression of endless duration. It seemed to him not only would this ambience of light and mood persist forever, but that it had always been, and no entry or departure of his could ever affect its validity. He sat down opposite the daughter of the manor and was moved to try to tell her of this queer feeling of permanence.

The girl's face warmed slightly.

"I believe I can guess why you feel like that."

"Why?"

"You've been thinking about coming here, haven't you, Mr. Petrie? ... You've wanted to come to see me ... haven't you?"

As Marsan asked this the familiar background was almost obliterated in her eyes. She saw only Mr. Petrie with his dark eyes and the thoughtful unsatisfied planes of his face and felt the queer gravitational insistence of his body.

The school teacher said that naturally he had been wanting to come for a long time, and his voice set forth frankly why he had so desired to see her and why he had not.

"Maybe that's why," said Marsan, with a helpless feeling at the childishness and inexpressiveness of her own words.

The man shook his head slowly.

"I don't think so. I have wanted to go to places before without feeling this way when I got there. I think anything beautiful is so fit, so perfect that one can't imagine any alteration of line or color, and so it seems as if it had existed so forever."

Marsan lost some of her self-consciousness in what Mr. Petrie was saying.

"It always seems to me that beautiful things look young."

"I suppose they look neither young nor old, but timeless. In human beings beauty is a striking of an average. Beautiful persons are neither tall nor short; their heads are neither large nor small, their noses short nor long. They are the result of a long selection of ancestors in which the variation from the norm in one ancestor has been offset by a counter variation in another. Beauty is a synthesis of what has proved physically efficient. That is why, they say, persons fall in love with their opposites; they instinctively grope toward a coming physical and mental perfection in their children . . . toward a coming efficiency, that is, toward beauty."

A gratification so intense that it was almost painful filled Marsan, and with it came her first real remorse for having squandered herself on Red McLaughlin.

She recalled Red's rough possession of the surface of her body and compared it unconsciously to Mr. Petrie's subtle, complete, and tantalizing possession of her being with words. She felt as if he need never touch her at all; his words and thoughts caressed her eyes and neck and breast and body with intangible caresses. It gave her a feeling of faint sweet suffocation. She wished he would never quit talking, never take his eyes off her face; that she might remain like this on and on, amid this intimate, sweetly embarrassing sensation of sitting before him thus, naked in body and mind.

He began talking of other things.

"Your father came to see me at my boarding house the other day, Marsan."

The girl opened her eyes with a touch of apprehension for something that already was past.

"Why, I didn't know that . . . I didn't know that he went to you."

"Yes, he came to me to . . . to find out something. I'm sure that's why he came, although he never did ask any question at all."

The color fell out of the girl's face.

"Why . . . should he have thought you knew?"

"I am your teacher; he must have guessed at once what he wanted to know had something to do with the school."

"Yes," said Marsan faintly, "but . . . I—I wouldn't have thought that he . . . would have gone to a third person." She sat looking at Mr. Petrie, still frightened at what she suspected must have been the mission of her father.

"Yes, he did, and, Marsan, he explained something to me that I had wondered and wondered about, something insoluble . . . until he came."

Marsan nodded her question, staring intently at him.

"It was the explanation of you," said the man in a gray voice. "I know women have lovers, some of them do. I know there isn't much to restrain them except convention and taste. I have always known that convention didn't enter into your life at all, but you always seemed to me a person of the most exquisite taste . . . of course taste is nothing but inherited feeling for convention. . . ."

Marsan felt a sinking feeling, as if her lawn chair were being lowered.

"You mean you thought I—I had terribly bad taste . . . with . . ." She left the name blank. This was one of the most dismaying suggestions that had come out of the whole affair. No matter how wealthy she was, if she didn't have taste she was lost; the more wealth she had, the higher her material position, the more hopeless was her loss. Marsan knew that, she felt it down to her trim toes.

"I simply couldn't understand it," repeated the school teacher, "until your father explained that this—this man had defended his name from insults by the mob. Of course, that would have a terrific pull for you, Marsan. I see that."

Marsan moistened her dry lips. They trembled so she had to bite them.

"You see . . . I was terribly excited . . . driving so fast in the car . . . and being stopped by the guards."

Her words painted a whirling, undefined picture before Petrie.

"And then the fact that you—you told me what you had done afterwards?" went on the man in a questioning tone, as if this too were a point to be cleared.

Mr. Petrie's eyes, looking into her own, became blurry and then were lost.

"I—I thought you loved me," she gasped, "I . . . I just the same as said that, Mr. Petrie, when . . . when I told you." At a movement of the man from his chair, the girl whispered, "Wait, Mr. Petrie . . . don't . . . don't . . . I—I'm going to have a . . . baby."

"I know it."

His voice sounded far away.

"You . . . knew it?"

"I knew it from your father's coming to see me. There could have been no other reason."

"Oh!"

"That's why I wanted so badly to come and see you. What are you going to do?"

"I . . . we don't know. . . . Mamma wants . . . I mean she doesn't want it . . . I had planned to run away with Porter and Lizzie. . . ."

"You mean your mother wants . . . to dispose of it?"

Marsan nodded, compressing her lips, then broke out suddenly.

"But I—I'm not going to have it! I won't have it taken away from me . . . the poor little tadpole sort of thing . . . not even a human being . . . groping and groping. . . . I'm its whole world, its sea and sky and land. . . . Suppose a hundred million years ago, when we were tadpoles, God had operated on the world and killed Life, and all this . . . everything . . . was a blank." She began weeping unrestrainedly. "I—I won't have it!"

Petrie was with her in her chair.

"Hush, hush, Marsan, nothing like that will happen. You and your baby are quite safe. Your mother, people of her age and generation, have a queer reverence for surfaces, Marsan, the surface of conduct, the surface of thought, the surface of life." He lifted the double life in his arms and fitted himself with her into the lawn chair. "Your assumption, when you told me what you and Red McLaughlin had done, was very, very true, Marsan, and it will always be."

CHAPTER FIFTY-ONE

Marsan vaiden's wedding to Mr. J. Adlee Petrie was a very quiet affair: the bankruptcy of the Second National Bank and the suit filed against the Colonel necessitated that. The actual wedding took place in the Vaiden home. Marsan had a girlish notion that she would like to have it in the old Lacefield manor down in the Reserve. She had heard so many tales of the old plantation life, the war, the romance of her great-uncle, A. Gray Lacefield, and her aunt, Marcia Catlin, who had been born a Vaiden, that she had longed to make her own marriage in that storied scene. She and Adlee did motor down one day, to BeShears Cross Roads and then into the Reserve. It was a flat, monotonous succession of worn fields and negro cabins. All that remained of the old manor were roofless brick walls penetrated here and there with broken holes for windows. Behind this ruin lay a small depression choked with weeds which Marsan surmised must have been the greenhouse of which she had heard Drusilla speak. Across from the ruin lay the old pasture, overgrown now with sassafras sprouts and blackberry vines. Here the Union army once encamped, and her paternal grandfather, old man Jimmie Vaiden, had come and tried to reclaim a runaway slave girl named Gracie.

The ruinous scene created in Marsan a melancholy, almost a homesick feeling, that was heightened by her own condition. Involuntarily she compared the purity, the honor, the chivalry of the old South with her own questionable estate. In other places she was less disturbed by approaching motherhood. She regretted it keenly for Adlee's sake. She wished from the bottom of her heart that she had saved every emotion she had ever felt for him. But beyond her future husband she was not greatly concerned.

Now, for such casualness of life and manners and morals, the walls of the old manor reproached her. The world that once encompassed this estate would never have forgiven such a misstep. She could not imagine her mother, Sydna, committing such an act, and Sydna, really, was not of the old school. As for her grandmother, Drusilla, it was unthinkable.

To Aurelia, Jerry Catlin's wife, the approaching wedding was a source of much pain and heartburning. She did not want Jerry to perform the ceremony; she said it would throw Jerry into too close an intimacy with Sydna.

Jerry protested that he had not been asked to perform the marriage ceremony, and Aurelia replied bitterly that that was just a getting-out place, that he knew he would be asked.

The Reverend Catlin looked at his wife in utter hopelessness and said, "Suppose I am, how could that possibly throw me into any kind of intimacy with Sydna? Somebody will have to officiate, will that person be intimate with Sydna?"

"Well . . . no-o . . . that person wouldn't."

"Then what do you mean by saying such a thing?"

Aurelia gave him a reproachful look and said:

"You understand other women without a single word, but I must explain and explain. . . ."

She was so mistreated, she wept.

To divert her mind from her wrongs, Jerry asked his wife to take him to the bus station in her car, but she sadly told him no, he would have to walk. She said it made her nervous so that it affected her piano playing to drive around in cars with persons who did not love her, and she put her music before everything.

Jerry set off on foot down Carver's Lane, inwardly amused at his wife. Her little revenge in making him walk would smooth over the wrong which she had cooked up for herself, and he expected to find her in good spirits when he came back home. As he walked along, a number of negroes with guns passed him. They were very glum black men, but he called to them with a Southern man's impulse to be cheery with the colored people and asked them where they were going.

One of the negroes mumbled out they were going rabbit hunting.

"How many men does it take to kill a rabbit?" laughed Jerry.

"Owin' to how many they is . . . an' how big they is," flung out a brown man.

Another, franker, gun bearer said:

"We's proputy holdahs in Jericho, an' 'em white men keep rollin' off our houses."

Jerry became concerned.

"Well, I hope you are not going to try to stop that with guns . . . that's legal, you know."

"Ya-as suh," nodded another negro, "but when a man is daid he kain't wuck de law on you."

"Look here, you numbskulls," reproved Jerry earnestly, "you look to me as if you were hatching up a lot of trouble for yourselves. . . . You take those guns home and put 'em up . . . who you going to shoot, the workmen who are rolling away your houses? . . . they haven't got a thing in the world to do with it. . . ."

At this point Jerry was interrupted by the sound of a car coming up behind him. It was Aurelia. She stopped her car and held a newspaper toward him, calling out in shocked and sympathetic tones:

"Jerry, honey, look what she's done, look!"

She rattled her paper indignantly at her husband.

Jerry went to her with concern.

"What is it, darling? What's happened?"

"That heartless aunt of yours . . . she's the most outrageous person." She pointed out an article in the *Florence Index*. It was an announcement of the approaching marriage of Miss Marsan Vaiden and Mr. J. Adlee Petrie; she was a popular young society bud, he held an executive position with the public school system (it sounded something like an auditorship or a superintendency in the paper), and the *Index* wished, etc., etc.

"I don't see anything wrong about that," said Jerry; "the notice is only a column and a half long, but they made it short because they wanted to keep it as quiet as possible."

"That isn't what I'm talking about . . . look what it says . . . . Dr. Blankenship officiating . . . he's the one to say the ceremony! Oh, Jerry darling, this is a cut at you because you married me!"

"No, no, it isn't," comforted Jerry, with an odd feeling that Dr. Blankenship should perform Marsan's marriage ceremony.

Aurelia drew Jerry's face down under her neck,

"Oh, my darling, I'd a thousand times rather she'd insulted me than you. You love her, I know you do, and for her to treat you so cruelly. That's all right, sweetheart, you have my love! And I won't go to their wedding . . . I'll show them they can't trample on my husband. . . ."

"But listen, darling, don't do that . . . go over and help with the decorations, honey . . . return good for evil . . . that would be a lovely gesture on your part."

"Help that cat! Huh, I'll never do it."

"Well, you will at least go to the wedding?"

"I don't think much I will. . . . Well, good-bye, I'm going back home . . . I just drove up here to show you this paper."

Jerry knew very well that in her sympathy for him about the ceremony she had come to drive him over to Florence and make up to his wounded feelings that much, but she had become miffed again, and he watched her turn around and drive back home.

When Jerry reached the Second National Bank he was surprised to find it had reopened and that there were half a dozen men in the lobby waiting to see his uncle. Miss Katie, however, admitted Jerry at once to the president's office. To Jerry's astonishment, he found Miltiades closeted with Sandusky, the lawyer. The two had three large safe deposit

boxes full of legal-looking papers which Sandusky was read-
ing and listing.

When Jerry inquired what was being done, the Colonel
told him they were mortgages whose payments were in de-
fault and which he was having Sandusky foreclose.

"But, look here, until your suit is settled, do you think it
is a good time to foreclose your mortgages, Uncle Milt?"

Sandusky looked around with a dry smile on his lined and
wizened face.

"Well, if here isn't old man Jerry . . . advising me what
to do in a lawsuit!"

Jerry was taken aback on several counts, one of which was
Sandusky's evident age. Sandusky was old. He looked almost
as old as the Colonel, and Jerry and Sandusky had gone to
school together. Therefore, he, Jerry, must be getting old.
Another count was that Sandusky always had talked to him,
Jerry, as if he, Jerry, were a fool, and he was doing so now.
It was discomforting to Jerry that Sandusky had not seen fit
to change his opinion.

However, Sandusky now made amends for his rudeness
by saying:

"Look in the paper there, and you'll see all that has blown
over."

He indicated another copy of the same *Florence Index*
that Aurelia had shown him. Jerry looked at the headlines
and saw that his uncle had quashed the proceedings brought
against him by the depositors in the bank. The judgment of
the chancellor read that Miltiades Vaiden had, as a private
citizen, sold his real property to speculators. The Second
National Bank had furnished the money to these speculators
each time against the advice, judgment, and vote of Miltiades
Vaiden, as director of the bank. Thereupon, Miltiades
Vaiden, as a private citizen, had taken said money and de-
posited it in a Louisville bank to his private account, be-
cause he felt the Second National Bank was no longer firm
and safe. The contention of the plaintiffs that this with-
drawal was what had made the Second National weak and

unsafe was dismissed by the chancellor as irrelevant, as Miltiades Vaiden, as a private citizen, had a right to place his money in whatever bank he desired.

The court therefore held the respondent guiltless and charged the costs of the suit to the complainants.

The *Index* required five columns of unleaded type to say this, and Jerry sat by the window until he had read every word of it.

As he went over the account an irrepressible doubt made the assistant minister wonder how closely the chancellor's opinion followed the inner purpose of his uncle in this whole affair. He wondered if the Colonel had not known all the time that his dry epigrammatic dissuasion would not urge the fortune hunters to a blinder purchasing than ever. He wondered if, had his uncle sincerely wished to stop his own bank from making its short-sighted investments, he could not have done so? These were questions, futile to ask and impossible to answer. He laid the paper aside.

Sandusky had gone, and another man had taken his place in his uncle's "visitor's chair."

From snatches of their conversation Jerry gathered that this second man was an architect who was explaining to Miltiades some blueprints for the building of a church.

Jerry came out of his absorption to ask in astonishment if the Colonel were interested in building another church.

The old banker laughed and said dryly:

"No, this is the same cathedral, Jerry, but I thought, since I am paying for it, I might have exactly what I want."

Then he introduced to Jerry a Mr. Ollendorfer, a member of the firm, Speight, Canary and Ollendorfer, of Birmingham.

". . . and my nephew here is assistant minister in the cathedral, Mr. Ollendorfer," concluded the Colonel.

"Then you are interested in this too," said the architect, moving the blueprints so Jerry could see them.

"What are you doing to it?" asked Jerry curiously.

"Restoring it to its original classical style and incorporating as much of the present work as possible," explained

Ollendorfer. "It will be a basilica in pure Greek patristic mode."

This term suggested to Jerry a low heavy dome and a colonnade fronting heavy walls.

. "Will you be able to use much of what is completed?"

"Almost everything . . . I was just going over the details with your uncle."

"Does the work extant fall into the Greek style?"

"Quite closely. What we have will produce a few of those charming variations which are analogous to accidentals in music . . . you know music, Dr. Catlin?"

"Very well," said Jerry, perceiving Ollendorfer was at least a good salesman, if not an architect.

Ollendorfer was the last man Miltiades would see, and soon afterwards he started to the manor with Jerry.

"I have been dictating some letters," he began, "trying to get a place for young Petrie in the research department of some laboratory . . . what do they do in such a place, Jerry . . . invent things?"

"No, they try to find out the fundamental facts on which other men invent things."

Miltiades frowned.

"What does the research man get out of it?"

"Why, nothing, except he just finds out these facts."

"Does he . . . patent 'em?"

"No, he can't patent anything, he just finds it out."

"Then he gives it away?"

"It amounts to that. If I discover that wood will float and tell you about it, there is nothing to prevent your building a boat."

The old Colonel shook his head.

"Imagine . . . imagine Marsan fancying a man like that . . . wants to give away his work."

"There are men like that," smiled Jerry, "you may have heard of them, Helmholtz, Cuvier, Pasteur, Faraday. . . ."

"M—m . . . yes," said the Colonel, not impressed with this compliment Jerry was paying the school teacher. "I knew

Petrie had a damn poor business head on him. He came to me once wanting me to advise him to buy a lot from old man Bill Bradley at some outrageous figure, I forget what, way up in the thousands. He was going to buy it, but I persuaded him out of it. Well, during the crash, old man Bill offered Petrie this same lot for another outrageous price, three or four hundred dollars . . . too little this time. Old man Bill said Petrie gave him the glassy stare and said he wasn't in the market at any figure. I remember how I laughed over it when Bill first told me that. It was so damned typical. I didn't know then that Petrie was going to be my son-in-law. . . ." The Colonel drew out his case and offered Jerry a cigar. "Well, I hope I can arrange things so Mr. Petrie can give his work away . . . apparently he can't do it for himself."

The Colonel evidently was badly hurt at Marsan's choice of a husband. He walked on slowly, for he had chosen this mode of going home.

"Jerry," he began again, "you're going to the General Conference at Wetumpka, aren't you?"

"Yes, I am. It will be around the first of next month."

"I've been talking things over with Dr. Blankenship . . . you know I'm finishing the cathedral myself in my own way . . . Blankenship agreed to that."

"I'm glad he did."

"Oh, he didn't want to, but he did."

"All of his other financial sources have dried up," observed Jerry, unnecessarily, perhaps.

"Yes, and I told Dr. Blankenship frankly that I thought a church, even a modern church, ought to resemble a church more and everything else less."

Jerry licked a smile off his lips.

"That must have pleased him."

"I also told him, Jerry, at Wetumpka . . . now I want you to get this . . . I told him at Wetumpka, you were to get at least half the credit for getting the cathedral started at all . . . for that's a fact, Jerry, if it hadn't been for you I never would have gone into the proposition."

Jerry was wonderstruck.

"I . . . get credit for . . . for building it!"

"And I'll tell you why," said the Colonel: "I'm having half of it put to your credit because I believe it'll do you good. It'll forward you in your work. Now, you may not believe it, Jerry; it may sound incredible to you, but there has been a suspicion latent in my mind for many, many years that the Methodist preacher who turns in the biggest budget to the Methodist General Conference gets the fattest jobs . . . that's why."

"I can't believe it," cried Jerry.

"I'm sure you don't, I told you it was incredible."

Both men laughed: Jerry self-consciously, the old Colonel dryly.

"Joking aside, I appreciate this, Uncle Milt, more than I can say . . . and I really didn't have a thing in the world to do with the cathedral . . . I mean I, actively, as a preacher, against I, passively, as your nephew."

"Well, I hope you won't feel it necessary to explain that to the presiding Bishop and his board of elders. Blankenship is not going to. You see if I drop this thing his entire work for the last four years here in Florence will tot up to exactly nothing at all, and half of anything is more than all of nothing, Jerry. It took me about two hours to explain that to Blankenship . . . I hope you can see it at once."

Jerry was really disturbed.

"Look here, Uncle Milt, I . . . I wouldn't want to take credit that didn't really belong to me. . . ."

"Listen," interrupted the old man, "a man deserves what he gets if he can use it . . . that's the only test there is . . . not how you get a thing, it's what you do with it. . . . You know, Jerry, when we come to die, I believe even God will see that point."

As the Colonel was saying this the two came into sight of the construction work on the new cathedral. To Jerry's blank surprise it swarmed with workmen, negro workmen. There were negroes everywhere, making up mortar, rolling wheelbarrows, hammering scaffolding, laying stones. Their color lent a touch of the picturesque to the white marble edifice on which they toiled.

Two or three white men were standing looking at the construction of the church. One of them stepped forward and touched his hat to the banker.

"Colonel Vaiden, we have been stationed here by the union to protest against this all-nigger labor on the church. We spoke to Dr. Blankenship, and he said see you."

Miltiades looked at the workman.

"That's right, I'm running this now."

"Well, these niggers are scabs, they've never joined our union."

"They work cheaper than the union men, don't they?"

"Certainly they do."

"Do you know why?"

"They want the work."

"Oh no . . . they are making a contribution to the church."

The walking delegate appeared a little taken aback, but after a moment suggested:

"Suppose you pay them regular union wages and let them make their donations in cash."

"My boy," said the Colonel, "when I was your age, I went out with a lot of other men into the woods, cut down trees, hewed them, and helped build the old Gravelly Springs Baptist Church. If somebody had been forced to pay us money and let us pay it back there wouldn't have been any church because there wasn't any money. That's our position today, Florence is broke."

"Well," said the delegate, "turn off three fourths of these niggers and put in white men at the same wages."

Miltiades looked at the fellow oddly.

"Young man, listen, niggers earned every penny of my fortune, they are going to lay every marble block in my tomb."

CHAPTER FIFTY-TWO

W<small>HEN</small> the wedding was over and Marsan was gone North on her bridal tour, Sydna lingered in the manor for two or three days, when she received a telegram from her genealogical expert and was compelled to go to Washington.

The telegram, which consisted of five hundred and thirty-one words, day rate, collect, explained that the expert had unearthed a new stirps connected with the Lacefield family which led directly back to Light Horse Harry Lee. Sydna immediately prepared herself for a month or two's sojourn in the nation's capital and set forth to see about it.

Wilson motored her to Nashville in order that she might not be aroused in Florence at an inconvenient hour of the night to catch the Washington sleeper. She stopped at the bank and told Miltiades and Jerry good-bye (which was out of her way, because she had to turn around and pass the manor again, going North to Nashville). She took with her a copy of that section of her genealogy which she hoped to link to that of Light Horse Harry Lee, six packages of cigarettes which she smoked in private for the benefit of her figure, and some novels to read on the train.

Jerry had had no idea how lonely Florence would be without Sydna and Marsan. Owing to the dislike and jealousy of Aurelia, Jerry had not seen either of them very often, but the mere knowledge that they were at home in the manor, accessible to him, had given him a comfort of which he had been unaware.

Their going loosened his tie to Florence and to the cathedral. In fact, he had only one more real duty to perform under Dr. Blankenship: that was to go to Waterloo and try to cement the schism made in the Methodist Church in that village by the new and absurd sect of the Drownders.

He chose the day after Sydna left town for this duty. It promised him something else to think about besides Sydna.

He borrowed his uncle Miltiades' small car for the Waterloo trip, and before he went away the old man asked Jerry if he and Aurelia would not come and stay at the manor until Sydna returned.

"Drusilla doesn't like it there alone," explained the old man; "she says the house never did look like a home since I fixed it up; she says it looks more like a museum or the capitol of something or other, and for me to get you and Aurelia to come over and help her keep it inhabited."

Jerry said he would speak to Aurelia and put it before her in the best light.

"All right, Jerry, you do that," nodded the Colonel, seeing that Jerry himself had no idea which way the cat would jump when he spoke to Aurelia, and feeling disappointed that a scion of the Vaiden blood was not the head of his own family.

When the assistant minister reached Waterloo he found that the new sect of the Drownders had spread like a grass fire not only through the membership of the Methodist Church, but through the Presbyterian and Baptist as well.

Waterloo was undergoing one of those characteristic religious orgies of the South. The village stores remained closed part of each morning and afternoon to give time for the meetings unhampered by business. Both the public grade schools and High Schools had been practically discontinued, and the young folks had been organized into a Drownder chorus who practised religious songs most of the time.

Family feuds in Waterloo of years' standing were being settled not only amicably but lovingly; lifelong enemies shook hands and embraced every morning and night amid religious raptures.

Willie Rutledge of Decatur, Alabama, was the Drownder preacher. He had two men and a woman to assist him and lead the songs. One of the men played a guitar.

The Drownders took up no collections.

When Jerry arrived in Waterloo, he found the local Methodist, Baptist, and Presbyterian ministers in a very low state. They were greatly heartened by the Reverend Catlin's appearance in Waterloo. The fact that he was a preacher from the new quarter-of-a-millon-dollar church that was going up in Florence caused them to attribute to Jerry a power of persuasion and debate which perhaps he did not possess.

Willie Rutledge, the Drownder preacher, had been holding his morning meetings in the Presbyterian Church and his evening meetings in the Methodist Church, to show, he said, that he was in fellowship and brotherly love with all denominations.

This had all been going very well until Jerry arrived. He collected the three other ministers, the stewards, and the deacons of the established churches, and planned what to do about Willie Rutledge and the Drownders. His first suggestion was that the three churches should lock their doors. This was done at noon. That evening a great crowd of Methodists, Presbyterians, and Baptists assembled at the door of the Methodist Church and could not get inside. Jerry and the stewards held the keys and kept out a congregation of three or four hundred Methodist laymen.

Rutledge got up on the steps of the church and asked why his brothers and sisters were not permitted to enter the house of their Father.

Rutledge was oddly changed from the man Jerry had helped resuscitate on the bank of Shoal Creek. His face was gentler and more serious; his eyes were larger and had the odd look of seeing distant things.

The ministers in charge had to answer Rutledge as to why he was not allowed to enter the church. The local Methodist minister got up on the steps and took the rather peevish stand that he and his stewards felt that guitar music had no place in religious worship and that therefore they had closed the doors of the church against the Drownders.

Rutledge immediately agreed to use the reed organ in the church if anyone in the crowd would play it, or he would dispense with music altogether.

The local minister then said he would ask the Reverend Jerry Catlin of All Souls Cathedral in Florence, Alabama, to speak in his stead.

"The Reverend Catlin," added the minister, "is a nephew of Colonel Miltiades Vaiden, who is building the new marble cathedral entirely out of his own private funds. We would therefore do well, brothers and sisters, to pay heed to a minister from such a family."

With an odd distant impression of his boyhood dreams and religious air castles, Jerry arose on the church steps and began his address.

He said that he had helped resuscitate Brother Rutledge when the latter was almost drowned in Shoal Creek. At the time, Jerry said, Rutledge had been in a posse trying to lynch six negroes.

"Now, brothers and sisters in the church of God," proceeded Jerry, "I am by no means relating these facts to cast any reflections on Brother Rutledge's character, but to show you that at the moment when he was almost drowned he was laboring under the most intense excitement.

"That excitement caused him, as he was losing consciousness in the water, to imagine wild and miraculous things. He says he felt himself fly up into the sky through a hole in the water. Brothers, if there had been a hole in the water he need not have drowned at all. He could have breathed through it. The fact that he was almost drowned shows the water had no hole in it. Besides, every sensible person knows water doesn't have holes in it. If Brother Rutledge saw one at all, it was an imaginary hole; if he floated up in the air and saw angels, they were imaginary angels.

"But further than that, Brothers and Sisters, we don't need miracles in these modern times. Christ revealed himself once and for all over nineteen hundred years ago. We have the New Testament as the foundation and nourishment of our faith. Paul himself says so.

"In whom would you pin your faith, brothers and sisters, if you were approaching death, the apostle Paul, or Brother Rutledge? Could you possibly doubt the apostle Paul who, on the road to Damascus, saw a light around about his head and heard a voice saying, 'Saul! Saul! Why persecutest thou me?' Oh, friends, brothers, that question from God reverberates down the centuries; it rings in our ears today. Let us bend our hearts to the testimony God gives us in His book.

"As a closing thought, let me suggest to you that the Bible says, Six days shalt thou labor and on the seventh thou shalt rest. But Brother Rutledge closes the stores, stops the grist mills, draws the children from their school and the farmer from his crops . . ."

Here Rutledge himself interposed to ask what Jerry thought of the quotation, "Take no heed of tomorrow."

"People may have lived that way nineteen hundred years ago," said Jerry, "but people have too many expenses nowadays for such a motto as that. This is a practical world, and we have to meet it in a practical way. And since God made this world which we all find so very practical, it seems to me very reasonable indeed to assume that God means us to meet life in a calm, cool, practical way, which does not include shouting, playing truant from school, neglecting business and profitable industry.

"That is why we do not turn the key to this building over to Mr. Rutledge. I hope the gentleman has had his answer. . . . And now may the blessing of God and the communion and fellowship of the Holy Ghost rest and abide with you all, Amen."

The benediction was what really broke up the Drownder meeting. It had a subtle disruptive quality based on the habits of many generations of Methodists.

Rutledge's musician thumped his guitar, his man and woman singer wailed, "Come to Jesus, He will save you," but it was for nothing.

Rutledge himself called out to the people that he had been drowned under water and his soul had risen up in the sky, but it was to no avail. Jerry had questioned his vision, had tagged it imaginary, and under the assistant minister's skepticism it had melted into nothing.

The crowd gradually dispersed. The fire at which they had gathered to warm themselves in the chill religious autumn had been put out, and they wandered away in all directions through the night.

CHAPTER FIFTY-THREE

THE people of Waterloo were neither downcast nor resentful over the fiasco of the Drownders. They felt a little ironic at themselves, a little sheepish at having been cozened once again by religious mountebanks. They should have known better than to follow a prophet with a guitar. The warmth, the radiance, the brotherhood which for a moment had suffused their world faded away and left them once more to the bickerings, the isolation, the chill which were so natural that the Christian communicants of Waterloo did not even observe their return.

On the following morning, as Jerry returned from Waterloo to Florence, he witnessed a queer ceremony. Willie Rutledge and his three disciples, the two men and the woman, were seated by the roadside; they had taken off their shoes and were shaking and blowing them. Not until Jerry had motored a mile or two further did it occur to him that the Drownder evangels were following literally the injunction to the apostles to shake from their feet the dust of villages that would not receive them. It was an odd and somehow a pathetic proof of their sincerity, and also, of course, of their ignorance and illiteracy. They were as crude as those first fishermen must have been who wandered after a carpenter nineteen centuries before.

When Jerry reached Florence and returned the motor to his uncle he found the Second National Bank in a subdued uproar; several merchants, a dozen realtors, a number of laboring men, clerks, small shopkeepers, a baker, two cobblers were in the Colonel's reception room and were asking through Miss Katie to be admitted as a delegation.

Jerry waited with the crowd and heard them asking one

another whether the Colonel would do it or not, and saying that the Colonel was a very rich man with more money than he could spend in a dozen lifetimes.

What their idea was, Jerry did not find out until they all went in together. Then the spokesman explained that they were the complainants in the suit instituted against Miltiades, and that almost every man in the room had been a witness in the Colonel's behalf. All of them had testified that the Colonel had earnestly advised them against buying Florence real estate when its price was so high; nevertheless, they had bought it. This evidence, taken with the minutes of the board meetings, had cleared the Colonel of all unethical intent. The group admitted that they themselves now saw the Colonel's innocence, and they came apologetically as brother man to brother man and asked the Colonel to keep all the money that he had collected from them and to resume the property, which he had reclaimed through foreclosure proceedings, but not to ruin them utterly by levying on their homes and their businesses for the still outstanding balance on their debts.

The Colonel was sorry for them, but he was unable to get their business point of view.

"These debts are mine," he explained, "and enough property of yours to satisfy them really belongs to me. I don't see how you gentlemen can ask me to make you a present of seventy-six thousand dollars. If the property had advanced and you had made that much money, I would not have expected you gentlemen to refund me the money I lost through poor business judgment."

"But we are ruined," said one of the men plaintively.

"I would be ruined too if I attempted to make good the losses of every unfortunate investor in Florence."

A horsy-looking man said when a gambling house broke its patrons it gave them a stake and let them go.

The Colonel was amazed that anyone should compare the most conventional of American businesses with a gambling house.

When the delegation had departed, the old banker turned
to his nephew and shook his head.

"The trouble with American business, Jerry, is that it is
founded on optimism. All the channels of American publicity
inculcate optimism. Papers print it; preachers proclaim it;
statesmen advocate it; poets rhyme it; Lions, Rotarians,
Kiwanians say grace over their luncheons and ask God in
His benevolence to renew their stock of optimism. That is
to say, they ask the paraclete to descend upon them and in-
spire them with the holy American faith that the ratio of
gold to other commodities is higher than it actually is . . .
and He does it . . . over and over."

Jerry felt a dubious admiration for his solitary old uncle.
He got on much better with him now than he did when he
was a boy. He understood him better, much better than
formerly.

The Colonel began talking about Marsan. She had tele-
graphed him that she and Adlee had flown from Atlanta to
Chicago and that they were now very air-minded and happy.

"That girl wouldn't be afraid to tackle anything," ex-
claimed the Colonel proudly; then, after a moment, he asked
Jerry what was the mortality rate in air travel.

"You and Aurelia . . . you are coming over to stay with
me and Drusilla, aren't you, Jerry?"

Jerry said Aurelia had it under consideration.

"Tell her we have rooms to let. Tell her she can get lost
in them if it's privacy she's after."

Jerry had seldom seen his uncle in so jolly a mood. As
he went on with his dignified waggery, his desk telephone
rang. The old banker picked it up smiling, listened a few
moments, then turned to Jerry.

"Bodine wants to see me. He'll hint for you to get out
of the office. Don't you do it, just stay where you are."

The Colonel opened a drawer and laid an automatic pistol
out on his desk.

Jerry straightened.

"You're not expecting trouble with him?"

"Not now."

A few seconds later the thick-bodied organizer entered the private office and sure enough did ask if he could have a private conversation with the Colonel.

The old banker explained politely that he and Jerry were in conference about a family matter and he had admitted Bodine for a few minutes not to keep him waiting all afternoon. The Colonel's whole concern was clearly for Bodine. The automatic he probably used around the office as a paper weight.

Bodine drew a long breath.

"Well, Colonel Vaiden, you know I invested some money in the Cypress Creek property."

"Oh, you did go ahead and buy it against my advice?"

"Yes," nodded Bodine dryly, "and I did it with the Association's money."

The Colonel leaned forward, perturbed.

"You don't mean to say you probably exceeded the authority . . ."

"No, no, that's not what I mean at all," assured Bodine in a hard voice. "I am the officer designated to invest the Association surplus, I have the authority all right."

"I am relieved," said the Colonel.

"What I came to see you about is the Cypress Creek property. The Association has already paid you more money than the property is worth, Colonel."

"You mean more than the property is now worth?"

"Yes."

"You haven't paid me as much as it will be worth ten years from now."

"Yes, but we are trading now," said Bodine.

"I'm not, I traded yesterday," replied the Colonel crisply.

"The Association," said Bodine, choosing his words carefully, "has paid you what the property is worth *now*, and it would greatly appreciate it if you would cancel that mortgage on it that you are trying to foreclose."

"Wouldn't that be unprecedented?" inquired the Colonel.

"It probably would be," agreed Bodine with a faint smile.

"And quite outside the directions of the law?"

"I have heard men say that is where the Association begins its operations, Colonel," laughed Bodine. "Now, laying all joking aside, won't you open up your heart and let us off with those last payments? Don't kick an association, or a sleeping dog, when it's down, Colonel."

"Laying all joking aside, I certainly mean to foreclose the mortgage on the Cypress Creek property, Mr. Bodine."

Bodine stood looking at the old banker for a space of ten or fifteen seconds.

"Well . . . that's what I came here to ask you to do. . . . Good-bye, Colonel."

And he turned and walked out.

CHAPTER FIFTY-FOUR

BODINE'S remarks disturbed Jerry. He wanted his uncle to
take precautions against the organizer, but Miltiades pooh-
poohed the idea of danger. He said blow-hards never did
anything. But if the Colonel had wanted to make some de-
fense against Bodine, Jerry did not see exactly what it would
be.

Half an hour later the assistant minister took a bus to the
Swartout home in Sheffield, and when he arrived he told
Aurelia of his uncle's invitation to the manor.

Aurelia began to make objections when Jerry explained to
her his uneasiness about his uncle. His fears finally infected
Aurelia, and she began to make ready to go to Florence for a
prolonged stay. As she got her things together, old Mrs.
Swartout came in and began the latest doings of Junior
Petman. Jerry began laughing.

"Before you go any further with Junior Petman, I'd like
to ask, do you know who Luggy is?"

"Why, no more than he is just Luggy," said the old
woman.

"He's a negro," said Jerry and began laughing again.

The old woman stared at him blankly.

"A nigger!"

"Isn't it the most ridiculous thing you ever heard of?"

"How do you know Luggy's a nigger?"

"Was talking to Junior and just happened to catch on."

Old Mrs. Swartout thought a moment.

"Maybe you can see black ghosts in the daytime and white
ghosts at night?"

"There you are, that's a good working hypothesis," de-
clared Jerry, amused again.

343

When Jerry finally got Aurelia over to Florence and domiciled in the manor, she was delighted. She had really never before been in the Vaiden residence. When she looked through the windows of the rooms to which Drusilla assigned them she saw the manor park in its autumn tints and cried out excitedly:

"Oh, Jerry . . . where's the piano? I wonder, would they bring the piano in here?"

"I'll take you to one," said Jerry, "you are the more easily moved."

They found an instrument, and Aurelia twirled the stool to the proper height. She looked intently into the color outside.

"That's Debussy," she declared. "'The Afternoon of a Faun.'" And she began playing the exotic unpredictable dissonances of the Frenchman.

As the music filled the long silent manor, the colored maid came and listened just outside the music-room door. Drusilla presently appeared. She nodded at Jerry and pointed at Aurelia to indicate how lucky he was to win such a wife. Jerry nodded back, acknowledging the fortunate chance of his marriage and his gratefulness for it. In Drusilla's mind was a memory of Jerry lying in bed day and night for over a week in his aunt Rose's boarding house just after Sydna had married Miltiades, and how Jerry's uncle Augustus had fussed over Jerry's malingering, not recognizing heartbreak as a masculine malady. It was sweet to know now that Jerry had married such a musician as Aurelia.

Miltiades came up beside Drusilla. After a space he whispered:

"Does she ever play a tune?"

"Real musicians like that never play tunes," said Drusilla. The old Colonel seemed excited.

"I have a telegram from Marsan."

"What's in it?"

"Come to the living room, I'll read it to you."

Drusilla turned from the door and followed Miltiades to

the living room. Miltiades led the way to an armchair and placed Drusilla before the fire. As he pulled up a seat for himself he drew out the telegram with shaky deliberation.

"All right, it's from Baltimore . . . read it for yourself."

The white-haired, dark-eyed old lady took it. She read without glasses:

MILTIADES VAIDEN PETRIE HAS JUST CALLED ON US IN JOHNS HOPKINS. HIS HEALTH SEEMS EXCELLENT. THE THREE OF US ARE NOW AT THE HOME OF MR. ATKINS, WHO DID YOUR LANDSCAPE.

MARSAN AND ADLEE.

The white-haired Drusilla stared at Miltiades with wide eyes.

"Milt! Just think of that! And it's named Miltiades!"

"Petrie . . . there's a Petrie onto it," said the Colonel.

"And a very fortunate thing it is, too," put in Drusilla.

"Yes . . . yes . . ." admitted the banker; after a moment he added, "I'll venture Sydna's there . . . or on her way there."

"Oh, of course, of course."

"And you know," said Drusilla, "it won't make a bit of difference to either of those women in no time."

"Yes, I understand they are very ingratiating," admitted the Colonel.

"You know, Milt, there is a lot of fuss made over a lot of things that is perhaps unnecessary. . . . I don't believe you are entirely happy, Milt?"

The Colonel walked over and poked the fire.

"No-o . . . I'm not."

The old lady pointed a finger at him.

"Now, look here, babies are babies; if conception is a sin, deliverance is a virtue; the fact that Marsan was married afterward is a detail. . . ."

The Colonel frowned.

"That's what I really object to."

"The . . . what . . . marriage after?"

"Yes . . . yes," declared the Colonel. "By the Eternal, Drusilla, if Marsan hadn't married, there would have been another Miltiades Vaiden in the world. There would have been another new branch starting out with the Vaiden name. . . ."

"Miltiades Vaiden!" cried the old lady, horrified, "you didn't want her to have the child before she married!"

"What difference would it have made?"

"All the difference in the world . . . convention . . . this is a lot closer to convention than . . . than the other way around."

"Yes, but look what it is . . . a Petrie!"

"What earthly difference does that make?" ejaculated Drusilla.

"Everything," said the Colonel. "That would have been as near as Marsan could have come to being a son to me."

In the midst of this unconventional and purely family discussion, Wilson knocked at the door. He told the Colonel that a lot of poor white trash had been bothering the niggers who were working on his church.

"Are they working this late?" asked Miltiades surprised.

"Was when I left," said Wilson; "'at's one thing the po' johns was fussing about."

"What made them keep on so long?"

"Well, suh, a lot of 'em was niggahs off'n yo' plantations, Col'l Milt, an' they figgahed you'd speck dem to wuck tull sundown jess same as old times."

The old banker got his hat, laughing.

"I'll go down and tell 'em there's a difference between town and country, that the city has an effeminating influence. . . ."

"Milt, I wouldn't do it," advised Drusilla.

"Maybe I can straighten 'em out with the union . . . it doesn't sound difficult, to stop negroes from working."

"It's too close to supper."

"Don't put in the biscuits till you see me coming back," suggested the Colonel.

The biscuits, however, must not have been what disturbed Drusilla. After the Colonel had gone, she went up to Jerry's room again and asked him to follow his uncle and see that he took no part in any quarrel between the negro workmen and the white union pickets.

She found Jerry at work and by questioning learned that he was making out a report which he had to deliver to the Conference in Wetumpka.

It seemed somehow droll to Drusilla to see a minister writing out his reports like a traveling salesman. It reminded her of Slim Bivins, who years before had been an ardent suitor of Sydna's.

"How much have you got to write, Jerry?" she asked from the door of his room.

"What can I do for you?" he inquired beginning to push away his papers.

"No, tell me what you've got to do first."

"Well, I send in a report on the Sunday schools, the Woman's Missionary Society, the Help for the Poor fund, home missionary and foreign missionary collections, church training work, money subscribed for hospitals, Kingdom Extension work, number of church papers sold . . . why do you want to know?"

Drusilla went to the window and sat in the window seat.

"I just wanted to know what sort of reports a real nice minister would make."

From where she sat she could see Miltiades walking down Pine Street; he moved with the ratchety quickness of an excellently preserved old man. He passed on out of sight in the direction of the cathedral.

Colonel Vaiden himself walked along Pine Street thinking, of course, of Marsan and her baby. He was glad she was at the home of Mr. Atkins, the landscape gardener who had arranged his lawn. That fact had a comfort to it. Mr. Atkins himself no doubt had a beautiful park to cheer the eyes of the young mother.

He hoped Petrie did not feel too bad about everything.

Petrie, he knew, eventually would possess everything that he possessed. He hoped the scientist would not be so foolish as to lose it completely. There really ought to be in America the English law permitting entail . . . to build up an estate like his own and then be forced to allow the first nincompoop, like Petrie, to scatter it to the winds, utterly to dissipate the Vaiden prestige! Well, that was what the marble cathedral, the housing of his tomb, would to some extent prevent. When Marsan was gone, when her baby was gone, when the children of that baby were vanished from the world, this white columned building would preserve his name and dignity.

By this time he had reached the new church. He stopped and looked at it. The white half-raised building was deserted. The negro workmen had been persuaded, perhaps, to quit before sundown.

The Colonel moved slowly among the pillars with the pensive satisfaction the building always brought. He did not know it, but the cathedral was all of heaven that Colonel Vaiden divined; lying in state in these white column-fronted walls; lying motionless in this white marble prayer.

Some of that coming peace entered the old man's heart. In years to come, this tomb would tell the passer-by that Colonel Miltiades Vaiden had lived.

A small shabbily dressed countryman came up the leaf-strewn sidewalk carrying a little bundle in his hands. He walked oddly, not fast, indeed rather slowly, but with a faint jerkiness of gait, as if there were something wrong with his legs. He was passing the church, scanning intently the park-lined street. The Colonel turned to watch him, and the slight movement caught the rustic's attention. He whirled about as if the old man had touched him. He called:

"Good-evenin', good-evenin', could you tell me where Colonel Vaiden lives?"

"Right on up the street. . . ."

"Why, that's you yourse'f, ain't it, Colonel?"

"That's right," said the Colonel.

"Now, I vence you don't know me?" called the rustic in backwoods style.

"No-o . . . I'm afraid I don't. . . ."

"Eph Cady."

The old banker repeated the name, still not recalling who the man was.

"My pap, Alex Cady, was a share cropper on one of yore farms down in the Reserve a long time ago."

"Oh, yes, I remember, but I didn't know Alex had a son . . . he had a daughter Mamie. . . ."

Cady gave a laugh that pulled the wrinkles of his face in a queer way.

"Yes, an' I allow, too, you remember of puttin' Pap in jail because he took it into his head to burn up his own waggin 'stid o' turnin' it over to you an' Shurf Mayhew?"

The rustic took something from the package, put it in his mouth, drew a match across the seat of his trousers, and lighted it. It began sparkling in an odd manner for a cigar.

"Why, yes, I remember that," recalled the Colonel soberly, "but that wagon really belonged to me, Mr. Cady; I traded your father eleven dollars and a dog for it."

"When you say you owned it," said Cady, "you're a god-damned yellow old liar . . . an' you can take that for puttin' Pap in . . ." He threw the thing he had taken from his mouth.

The Colonel started running stiffly toward the church, away from the missile. He had made five or six steps and was passing a column when a fountain of fire filled the half-built porch. When the flash winked out of the air the Colonel found himself on his back. He saw a column shattered, the bottom blocks knocked out. The shaft with its Corinthian capital swayed toward him. It swung over with curious deliberation. It was coming down right over him. It seemed to grow larger, it widened, it was vast. It seemed to the Colonel that it struck the tessellated pavement where his legs and hips were.

Of the explosion, of the smash of the capital through his body, the old banker neither heard nor felt anything. He saw the capital lying where he had been for perhaps a second, or it may have been less time than that.

At the manor, Drusilla Crowninshield, sitting in the window, heard the explosion. She screamed out:

"Jerry! Jerry! Something terrible has happened to Miltiades!"

CHAPTER FIFTY-FIVE

Wʜɪʟᴇ the funeral awaited the return of Sydna and Marsan, the body of Colonel Miltiades Vaiden lay in state in the manor.

At all hours during these two days little groups or single visitors came and went. Among them were negroes to stand with poor hats in black hands to look at the still aristocratic face of the Colonel. He lay on his bier, banked in flowers, with a faded and brittle flag spread over his crushed body.

Mary, the colored maid, would explain to each visitor, be he high or humble:

"Them's the bank's flowers; them's the Rotary flowers; them's the church's flowers; Mr. Knoblett sent that flag out of his museum in Sheffiel'."

An effort was made to notify the Vaiden relatives in Arkansas and Louisiana, but neither Jerry nor Drusilla knew their addresses. Miss Katie, at the bank, made a long search through the Colonel's correspondence, but for five years he had received no communication from either Sylvester or Lycurgus. A notice was telegraphed to the Memphis and New Orleans papers directed to Lycurgus or Sylvester Vaiden, notifying them that the body of their brother, Colonel Miltiades Vaiden, was to be buried in the Florence cemetery on Monday at eleven o'clock. Nobody in Florence knew either of these brothers. Drusilla had seen Sylvester once, decades ago, at the burial of Polycarp.

The two Vaidens to whom these notices were addressed, Jerry Catlin felt sure, were dead. With the going of Miltiades, the house of Vaiden was no more.

To Jerry, the rigid yellow face of his uncle among a room

of flowers renewed in a strange way the deaths of his uncle Augustus and his aunt Rose, his aunt Cassandra and his mother. Somehow, it was as if they had all died anew in the death of Miltiades.

It seemed unbelievable to Jerry that all of the Vaidens were gone; that of all that numerous brave and high-hearted family not one single member remained: his uncles, his aunts, his mother; it was as if some bold vista that lay in the sun of the past had darkened into night. With his uncle's death, Jerry found his own life painfully contracted.

At the station Jerry and Drusilla met Sydna Vaiden and Marsan and Adlee Petrie. Marsan, holding her tiny baby, looked worn and white from her travail. Drusilla brought them up the blind steps over the porte-cochère to avoid having them immediately see the funeral flowers all over the lower floor. But the old Colonel's room at the top of the hidden stairway was as pathetic with his departure as the very bier on which his body lay below.

Marsan began weeping and took her baby and went down the grand staircase to her dead father's body.

What Marsan thought, Jerry did not know, but when he saw the daughter holding the little flannel bundle which was Miltiades Vaiden Petrie, and saw Colonel Miltiades Vaiden, fixed and immovable beneath the ancient battle flag, he saw a symbol of the change that had come over the South. The old order passeth; the new order cometh. A volume closed and placed on the shelf of History.

The plan of laying the Colonel in the cathedral had to be abandoned. Jerry suggested the family burial ground in the country beside Ponny and Polycarp Vaiden, but both Drusilla and Marsan objected to that. Drusilla, weeping, said the Colonel was not of the country and it would break her heart to have him interred on a lonely little hillside where nobody came. Then she said a strange thing, "It took crowds for Miltiades even to be lonely in."

Marsan remembered the miniature sarcophagus which she had seen in the old Pine Street Church. Her father had liked that, and so let one be erected on the highest point in the cemetery, with the rest of Florence sloping away below.

The funeral train extended from the manor to the ruins of the cathedral. Mounted officers of the Florence Fencibles kept the line in order.

After the hearse came Sydna and her family; then Jerry and Aurelia. Behind them, three stooped old veterans in an open car carrying a flag, and behind them marched the Florence Fencibles.

A military band played the Marche Funèbre, and to its stately grief the cortège moved away. After them motors passed the manor gate unendingly, women's organizations, the bank officials, luncheon clubs, lodges, physicians and surgeons, private automobiles, until finally came negroes in their ramshackle vehicles and a long line following on foot.

In the first of the negro cars sat a thin worn yellow old woman in melancholy thought; by her side rode a small yellow negro boy in knickerbockers.

Dr. Blankenship preached the sermon.

He told of the dead man's charities, his munificence to the church, how he had been struck down by an assassin's hand in the midst of his great good work.

Then the good Doctor pointed out that Miltiades' life was an example of wisdom. If there were a God, the simplest good sense and foresight directed one and all to follow Miltiades Vaiden's example. If there were no God, the religious man had lost nothing, forfeited nothing; because a Christian life bestows on its adherents blessing not only in a heaven to come, but it makes a heaven on earth as it is. So no matter what be the truth of religion, how infinitely better is the lot of the saint over the lot of the worldling. . . . It was the final pathetic defense of skepticism before the open grave.

When the funeral sermon was over and the flowers piled on the mound, taps was sounded, the Florence Fencibles fired a volley into the air; the band struck up a brisk air, and the soldiers turned and marched away with eyes forward, toward the future.

CHAPTER FIFTY-SIX

With the Colonel gone, life was at odd ends in the manor. Petrie moved about the grounds with the aimlessness and dulled emotions which strangers always feel in a home where death has passed. He encountered Jerry in the garden and said he supposed now he would have to give up his idea of research in pure science.

"Have you got a place yet?" asked Jerry.

"Yes, I have. I think the Colonel must have written some letters about me. I received two tentative offers. One from Schenectady. It begins the first of next month."

He spoke unhappily, as if the stewardship of a million dollars were an irksome and disconcerting thing. Jerry listened with a sympathy that was little more than academic. His experience as a minister with the difficulty of collecting money gave him scant patience with Petrie. Besides that, he never really had liked the fellow with his gloomy eyes and face. The assistant minister was minded to say satirically that the scientist would find it very easy to give over the Vaiden fortune and carry out his own plans, but he knew that was not true. To disentangle one's self from money and the hope of money, Jerry had found in his adolescence and in his middle age the most difficult thing in the world.

The two men really had little to say to each other. Jerry ended the talk by pointing out a cherry tree that was blooming untimely in the autumn, and then the uncongenial pair moved slowly away from each other, impelled by some spiritual centrifugal force that neither of them desired to control.

Petrie's problem vanished immediately from Jerry's mind. The assistant minister was intently engaged in the odd task of not thinking a certain thought. He was putting an increasing strength into his repression of the undesired imagining. That was why he had come into the garden in the first place, to cling to surfaces, to look at the flowers, to watch the red leaves fall to the redder rose below, where a failing butterfly clung to a life past due.

Now Petrie had broken the spell of the garden, and Jerry turned inside again. He met Drusilla at a side door. She looked worn and old, as if a mantle of age had fallen on her. She stopped Jerry and said she had been trying to get Sydna in the notion to sell the manor, that the two of them could live more simply and with less loneliness in a cottage; what did Jerry think?

"You couldn't sell it now, during the depression," said Jerry.

"I suppose that's true," nodded the old woman dolorously. "Around Miltiades one fell out of the habit of thinking about money. I suppose we'll have to start again."

"There is nothing to do except direct what shall be done."

Drusilla responded with a faint touch of her old irony:

"Yes, nothing to do except direct a fortune, a preacher would say that."

She passed on into the garden with a pannier to gather the last of the flowers.

Jerry went on upstairs to Aurelia. He dreaded being with her for any length of time lest she read the private thought that stirred and stretched down underneath the things he was doing. The musician had a queer facility of getting at these obscure movements of his mind. As he climbed the stairs he fixed his thoughts intently on the reports which he had not yet finished.

When he entered their apartment he found his wife arranging her things in her dressing case. She was very grave, and the appearance of her eyes showed that she had been weeping. He watched her a few moments and finally asked mildly why she was packing her bag.

She stopped and looked at him with a peculiar expression,

so that Jerry was afraid she would break out into reproaches. Instead of that she began sobbing under her breath:

"Oh, Jerry, what have I done! What a terrible thing I've done to you!" And she went to the bed, flung herself face down, and wept in the counterpane.

The assistant minister went to her in distress.

"Darling, hush, darling, you haven't done anything to me . . . what do you think you have?"

"You know."

"N-no, darling, I don't really," stammered the minister.

She lifted herself on her elbows, stared out of the window, and said in a pathetic voice:

"You are a preacher, you will never get over trying to comfort people with lies. . . ."

"Why, Aurelia!" cried the assistant minister, really hurt.

She looked at him sadly.

"You know it's true. All last night you lay and thought about her . . . and the manor . . . and the fortune . . . all three are so exactly alike, finished, conventional, and beautiful . . . and so are you. . . . I feel like I've smothered a goldfish in the air."

Jerry passed over the figure of the goldfish . . . it was ludicrous applied to his penurious life . . . and reassured her again, but she got up and resumed her packing.

"Honey, it's the funeral that's upset you," suggested Jerry.

"No, it isn't . . . I didn't like your uncle . . . he robbed my father of his home."

Jerry was silent for a space, thinking how far such an answer would have been from Sydna if the relationship had been reversed.

"What are you going to do?"

"I'm going home . . . you can stay here."

"Oh, don't do that, please, Aurelia . . . the manor is empty enough as it is."

"Yes, but it's emptier when I'm here than when I'm not here. . . . Besides, Mother and Father need me."

"Honey, they're all right."

She looked at him and gave a mirthless smile.

"You needn't beg me so hard to stay, Jerry, you don't have to go because I do."

"Darling, it isn't that at all . . . but ought I to stay here without you?"

"Why, Jerry . . . of course . . . you have to stay and help them get things straightened out . . . you're needed here . . . it would be wrong of you to come home with me."

She went downstairs into the garden and found Drusilla. She kissed the old woman's colorless cheek.

"Mother and Father are by themselves and I have to go back. Jerry can stay. I'll try to come over and see you all tomorrow or the day after. Tell Marsan good-bye for me . . . and Sydna."

Jerry went with her to the garage where her shabby car was housed.

"Why don't you go hunt up Sydna and tell her good-bye for yourself?"

Aurelia simply looked at Jerry.

In the garage Wilson tried to get out Aurelia's car, but it had reached that age in an automobile when it would not start for anyone except its owner. Aurelia got in it herself and drove away from the manor.

Jerry walked slowly back to his reports, which, like friendly ogres, gave him enough trouble to keep his thoughts from more unpleasant things.

But as he climbed the stairs the irony of his life came to him; he had remained a bachelor on account of Sydna right up to the year of his uncle's death. Then, to protect himself and Sydna from any possible mental unfaithfulness to his uncle, he had married Aurelia . . . and Sydna was freed. That was the jibe the garden could not hush.

He needed some references for his reports and walked down to the old Pine Street Methodist Church to get them.

Miss Chisem, who was staying on in the office until she saw what changes would be made, asked Jerry if he thought the cathedral would be finished.

"Finally," said Jerry; "there has been too much spent on it not to be. The Methodists wouldn't allow city property to lie idle."

"Will it be in time for me to hold my place here?"

Jerry shook his head; he didn't think so.

"I don't know what I'll do," said the secretary; "there are no jobs anywhere now. I have two town lots . . . but they aren't worth anything."

"Why did you want to speculate?" asked Jerry curiously.

"I didn't want to speculate. They told me real estate was safe, it couldn't burn up or blow away."

"They failed to mention that the price could vanish."

"Well, I'm better off than I would have been if I had kept my money, the bank where I kept my deposit broke, and that's all completely gone. If I can't find another job I suppose I'll have to go and try to live on two vacant lots." She gave a pale smile at her little attempt at a joke and set to work copying the notes Jerry needed.

When Jerry started for the manor again he had an uncomfortable feeling about going back. He wished Aurelia had remained at the Vaiden home. He knew that his stay in the manor would torture his wife with jealousy, but, as far as that went, if he returned to Sheffield, it would be the same thing. The musician was an idealist, she struggled without cessation toward a perfection which she, and which no one else, would ever reach. It suddenly occurred to Jerry that the reason his wife had never become a great musician was because she would never settle on a rendition and stereotype it. She was experimental, impulsive, and without even the desire for self-control. Her outbursts of temper were luxuries to her.

He wished to heaven she had remained at the manor. He thought of calling her up on the phone and asking her to return, but he knew it would do no good.

As Jerry approached the manor, he saw the postern gate open and a man come out. The man, Jerry thought, was a stranger, and he hoped that nobody was visiting the manor on a point of business so soon after his uncle's death. Twenty or thirty steps further on the features of the visitor became abruptly familiar, and a profound shock traveled through Jerry which for a moment left him with a feeling of speechlessness.

The man was Lucius Handback. To see Lucius Handback coming out of the manor gate was so incredible that Jerry could hardly believe his eyes. He had never liked Lucius for a number of excellent reasons.

Mr. Handback came up to Jerry with the quiet earnest air of those who sympathize with the relatives of the dead.

"I want to tell you how sorry I am, Jerry, for you and Miss Sydna and all of you. I hope you won't think it strange of me saying this. The difficulty between my father and your uncle is past, and, I hope, buried with the two men. You will believe me, won't you, when I say I feel for you in your sorrow and that I'd like to be friends again, if I may?"

Such a speech from Lucius was even more surprising than his presence.

"Why, Lucius, you know I have nothing to forgive. You were the one who was wronged. I hate to say it, especially now, but after what you've said . . . after what you've had the generosity to say . . . I can't do anything else."

"Well, I wanted to tell you, Jerry, and I wanted to tell Sydna how I felt."

Jerry observed the intimate use of "Sydna," but Lucius had a right so to use it. He had been a suitor of Sydna's before he, Jerry himself, had ever seen the girl.

Here the thought of Sydna in her girlhood, in the period of her almost unbearable attraction for him, sent a kind of quiver through Jerry and set his heart beating. Lucius continued talking:

"And there was something I wanted to see you personally about, Jerry; that's another reason why I came here."

"Yes, what is it?" asked the assistant minister wonderingly.

"Why . . . the man who killed your uncle . . . Eph Cady."

"Do they know who assassinated him?"

"Didn't you know that? Yes, a negro saw him throw the bomb. When it exploded, it knocked Cady down too; then he got up and ran off."

"No, I hadn't heard. . . . I've been here in the manor. . . ."

"I suppose nobody wanted to disturb the family with it. They have Cady in jail now, that's what I wanted to see you about."

"Yes . . . and what about it?"

"Don't you think you had better get a lawyer to assist the states attorney in prosecuting Cady? You know he will have the best defense in Florence."

"Is he rich?"

"He has nothing at all, but you know as well as everybody else that Cady was paid to do what he did. He claims he did it because the Colonel once put his father, Alex Cady, in jail . . . there's no sense at all to that."

"I didn't know he even claimed it."

"Yes, that's the statement he made to the sheriff."

Jerry stood brooding.

"It looks as if the people would rise up and lynch Cady, doesn't it? . . . such an atrocious crime . . . bombing a man in the very church he was building!"

Handback shrugged.

"The labor union would bomb heaven, Jerry, if they were roused up enough, and Bodine's association would keep a jump ahead of the union in terrorism. And all the wealthy men in town who have lost their money and property and now are about to lose their homes on the Colonel's mortgages . . . there's not a bit of telling who is standing back of Cady. I don't see how you are ever going to convict him myself. You'll certainly need a clever lawyer."

Jerry said he would take the authority on himself to employ one. He walked back down the street to Handback's car and drove to town with him.

When the two men reached the business section and made a canvass of the legal offices, they developed the disheartening fact that every able lawyer in town had been retained to defend Cady. Mr. Jefferson Ashton was available for the prosecution, and two or three others of his sort.

Lucius said this proved that Cady was being defended by a large group of men, and the reason the group wanted an out-of-town attorney to help prosecute the case was to enable them to place several of their own men on the jury. A strange lawyer, just coming into Florence, would not know which men to challenge on the jury.

The assistant minister remained downtown for an hour or two with a feeling of recess from the funereal manor. Here, among the commonplace stores, he felt a relief even from the beauty of the manor and its grounds. It was like a dish of simple food after a surfeit of confections. And the queer thought came to him, if Marsan had been reared among these middle terms of Florence life, would she have conceived a child without marriage? Was her act the result of lifelong surroundings of sensuous loveliness? Did humdrum, middle-class, unexciting stores and homes produce the humdrum, middle-class, conventional morals upon which the national life of the South was securely founded?

He did not know, but the very look of the dull stores warned Jerry that, if he went back to the manor, in some way or other he would have some ill-starred passage of tenderness with Sydna. How it could come about he did not know, nor could he imagine, but the shabby appearance of Courthouse Square with the autumn sunshine falling coldly upon it, the undistinguished crowd moving across it, filled him with a premonitory shiver of Sydna's sympathy and warmth and luxury.

He decided that he would go home . . . to the Swartout home . . . for the night. The next morning he would come over and see if there was something he could do. He went to a telephone booth and called up the manor. Mary, the colored maid, answered him. Her usual soft drawl was edged with excitement; she cried out:

"Mist' Jerry, I been tryin' to telephone you evahwha'.

Miss Drusilla is bad sick. She's down in huh stummick. If you kin fin' Doctah Lovell bring him quick! Miss Sydna's got Doctah Thomas an Doctah McLeroy an' Doctah Sanford, but Miss Drusilla say she want Doctah Lovell, because Doctah Lovell waited on huh when Miss Sydna was bawn."

Jerry snapped up the receiver and called to the drugstore proprietor:

"Jim! Jim! Where's Dr. Lovell?"

"Why, who's sick?"

"Miss Drusilla!"

"Why, doc's right back there behind my screen playing checkers with old man Bill Bradley."

CHAPTER FIFTY-SEVEN

QUIET was over the manor again, a different kind of quiet, the whispering, moving quiet of the sick and not of the dead.

There was nothing so very wrong. Drusilla's digestion was out of order, that was the conclusion reached by the combined wisdom of all the doctors in Florence. The younger doctors did not see how it could amount to much; the older doctors knew that the digestions of old ladies lean more closely upon their affections and their hearts than upon their stomachs.

Old lady Drusilla had eaten a little soft toast and milk, and it had disagreed with her acutely; indeed, it was almost as if she had swallowed glass.

It was not till after nightfall that her stabbings of pain had died away and she fell asleep. Finally the last and most pessimistic of the doctors agreed that Drusilla's "spell" was over and that in the morning she would be all right . . . weak, of course.

Drusilla had never before been an old lady. Now she was very old. It was as if the death of Miltiades had taken from her some profound source of comeliness and strength and left her a poor shrunken old woman with even the loveliness of her eyes faded, and nothing left but the white beauty of her hair. But she was better; she had passed the crisis brought on by a little soft toast and milk; she would get along all right now; and the doctors went away.

Jerry told Sydna to go to her room and sleep, as there was no use in both of them sitting up.

"You needn't either," said Sydna. "Mary sleeps in the

next room with the door open. She hears every breath Mother draws."

Here Mary appeared in the doorway with apron and cap.

"You-all don't have to sit up and watch, Mist' Jerry. She's all right now. She's had these spells befo' when somep'n happen."

Both Sydna and Jerry were far more reassured by Mary's words than they had been by the doctors. They went upstairs together, and at the top, took each other's hands and said good-night. Then they went their different ways.

As Jerry walked along the hallway he had a queer impression that he was high above the earth, and the dim hall in which he picked his way was very, very long. It seemed as if Sydna, walking in the opposite direction along the passage, were leaving him at some great distance. He went on to his room and entered without looking back.

In the suite that had been assigned to him Jerry made himself ready for bed. An impression of the Colonel and of Sydna surrounded him; it was in the hangings of the windows, in the period furniture, in the four-poster with its canopy. The quiet harmony of the room made him feel that Sydna stood everywhere he looked, an almost visible wraith of loveliness, a household goddess presiding over her demesne.

When he turned out the indirect lighting and opened the French window, a quarter moon swimming above the garden filled the room with a faint crystalline radiance.

The thought of Sydna lying awake in the moonlight down the hall lay on Jerry's pillow. The man drew a long breath and tried to sleep. He turned in his bed. His arms and legs were filled with a kind of restlessness of their own. He looked at the moon over the garden. In the arms of the quarter moon, clasped like a lover, lay the ghost of the moon that was gone. It called to his mind Sydna and his dead uncle, and the symbol so horrified him that he sat up on the side of his bed.

He decided that he could not sleep at all and thought of dressing himself and going home. The buses had quit running, and he pondered waking Wilson and having the colored man drive him to Sheffield. Then this too became a mere idea, and presently he thought he was sitting up in Wilson's car, very, very tired, going to Aurelia.

In the midst of this mixture of dream and waking a shock went through Jerry. He became completely awake. He listened intently for something that he had heard and could not identify. Then he heard repeated a rustling in the hall outside his door.

He sat listening intently, breathing through open lips until his mouth was dry. As he heard nothing more he got to his feet with a sharp internal trembling and moved to the place where he could make out the tall rectangle of the door. When he was almost to it, he heard a faint tapping on the outside panel. He put a hand to the knob and opened it silently.

A faint night light in the hallway revealed a glimmer of her negligee, her dark eyes and hair set against the pallor of her face.

"Jerry," she whispered unsteadily, "I . . . I hope you'll pardon me—I knew you were awake—I—wanted to tell you something."

He found her hand in the darkness and drew her silently inside, with a heart pounding in his chest. Her fingers were free of rings and seemed to melt into his own. He moved toward the bed, but Sydna drew a little back.

"Let's not go there."

"No," agreed Jerry, and did not know where to go

"I wanted to tell you this, Jerry . . . privately . . . and intimately . . . and—and . . . oh, I don't know . . . let's do sit down . . . I feel . . . about to fall."

He put an arm about her unconstricted body, and they went on to the bed.

They sat side by side with their damp palms locked to-

gether, when, amid his dizziness, Jerry remembered that
she had come to tell him something. He turned and asked
her in a whisper what she wanted to tell.

"Oh, Jerry," she breathed, staring into the garden, "not
now . . . not right now."

A premonition of pain went through Jerry at her reticence,
and then this faded in the utter sweetness of her presence,
in the feel of her palm pressed to his own, in the faint nes-
tling movements of her fingers. It was strange how this
slight contact sufficed, a touching, an intertwining of
fingers, and something ecstatically sweet flowed into each
other's veins and nerves and bodies.

After a while she drew a long breath, squeezed his hand
nervously.

"I might as well tell you."

He became apprehensive again and looked at her.

"Yes, Sydna . . . what is it?"

"Jerry . . . I'm going to . . . marry."

For almost a minute the man sat perfectly still, then he
asked incredulously:

"You mean . . . someone else?"

The woman nodded without looking at him in the thin
radiance.

"I wanted to tell you first . . . to sort of . . . explain to
you, Jerry. . . . You see . . . I've been a widow for a long,
long time, Jerry. I . . . I persuaded Miltiades to make you a
place here in Florence. . . . I believe he knew what I meant
and . . . did it for me."

Jerry drew breath to start a sentence, but there was
nothing to say, there was nothing he could say; then the
reproach which filled his body with its wordlessness shivered
out:

"Why couldn't you . . . at Shiloh . . . just a hint . . ."

"Jerry! Jerry! I was his wife . . . you had just announced
to me your engagement . . . and even I didn't know it, you
know what I mean, *know* it until the Colonel was gone . . .
there had been a kind of hazy sweetness in your coming."

"Sydna . . . if you had only said . . . anything. . . ."

The woman gave a long sigh.

"I am not Marsan, Jerry . . . I don't belong to the new generation."

The two sat silent, watching the new moon sink downwards with her hoary lover in her arms.

"I can think now what we would have been, Jerry, if we had married years ago at the proper time; children and cares, and love a habit, not a passion. And that last is what our lives would still fall into, Jerry, if you hadn't married Aurelia. I think our two families were born to love each other . . . not to marry. Drusilla once told me that on the Vaiden and Lacefield lovers God had bestowed his cynical blessing of separation."

"I—I can't imagine you ever becoming . . . a habit, Sydna."

"Oh, Jerry, no, no, no . . . you don't dream I believe it!"

Presently a painful question lodged in Jerry's thoughts. He tried to put it aside. He thought to himself, "If she had wanted me to know . . ." but presently did say:

"Sydna, would you . . . if you don't mind saying . . ."

"You mean . . . him?"

"Yes."

"Why, you see . . . most of this . . ." she made a little gesture in the frail light, "most of it belongs to him anyway . . . and he has cared for me too, Jerry . . . a long, long time. I told him frankly that I loved you, that I never really had loved anyone but you, Jerry, and I never would. I told him I wouldn't marry him unless he made friends with you . . . because I loved you. . . ."

"Yes . . . I see."

Jerry sat with Lucius Handback's overture of reconciliation going through his mind like the intermezzo of a tragedy . . . Sydna . . . to go at last . . . to Lucius Handback!

She answered his thoughts.

"We have many things in common, Jerry. I don't think we will be lonely with each other. Mother can't stay here long, Jerry, with Colonel Milt gone. And Marsan is gone now . . . or rather she never was here. I knew a baby once, Jerry, named Marsan, but she left me a long, long time ago." Sydna began weeping and put out her arms.

"Kiss me good-bye, Jerry."

CHAPTER FIFTY-EIGHT

THE conference of the Methodist Church South at Wetumpka, Alabama, was a profound relief to Jerry Catlin. It took him away from Aurelia, who had received him in a disquieting solemn fashion after his night at the manor. Jerry did not like Aurelia to receive him without reproaches and with somber eyes. He would have much preferred her old understandable vituperative self.

Another comfort of the conference was that it took Jerry out of Florence on Sydna and Lucius Handback's wedding day.

Quite naturally Sydna Vaiden haunted the car Jerry took to Wetumpka. In the seat ahead of him he saw a woman with hair as dark as Sydna's, and it set his heart beating until he walked past her for a drink of water and saw her face.

Jerry's seat mate, after the companionable manner of Southern traveling folk, asked Jerry his name, where he lived, what he did, where and why he was traveling, and the two presently developed some mutual acquaintances whom Jerry had known at a former pastorate in Dothan, Alabama.

In the midst of this prolonged catechism the fellow ejaculated:

"That reminds me, here's an article in the morning paper." And he drew out the paper and showed Jerry an account of a Dr. Buckley, pastor of the Southbridge Methodist Church in Columbus, Georgia, eloping with a Mrs. Ann Struthers, wife of George Struthers, a prominent lawyer of that city.

Jerry's seat mate, who was a country physician and a
very simple fellow, discovered the usual layman's pleasure
in assisting as far as he could in the pillorying of an ec-
clesiast.

"You preachers won't do," he said jocularly.

"This two-column headline says we will do," returned
Jerry absently.

"How do you figure that?" asked the medico in surprise.

"Well, if a country doctor had eloped with another man's
wife, it would not have been unusual enough to get into the
Associated Press, but out of the tens of thousands of preach-
ers over America, if a single one goes wrong, every paper
billboards it. It's news, it's unusual, it hardly ever happens.
Your article is a fine testimonial to the character of preach-
ers in general."

The simple fellow was amazed.

"Well, I be derned, I've heard the devil could quote the
preachers for his purpose, but I never knew that preachers
could quote the devil for theirs," and he broke into hearty
self-appreciative laughter at his paraphrase.

Wetumpka was full of Methodist preachers who had fore-
gathered from every town and village in the state and who
represented every social plane in Southern life. They were
a jolly, laughing, joke-cracking bunch, foregathered in and
around the church, talking and electioneering for the forth-
coming appointments. Not many felt really uneasy, for
most of them were sure that they would return to the
church from which they came; others, however, would be
transferred to worse or better churches.

The Presiding Elders were the most popular and courted
men because they formed the Bishop's cabinet and recom-
mended the changes to be made.

The general appearance of the preachers sitting in confer-
ence reminded Jerry of a group of farmers turned business
men. Their faces, nearly all of them, were farmer faces,
honest, well-met faces of the out of doors. Even the metro-
politan ministers, with the pallor of their studies on them,

held the lines of their country origin in their eyes and mouths and sometimes in their speech. That they were business men needed no analysis. They represented, as a corporate body, the most heavily capitalized industry in Alabama. Its tax-free property amounted in money valuation to something over a quarter of a billion dollars. It possessed church buildings, hospitals, orphanages, bookshops, printeries, libraries, colleges. It was the biggest single industry in the state. And it had accumulated this mass of wealth and property for the curiously ethereal and unverifiable purpose of saving dead men's souls.

There were some new ministers, young men, to be ordained, and the old ministers came around and laid their hands on the new ministers' heads, and then went on with their quarter of a billion dollar business.

The important work for the Conference to do was to collate the financial reports of the various ministers and then redistribute these ministers among the churches, some consideration being paid to how much money a given minister had collected in the post he had just occupied.

As Jerry Catlin sat in the Conference he thought of the Drownders, whom he had helped displace from Waterloo. He recalled how they had stopped the stores and the mills and the schools, and with no effort toward the collection of money had produced the strange ecstasy in which he had found the village. And he remembered, too, when the Drownders were turned out of the churches, how Rutledge and his three companions sat down by the roadside and brushed the dust of Waterloo from their shoes.

The business sessions of the Conference were held in the mornings, but many of the afternoons were given over to the preaching of what might be called "sample sermons." The importance of these sample sermons lay in the fact that within the organization of the Methodist Church South were congregations of all kinds and varieties of beliefs, from rural churches which accepted the Bible literally, through the larger town churches which believed in a factual

God but accepted the Bible figuratively, up to the great metropolitan churches which accepted God as an ideal and looked upon the Bible as the most inspiring and helpful collection of folklore which the human race had produced.

The solitary bond which held together these heterodox churches was their common necessity of obtaining funds for their educational, charitable, and religious organizations.

Analogous to this diversity in congregations was an equal diversity in the beliefs of the preachers. And here was the point of these afternoon sample sermons. They helped the Bishop and his Board of Elders to place a minister of a certain faith in charge of a congregation holding a similar creed. For while a correspondence in faith between a minister and his charge was not absolutely essential, still, much better results, both financial and spiritual, could be obtained when such an arrangement was possible.

Now, much of this fitting together of preacher and congregation depended upon these sample sermons; hence their importance.

It was the Reverend Jerry Catlin's fortune, whether good or evil, he did not then know, to receive on the morning before he was to deliver his sample sermon, a formal hand-written invitation from Sydna to her wedding.

It was odd how the actual receipt of the invitation and the setting of the date made real and concrete a marriage which up until that moment had seemed vague and improbable. The approaching marriage somehow emptied the universe of purpose for Jerry. It coincided with Petrie's bleak materialism.

Therefore Jerry approached his sample sermon in the Conference, not with his faith shaken, but certainly with a subtler understanding of the weaknesses of others.

On the appointed afternoon, in the bleak flower-screened bareness of the auditorium, Jerry spoke on the theme, "If there be no God the Christian attitude is best."

He showed that not only was it best ethically, spiritually, and socially, but it was best biologically. Only religious nations were crescent nations. Only religious peoples with the vision of God in their hearts moved undauntedly forward through the accidents and disasters of this life to high racial destinies.

That ancient illustration in Exodus, God led the Children of Israel as a pillar of fire by night and a cloud of smoke by day is as true of modern nations today as it was of a handful of wandering Jews three thousand years ago.

"I do not ask you, friends," said Jerry in his peroration, "what is your literal faith. I am no inquisitor probing the cloistered chambers of the soul. All that I ask is that you lift your eyes to the noblest, the most inspiring ideal ever figured on the heart of man. Be that figure real or ideal no man may say, but the categorical imperative of its existence in the lives and hearts of humanity today, no skeptic can question."

Jerry closed his manuscript, turned from the pulpit leaving his audience with that queer subtle feeling of inconclusiveness used so often and with such telling effect by modern ministers. He turned and seated himself in the chair beside the Bishop.

The lay members of the Conference were sitting upright, paying a concentrated attention. Even some of the other preachers listened.

After the benediction the congregation streamed up to congratulate the speaker. The idea that a man could join Jerry's church and receive the great uplift of religion without any real belief in God seized on the secret foible of almost every man in the building.

Among the stream of congratulations one smart business man held Jerry's hand longer than usual, leaned across and said:

"I've been keeping a lookout for you, Brother Catlin. That is the most liberal sermon I've heard since I came South six years ago. Where are you stopping?"

This use of the word "stop" told Jerry he was speaking to a Northern man. He gave him the address. The man then made an appointment to call on Jerry at six-thirty that afternoon and moved away in the line.

When Jerry found a moment, he asked the Bishop who it was, and the Bishop, in astonishment that Jerry did not know, replied, "Why, that's Atkins of the New Methodist Church in Birmingham!" but still it meant little to Jerry.

The interim between the sermon and six-thirty Jerry spent in that excited, nervous, and bleak period of reaction which follows the successes of actors, orators, and ministers.

Jerry was staying in a private home, and his hostess was anxious to minister to his recuperation after his effort. She offered him coffee, tea, chocolate, and admitted in a very vague way that her husband took other things when he was extremely exhausted, which had the recommendation of St. Paul and which were procurable in their home.

Jerry took nothing at all. He went up to his room with his periods still rolling through his head. He remembered points which he should have put in but did not; he recalled one or two words which would have been better omitted or changed. But behind it all lay a sense of emptiness and futility; a feeling that if Sydna never could hear him, of what use would be his eloquence? And the strange part of it was, he knew Aurelia would have been tremendously more moved by his rhetoric than Sydna. Aurelia would have caught fire; Sydna would have enveloped him in a cool beatific calm; she would have been curving strand and evening sky and the murmuring calm of the sea.

There came a faint tap on his door. . . . Sydna's tap flickered through his head and vanished. He called, "Come in." His hostess barely opened the door and said in a low tone that a Mr. Atkins had called by appointment.

Jerry arose, asked that Mr. Atkins be shown to his room. In the interim Jerry bathed his face, for he had a slight headache.

When the caller entered the room he was still moved to felicitations.

"I would like to say again how much I enjoyed your sermon . . ." he hesitated a moment, then gave Jerry a frank intimate smile.

"May I ask one question?"

"Certainly."

"Was that a—a pet sermon? . . . had you used it a good many times?"

Jerry was amused. He began to like Mr. Atkins.

"No, it wasn't at all . . . I just said what I thought."

"By George, it sounded like it," ejaculated Atkins. "We decided we wanted you, Dr. Catlin, if it was a pet sermon, because it didn't sound like one, and we wanted you if it was not a pet sermon, because it did sound like one, if you know what I mean."

Jerry laughed outright; his slight headache vanished. He decided that Mr. Atkins was an advertising man.

"Who is the 'we' you mention?" inquired Jerry.

"Three more members of the New Broad Street Methodist Church in Birmingham. . . . You remember, I spoke to you at Mr. Ponniman's reception in Florence. Colonel Vaiden and his charming wife and daughter and another young man were in the car."

"Certainly, I remember that," assured Jerry, but he gave himself away somewhat by adding, "Colonel Milt had a landscape gardener named Atkins . . . he lived in Baltimore."

The Birmingham Mr. Atkins waved aside the Baltimore Mr. Atkins.

"Listen, Dr. Catlin, my delegation has decided it wants you if you are available. We want a man who can persuade the Florence realtors to subscribe a thousand dollars a month to the cathedral, and who is a preacher, too. Why, Dr. Catlin, you don't know how rare a combination that is! We stewards of the New Methodist Church had seriously considered calling two men, a financier and a preacher."

Jerry laughed.

"I never heard that idea before."

"No, we're a new church. Now . . . to get down a little closer to business, have you made any commitments yet?"

"No, I haven't," said Jerry.

Mr. Atkins became grave.

"We hope you feel you could be of service in Birmingham, Dr. Catlin. You will find the heartiest coöperation among the membership and the Board of Stewards of the New Methodist Church."

"I am sure I should, if you are a fair sample," said Jerry.

"There is just one drawback," said Atkins, with a worried expression: "the Bishop has already brought it up. I talked to him about you."

A little thrill went through Jerry as he wondered if this objection could possibly concern Sydna.

"What is it?" he asked.

"It's in the exchange of ministers," explained Mr. Atkins. "The Methodist Church has a rule, you know, that if a new minister be brought into a district, a minister must be taken out by the district sending the new minister in. Of course, that's a good rule. It protects all preachers and is a kind of job insurance, but we are going to have trouble with that rule, especially with you."

"Why me?" asked Jerry thinking uncomfortably again of Sydna's unconventional call in his bedchamber.

"Because there aren't many modern churches in Alabama. Men who can fill that type of pulpit receive satisfactory perquisites and . . . they are not changed easily. There is no modern church in Florence, so our preacher, Dr. Daviscourt, would have nowhere to go in the Florence circuit. However, before you can come to the New Methodist Church Dr. Daviscourt has got to be placed somewhere. Now, Dr. Catlin, that is the lion in our path."

Jerry sat considering the matter.

"The Bishop feels that way too?"

"Oh, certainly, it's a hard-and-fast rule. However, I will say this: we Birmingham business men have often gone after things that are not in sight but which later we made visible. We are going to work for your exchange in the Birmingham spirit, Dr. Catlin."

"That's very hopeful," said Jerry, somewhat encouraged by Mr. Atkins' optimism.

"Oh yes, yes, Birminghamers are always hopeful. I wanted to know personally how you felt before we went on with our plans, and—er—I might mention that the honorarium which usually attaches to the field open to you is twelve thousand, five hundred per annum . . . that's secondary, of course, any figure convenient to you could be arranged."

CHAPTER FIFTY-NINE

Before Jerry returned to Sheffield he saw Atkins two or three more times. Each time the Birminghamer reported that while the Bishop had not been able to arrange Jerry's transfer to the New Church in Birmingham, he, Atkins, continued to be full of hope.

There was something rotarian in the man's invincible optimism. It was mechanical and automatic. It seemed to require no moral effort whatever. Mr. Atkins worked at the proposed change with a kind of routine enthusiasm. He outlined some of the plans of the stewards of the New Church to Jerry: recreation camps for the poor, a new wing to the Methodist hospital, an American citizens' training course for the foreign population in Birmingham, the milk fund, and on and on . . . all most excellent projects.

The moment Jerry boarded the train for Sheffield and removed himself from the Birmingham man's technique of enthusiasm, thoughts of Sydna rushed in on the assistant minister. He looked at his watch, and it came over him that Sydna's wedding would take place at some point in that very hour. This fact suddenly connected the manor in Florence with the train in one link of time. It was as if the two places, separated by half the state, had somehow coalesced. It was as if Sydna were being married under his very eyes in the impalpable dimension of Time.

For a space he sat, watch in hand, glancing now at its dial, now at the brown woods and dead fields that lay in the same charmed sunlight that fell on the manor in Florence. The train might have been running, somehow, in the midst of the wedding decorations in the Vaiden mansion; in the clash of its wheels there sounded as faint overtones the murmur of wedding guests. The engine's whistle, far ahead, brought a phantasmal ceremony to a close. The train slowed down and stopped at a way station.

It moved on again, and presently the conductor made his round, punching the tickets of the new passengers with an impassive deliberation.

A shabby man came walking up the car hunting a seat. He paused beside Jerry and sat down.

The assistant minister paid the newcomer no further attention than to pick up his newspaper out of the seat and open it at random.

The headlines spread before Jerry's eyes in words which his mind did not hold tightly enough to connect into sentences . . . drought in Texas . . . millions of bales overplus ruinous to cotton growers . . . oversupply of apples depresses orchardists . . . glut of hogs . . . nakedness and starvation ravaged the land because the people had produced more than they could eat and wear . . . a jeweler murdered in Memphis . . . labor troubles in Florence . . . entire white Swartout family in Carver's Lane murdered by negroes in Sheffield . . . Grey Mule Hill and Jericho wiped out in retaliation . . . divorce in Reno . . . Gilded Boy wins at Pimlico . . .

It all slid without impression across Jerry's retina. He glanced involuntarily at his watch. The hour was gone. Sydna Vaiden's life had veered sharply and finally from his own. The sympathy and comfort which they had brought to each other in the past would of course be impossible between him and Mrs. Lucius Handback . . . the very name stood before his mind as a sardonic mocking symbol for Sydna . . . . Mrs. Lucius Handback . . . Sydna . . . Mrs. Lucius Handback . . . because he had married Aurelia.

The man on the other half of the seat kept glancing across until Jerry offered him the paper. The shabby fellow took it, held it irresolutely in his hands, finally moistened his lips and spoke in a voice just loud enough to carry above the rattle of the train:

"Excuse me, sir, maybe I oughtn't to be talking to a gentleman like you about it, I'm sure you're a much better man than I am. . . ."

Jerry looked at him without knowing whether his words were coherent or not. He started to ask him what he had said, but if the sentence were repeated it would slip away just as it did before.

"Both of us have to die," said the shabby man.

Jerry looked at the man's rough face and earnest eyes against the indefinite background of the coach.

"Yes, that's true," nodded Jerry, his attention caught by the oddity of the statement.

"And do you dread it?" asked the man earnestly, leaning over the paper and peering intently at the assistant minister.

"Well . . . ye-es . . . no . . . no, I don't dread it." His eyes went involuntarily to his watch again, and he thought, "Two hours ago I would have," and then he reflected with the comforting cynicism of middle age, "two days, two weeks, two years from now, I'll dread it again, because love dies. My first love for Sydna died . . . and so will this. . . ." And yet this comfort in his thought was more tragic and more pathetic than his wound itself, because it gave up all love . . . it abandoned his own and every mortal soul to a final, utter loneliness.

The unkempt questioner at Jerry's side continued his scrutiny.

"Aren't you in trouble, brother?" he asked at length.

"I'm not exactly happy," said the assistant minister with a shadow of a smile.

"Have you lost money, brother?"

"No . . . I didn't have any to lose, or I'm sure I would have . . . everyone else did."

The man disregarded this faint touch of lightness with the certainty of a hound passing over a false trail.

"Have you lost a friend, brother?"

Jerry compressed his lips and ran his tongue around his teeth to conceal his expression.

"Yes."

"Is—is she dead?"

"No."

The man moved his hands and rattled the newspaper. He looked at Jerry, then out of the car window at the revolving landscape . . . from far ahead came faint blasts from the engine, hailing other people at other stations.

"Brother," said the shabby man, "had you thought what a little while you would have had to stay with this—this friend of yours . . . a few more years . . . not long . . . but when you join her after that, brother, this—this thing we call Time ain't going to be no more. It kain't be, because the sun won't go around the earth where you and her are. The earth'll turn under you, but you'll be in the sunshine. Nobody can take her away from you, brother, because what'll hold you together will be your love, and if he loves her too, why, you'll both just love her, that's all. . . . Is it so terrible, brother, that another man loves her down here like you do . . . can you blame him, even down here . . . ain't his heart got a right and a joy to reach out after what's beautiful and sweet and holy . . . even down here, brother? . . . Well, if you can see that so simple now, what must it be like up there in God's sunshine?"

"Listen, listen," cried Jerry, staring at the fellow, "I know you are an uneducated man, but can even you really believe such nonsense? Don't you know that up in the sky there is just space, cold interstellar space . . . absolute zero? . . ."

The man loosed the paper to hold up a hand and a forefinger.

"There, that's the point, brother, exactly. I—I don't believe because I read about it or figgered it out, not at all, not the least bit . . . a friend o' mine's been there . . . he really has. He was drowned in a creek up clost to Florence. . . ."

Jerry turned his face from the fellow.

"Oh, my goodness . . . I know who you're talking about . . . I was there."

A rapt expression came on the man's face.

"Was you . . . was you, brother?"

"Yes, and it was just the ordinary hallucination of a drowning man. It has occurred over and over and over."

The man pondered.

"I know it occurred once before, brother, angels came and attended to a man once in a garden called Gethsemane."

"That was a long time ago," said Jerry; "that really happened. That went down on record for the faith of mankind, but since then there have been no miracles, nothing but hallucinations."

The man gave a puzzled frown.

"Brother, may I ask you what is your trade, a doctor, or lawyer?"

"I'm a minister," said Jerry.

"Oh . . . I see . . . well, you must excuse me, brother . . . I took you for a business man of some sort. . . ." The train was slowing down, the man got up. "I get off here, brother. God bless you. . . ."

And as the Drownder went down the aisle to the door, Jerry noticed him sliding his feet along the runner, and once he wiped his shoe against the standard of a seat.

Jerry could see that the Drownder had once been a farmer, as had he, himself, as had three fourths of the ministers who attended the conference at Wetumpka. And Jerry remembered how this simple evangel sent out by Rutledge to sympathize with and to try to comfort the world was the very spirit and image of what he, Jerry Catlin, once had dreamed of being. And so, Jerry suspected, lay a smothered similar dream in the heart of every minister at the Conference.

But they had all learned better. Amid the practical necessities of the world, amid schools and hospitals and churches and libraries and printeries, they had recovered from their romantic youth, they had recovered from romanticism, which another youth, twenty-six years old, had started in a vast wave around the globe, from a Cross.

The porter came through the train paging someone. After

two or three repetitions, Jerry recognized his own name. He called to the black man and received a telegram. It was from Atkins. It read:

VAN WEY, CHATTANOOGA, TRANSFERRED TO SOUTHBRIDGE METHODIST CHURCH, COLUMBUS, GEORGIA; WHITESIDE, MEMPHIS, TRANSFERRED TO CHATTANOOGA; LARKIN, DALLAS, TRANSFERRED TO MEMPHIS; DAVENPORT, BIRMINGHAM, TRANSFERRED TO DALLAS; CATLIN, FLORENCE, TRANSFERRED TO NEW BROAD STREET METHODIST CHURCH, BIRMINGHAM. . . . CONGRATULATIONS.

Atkins and his delegation had traded ministers among half a dozen Methodist Conferences to obtain their end. They needed a practical financier for their endless good and necessary works. The world might possibly lay claim to a soul; no one knew, no one was sure; but it was possessed by a body.

At the next station Jerry telegraphed back his acceptance.

THE END

FAMILY HISTORY
AND THE DESTINY OF A NATION

"EACH GENERATION *quickly and completely forgets its for-bears. I was filled with a profound sense of tragedy that my own family, my neighbors, the whole South surrounding me would be utterly lost in the onrushing flood of the years. History will not rescue it from oblivion because history is too general to be human and too remote to be real.*"

So Mr. Stribling took upon himself the task of painting a real picture of the South, and the North as it influenced the South, precisely as all these different forces were, and not as one might wish them to be. The result is the tremendous trilogy upon which he has been working for the past six years, a trilogy which has won its author the greatest honors of this decade.

THE FORGE

THE FORTUNES of old man Jimmie Vaiden, the "meat-eating Alabama Baptist" and his two sets of children—three if one counts Gracie the quadroon—as they are drawn into the Civil War. With sympathy, breadth of understanding and shrewd humor, Mr. Stribling portrays the upheaval of a whole civilization. "The Forge" was the first American novel chosen by the English Book Society.

THE STORE

On a tapestry even wider and richer in scope than "The Forge" one sees the drama of Pap's son, Colonel Milt Vaiden, who attempts to restore to the somnolent backwash of Southern life in the '90's something of the spaciousness of the days before the war. Blacks, whites, crooks, storekeepers, politicians, dreamers, are knit together in this graphic social history of the reconstructed South. "The Store" was selected by the Literary Guild and was awarded the Pulitzer Prize for 1932.

UNFINISHED CATHEDRAL

At ninety Colonel Milt Vaiden is the financial lord of his Alabama city, prime mover in a big real estate boom, chief patron of the projected All Souls' Cathedral which is to house his bones. Rotarys, lynchings, high pressure go-getting, quick wealth, the fragrance of magnolia and wisteria at dusk, the swift incredible drama of the great boom years. So closes the story of the Vaidens which is more or less the story of every Southern family and in a little more generous degree the story of every family North or South, "so closely are our family histories bound with the destiny of our nation." "Unfinished Cathedral" is also a selection of the Literary Guild.

TRIUMPHANT IN SUFFERING

Triumphant
in Suffering

by MERLIN L. NEFF

Author of "Life Begins With God,"
"The Bible Pageant," "The Glory
of the Stars," "Power for Today"

PACIFIC PRESS PUBLISHING ASSOCIATION
Mountain View, California

Brookfield, Illinois   Omaha, Nebraska   Portland, Oregon

ACKNOWLEDGMENTS

Many of the Bible texts in this publication are from the *Revised Standard Version of the Bible*, copyrighted 1946 and 1952.

I wish to thank the following publishers for their co-operation in allowing me to quote from books bearing their imprint. Quotations are used with their special permission.

LEWIS, C. E., *The Problem of Pain*, The Macmillan Company, New York.

STEWART, JAMES E., *The Strong Name*, Charles Scribner's Sons, New York.

BOWIE, WALTER RUSSELL, *The Interpreter's Bible*, volume 1, Abingdon Press, Nashville.

SHIRES, HENRY H., and PIERSON PARKER, *The Interpreter's Bible*, volume 2, Abingdon Press, Nashville.

BUTTRICK, GEORGE A., *The Interpreter's Bible*, volume 7, Abingdon Press, Nashville.

GOSSIP, ARTHUR JOHN, *The Interpreter's Bible*, volume 8, Abingdon Press, Nashville.

SHORT, JOHN, *The Interpreter's Bible*, volume 10, Abingdon Press, Nashville.

REID, JAMES, *The Interpreter's Bible*, volume 10, Abingdon Press, Nashville.

CONTENTS

DEDICATED

To E. W. E., whose courage and fortitude
in the ordeal of suffering and sorrow has
been an inspiration in writing this volume.

PROLOGUE

To write about suffering, pain, and sorrow is one thing; to accept these unwelcome visitors when they come is quite another matter. I hesitate to write on this subject because I have not always triumphed in test. True, I have known weeks of illness and hours of intense pain, and at times it seems that from a horizontal position in bed I have gained a truer perspective of life, of my friends, and, most of all, of a loving God. But in some trials I have been bitter and rebellious; I have not accepted them patiently, and it has been difficult to pray, "Thy will be done." It is in these crises that I have devoted hours of study to find how it is possible to triumph over suffering.

No one enjoys suffering, and I am sorry to say that I believe it has often destroyed the best and noblest in human character. There are too many who feel as Somerset Maugham did when he expressed his views in these words: "I knew that suffering did not ennoble; it degraded. It made men selfish, mean, petty, and suspicious. It absorbed them in small things. It did not make them more than men; it made them less than men; and I wrote ferociously that we learn resignation not by our own suffering, but by the suffering of others."

This has been too often true, for man in his unconverted state is self-centered, not God-centered. And when there is faith in divine Providence, it is not always easy to "practice what we preach." Richard Sheppard, who endured torturing pain, wrote a friend: "I do not love suffering, so you must not worry about me in that way, and I dislike all that talk about how lovely it is to suffer. I think it is a rotten process, which has nothing whatever to do with God; at least, if God causes suffering and delights in it, I do not delight in believing in

Him. I know it may do me good—that is, if I take it decently, but I know it is as likely to embitter mankind as to convert him. There is a great deal of rot written, isn't there, about how beautiful it is for us to suffer?"

There is a great deal of truth in these cynical words. When men blame God for suffering, pain, and death, they turn against Him. Unless the thinking is straight and God's love is in the heart, suffering can turn a man from the way to heaven and drive him to destruction. It is of vital importance, then, that we face the truth and learn how to meet the universal problems that haunt men more today than in any previous age in history.

It is not the fleeting sorrow or the sharp pain of the moment that does the damage to the soul. A man who had suffered but little said, "I like pain, it brings me to God." Yet, later, when he had agonized for weeks and months, he grew disillusioned and cursed God. It is the suffering that goes on endlessly, the trial that seems purposeless that breaks the spirit. In the time of unceasing trial comes the greatest test. The nobility of character of men and women who have come through the dark valley of the shadow by trusting in a loving God who is at their side is the strongest proof that there is a better way to face tragedy. And the paramount proof is the example of Jesus Christ, who accepted the cup of sorrow and drank it to the dregs, for He was made "perfect through sufferings."

To our Example, our Saviour, we turn for lessons of faith. To Him we call: "Teach us how to be triumphant in suffering. Help us to find the divine answer for each trial and tribulation, that we may be conquerors through Thy name."

This is the fervent desire of the author for every reader and for himself.   THE AUTHOR.

Los Altos, California.

IS THERE AN ANSWER?

How Sin and Suffering Came to Be

WHAT mysteries remain unsolved in this life! A sweet-faced little girl, innocent of wrong, lies in the hospital dying of a malignant tumor of the brain. Why should pain and death come to a child so young and eager for life?

A devoted minister of the gospel, driving through the night on a mission of mercy, sees the flash of headlights in his eyes, and then there is a crash. A drunk driver had swerved across the center line to hit the minister's car head-on. A godly man is killed instantly. Why did it happen to him when he was giving his life to the service of God?

Here is a Christian wife who has done all in her power to make a happy home for her husband and children. Now her happiness and security are shattered, as she becomes the victim of heartless desertion. Does God have an answer for this?

How are we to meet the bitter cup of pain and suffering? What is our reaction when heartaches and disappointments come? There are several ways human beings respond to suffering and sorrow. Some persons become bitter and resentful. They say, "If there is a God, why does He permit such things to come? I don't believe He loves me." Dr. Harry Emerson Fosdick tells of a man who said, "I don't know what I believe, but I don't believe all this 'God is love' stuff. I've been in two world wars, been unemployed eighteen months on end, seen the missus die of cancer, and now I am waiting for atom bombs to fall. All that stuff about Jesus is no help."

Others are stoical to calamity. They shrug their shoulders, act calloused, and refuse to allow suffering to touch their hearts. They consider life a mystery and simply say, "This, too, will pass."

There are folk who pity themselves when faced with sorrow. With whimpering moans they say, "I must be a terrible sinner, since all this trouble comes to me. I guess I was born to suffer."

Then, again, there are a few men and women who do not believe sorrow and pain exist. They attempt to deny the reality of suffering, and say that there is no such thing as death.

Heartaches drive some persons to seek consolation in alcohol, frivolity, or riotous living, where they hope to drown their sorrows. "Why not forget," they shout; "we only live a little while, so why not have fun?"

Christianity Increases the Problem

We can see these reactions in the lives of those about us if we only take time to look for them. Multitudes of Christians have been puzzled as they attempted to reconcile faith in a loving God with the bitter tragedies of life. One clergyman says he has found it harder for Christians to accept and overcome sorrow than to gain the victory over doubt and sin. In one sense this is true, for the person who does not accept the gospel of Jesus Christ has no mystery to solve and no conflict in his soul. The man without faith in Providence simply submits to what he calls "inevitable fate;" but the Christian declares that "God is love." The trusting soul must reconcile the dark and tragic experiences of life with his faith in the sovereignty of God. Thus, the Christian gospel of an all-loving heavenly Father thrusts the problem of suffering upon every believer, and it must be faced.

The mystery of suffering has been with mankind ever since the first family were upon the earth; however, the tensions and uncertainty of our day cause the questions to pile up with terrible urgency. Death comes suddenly, and millions of persons live on the razor's edge because of the ravages of war, famine, and disaster. The heavenly Father seems so far away from earth's welter and confusion that men lose their way in the darkness.

Since God is love and the basis of His government is the law of love, why are pain and sorrow and tragedy the lot of men? Only when we turn to the Bible do we find an answer that helps us to understand the problem. We shall never have the complete solution for the mystery of suffering, but we can fathom much of the divine plan for human beings.

To Goethe's statement, "If I were God, this world of sin and suffering would break my heart," I would answer, "That is what sin did to our Father's heart of love and to Jesus, our Saviour." Before this world was brought into existence, God faced the horrible menace of sin. Lucifer, the brilliant leader among the created beings of heaven, purposed in his heart to rebel against his Maker. The power of choice—a fearful instrument—had been given to the angelic host. They could love and obey God or they could follow their own selfish way. Lucifer decided to make self his god, for he exclaimed, "I will ascend into heaven, I will exalt my throne above the stars of God: I will sit also upon the mount of the congregation, in the sides of the north: I will ascend above the heights of the clouds; I will be like the Most High." Isaiah 14:13, 14.

Rebellion against God is sin. Thus when Lucifer and his cohorts made their fateful decision to revolt, they brought sin into a perfect universe. God permitted Lucifer, or Satan, to come to this earth. This rebel determined to tempt Adam and Eve, who were free moral agents, able to think and act as they chose. But the gift of freedom also carried with it the danger that man might forget his Creator and make the wrong choice.

God created this earth for perfect beings who would desire to follow His blueprint and obey His laws. Adam and Eve decided to turn the Garden of Eden into a place where they could do as they pleased. Their rebellious actions brought pain, sin, and death to the world.

The all-powerful God could have taken away the results of the first disobedient act of Adam and Eve; but then sin would have gone on and on unpunished, for the law would have been nullified. There would have been no consequences for wrong-doing, and no difference between good and evil. It would have robbed man of his power of choice since "sin is the transgression of the law," and where there is no law, there is no sin. The end result would, therefore, have been to make sin righteousness, for any code of law to be effective must have its penalties for disobedience.

As members of the human family we must accept the legacy of sin which is our inheritance; we cannot escape it. The apostle Paul describes man's plight in these words: "Therefore as sin came into the world through one man and death through sin, and so death spread to all men because all men sinned." Romans 5:12, R.S.V. The virus of evil spread throughout the world, and no one, except Jesus Christ, has been able to resist its deadly power, and that is why "the whole creation has been groaning in travail together until now." Romans 8:22, R.S.V.

What Causes Suffering?

This brings us face to face with the paramount issue: What are the causes of suffering? If we consider the chief reasons why pain and sorrow come, we shall know better how to relate ourselves to the problem.

1. *Suffering comes from the transgression of natural laws.* We live in a world where natural laws are in force. If they are disregarded or broken willfully, suffering is the result. A small child does not know about the law of gravitation, yet he toddles over a wall and falls to the hard pavement. He suffers pain as the penalty for breaking the law even though he did not know it existed. Should natural laws be suspended to save the innocent or ignorant from disaster? That is impossible, for everyone in the world would face chaos and destruction without these protective laws.

2. *Suffering may result from the wrong use of the power of choice.* Like Adam and Eve, modern men and women have brought disaster upon themselves by choosing the wrong course of action. Since we are free moral agents we can decide our course of action, but in the end we may find ourselves on the way of death. God could prohibit us from making foolish decisions, but by such intervention He would rob us of our freedom. Therefore, much of the pain and sorrow come upon us because the heavenly Father will not force us to do what is for our best good.

3. *Tragedies may result from man's greedy exploitation of nature.* Sometimes human beings blame God for the disasters in nature, such as floods and pestilences. While they are beyond

the control of the individuals who suffer, yet some of these catastrophes are the result of the selfish actions of men. A flood may sweep away a thousand homes and cause the death of five hundred persons; but the real reason for the disaster is man's ruthless, wasteful destruction of the forests which once held back the flood waters. We cannot squander the natural resources given us by the Creator without paying the penalty.

4. *Some tragedy and disaster is brought about by satanic power operating on the forces of nature.* Certain destructive forces, such as earthquakes and tornadoes, are beyond man to influence or control; yet they are not acts of a loving Father. When man lost his earthly dominion, Satan became "the prince of the power of the air." Ephesians 2:2. Unless restrained by God, this fearful enemy can wreak havoc and death by making nature a destroyer. "In accidents and calamities by sea and by land, in great conflagrations, in fierce tornadoes and terrific hailstorms, in tempests, floods, cyclones, tidal waves, and earthquakes, in every place and in a thousand forms, Satan is exercising his power. He sweeps away the ripening harvest, and famine and distress follow."—*The Great Controversy,* pages 589, 590.

5. *Pain and death may result from the careless mistakes of human beings.* Since we live in an imperfect world where men make mistakes or shirk their responsibility, accidents are bound to occur. An airplane crashes, snuffing out sixty lives. If the truth were known, the airliner came to grief because a mechanic was careless in his work, the inspector had not checked the equipment thoroughly, or the pilot was weary and misjudged his position. The God who loves men does not always see fit to perform a miracle to save the innocent from human error or poor judgment.

6. *Heartaches and bloodshed are caused by political and*

economic dictators. Suffering and sorrow have been the fate of millions of innocent souls because of oppressors. Tyrants have risen in power and sent armies marching to their death. God does not instigate wars; He is a loving Father who knows only love and peace. War is basically the result of man's rebellion against the divine will; and the dead and wounded, the displaced persons and innocent children, suffer because of man's inhumanity to man, not because God wants the ordeal of blood and tears.

The Christian can be certain that the basic cause of all sorrow and suffering is sin—not God. "Sickness, suffering, and death are work of an antagonistic power. Satan is the destroyer; God is the restorer."—*The Ministry of Healing,* page 113.

A Call to the Prodigal

God may permit trial and tragedy to test His children, but "He does not willingly afflict or grieve the sons of men." Lamentations 3:33, R.S.V. Suffering and loss may be the only way that a loving God can penetrate the calloused shell of the person who rests smugly in his carnal pleasures, his foolish thinking, and his sins. Rich and increased in material blessings, he finds no need of God until pain and sorrow strike. C. S. Lewis well says: "God whispers to us in our pleasures, speaks in our conscience, but shouts in our pain: it is His megaphone to rouse a deaf world."—*The Problem of Pain,* page 81.

To the Christian, then, suffering is not so much a mystery to be solved as a challenge to be met. We have the assurance that we are not alone in the darkness, for God is by our side. The sweet comfort of the twenty-third psalm centers in the knowledge that the Eternal One is with us. "Yea, though I walk through the valley of the shadow of death, I will fear no evil: for Thou art with me."

In the final chapter of *A Tale of Two Cities* Charles Dickens gives a moving description of two prisoners in Paris riding in a cart to the guillotine. One is a brave man who had once lost his way but had found it again, and who is now dying for a friend. Beside the man is another prisoner—a young girl. She saw the gentleness and courage of this man at the prison, and as she faces death, she asks to ride in the cart with him. "If I may ride with you," says the frightened girl, "will you let me hold your hand? . . . I am little and weak, and it will give me more courage."

So the two prisoners ride in the cart to the place of execution. As the girl gets out of the cart, she looks into the face of the friend and says, "I think you were sent to me by heaven."

In a far closer way Jesus Christ is with us in every hour of trial and sorrow. When Israel suffered at the hand of enemies, these words of comfort were spoken: "In all their affliction He was afflicted, and the angel of His presence saved them: in His love and in His pity He redeemed them; and He bare them, and carried them all the days of old." Isaiah 63:9.

If at each day's beginning we will place our hand in the hand of Jesus, the ever-old, ever-new miracle will take place again, and our broken hearts and tear-dimmed eyes will find comfort as we look up with hope into the face of our loving heavenly Father who does all things well.

MEN WHO ENDURED
SUFFERING

∾2∾

Abraham, Jacob, Moses, and Paul

IT IS one thing to theorize as to how suffering should be accepted; it is quite another matter to experience it. I have known ministers who preached submission to God's will for years, but when tragedy came they rebelled against it in a fury of bitterness. The problem of pain never seems urgent or imperative until it comes into our own life. I remember a man who visited me in the hospital after I had gone through months of suffering. He had never been sick in his life, but he glibly said, "I sympathize with you in your illness." I also remember when a relative sat beside me and with deep emotion said, "You have suffered a great deal. I know, for I've been through the same attacks again and again."

Talking about sorrow and suffering from a distance is easy, but looking at pain from the inside through tears makes a person humble and silent. It is well, therefore, to look at the lives of men of the Bible who are examples of faith and patience in trial and suffering. We are admonished by the apostle

James to consider the prophets as "an example of suffering affliction, and of patience." James 5:10.

To see a fellow traveler on life's highway endure the same tests and temptations that we experience and come through triumphantly is a source of spiritual strength. That is why the experiments in the laboratory of life recorded in Holy Writ are so precious to the trusting Christian.

"These examples of human steadfastness, in the might of divine power, are a witness to the world of the faithfulness of God's promises—of His abiding presence and sustaining grace. As the world looks upon these humble men, it cannot discern their moral value with God. It is a work of faith to calmly repose in God in the darkest hour—however severely tried and tempest-tossed, to feel that our Father is at the helm."—*Testimonies,* vol. 4, p. 525.

In the lives of the four characters to be considered in this chapter, we find four types of sorrow and suffering. Abraham's greatest ordeal was a trial of faith. Was he willing to obey God by offering his son as a human sacrifice? The suffering and anxiety of Jacob was largely the result of sin in his own life. He reaped the harvest of his own sowing, yet from the bitter experience he came forth a new man. Moses accepted the cup of humiliation, personal loss, and tribulation, because he loved his people. He was willing to give up honor and wealth to obey God's call. Finally, Paul is a study of a valiant man who knew physical and mental agony. He was persecuted because he preached the gospel; yet in the midst of fiery trials he rejoiced to be worthy to suffer for Christ.

Abraham, a Man of Faith

Faith does not spring full-blown in the life of a great man; it is developed through years of testing. Such was the experience of Abraham, the pioneer, who left his Chaldean homeland, his friends, and most of his relatives for a strange country whose distance to him could be compared only with a journey halfway around the world today.

God's purpose gripped the adventurer as he set out, "not knowing where he was to go." This patriarch had many detours on his way. He stopped first in Haran, where he lived long enough to feel at home and where he was tempted to remain in a comfortable existence. He could have reasoned that this was all that God could expect of him. Why go farther? But Abraham was made of stronger stuff; he was not disobedient to the divine call. He pushed on and arrived in Canaan, where "by faith he sojourned in the land of promise, as in a foreign land, living in tents." Hebrews 11:9, R.S.V.

A detour into Egypt, the lack of co-operation on the part of his nephew Lot, and the necessity of rescuing him from kidnapers, were troublesome episodes in Abraham's development. Poor Lot was weak spiritually. He "lifted up his eyes" toward Sodom, and he "pitched his tent toward Sodom," then he "dwelt in Sodom." Finally, when escape from the wicked city was offered to the vacillating man and his family, "he lingered" in Sodom. Yet through all his trials, and in spite of family burdens, Abraham did not waver, for he was bound to God by cords of faith.

However, the most severe ordeal came in the sunset years of Abraham and Sarah's life, after they had been given Isaac, through whom God promised to develop the chosen nation. Abraham must have staggered when he received the divine command: "Take now thy son, thine only son Isaac, whom thou lovest, and get thee into the land of Moriah; and offer him there for a burnt offering." Genesis 22:2.

Human sacrifices to pagan deities were a common practice

among the Canaanite tribes; but the true God had never asked
His children to take human life. Abraham must have won-
dered at times if he should not be willing to do as much as
the pagans did, if his God commanded.

We must never minimize the suffering and sorrow that this
man of faith endured. It was, no doubt, the greatest anyone
had experienced up to that time. "The trial was far more severe
than that which had been brought upon Adam. Compliance
with the prohibition laid upon our first parents involved no
suffering; but the command to Abraham demanded the most
agonizing sacrifice. All heaven beheld with wonder and ad-
miration Abraham's unfaltering obedience. All heaven ap-
plauded his fidelity."—*Patriarchs and Prophets,* page 155.

The test ended in victory! God could say to His servant,
"Now I know that thou fearest God, seeing thou hast not with-
held thy son, thine only son from Me." Genesis 22:12. What
do we attempt to hold back as too precious to place on the
altar of sacrifice? Only a boundless devotion, an unlimited
commitment, will stand the test. Like Abraham, each of us
is faced with a supreme moment when we must decide if we
will pay the price to follow God all the way. May it be said of
us, as it was of this patriarch of old, "By faith Abraham . . .
obeyed."

Suffering for His Sins

Although man brings sorrow and suffering upon himself
because of his sins, yet if he is truly repentant he can, like
Jacob, gain a blessed victory. The early pages of Jacob's life
present him as a rogue and a rascal. It all began in a home
where parental love was divided, where jealousy and dissension
reigned. As Robertson points out, "Rebekah loved her son
more than truth, i.e., more than God. . . . Abraham was ready

to sacrifice his son to duty. Rebekah sacrificed truth and duty to her son."—*Sermons on Bible Subjects,* pages 27, 28.

By seeking the birthright, Jacob revealed his longing for spiritual values and his need for a close relationship to God; but he lacked faith. Therefore he endeavored to work out his salvation in his own way, and this brought him sorrow, suffering, and very nearly cost him his life.

As a refugee in Haran, Jacob received some of the treatment he had given to others—he was deceived and cheated. The years passed and Jacob realized it was time for him to take his large family back to Canaan if he would keep them in the faith of the true God. But the supplanter must face his brother, and what would be the outcome of this meeting?

"Jacob was greatly afraid and distressed" when he found that Esau was coming to meet him with four hundred men. The angels of God stood by Jacob on the way, and they gave him renewed courage, even as they had done years before at Bethel. He called the place Mahanaim, which means: "This is God's army!" Genesis 32:2, R.S.V. But the man had not completed his course in humility; he must be humbled and chastened by suffering and by a night of wrestling at the brook Jabbok.

Through the dark hours Jacob struggled with his supposed adversary. "While he was thus battling for his life, the sense of his guilt pressed upon his soul; his sins rose up before him, to shut him out from God. But in his terrible extremity he remembered God's promises, and his whole heart went out in entreaty for His mercy."—*Patriarchs and Prophets,* page 197.

Haunted by uncertainty and burdened by our sins, how many of us wrestle blindly as did Jacob! We could have comfort and help in the instant of our need; but we fight on, hoping to gain the victory in our own strength. Finally, in our helplessness we cry out for divine strength and blessing; and, lo, God has been at our side all the time! Jacob wrestled from darkness to sunrise, for we read that "the sun rose upon him as he passed Penuel."

Victory came to Jacob as he held on to God through pain and tears. "Caught in the grip of judgment, his prevailing desire was not for escape. He would hold on until something decisive happened. . . . The shallow man may ignore his sins; the cowardly man may try to evade their consequences; but Jacob now was neither one."—*The Interpreter's Bible,* vol. 1, p. 724. Now Jacob was "a prince of God," for he had found the true source of power—a humble and contrite heart obedient to God.

Moses, Patient in Trial

The greatest men in history are those who have cast their lot with the oppressed and downtrodden. Again, some of the best work has been done by those who felt unfitted for the task. Moses is classified with both of these groups. He chose "rather to share ill treatment with the people of God than to enjoy the fleeting pleasures of sin" in the idolatrous land of Egypt. Hebrews 11:25, R.S.V. He joined his people in their suffering and slavery, for "he considered abuse suffered for the Christ greater wealth than the treasures of Egypt, for he looked to the reward." Verse 26, R.S.V.

Here was the secret of the man's power: By faith Moses looked beyond the trials and tribulations of the moment to the final reward. "He looked beyond the gorgeous palace, beyond a monarch's crown, to the high honors that will be bestowed on the saints of the Most High in a kingdom untainted by sin. He saw by faith an imperishable crown that the King of heaven would place on the brow of the overcomer. This faith led him to turn away from the lordly ones of earth, and join the humble, poor, despised nation that had chosen to obey God rather than to serve sin."—*Patriarchs and Prophets,* page 246.

"Why do you say Moses suffered ill treatment with the people of God?" someone may ask. "He was the leader of the nation. Surely he had power and honor in his position." When Moses accepted the divine call to lead Israel from Egypt he took upon himself a lonely, thankless task in which he would be misunderstood by the multitude. He was an outcast from all his Egyptian friends; his own brother and sister arose against him on occasion, and the thousands of Israelites rebelled against his leadership and threatened to kill him.

Yet, when the way became too rough and rebellion was in the camp, Moses pleaded with God for strength and courage. When the nation sank into idolatry and God was ready to destroy the people for their sin, Moses stood firm in intercession for them. He courageously asked that his name be blotted out of the book of life if God could not save the nation. In other words, Moses loved his people so completely that he was willing to face annihilation with them if they could not be forgiven.

Yet this Gibraltar of a man failed in a minor crisis! At Meribah the people shouted for water, and God commanded Moses and Aaron to "tell the rock before their eyes to yield its water." Numbers 20:8, R.S.V. But Moses called the thirsty crowd "rebels" and struck the rock twice. God did not fail to supply the people with water, even though Moses had disobeyed. The rock, a symbol of Christ, had once been smitten; it should not have been struck again. But in this moment Moses lacked faith, and he "lost sight of his Almighty Helper. . . . The man who might have stood pure, firm, and unselfish to the close of his work, had been overcome at last."—*Patriarchs and Prophets,* page 418.

Now Moses suffered before the entire nation. Every Israelite knew their leader had sinned and that he must receive humiliating punishment. He had given his life for the nation, and he longed to lead them triumphantly into the Promised Land; but it was not to be. Listen to his farewell speech to the throng standing before him: "I am a hundred and twenty years old this day; I am no longer able to go out and come in. The Lord has said to me, 'You shall not go over this Jordan.'" Deuteronomy 31:2, R.S.V.

In seeming defeat, the mighty warrior for God was not bowed or broken. He introduced Joshua as the new leader and then gave this ringing testimony: "Be strong and of good courage, . . . for it is the Lord your God who goes with you; He will not fail you or forsake you." Verse 6, R.S.V.

Suffering, trial, and disappointment faded from the mind of Moses. He had confessed his sin, received forgiveness, and he was now ready for a mountaintop experience with his God. "From the human point of view, which loves happy endings, the story should have been rounded out with Moses leading his people over the Jordan. . . . If God chooses to close a door, no lasting disappointments can beset the life which is fully committed to Him."—*The Interpreter's Bible,* vol. 2, p. 535.

Moses needed no tomb or monument to mark his resting place, for soon after his death he was raised to life and ascended with his Deliverer to the glories of heaven.

Paul, a Triumphant Sufferer

If any Bible character was truly qualified to write on the subject of suffering, it was Paul, who loved the title "an apostle of Jesus Christ." He endured physical infirmity, which he called his "thorn in the flesh;" and although he prayed earnestly that it be taken away, it was not God's will to remove it. For years Paul experienced bitter persecution—physical and mental —in order to preach the gospel of his Lord. In addition to this he had heartbreaking disappointments because of strife among the church members and the apostasy of some believers. Paul declared that suffering was a part of the Christian's life, and he affirmed that where sin and suffering abounded, the grace and comfort of God must much more abound.

What physical ailment Paul suffered, we are not informed. He "suggests that it was painful, crippling his enjoyment of life, and frustrating his full efficiency. It was also humiliating, for it awoke in others the pity which is sometimes mingled with contempt."—*The Interpreter's Bible,* vol. 10, p. 407. The apostle says it was given "to harass me, to keep me from being too elated. Three times I besought the Lord about this, that it should leave me; but He said to me, 'My grace is sufficient for you, for My power is made perfect in weakness.'" 2 Corinthians 12:7-9, R.S.V.

God answered Paul's prayer with "No." A true Christian will be content with this answer, for he is submissive to God's will. In the case of the apostle, God assured him that there was ample strength and grace from heaven to meet his need. So Paul could say, "I will all the more gladly boast of my weaknesses, that the power of Christ may rest upon me." Verse 9, R.S.V.

Here is a statement of what suffering can do to the spiritually minded man. The weakness, the pain, the physical defect, can be transformed into a blessing! Suffering oftentimes breaks down our self-sufficiency and makes us willing to follow the Holy Spirit's leading. Tragedy can take boasting from our lives and cause us to glory in the cross of Calvary. Writing of John Bunyan's trials, W. Hale White declares, "The Creator gets the appointed task out of His servants in many ways. It is sufficient to give some of them love, sunrises and sunsets, and primrose woods in spring: others have to be scourged with bloody whips . . . before they do what God has determined for them."—*John Bunyan,* pages 25, 26.

Paul was reminded again and again that he was "a frail vessel of earth." 2 Corinthians 4:7, Moffatt. Yet he was made of the toughest metal, for he endured the ordeal of beating with rods, stoning, shipwreck, imprisonment in dungeons, as well as hunger, cold, and nakedness.

Near the beginning of his ministry, Paul, accompanied by Silas, was illegally beaten, thrown in prison, and fastened in stocks. Yet the two missionaries prayed and sang while they suffered in the Philippian jail. "From the inner prison, voices broke the silence of midnight with songs of joy and praise to God. These disciples were cheered by a deep and earnest love for the cause of their Redeemer, for which they suffered."— *Testimonies,* vol. 3, p. 406.

In his second letter to the church at Corinth, Paul gives a series of four dramatic contrasts in his experience. He says, "We are afflicted in every way, but not crushed; perplexed, but not driven to despair; persecuted, but not forsaken; struck down, but not destroyed." 2 Corinthians 4:8, 9, R.S.V.

When we realize that these experiences came to Paul *because* he was following Jesus Christ and preaching His gospel, we catch a deeper insight into the apostle's dauntless spirit. No wonder John Buchan has said: "I reckon fortitude's the biggest thing a man can have—just to go on enduring when there's no . . . heart left in you. . . . The head man at the job was the apostle Paul."—*Mr. Standfast,* page 177.

How much it means, then, for Paul to write of the "God of all comfort, who comforts us in all our affliction." 2 Corinthians 1:3, 4, R.S.V. Comfort is not a sedative to deaden the pain; it is a strengthener. The word comes from the same root as "fortify." God was with Paul, comforting, or building him up, in all his afflictions. The comfort from our heavenly Father comes through facing the truth about ourselves and accepting the divine will for our life. Like the man of Tarsus, we must come to the place where we will say, "I can do all things"—suffer, face perplexities, come to the end of all my resources, lose loved ones, and meet death—"in Him who strengthens me."

Most amazing of all, Paul could declare truthfully that "we rejoice in our sufferings, knowing that suffering produces endurance, and endurance produces characer, and character produces hope, and hope does not disappoint us, because God's love has been poured into our hearts through the Holy Spirit which has been given to us." Romans 5:3-5, R.S.V. The apostle saw that the fire of trial and affliction burned out the dross and, with the help of the Holy Spirit, developed character that would be fit for heaven.

Finally, Paul, the dynamic man of action, was in prison— first in Jerusalem, then in Caesarea, and finally at Rome. These must have been tedious months and years for the apostle who had known so much activity. During this time some of his fellow workers were called away or gave up the faith. When trial and imprisonment came, Paul watched for God's plan to turn barriers into blessings for the furtherance of the gospel.

The lesson was so indelibly written in Paul's life that he longed to share Christ's sufferings. Philippians 3:10. Like a trumpet peal his message sounded to Timothy: "The time of my departure has come. I have fought the good fight, I have finished the race, I have kept the faith." 2 Timothy 4:6, 7, R.S.V. Beyond all suffering and tragedy, Paul saw Jesus at the end of the road with the crown of glory. The doughty apostle had lived a committed life, and for him the reward was sure!

DAVID'S VICTORY OVER SORROW

$\sim 3 \sim$

A Man Who Faced Many Crises

TO FEEL deeply one must have strong emotions and keen senses. Such a person knows the height of gladness and feels the pangs of sorrow more intensely than does the average man in the street. David, the son of Jesse, was extremely sensitive to beauty in nature, to the Creator's handiwork and power, and to love. He could be described as a man with a poetic soul who yearned for the presence of God in his life.

While caring for his father's sheep on the hills of Bethlehem, the young man may have composed and sung many spiritual psalms, such as this:

> "The heavens are telling the glory of God;
>   and the firmament proclaims His handiwork.
> Day to day pours forth speech,
>   and night to night declares knowledge.
> There is no speech, nor are there words;
>   their voice is not heard;
> yet their voice goes out through all the earth,
>   and their words to the end of the world."
>   Psalm 19:1-4, R.S.V.

Or again he may have blended his voice with the music of his harp to sing:

> "As a hart longs for flowing streams,
>   so longs my soul for Thee, O God.
> My soul thirsts for God, for the living God.
> When shall I come and behold the face of God?
> My tears have been my food day and night,
>   while men say to me continually,
>   'Where is your God?'"
>
> Psalm 42:1-3, R.S.V.

Because he was of a sensitive nature, David suffered intensely when he sinned or when sorrow and loss bowed his spirit. "The love that moved him, the sorrows that beset him, the triumphs that attended him, were all themes for his active thought. . . . While he was absorbed in deep meditation, and harassed by thoughts of anxiety, he turned to his harp, and called forth strains that elevated his mind to the Author of every good, and the dark clouds that seemed to shadow the horizon of the future were dispelled."—*Patriarchs and Prophets,* pages 642-644.

Called to Be King

We first see David as a youth hurrying in from the meadow at the command of his father. The bronzed shepherd boy, who lived much in the outdoors, was met by the prophet Samuel; and before Jesse's seven other sons the youngest member of the family was anointed king of Israel. The character of David at this period of his life is revealed in the testimony of one of Saul's servants. "Behold, I have seen a son of Jesse the Bethlehemite," he declared, "who is skillful in playing, a man of valor, a man of war, prudent in speech, and a man of good presence; and the Lord is with him." 1 Samuel 16:18, R.S.V.

Indomitable faith in the Lord was shown by David when he stood before giant Goliath and said, "You come to me with a sword and with a spear and with a javelin; but I come to you in the name of the Lord of hosts, the God of the armies of Israel, whom you have defied." 1 Samuel 17:45, R.S.V. With exultant courage young David added, "The battle is the Lord's and He will give you into our hand." Verse 47.

The first period of suffering in the life of David was the unjust and undeserved persecution by King Saul. The acknowledged leader of God's people had departed from God's way, and at this time he was actually an impostor. It must have almost shaken David's faith to receive such cruel treatment from the reigning monarch, especially after the youth had been told by the prophet that he was the true king! After all, a child of God suffers no more baffling discouragement than to find cunning, sinister evil wrought against him by a professed leader in God's cause. When the wrath of the half-insane king fell upon David, the youth became a fugitive, fleeing day and night for his life, for "Saul became David's enemy continually." 1 Samuel 18:29. The young man who had a short time before been set apart as God's choice to rule Israel was now an outcast, forced to desert his wife and friends, and to wander in deserts and hide in caves—even seeking refuge among the despised Philistines.

Recounting these years of sorrow and suffering, David wrote:

"I call upon the Lord, who is worthy to be praised,
    and I am saved from my enemies.
The cords of death encompassed me,
    the torrents of perdition assailed me;
the cords of Sheol entangled me,
    the snares of death confronted me."
                              Psalm 18:3-6, R.S.V.

The psalmist realized that suffering could change character and alter one's attitude toward life. The word "character" comes from Greek derivation meaning *to cut out, to carve or engrave* as with a graving tool. Affliction is the sharp instrument with which much of the divine carving is accomplished. If we allow the knife to cut away defects and shape us, we shall eventually be fashioned according to the pattern of the Master.

During the months and years that Saul persecuted David it was difficult for the sufferer to see the hand of God in his stormy experiences. Yet we are told that "it was the providence of God that had connected David with Saul. . . . The vicissitudes and hardships which befell him, through the enmity of Saul, would lead him to feel his dependence upon God, and to put his whole trust in Him. . . . In all these things, God was working out His gracious purposes, both for David and for the people of Israel."—*Patriarchs and Prophets,* page 649.

David Ascends the Throne

After the death of Saul, David was crowned king of Israel, and during his reign he established his court at Jerusalem. For many years he was a faithful ruler, bringing the golden ark to the new capital city and setting his people an example in devotion and worship of the true God. The nation prospered in an era of peace, and when enemies rose up—as did the Philistines and Moabites—David's armies subdued them in glorious victories.

Finally, a group of enemy nations swept down from the north and east to attack Israel. Joab, the general of David's army, possessed the courage of his king, for he called upon his men to put their trust in God. "Be of good courage," he said, "and let us play the man for our people, and for the cities of our God; and may the Lord do what seems good to Him."

1 Chronicles 19:13, R.S.V. While the armies were marching, David was humbly praying for the salvation of his people. "The dangers which had threatened the nation with utter destruction, proved, through the providence of God, to be the very means by which it rose to unprecedented greatness."—*Patriarchs and Prophets,* page 715. Later the king sang praises to God for victories won:

> "The Lord lives; and blessed be my Rock,
>   and exalted be the God of my salvation,
> the God who gave me vengeance
>   and subdued peoples under me;
> who delivered me from my enemies;
>   yea, Thou didst exalt me above my adversaries;
>   Thou didst deliver me from men of violence."
>   Psalm 18:46-48, R.S.V.

However, it was in the time of his greatest prosperity and martial triumph that David was in the greatest danger. It is not easy to carry the brimming cup of success with Christian humility. In his self-sufficiency, the king forgot God and yielded to subtle temptations of the flesh. Adultery was written against David's name, and when, as the result of his illicit passion for Bath-sheba, he was trapped, the king attempted to cover one transgression with still another—the murder of Uriah. David should have remembered the wise words of Moses that echoed down the centuries: "Be sure your sin will find you out." He should have realized that he could not hide his evil course from the eyes of God. For about a year he seemed to be secure in his wickedness, although his conscience gnawed within him. Later he described his agony in these words:

> "When I declared not my sin, my body wasted away
>   through my groaning all day long.

For day and night Thy hand was heavy upon me; *
   my strength was dried up as by the heat of summer."
                  Psalm 32:3, 4, R.S.V.

Then into the court of the king came the prophet Nathan
with a divine accusation. He described the cancer of sin, and
then said to David, "Thou art the man." Judgments were to
fall in succeeding years upon the king's head, for the prophecy
declared that "the sword shall never depart from thine house."
The news of David's sins was broadcast throughout the nation,
and the people recognized that he should rightfully receive the
punishment of death; yet no man dared lift his hand against
the ruler.

Staggered by the enormity of his evil deeds and broken
in spirit, David confessed his transgressions. "I have sinned
against the Lord," he whispered with bowed head. In such an
hour Satan must have gloated, for here was the one person in
all Israel he desired most to bring to ruin. Was he not the
anointed king that had been chosen by the Lord? Was he not
the spiritual leader of his people? Behold him now, crushed,
defeated, and seemingly lost!

But in the agony of his suffering, David found the divine
healing balm of forgiveness. Nathan said to the king, "The
Lord also has put away your sin; you shall not die. Neverthe-
less, because by this deed you have utterly scorned the Lord,
the child that is born to you shall die." 2 Samuel 12:13, 14, R.S.V.

We will never fully understand why the innocent must
sometimes suffer for the sins of others; yet a gleam of light
breaks through the clouds and we faintly comprehend. In this
instance we see that God used the loss of the innocent baby to
bring David to full repentance. In this experience "the king
was given opportunity for repentance; while to him the suffer-
ing and death of the child, as a part of his punishment, was far

more bitter than his own death could have been."—*Patriarchs and Prophets,* page 722. When our path goes through some of the darkest chasms of suffering it would be far sweeter to lie down and rest in death than to fight on through blood and tears. It is sometimes far greater punishment to live and endure the ignominy and pain than to be able to by-pass it by the sleep of death.

When the message reached David that his little son was dead, the king bowed his head and accepted the decree of the Almighty. We can better understand David's spiritual struggle, his suffering, and his final victory over sin when we read these verses from the fifty-first psalm:

"Have mercy on me, O God, according to Thy steadfast love;
    according to Thy abundant mercy blot out my transgressions.
Wash me thoroughly from my iniquity,
    and cleanse me from my sin!"

Verses 1, 2, R.S.V.

In these four lines of poetry David uses three words to describe his sin. *Pesha,* "transgression," is the act of setting one's self defiantly against God's will and rebelling against His eternal law. *Awon,* "iniquity," best describes a "warped" or "crooked" course. And *hatah,* "sin," means "to miss the mark." Therefore the psalmist recognizes that sin is a rebellion against God that leads to a crooked course of action, a course that takes one far from the mark God has set before us. David longed for his sins to be blotted out so that he might stand clean and pure before his Maker. This is the keynote of his soul-searching petition, as found in verses 10 to 12:

"Create in me a clean heart, O God,
    and put a new and right spirit within me.
Cast me not away from Thy presence,
    and take not Thy Holy Spirit from me.

Restore to me the joy of Thy salvation,
and uphold me with a willing spirit."

How wonderful it is to know that sins are blotted out and
to feel peace come to the troubled conscience! This assurance
of pardon, forgiveness, and a return to sonship in the Father's
house has been made certain for every sinner through the
death of Jesus Christ. Our Saviour is a mighty Redeemer, and
through Him we can know the joy of freedom from all sin!

Suffering Because of Weakness

There is no greater tragedy than for a father, who dearly
loves his son, to be so indulgent of the youth that he winks at
his faults and fails in discipline. Then the day comes when an
avalanche of sorrow crashes down on the father's head because
of the crimes of the wayward boy—crimes for which the father
is actually responsible. This was the additional suffering that
David had to endure.

The king of Israel failed to punish his first-born son Amnon
for his shameful crime. No doubt David refused to act because
he was haunted by the weakness in his own character. When
two years were allowed to pass without the indulgent son's
being punished, Absalom stepped in and murdered his brother.

The real reason for the tragedy in the family is found in
these words: "David had neglected the duty of punishing the
crime of Amnon, and because of the unfaithfulness of the king
and father, and the impenitence of the son, the Lord permitted
events to take their natural course, and did not restrain Absa-
lom. When parents or rulers neglect the duty of punishing
iniquity, God Himself will take the case in hand. His restrain-
ing power will be in a measure removed from the agencies of
evil, so that a train of circumstances will arise which will
punish sin with sin."—*Patriarchs and Prophets,* page 728.

Many a brokenhearted father or mother has pleaded with God to turn a prodigal son back to the path of right, to save the child from sin, when if the truth were known, the youth had been petted, pampered, and allowed to go in a rebellious course during the years of childhood. In later life he reaps the harvest of his and his parent's sowing. God cannot step in and force the sanctity of the human will, even to save a rebellious child from his crimes that will disgrace the family and bring unmeasured suffering to the parents.

After his failure with Amnon, David also blundered in his dealings with Absalom. First he alienated him for his crime, and later he allowed him to return to Jerusalem but refused to make peace with him. Absalom courted the favor of the citizenry until he "stole the hearts of the men of Israel." Soon there was open rebellion and revolt, and David fled from Jerusalem for fear of being assassinated.

We see the full cup of sorrow that the king must drink as he once more became a pitiful fugitive. "In humility and sorrow, David passed out of the gate of Jerusalem,—driven from his throne, from his palace, from the ark of God, by the insurrection of his cherished son. The people followed in long, sad procession, like a funeral train."—*Patriarchs and Prophets,* page 731.

Wise, indeed, is the person who sees the meaning of sorrow and profits by it. David "saw in his own sin the cause of his trouble," and again he turned to God for mercy and pardon. The Lord permitted "David to pass under the rod, but He did not destroy him; the furnace is to purify, but not to consume." —*Ibid.,* p. 738. Our heavenly Father seeks to purify the character, not to consume the life of His beloved child.

Forgiveness is not all that the Christian needs. Each follower of the Master must also have the sustaining love of God, the upholding power of the everlasting arms. David's sins were blotted out, but the scars—the remorse, the heartaches—remained. The prophet had told him, "The sword shall never depart from thine house." His little son died, and his other sons brought him disgrace. In his sunset years, when men long for peace and calm, David was crushed by Absalom's rebellion and death. Yet through the dark hours—and there were many in David's life—he learned to wait for the deliverance that came from heaven. He exclaimed:

> "My soul waits for the Lord
> more than watchmen for the morning."
> Psalm 130:6, R.S.V.

Truly "the psalms of David pass through the whole range of experience, from the depths of conscious guilt and self-condemnation to the loftiest faith and the most exalted communing with God."—*Patriarchs and Prophets,* page 754. That is why every Christian finds comfort and strength there, for in them he learns that God is his Comforter and Shepherd, his Refuge and Rock of salvation.

Shadows may have a valuable place in life, as explained by Thomas R. Henry in writing about the cold continent of Antarctica. He says, "In white darkness there are no shadows; these are seen only when the sun is high in a cloudless sky. As a result Antarctica most of the time is a shadowless land. On a cloudy day the illumination of the landscape is so diffuse that there is no perspective by which one can estimate the contours, size, or distance of white objects. The feet cannot find the snow underfoot. One staggers and stumbles like a drunken man. Walking becomes extremely difficult and tiresome. Sledge and tractor drivers cannot move for days at a time until shadows reappear by which they can detect the parallel ridges which indicate the presence of crevasses. Otherwise they might well stumble blindfolded into an area crisscrossed with thousand-foot-deep rifts in the ice which are the death traps of polar explorers.

"Elsewhere, perhaps, shadows do not play an important part in life. But in the infinity of whiteness, black images on the snow provide a pattern by which the human mind can function. Without them the difficulties of finding one's way are enormously multiplied. They may mean the difference between reason and utter confusion—in extreme cases between life and death. Where all reality is white it vanishes in whiteness, and the world is left empty of substance."—*The White Continent,* pages 39, 40.

The shadows helped David find the true persepective in life as he turned to God with all his heart. If the Eternal One allows us to pass through deep waters, may we, like the psalmist, be able to say:

"Search me, O God, and know my heart!
Try me and know my thoughts!
And see if there be any wicked way in me,
and lead me in the way everlasting!"
Psalm 139:23, 24, R.S.V.

"I SHALL COME FORTH
AS GOLD"

ᘒ4ᘓ

A Saint Suffers for His Faith

SOONER or later everybody needs a faith or philosophy of
life big enough and strong enough to stand up to disaster,"
said Leslie D. Weatherhead. "Blessed is he who has his
anchor secure before the storm breaks. When what we call
disaster breaks upon us, we are too stunned to be able to ar-
range our ideas, too bewildered to begin to erect our faith."

Job came to terms with God before he faced the white-hot
flames of suffering, and he knew he could depend on his
Redeemer. Yet the mystery of suffering Job faced was so
baffling, that although the Lord said this man was "perfect
and upright, and one that feared God, and eschewed evil" (Job
1:1), yet when sorrow cascaded over the poor man, he cursed
the day he was born and wished he were dead.

There is a significant warning in the book of Job—a warn-
ing against twisted thinking that believes doing right guaran-
tees prosperity and that wickedness always reaps its harvest of
tears in this life. It has always been easy to believe that wicked
men suffer for their sins; but it is difficult to find the reason for
good men suffering when they are good. From Job's experience

we learn that troubles may overwhelm the righteous, not as punishment for wrong, but as a test of their integrity.

In the land of Uz there lived a prosperous, godly man who loved his family and thanked the Lord for his blessings. He seemed to have security that would last for many years, but he was to learn that ruin can come swiftly. Job did not know how the divine plan was evolving, and all he could do was trust his heavenly Father. Now the good man had caught the attention of Satan, and the enemy of man appeared before God and challenged Job's religion. How many times our profession of Christianity is challenged today by men and women who say, "Let's see a genuine follower of Jesus Christ"? Can God testify of us as He did of Job: "Hast thou considered My servants, Neighbor Bradley or Dr. Freeman?"

Satan accused Job of doing right merely because of what he got in return. Job's piety was declared to be merely a matter of self-interest. The Lord said to Satan, "Behold, all that he has is in your power; only upon himself do not put forth your hand." Job 1:12, R.S.V. Even though the enemy may come upon us with his fierce attacks, it is comforting to know he can go no further than God permits.

The first blow was struck against Job's cattle and sheep and camels. These valuable possessions were swept away as in a moment. The second tragedy was the result of a tornado that wrecked the house where his sons and daughters were gathered, and killed all his children. Calamity was heaped on calamity!

In these tragic events Job did not sin or blame God for the trouble that befell him. The patient man might have asked, "Are all my prayers for my children in vain? Why would a loving God allow all these faithful young people to be taken away?"

As Robinson states, the messengers brought "crushing tidings for a father's ears. All dead, dead all at once—dead prematurely—dead by a sudden, unusual, and miserable death, dead as if by the hand of God Himself." Yet in this hour of staggering blows, Job held on to God.

Job was resigned to God's will, for he said, "The Lord gave, and the Lord hath taken away; blessed be the name of the Lord." Job 1:21. All of us must experience some form of resignation. Some must give up earthly happiness, some must be without love, some must renounce cherished hopes and plans. Resignation is not merely grinning and bearing it; it is accepting the divine will with good grace. Charles Lamb once paid this tribute to one who had suffered: "He gave his heart to the Purifier, and his will to the Sovereign Will of the universe." Only thus can we reach the experience described by Dante in the *Paradiso:* "In His will is our peace."

When Sickness Comes

Job's health was the next target of the evil one. A painful disease attacked the man, and he had no rest day or night, for in those days there was no sedative a physician could give that would lull the patient into slumber. The excruciating pain weakened Job and made him more susceptible to temptation.

See the sufferer, a man of prominence in his city, who is almost deserted by friends and loved ones. In those times, sickness was considered to be the curse of God, and men fled from it in fear. Job, who had once known the respect of young men and the honor of the aged, now says:

> "My kinsfolk and my close friends have failed me;
>   the guests in my house have forgotten me; . . .
> I am repulsive to my wife,
>   loathsome to the sons of my own mother."
>   Job 19:14-17, R.S.V.

To climax his troubles, Job's wife refused to stand by his side and encourage him. Scorning her husband's persistent faith, she said, "Do you still hold fast your integrity? Curse God, and die." Job 2:9, R.S.V. Gordon Chilvers makes this astute observation: "Satan had taken away Job's wealth, his children, and his health, but he did not take away his wife—her influence was used to make Job's trial greater. . . . The severity of this trial lay in this fact that the one who should have been his help and source of comfort in time of trial became his temptress and the tool of Satan."—*Moody Monthly,* July, 1953.

If ever a man might be justified for losing his temper it would be when Job's wife turned against him after he was saddled with the full burden of loss and grief! If ever a man seemed to have an excuse to flare up and shout angrily at his spouse, it was then. But the Bible states plainly: "In all this Job did not sin with his lips." Job 2:10, R.S.V. It would seem that the book of Job is asking again and again: "Is there such a thing as a sincere, wholehearted person who serves God just because it is the right thing to do?" And the life of Job proclaims the answer: "Yes!"

Troubles come to all of us, but they come without our choosing. We are not permitted to go to a store and select the "trouble" of our choice, and if it were possible none of us would be satisfied with our "bargain." No man would ever be willing to choose a trial or select his suffering.

Joseph Addison gives us a vivid lesson in his essay. He dreamed that the ruler of the world proclaimed that every person should bring his troubles and sorrows to a certain broad plain on a definite day. Humanity came like a vast army and piled their troubles high. Then a second order was given commanding everyone to choose another burden or trouble from the pile. The mortals rushed forward to make their choice, but they soon discovered that their new trouble was worse than their former one. Then, in the dream, the ruler of the world allowed each person to resume his own burden. When he had done so, the troubles of life seemed to shrink to about a third of their former size. With the help of our Saviour, our burdens grow lighter still and we can go forward, knowing that He cares for us.

The Test of False Philosophy

The next torturing ordeal that came to Job was the visit of his friends with their false accusations and distorted religious views. "Now when Job's three friends heard of all this evil that had come upon him, they came each from his own place. ... And when they saw him from afar, they did not recognize him; and they raised their voices and wept; . . . and they sat with him on the ground seven days and seven nights, and no one spoke a word to him, for they saw that his suffering was very great." Verses 11-13, R.S.V.

Finally, Eliphaz led the round of arguments by asking Job, "Think now, who that was innocent ever perished? Or where were the upright cut off?" Job 4:7, R.S.V. In other words, it was plain to this friend that no innocent person ever reaped trouble or sorrow. He was attempting to show that God bestows happiness and prosperity in proportion to man's obedience. There was some defect of character, some secret sin in Job, so Eliphaz believed, that caused all this suffering. Zophar emphasized the same thought with these smug words: "Know then that God exacts of you less than your guilt deserves." Job 11:6, R.S.V.

Furthermore, the "comforters" told Job that death came to his children because of their evil-doing. Bildad said, "If your children have sinned against Him, He has delivered them into the power of their transgression." Job 8:4, R.S.V. These words must have cut like a knife into the heart of the patient sufferer, for he had brought his children up to have faith in God and to obey the divine commandments. Here Bildad assumed something for which there was no proof.

When the "friends" could not point to specific sin in Job's life, they began to surmise that he mistreated the poor and the orphans. Job 22:5-9. But by this time the sufferer had quit attempting to defend himself, for he cried out:

> "Oh, that I knew where I might find Him,
>   that I might come even to His seat!"
> "But He knows the way that I take;
>   when He has tried me, I shall come forth as gold."
>   Job 23:3, 10, R.S.V.

Now even saintly persons can be wrong in their thinking, and this was true when Job thought that his trouble was from God. He cried out:

> "For the arrows of the Almighty are in me;
>   my spirit drinks their poison;
>   the terrors of God are arrayed against me."
>   Job 6:4, R.S.V.

God had not shot the arrows of suffering at His faithful servant; but He had permitted the test to prove Job's integrity. Let us be certain that we do not blame God for what He never sends.

Were Job's friends correct in their philosophy of sin and suffering? They were religious men who were convinced that God deals out judgment according to a man's sin. They looked upon Job as proof of their belief, but they were wrong, woefully wrong. We read: "Job's professed friends were miserable comforters, making his case more bitter and unbearable, and Job was not guilty as they supposed."—*Testimonies to Ministers,* page 350.

The Voice of the Almighty

God steps into the drama through the Voice in the whirlwind, and He challenges puny man to answer the basic questions concerning creation and the wonders of the universe. After some eighty-two questions have been propounded, none of which Job can answer, the humble sufferer says:

> "Behold, I am of small account;
>   what shall I answer Thee?
>   I lay my hand on my mouth."
>
> Job 40:4, R.S.V.

The Almighty states plainly that the views of the three friends are false. "My wrath is kindled against you and against your two friends," God says to Eliphaz; "for you have not spoken of Me what is right, as My servant Job has." Job 42:7, R.S.V.

If Job was able to speak that which was acceptable to God, it was because the man had knelt humbly on "the world's great altar stairs which slope through darkness up to God." From the despondency of the ash heap Job arose to mountain heights of trust, for in the supreme moment we hear him exclaim, "Though He slay me, yet will I trust Him."

Job was so pressed down by the burden of suffering and calamity that he longed to weigh it on the scales. Job 6:2. But there are no scales that can measure humanity's load of sorrow, for each one thinks his own is the heaviest. However, we can be sure that the heavenly Father will allow no trial to come that is greater than we can bear. And in the maelstrom of suffering Job found divine power to keep him from ruin.

When the Almighty spoke from the whirlwind, Job and his friends stopped their arguments. There is a wonderful lesson for every Christian in this experience of listening to God. May we come to the same conclusion that Job reached when he said to God:

> "I know that Thou canst do all things,
> and that no purpose of Thine can be thwarted."
>
> Job 42:2, R.S.V.

Job's Captivity Ended

The testing fires of pain and sorrow were finally quenched. Although Job did not know it, he had outwitted the cunning of Satan and vindicated God's confidence in him. Job must have felt a wonderful peace, for he had "come forth as gold" through the help of the Spirit of God.

The three friends who had not spoken "what is right" were instructed to offer sacrifices to the Lord and to ask Job to pray for them. "And the Lord restored the fortunes of Job, when he had prayed for his friends; and the Lord gave Job twice as much as he had before." Job 42:10, R.S.V.

Long arguments and endless debates did not change the views of the three friends concerning religion; but Job's unwavering faith, consistent life, and prayers brought them to see their great need. Human nature has not changed, and today, even as in Job's generation, a godly life is the most powerful argument for the truth. "Not all the books written can serve the purpose of a holy life."—*Testimonies,* vol. 9, p. 21.

Job's patient endurance became the ideal of the Jewish people, and in the New Testament the apostle James writes to the church: "You have heard of the steadfastness of Job, and you have seen the purpose of the Lord, how the Lord is compassionate and merciful." James 5:11, R.S.V.

How changed our view of calamity and sorrow can be if we see "the purpose of the Lord." Our chief concern with the problem of suffering is not to find an explanation for it, but to find victory! "I do not want to die," wrote Katherine Mansfield, "without leaving a record of my belief that suffering can be overcome. For I do believe it. Everything in life that we really accept undergoes a change. So suffering becomes love."

If Paul and Job could have recounted their tribulations, the physical pain, their bitter treatment by others, I am sure they would have joined in saying, "In all these things we are more than conquerors through Him that loved us." Romans 8:37.

"It is precisely from the company of the sons and daughters of affliction that the most convinced believers of all the ages have sprung. Who are the men whose names stand on the dramatic roll call of the faithful in Hebrews? Are they men whose days were happy and unclouded and serene, souls for whom the sun was always shining and the skies unvisited by storm or midnight? If anyone imagines that such is the background of faith, let him listen to this—'They were stoned, they were sawn asunder, were tempted, were slain with the sword, destitute, afflicted, tormented; they wandered in deserts, and in mountains, and in dens and caves of the earth.' That, declares the New Testament, has been in every age faith's grim heredity! And it is not from sheltered ways and quiet, sequestered paths, it is from a thousand crosses, that the cry ascends—'Hallelujah! For the Lord God omnipotent reigneth.'"—James S. Stewart, *The Strong Name*, page 153.

WHY JESUS SUFFERED

∽5∾

"A Man of Sorrows"

JESUS CHRIST is our Example in all things, even in suffering. He did not seek martyrdom, neither did He run away from it. He understood suffering to be an appointed means of accomplishing His Father's will, and when it came upon Him like a flood, He was able to pray, "Thy will be done."

Our Saviour was not triumphant in suffering because of His divine nature. No, He laid aside all of heaven's glory and took all the weakness of humanity, even "the seed of Abraham" and the body of our humiliation. As a weak human being He knew all about the pain, the disappointment, the trials and sorrows that mankind faces. Jesus can sympathize with humanity's suffering in a way no other being in the universe will ever know, for He spent nights in prayer; He felt hunger, pain, mental torture, fatigue, discouragement, and despair.

In Jesus we have the supreme example of vicarious suffering. There are occasions when men have taken the penalty of a crime for a friend or loved one; but while mankind was at enmity against God, Jesus came and suffered and died—not to save Himself but that we might have eternal life. The Son of man fasted forty days and when physically depleted was tempted of the devil; He suffered ignominy and shame; He faced the terrors of death in Gethsemane and longed to escape them; He took the mocking and ridicule of pagan soldiers and hypocritical Jewish leaders, and finally He died on Calvary. Why? He did all of this for one purpose—to save us from sin. His pure heart felt the degradation, the guilt, and the utter lost condition of the sinner in order that He might know how to enter into the experience of every man and faithfully intercede for him in heaven's tribunal.

The vicarious suffering of Jesus is portrayed in Isaiah's prophecy, where we see the suffering Servant bowing under man's horrible burden of woe. In all our "affliction He was afflicted." Isaiah 63:9. The sorrows He endured were ours, not His. "Surely He has borne *our* griefs and carried *our* sorrows; . . . He was wounded for *our* transgressions, He was bruised for *our* iniquities." Isaiah 53:4, 5, R.S.V.

The Pathway of Suffering

If today we could have a clear and reasonable explanation of all pain and suffering, that would be of little help in our dire need. We must have grace and help to bear it. *This is why Jesus suffered*. To be a perfect and faithful representative of man, Jesus Christ must know how humanity has been tortured by sin. "Therefore He had to be made like His brethren in every respect, so that He might become a merciful and faithful high priest in the service of God, to make expiation for the sins of the people." Hebrews 2:17, R.S.V.

If Jesus could not have sinned He could not have been tempted. A man who is blind cannot be tempted to see evil pictures. We can be tempted only because we are able to succumb to sin. Therefore, "because He Himself has suffered and been tempted, He is able to help those who are tempted." Hebrews 2:18, R.S.V. This means that He knew the pull of sin, He knew tragic disappointment, loss, and pain; but He came through it all triumphantly.

For our sake God "made Him to be sin for us, who knew no sin." 2 Corinthians 5:21. The Saviour never yielded to temptation; therefore, He did not know sin as the result of His own evil-doing. However, He took on Himself the entire burden of sin—the shame, the suffering, and the judgment of God. Thus He was made "sin" for us.

"If we had to bear anything which Jesus did not endure, then upon this point Satan would represent the power of God as insufficient for us. Therefore Jesus was 'in all points tempted like as we are.' Hebrews 4:15. He endured every trial to which we are subject. And He exercised in His own behalf no power that is not freely offered to us. As man, He met temptation, and overcame in the strength given Him from God."—*The Desire of Ages,* page 24.

Obedience Through Suffering

Many a person has gone on in a defiant, headstrong way until suffering caused him to bow his head and seek God's will. Jesus Christ did not defy His Father's will, or rebel against the divine plan, but He did learn the way of perfect obedience as the result of suffering. "Although He was a Son, He learned obedience through what He suffered." Hebrews 5:8, R.S.V.

At no point in His earthly life did Jesus turn aside from His Father's plan. At the age of twelve years He said, "I must be about My Father's business." Luke 2:49. To His disciples Jesus declared His purpose in these words: "My meat is to do the will of Him that sent Me, and to finish His work." John 4:34. In Gethsemane the Saviour prayed, "Nevertheless not *My* will, but Thine, be done." Luke 22:42. And His obedience led Him to humiliation and death, "even death on a cross." Philippians 2:8, R.S.V.

If sorrow and trial are necessary to bring us to obedience, then let us welcome the ordeal. The Son of God learned perfectly all that the right use of suffering can teach us. And He says, "My child, trust and obey. Out of this suffering can come the sublime lesson that you need."

The Love Supreme

From the first moments of hunger in the wilderness of temptation until He cried, "I thirst," as He hung on the cross, Jesus endured much physical pain. He knew the brutality of Roman soldiers as they scourged Him, spat upon Him, and placed a crown of thorns on His head. He fell beneath the weight of the cross, and He felt the searing pain of nails driven into His sensitive hands and feet. In the hours of darkness on the cross His feverish body and tortured muscles found no surcease from pain. And then Jesus knew the agony of death. Why did He suffer? There is only one answer, and the apostle Peter states it bluntly: "Christ hath suffered for us in the flesh." 1 Peter 4:1. Yes, we were the cause for all His suffering, and "with His stripes we are healed."

Let no suffering child of God say that our heavenly Father does not love us. He poured out His heart for us through the suffering of His Son. Jesus shielded us from the penalty of sin because He loved us. An illustration of the length of human love that is a faint shadow of how Christ loves us is related by Dr. W. Russell Maltby in *The Meaning of the Cross:*

There was "a workingman in the North of England whose wife, soon after her marriage, drifted into vicious ways, and went rapidly from bad to worse. He came home one Sunday evening to find, as he had found a dozen times before, that she had gone on a new debauch. He knew in what condition she would return, after two or three days of a nameless life. He sat down in the cheerless house to look the truth in the face and to find what he must do. The worst had happened too often to leave him with much hope, and he saw in part what was in store for him. Now that a new and terrible meaning had passed into the words 'for better, for worse,' he reaffirmed his marriage vow. Later, when someone who knew them both intimately, ventured to commiserate him, he answered, 'Not a word! She is my wife, and I shall love her as long as there is breath in my body.' She did not mend, and died in his house after some years in a shameful condition, with his hands spread over her in pity and in prayer."

This is a feeble illustration of how our Lord, the Bridegroom and Husband of His church, has loved us with an everlasting love, even when we sank into the pit of sin. "Christ has shown that His love was stronger than death. He was accomplishing man's salvation; and although He had the most fearful conflict with the powers of darkness, yet, amid it all, His love grew stronger and stronger."—*Testimonies,* vol. 2, p. 212.

But the physical, outward ordeal of the Christ was only a symbol of the deeper spiritual suffering. Jesus was lonely, misunderstood, and rejected by the majority of those He came to save. He suffered the agony of rejection because sinners were blind to their need of salvation and they spurned the love of God manifest in His Son. We can never comprehend the Master's sorrow as He looked upon Jerusalem, the city that was turning its back upon Him and plotting to crucify Him.

"It was the sight of Jerusalem that pierced the heart of Jesus—Jerusalem that had rejected the Son of God and scorned His love, that refused to be convinced by His mighty miracles, and was about to take His life. He saw what she was in her guilt of rejecting her Redeemer, and what she might have been had she accepted Him who alone could heal her wound. He had come to save her; how could He give her up?"—*The Desire of Ages,* page 576.

The supreme portrayal of divine love is seen on Golgotha's cross where the Lamb of God was made sin for us. His greatest suffering was to be shut away from His Father. Hear His cry: "My God, My God, why hast Thou forsaken Me?"

"Sorrow is the consciousness of lack," says G. Campbell Morgan. "What is the sorrow of sickness but the consciousness of lack of health? What is the sorrow of bereavement but the consciousness of the lack of the loved one? . . . What is the sorrow of loneliness but the consciousness of the lack of companionship? All sorrow is lack. Then it follows by a natural sequence of thought, that the uttermost depth of sorrow is lack of God. There is no sorrow like it."—*The Crises of the Christ,* pages 299, 300.

Jesus experienced the agonizing despair of the lost sinner separated from God by an impassable gulf. This is the greatest suffering ever witnessed in the universe. It is the supreme demonstration of love!

The Fellowship of Christ's Sufferings

The privilege of sharing in Christ's sufferings was a blessed comfort to the apostle Paul in his trials and persecutions. To the church in Corinth, he wrote, "For as we share abundantly in Christ's sufferings, so through Christ we share abundantly in comfort too." 2 Corinthians 1:5, R.S.V. When Paul suffered for his faith as he ministered to the churches, he knew he was walking in the steps of his Master.

We, too, share the sufferings of our Lord when we take up our cross and follow Him. First of all, we can return to

Gethsemane and Golgotha and meditate upon heaven's sacrifice for us. "It would be well for us to spend a thoughtful hour each day in contemplation of the life of Christ. We should take it point by point, and let the imagination grasp each scene, especially the closing ones. As we thus dwell upon His great sacrifice for us, our confidence in Him will be more constant, our love will be quickened, and we shall be more deeply imbued with His spirit. If we would be saved at last, we must learn the lesson of penitence and humiliation at the foot of the cross."—*The Desire of Ages,* page 83.

There are particular elements in suffering where we have fellowship with Jesus Christ. He suffered because of the sins of others; He felt the degradation and the awful consequences of sin in a way the sinner never could. For example, a parent suffers in the same way, but to a lesser degree, for a son or daughter who becomes a drug addict. The child may think lightly of his evil course, but the parent's love and deeper knowledge of all that is involved make his suffering the greater.

Jesus was not indifferent to human grief. He wept when He saw Martha and Mary grieving at their brother's tomb. While hanging upon the cross, the Son of God was touched by the sorrow of the women who stood nearby. "Although full of suffering, while bearing the sins of the world, He was not indifferent to the expression of grief. He looked upon these women with tender compassion."—*The Desire of Ages,* page 743. As His followers, we share His suffering when we "weep with them that weep," and sympathize with those who pass through the valley of the shadow.

Many times we suffer when we are obeying God's will. We may be hated, reviled, and persecuted; but in this dark hour we experience fellowship with Christ, for He deserved none of the suffering that was His lot.

When we walk with Jesus our sufferings are His sufferings, our sorrow is His sorrow. We can receive the greatest comfort and blessing as we know God is with us in all our trials and afflictions. James S. Stewart declares, "It is as though God said, in the day of darkness, 'Here, My child, is something you can do for Me! Here is your little share in the burden which I have been carrying from the foundation of the world and must carry till the day break and the shadows flee. Here is your part with Me in the age-long cross I bear.' "—*The Strong Name,* page 165.

> All those who journey, soon or late,
> Must pass within the garden's gate;
> Must kneel alone in darkness there,
> And battle with some fierce despair.
> God pity those who cannot say:
> "Not mine but Thine;" who only pray:
> "Let this cup pass," and cannot see
> The purpose in Gethsemane.
>   —Ella Wheeler Wilcox.

Here is a new concept of suffering of which the world knows nothing. The Christian takes up his cross—a little share in the cross of Jesus—and bears the pain, sorrow, and tribulation, knowing he is in fellowship with his Master. Jesus is in it with us, and we are in it with Him. "And of all the gifts that heaven can bestow upon men, fellowship with Christ in His sufferings is the most weighty trust and the highest honor."—*The Desire of Ages,* page 225.

WE ARE NOT ALONE

~6~

God Is With Us in Suffering

FROM my own limited experience I agree with C. S. Lewis that "when pain is to be borne, a little courage helps more than knowledge, a little human sympathy more than much courage, and the least tincture of the love of God more than all."—*The Problem of Pain,* page viii.

It requires courage to face suffering at any time; but it takes all the fortitude a brave soul can muster to accept trial and affliction *alone,* without a friend or loved one to share the burden. Faith has ebbed from many a great man's soul when he was forced to fight alone.

Elijah, the militant prophet of Carmel, could defy the false religion of four hundred and fifty priests of Baal; but when he stood alone against the world and one woman's threatening, he was seized with panic fear. Elijah left his servant behind and ran until he was exhausted. As he sat under a tree he moaned, "It is enough; now, O Lord, take away my life; for I am no better than my fathers." 1 Kings 19:4, R.S.V.

Forty days later the prophet was found hiding in a desert cave near Mount Sinai, and fearfully he told the Lord: "I, even I only, am left; and they seek my life, to take it away." Verse

10. The prophet of God suffered deep mental anguish, for he believed that all he had struggled to win for the truth had been lost. He was without companionship or sympathy. "I am the only one left." "I *only* am left." This was his lamentation in loneliness. Yet, when Elijah was the most despondent, God came to His servant. Not in the storm, the earthquake, or fire did the message of love come; but in "a still small voice." The prophet was challenged to go forward on a special mission which took away his sorrow and loneliness. He was assured that he was not the only faithful follower of the true God, for there were seven thousand in Israel who had not worshiped Baal.

With new strength and vigor Elijah arose above his defeat and went forth a dedicated messenger of the Lord. "As the rock never appears more majestic than when seen standing alone, with the ocean billows rolling round it, so with one who is 'faithful found among the faithless,' cut off from all natural and human supports, isolated in a surrounding sea of indifference or iniquity."—*The Pulpit Commentary,* vol. 5, p. 474 (1 Kings 19:1-18).

David is another Old Testament figure who knew abject defeat and loneliness. His mental suffering must have been intense as he felt himself to be a "forgotten man." Psalms 10:1; 13:1. Yet the Lord of heaven was at his side to encourage him, and when his strength was renewed the psalmist could sing, "I will fear no evil: for Thou art with me." Psalm 23:4. When isolated by enemies, he could feel God's protection, for he said, "The angel of the Lord encampeth round about them that fear Him, and delivereth them." Psalm 34:7.

"If, under trying circumstances, men of spiritual power, pressed beyond measure, become discouraged and desponding; if at times they see nothing desirable in life, that they should choose it, this is nothing strange or new. . . . When we are encompassed with doubt, perplexed by circumstances, or afflicted by poverty or distress, Satan seeks to shake our confidence in Jehovah. . . . Abiding in God's love, you may stand every test."—*Prophets and Kings,* pages 173-175.

The Loneliness of the Master

Every human being desires to fit into his environment; he longs to be understood and accepted. It was the bitter cup of loneliness and misunderstanding that Jesus Christ drank throughout His earthly life. In childhood His playmates and brothers misunderstood Him. The Saviour mingled with the crowds in city or on the hillside, "yet through childhood, youth, and manhood, Jesus walked alone. In His purity and His faithfulness, He trod the wine press alone, and of the people there was none with Him."—*The Desire of Ages,* page 92.

After His baptism the Son of man went into the desert and for forty days experienced deepest solitude. No faithful companion shared His anguish of soul, no human helper was beside Him in the ordeal of temptation. Later Jesus called twelve disciples to follow Him, but even they could not fully appreciate His work. "Throughout His life His mother and His brothers did not comprehend His mission. Even His disciples did not understand Him. . . . Alone He must tread the path; alone He must bear the burden."—*Ibid.,* p. 111.

When human companionship failed Him, Jesus went to His Father in prayer. The climax of temptation came in the Garden of Gethsemane. In His humanity He asked His sleeping disciples in the garden, "What, could ye not watch with Me one hour?" Although the fate of all mankind hung in the balance, the uncomprehending disciples slept on while Jesus suffered alone! When soldiers came to take Jesus, the disciples were afraid, and "they all forsook Him, and fled." The Son of God, who had enjoyed the adoration of angels and the fellowship of heavenly beings, was deserted by His followers in His trial, scourging, and crucifixion. The Saviour knew that men would desert Him, for He had prophesied: "Behold, the hour cometh, yea, is now come, that ye shall be scattered, every man to his own, and shall leave Me alone: and yet I am not alone, because the Father is with Me." John 16:32. This was the secret of the Master's strength, and it is the source of power for every Christian today.

"Whatever our distress, we can be sure that God sees us and that God cares for us," says Clarence E. Macartney. "If ever we are tempted to cry out with the psalmist, 'No man cared for my soul,' let us remember that God cares for us and that His providence is over us. As Jeremy Taylor, the master of English style, once put it, 'We are safer in God's storm, with God present, than we are in the calm of the world.' Whatever our difficulties, let us have faith that God will open our eyes and that we shall see, as Hagar saw in the wilderness, a well of water springing up for our refreshment. We can answer every temptation to doubt and despair, every assault of the world and of the devil, with that beautiful confession of faith by the slave girl there in the lonely wilderness: 'Thou God seest me.' "

But the Son of God must go farther into suffering than any sinner will ever be called to go. Not only did Jesus face Pilate, Herod, the Roman soldiers, and the mob alone, but He died on the cross, shut away from His Father. While He suffered physical torture He knew greater mental anguish as He was reviled and mocked. He listened for some word of courage from His disciples that would reveal their faith; but they were silent. The only moment of comfort came to the Son of God when the thief asked for salvation; Christ promised him eternal life, though His own valley of the shadow was just ahead. All that He heard from the crowd was the sound of curses and jeers.

When the final dark hour came, the Father shut Himself completely from His Son. There was no comfort, no hope, no promise, for the dying Lord of heaven and earth! "The sins of the world were upon Him, also the sense of His Father's wrath as He suffered the penalty of the law transgressed. It was these that crushed His divine soul. It was the hiding of His Father's face—a sense that His own dear Father had forsaken Him—which brought despair. The separation that sin makes between God and man was fully realized and keenly felt by the innocent, suffering Man of Calvary. He was oppressed by the powers of darkness. He had not one ray of light to brighten the future."—*Testimonies,* vol. 2, p. 214.

> Though long the weary way we tread,
>   And sorrow crown each lingering year,
> No path we shun, no darkness dread,
>   Our hearts still whispering, Thou art near!
>
> When drooping pleasure turns to grief,
>   And trembling faith is changed to fear,
> The murmuring wind, the quivering leaf,
>   Shall softly tell us, Thou art near!
>   —Oliver Wendell Holmes.

No child of God will ever be called to drink the lonely cup of grief our Saviour accepted. He felt that the whole race of men had betrayed, deserted, or rejected Him, and there was no one to understand the poignancy of His grief.

Clarence E. Macartney has said, "Because Christ tasted that loneliness for us and drank our cup, no soul need ever remain in the lonely night and darkness of sin. Peter, too, sinned and went out into the night and wept bitterly, but he did not forget that look which Jesus gave him when He heard him cursing and denying that he ever knew Him. It was that look that brought him to repentance and gave him forgiveness. Are you lonely because of sin? Then that is the cure for you, that loving, yearning, forgiving look of that wonderful Saviour who loved you and gave Himself for you."—*You Can Conquer,* page 55.

God Stood Beside Paul

It was the thought that Jesus Christ had been triumphant in suffering that sustained the apostles through trial, imprisonment, and martyrdom in the early history of the church. When Paul was in prison in Rome he knew something of his Saviour's lonely vigil. To Timothy the imprisoned apostle wrote, "At my first defense no one took my part; all deserted me." 2 Timothy 4:16, R.S.V. But the next verse reveals the valiant warrior of the cross in all his fortitude, as he says, "But the Lord stood by me and gave me strength to proclaim the word fully, that all the Gentiles might hear it." Verse 17, R.S.V. Pagan, sophisticated Romans looked skeptically at this prisoner from Jerusalem. There was no friend or fellow Christian in the court at his trial. Yet in that heartbreaking hour Jesus Christ stood by his side, and Paul rejoiced.

How changed is the suffering we must endure when we know Jesus is by our side! When the three Hebrew worthies were thrown into the red-hot furnace, they were not alone. A fourth person was walking in the fire with them! "As His witnesses were cast into the furnace, the Saviour revealed Himself to them in person, and together they walked in the midst of the fire."—*Prophets and Kings,* pages 508, 509.

In a world bent and almost broken by pain, affliction, and

disillusionment, the Christian can be a comforter. God "comforts us in all our affliction, so that we may be able to comfort those who are in any affliction, with the comfort with which we ourselves are comforted by God." 2 Corinthians 1:4, R.S.V. There is a blessing in suffering we may not as yet have found— it can prepare us to be a sympathetic helper to those in sorrow and pain. We need compassion and sympathy such as Jesus had, for His heart of love went out to every poor, struggling soul.

We will never be able to enter fully into the sufferings of our brother man as Jesus did; but there is a sense in which we can follow His steps as we help lift the burdens and speak the word of cheer. "Suffering in which we have found for ourselves the comfort of God is an equipment for service. It puts us alongside of others. It gives us entry to their pain, making them willing to listen to us. We can speak with authority for we have been there."—*The Interpreter's Bible,* vol. 10, p. 281.

The Master's Commission

As Jesus met with His disciples after His resurrection, He found them afraid that the Jews would kill them. How comforting was the Master's assurance: "Peace be unto you." At that moment He gave them a definite commission: "As My Father hath sent Me, even so send I you." John 20:21.

The Son of God proclaimed His mission to men when He preached His first sermon in Nazareth, for He said:

"The Spirit of the Lord is upon Me,
  because He has anointed Me to preach good news to the poor.
He has sent Me to proclaim release to the captives
and recovering of sight to the blind,
  to set at liberty those who are oppressed,
  to proclaim the acceptable year of the Lord."
Luke 4:18, 19, R.S.V.

The same royal service of love has been entrusted to everyone who takes the name of Christ and follows Him. We are called to help the poor, the oppressed, the suffering, and heartbroken. "Never should we pass by one suffering soul without seeking to impart to him of the comfort wherewith we are comforted of God."—*The Desire of Ages,* page 505.

There are many lonely hearts who have never met Jesus Christ or learned to love Him. In their solitude and suffering they need our assistance, and through us they may find the Saviour. We can tell them of His peace that passeth understanding.

"Through all our trials we have a never-failing Helper. He does not leave us alone to struggle with temptation, to battle with evil, and be finally crushed with burdens and sorrow. Though now He is hidden from mortal sight, the ear of faith can hear His voice saying, Fear not; I am with you. 'I am He that liveth, and was dead; and, behold, I am alive for evermore.' Revelation 1:18. I have endured your sorrows, experienced your struggles, encountered your temptations. I know your tears; I also have wept. The griefs that lie too deep to be breathed into any human ear, I know. Think not that you are desolate and forsaken. Though your pain touch no responsive chord in any heart on earth, look unto Me, and live."—*The Desire of Ages,* page 483.

Thank God, we are not alone in this chaotic world. "There is a Friend that sticketh closer than a brother." Proverbs 18:24. The apostle Peter knew what Jesus had done for him, and he admonishes us to "cast all your anxieties on Him, for He cares about you." 1 Peter 5:7, R.S.V. Have you proved His love and found His comfort in your life?

THE SEARCH FOR GOLD

✎ 7 ✎

God's Purpose in Suffering

WHEN we surrender our will to God and follow His blueprint, living unselfishly in a selfish world, striving for purity in a corrupt generation, we are certain to have trials and troubles. This does not mean that the Christian flaunts his religion or deliberately walks into trouble, but he finds he is thrust into the same world of sin that rejected and crucified his Lord. James asks, "Know ye not that the friendship of the world is enmity with God? whosoever therefore will be a friend of the world is the enemy of God." James 4:4. Jesus never promised His followers a calm, untroubled existence in a world antagonistic to His message, for He said, "In the world you have tribulation; but be of good cheer, I have overcome the world." John 16:33, R.S.V.

Therefore suffering should be regarded as a normal part of the Christian's life. It is neither unusual nor strange. Many persons live to the sad strains of suffering; it is the dominant minor melody. Because of this fact, the apostle James makes the daring statement: "Greet it as pure joy, my brothers, when you encounter any sort of trial." James 1:2, Moffatt. Yes, the Christian is to accept the trials and afflictions seriously, willingly, and also *joyfully*.

The word *tribulation* means "to press or afflict." The ancient *tribulum* was a threshing sledge; therefore tribulation is related to the process of threshing grain, separating it from the chaff. For the Christian, tribulation may be necessary to beat out the worthless and cherish the rich grain of character.

The Fruits of Suffering

Rightly accepted, the experience of suffering does not destroy our faith; it strengthens it and causes the follower of Christ to bring forth fruit. The writer of the book of Hebrews tells us: "For the moment all discipline seems painful rather than pleasant; later it yields the peaceful fruit of righteousness to those who have been trained by it." Hebrews 12:11, R.S.V.

Suffering and trial are required courses in the college of Christlike living. If we are "trained" by hardship and pain we will be humble and teachable. If we refuse the course of study and turn away, we will become embittered and ignorant of God's plan for us.

Patience is a noble virtue that develops through a lifetime. No one ever saw a patient baby, for no one is born with patience. James says, "Let patience have her perfect work, that ye may be perfect and entire, wanting nothing." James 1:4. This is the kind of patience John Wesley's mother possessed. One day her husband asked her, "How could you have the patience to tell that blockhead son the same thing twenty times?"

"If I had told him but nineteen times," she quietly replied, "I should have lost all my labor."

"None who receive God's word are exempt from difficulty and trial; but when affliction comes, the true Christian does not become restless, distrustful, or despondent. Though we cannot see the definite outcome of affairs, or discern the purpose of God's providences, we are not to cast away our confidence. Remembering the tender mercies of the Lord, we should cast our care upon Him, and with patience wait for His salvation."—*Christ's Object Lessons,* pages 60, 61.

These are days when the tension becomes great and tempers are short. It is a time for "the patience of the saints" to be manifest. Enduring suffering and hardship with a calm, sweet spirit is an evidence of patience.

Clara Barton once advised her young niece to be patient. "Keep yourself quiet and in restraint," she said. "Reserve your energies doing those little things that lie in your way, each one as well as you can, saving your strength, so that when God does call you to do something good and great, you will not have wasted your force and strength with useless strivings, but will do the work quickly and well."

A patient man and an impatient one may both lose heavily on the stock market, or both of them may come down with the same disease. The trouble might be as near alike as could come to two humans, but the reaction of the two men will be vastly different. Why? Because of the strength of character in the patient man and the lack of stabiliy and fortitude in the other. Life's values can often be determined more by *reactions* than by mere actions.

Patience means more than passively accepting trial and difficulty. Patience suggests endurance, waiting for something to happen, for someone to help. "The patience of the saints" is an *active* experience; it is the certain belief that God will stand by His suffering child and give him strength to endure.

Accepting pain and suffering in the right spirit helps to draw man back to God. "The finest men and women have recognized the part played by suffering in the making of noble character and the achievement of human usefulness," says

James W. Wilson. " 'In the story of the great, one chapter is invariably entitled "Pain." ' Pain is one of God's hardest-to-accept means of transforming and redeeming a human life." —*Religion in Life,* vol. 19, p. 168.

The famous violinist Ole Bull was once giving a concert at Munich when his A string snapped. Without hesitation he finished the program by playing on three strings. How like the undaunted Christian, who, when handicapped by sickness or adversity, learns to get life's music from the strings he has left! There was John Milton, writing his most magnificent poetry after he was blind; Ludwig van Beethoven composing his richest sonatas when deafness had overtaken him. Nor can we forget the spirit of Louis Pasteur, who made his scientific discoveries after a paralytic stroke had crippled him at the age of forty-six.

Yes, pain and suffering, rightly used, have developed greatness in men because they allowed it to bring forth the precious gold of character. Disappointed hopes became the challenge to do great things for God and for the love of fellow men.

The psalmist recognized how sorrow could draw a soul to the path of right, for he said, "Before I was afflicted I went astray: but now have I kept Thy word." Psalm 119:67. Some of life's profoundest lessons have been learned in a hospital bed, in an iron lung, in a wheel chair, or in prison. The "suffering is not good in itself," C. S. Lewis points out. "What is good in any painful experience is, for the sufferer, his submission to the will of God, and for the spectators, the compassion aroused and the acts of mercy to which it leads."—*The Problem of Pain,* page 98.

We Are Not Judges

Let us agree, then, that a loving God is not in the pain, the sorrow, the dying, and the myriad tragedies of daily account.

These are all evil in themselves; yet out of the grief, the agony, and the suffering may come the gold of a Christlike character. It has been refined in the crucible of affliction.

No man has a right to be a judge over his fellow men in matters of suffering. Sometimes we hear shallow-minded persons say something like this: "The death of her husband came because she left the church." Or, "He has been stricken with that disease because he wasn't faithful to God." Such was the distorted thinking of many persons in Christ's time, for the Jews considered all sickness and pain to be punishment in this life for some wrongdoing.

Jesus exploded this fallacy when He healed the man born blind. The disciples asked Jesus, "Who did sin, this man, or his parents, that he was born blind?"

"Neither hath this man sinned, nor his parents: but that the works of God should be made manifest in him." John 9:2, 3.

Jesus healed the blind man—a direct answer to the questioning disciples. They "were not called upon to discuss the question as to who had sinned or had not sinned, but to understand the power and mercy of God in giving sight to the blind."—*The Desire of Ages,* page 471.

In commenting upon this experience of Jesus, *The Expositor's Bible* makes an excellent observation: "It was our Lord's intention to warn the disciples against a curious and uncharitable scrutiny of any man's life to find the cause of his misfortunes. We have to do rather with the future than with the past, rather with the question how we can help the man out of his difficulties than with the question how he got himself into them. . . . No matter what has caused the suffering, here certainly it is always with us, and what we have to do with it is to find in it material and opportunity for a work of God."—Vol. 5, pp. 180, 181.

Think what a load was lifted that day from the blind man and from his parents when Jesus answered, "Neither hath this man sinned, nor his parents." No doubt the parents had endured years of mental anguish, trying to search their souls for the sin that had caused the baby to be born blind. Now they were clear of blame.

In like manner let us remember this divine lesson when men and women suffer today, for much of it comes through no direct fault of their own. Let us leave the mystery to God and refrain from judging when we do not have, and cannot obtain, the evidence.

Dr. Arthur J. Gossip says, "No doubt at all, sin does have penal consequences; and sometimes some of them are physical. Any doctor will tell us that this very case of blindness from birth is sometimes the direct result of the father's or the mother's misdemeanors. Sometimes. But there are many other possibilities that may account for such catastrophes; and to read the sinister interpretation into every case would be monstrously unjust."—*The Interpreter's Bible,* vol. 8, p. 612.

A Test for Eternity

The fires of adversity can be the testing to prepare us for the final crisis. Faith is essential today, even as it was in the time of Abraham. Faith holds on when there is no human way out of the darkness. When we think of faith our minds turn to Hebrews 11:1. New light has recently been thrown on the word from the Greek which is translated "substance." According to Bruce M. Metzger, the verse might well be rendered: "Now faith is the *title deed* of things hoped for." The Greek words have been found in business documents and contracts and refer to the possession of a piece of property. By faith we have the title deed to our heavenly home, and if we

are ready to meet Jesus Christ when He appears, we will re-
ceive the reward. The fruits of the Spirit must be developed in
every child of God *now* if he expects to stand the final test.
"Many who profess the name of Christ and claim to be look-
ing for His speedy coming, know not what it is to suffer for
Christ's sake."—*Early Writings,* page 113.

Some professed Christians suffer, not for the sake of the
gospel, but because of their selfish, unregenerate hearts. They
are tortured because they want to hold on to the world with
one hand and to Jesus Christ with the other. The attempt to
compromise brings only frustration and unhappiness.

The surrendered life gives up to God's plan, and when
suffering comes, the Christian prays that it will better pre-
pare him to meet his Saviour. Have you suffered? Remem-
ber Jesus climbed Golgotha's hill and His hands and feet
were pierced for you. Have you been discouraged? Our
Saviour saw the last ray of hope fade and darkness settle
over the earth. We are told to expect suffering for the sake
of our faith in Jesus. The disciples heard the Master say that
enemies of truth would "lay their hands on you and perse-
cute you, delivering you up to the synagogues and prisons,
and you will be brought before kings and governors for My
name's sake. This will be a time for you to bear testimony."
Luke 21:12, 13, R.S.V.

In time of persecution, torture, and sorrow we are called
to witness to the love of Jesus! Never was a testimony for
Christianity of greater value than in periods of suffering and
tragedy. This is the greatest proof that our faith in God is
genuine. In such an ordeal the Master has promised to be at
the side of His faithful follower. "Never is the tempest-tried
soul more dearly loved by his Saviour than when he is suffering
reproach for the truth's sake. 'I will love him,' Christ said, 'and

will manifest Myself to him.' When for the truth's sake the believer stands at the bar of earthly tribunals, Christ stands by his side."—*The Acts of the Apostles,* page 85.

The experience of suffering will not destroy the faith of a genuine Christian; it strengthens it. There is a Swedish proverb that says, "Blessed is he who sees a dawn in every midnight." When suffering comes crashing in upon us and we have exhausted our resources, then we surrender to God's sustaining mercy and our hearts reach out for His love. The very trials that make us feel deserted are the ones that can draw us closer to Christ. As we come near with tear-filled eyes we lay our burdens at His feet, and in exchange we receive comfort and strength.

Will It Make "Brave Reading"?

Wonderful is the promise stated by the apostle James: "Blessed is the man that endureth temptation: for when he is tried, he shall receive the crown of life, which the Lord hath promised to them that love Him." James 1:12.

Listen to the words of men and women who have endured the test and come forth as gold: Esther in the palace casts her lot with her doomed people as she says, "If I perish, I perish." Esther 4:16. Joseph, faced with sinister temptation, exclaims, "How then can I do this great wickedness, and sin against God?" Genesis 39:9, R.S.V. Peter and his fellow apostles face a council that recently voted to put the Son of God to death, and the apostle says, "We must obey God rather than men." Acts 5:29, R.S.V. Martin Luther defies the emperor with his ringing testimony: "Here I stand. I can do no other; may God help me. Amen."

It was this same Martin Luther who, in a severe illness and writhing in pain, said, "These pains and troubles here are like the type the printers set; as they look now, we have to read them backward, and they seem to have no sense or meaning in them; but yonder, when the Lord prints us off in the life to come, we shall find they make brave reading."

The testing will come, for everyone has a date with trials and adversity. Let us remember that Jesus Christ sees in us something worth developing, for He would not waste time on that which is of no value. "The Lord allows His chosen ones to be placed in the furnace of affliction, to prove what temper they are of, and whether they can be fashioned for His work."—*The Ministry of Healing*, page 471.

May we endure the testing and come forth as pure gold!

BEYOND THE SHADOWS

~∂8∂~

The Christian's Hope

IN A famous art gallery of Europe is a statue bearing the title, "The First Death." The sculptor has portrayed a mother holding the lifeless form of her son in her arms, while at her side stands the boy's father, a look of bewildering sorrow on his countenance. This may specifically represent the suffering of Adam and Eve over the death of Abel; but it also represents the universal loss that overwhelms us as we stand by the open grave of a loved one!

"I wish someone would light up the way for me," pleaded John Burroughs. When the grim shadows hover about us, we long for a ray of light that will give safe footing on the path ahead, for we are lonely and lost. With tears in her eyes a mother tells us that no amount of money could reimburse her for the loss of her son. Precious companionship and enduring love can never be measured by houses and lands or replaced with gold.

In the time of trouble it is the most natural thing for man to appeal to the Supreme Being. David said, "I stretch out my hands to Thee." Psalm 143:6, R.S.V. The answer is certain: "For this God is our God for ever and ever: He will be our Guide even unto death." Psalm 48:14.

No matter how involved we are in trouble or how great our perplexity, the Eternal One is our strong tower forever. Our Father's "watchcare extends to every household and encircles every individual; He is concerned in all our business and our sorrows. He marks every tear; He is touched with the feeling of our infirmities."—*Testimonies,* vol. 5, p. 742.

The key to the mystery of death is found in the radiant words: "He is risen." The resurrection of Jesus is the triumph of Christianity, for He not only defeated death on that memorable morning He came from the tomb; but He is alive forever, and He is our resurrection and life. The apostle Peter called his Lord "the Pioneer of Life." Acts 3:14, Moffatt. Through our Saviour the life that was forfeited in Eden because of sin was regained for the human race when He broke the seal on the tomb.

We can see light in the valley of the shadow because the Son of God has passed through it.

> Christ leads me through no darker rooms
> Than He went through before.

Today the glorified Son of God proclaims, "I am the resurrection and the life; he who believes in Me, though he die, yet shall he live." John 11:25, R.S.V. No comment upon these glorious words is adequate. Indeed the message is beyond human comprehension, and all we can do is accept the promise by faith, and exclaim, "Thank God!"

"Without the conviction that Christ had conquered death, not for Himself alone, but for all who found life in Him, there would have been no Christianity," says Robert D. Bulkley. "All else was dependent upon this one central fact, that Christ was risen and that we, too, shall rise." We can claim the reality of Christ's resurrection, for it "has entered more deeply than any other historic event into the lives of millions since those early days. It gave the martyrs courage as they faced the perils of the amphitheater."—F. Townley Lord, *The Conquest of Death,* page 73. The early church read the Gospel of John and each member cherished the Saviour's words: "I am come that they might have life, and that they might have it more abundantly." John 10:10. This is the summing up of the purpose of Christ's first advent, and the ever-present hope of the church.

Our attitude toward death and the future life shapes our ideas concerning the purpose of our present existence. "If one then puts aside the existence of God and the possibility of survival as too doubtful to have any effect on one's behavior," says Somerset Maugham, "one has to make up one's mind what is the meaning and use of life. If death ends all, if I have neither to hope for good to come nor to fear evil, I must ask myself what I am here for, and how in these circumstances I must conduct myself."

The Universal Summons

Of the billions of human beings who have lived, worked, loved, and suffered on this earth, only two have escaped from it alive—Enoch and Elijah, who were translated to heaven. Every other being, including the Son of God, has tasted the bitter cup of death.

One man came back to live on this earth after he died and had been buried for four days; but when he returned he gave no account of any life beyond the grave, and he brought no message from the spirit world. That man was Lazarus, a friend of Jesus Christ. On one occasion Lazarus became ill, and before his friend Jesus arrived from a distant part of the country, the man was dead. As Christ and His disciples journeyed toward Bethany, the Saviour broke the sad news of

Lazarus's death. He said, "Our friend Lazarus sleepeth; but I go, that I may awake him out of sleep." And when the disciples were slow to comprehend, Jesus added, "Lazarus is dead." John 11:11, 14.

God's word plainly declares that the dead are asleep. In the day that a man dies his thoughts perish. Psalm 146:4. None of the mental faculties continue in death, for "the dead know not anything." Ecclesiastes 9:5. Each human being is given life, a time when he can decide to be noble, pure, and obedient to God or selfish, proud, and evil. In a world of sin such as ours, men cannot go on living forever. Evil would grow to mammoth proportions if human beings lived for centuries. Therefore a just God allows man to make his decision, to choose his course of action, and then comes the sleep of death. All human beings are left in this unconscious sleep, their life record kept by a merciful Father until the day of judgment and the resurrection.

A loving God shields the dead from the evil, strife, and bloodshed of a world of sin. Comforting is the promise: "He giveth His beloved sleep." Psalm 127:2. It is a rest from the labors and trials, the sorrows and disappointments, of this existence. Hamlet feared that in the "sleep of death dreams may come." But, no; there is nothing to fear, for in quietness and peace the dead rest until they hear the mighty voice of the Son of God.

They Shall Hear His Voice

"The hour is coming," said Jesus, "in the which all that are in the graves shall hear His voice, and shall come forth; they that have done good, unto the resurrection of life; and they that have done evil, unto the resurrection of damnation." John 5:28, 29. There are two distinct resurrections according to this text; the first, to restore the good to life, and the second, to call forth those who have persisted in evil.

The day of triumph over death for the saints who sleep will be when Jesus returns. Paul describes the event in these words: "For the Lord Himself shall descend from heaven with a shout, with the voice of the Archangel, and with the trump of God: and the dead in Christ shall rise first." 1 Thessalonians 4:16.

This is the "lively hope" that Peter speaks of in his first epistle where he emphasizes the promise of eternal life because Jesus was resurrected. The word "lively" means *living* or *full of life*. Truly, Christians have no dead creed; they have a living message: the Pioneer of Life reigns, and He is coming to give eternal life to His faithful ones.

For those who sleep, it will seem but a moment from the hour of their death until they hear the voice of the Son of God. They are unconscious of the passing of time. But suddenly the silence of the grave is broken by a shout of triumph, and the sleeping ones hear His voice! "The hour is coming," said Jesus, "and now is, when the dead shall hear the voice of the Son of God: and they that hear shall live." John 5:25. How fitting it is that those who have obeyed the teachings of Jesus and followed His commandments in this life shall hear Him at the first moment of their resurrection! It is the omnipotent voice of death's Conqueror, the One who, since the day of His release from the tomb, has held the power of death in His hands. When He comes, "then shall be brought to pass the saying that is written, Death is swallowed up in victory." 1 Corinthians 15:54.

We are interested in the exposition of the recently published Protestant commentary, *The Interpreter's Bible,* where a discussion of Paul's teachings on the resurrection is clearly set forth. John Short states, "Christian doctrine is not one of immortality but of resurrection. We shall do well to get this point clear. As expounded by the apostle Paul, whom we believe to have entered more deeply into the mind and spirit of his Lord than any other, man's hope of survival depends not on the inherent immortality of his soul, but on the act of God. ... There is nothing in Paul's writings nor in the New Testament to suggest that the soul is inherently immortal."—Vol. 10, p. 253.

The Gift of Immortality

The transformation from death to life is described in the Scriptures: "For the trumpet will sound, and the dead will be raised imperishable, and we shall be changed. For this perishable nature must put on the imperishable, and this mortal nature must put on immortality." 1 Corinthians 15:52, 53, R.S.V. The change of our bodies from disease and death to purity and immortality will be made at that moment. No man has earned it, for it is "the gift of God."

Our only knowledge concerning the form of the body after it has been invested with eternal life is drawn from the appearance of Jesus after His resurrection. The Gospel narratives reveal that our Lord retained His personality and His form so that He was recognized by the disciples. To doubting Thomas, Jesus showed His nail-pierced hands and His side which had been torn by the soldier's spear. John 20:27. Jesus ate food with His disciples. John 21:12, 13. There was, however, a power in the glorified body which was not confined to time and space. We are told that the resurrected Lord appeared in the room with His disciples when the door was shut. John 20:26. Again He vanished from the sight of two disciples after He had talked with them at the dinner table. Luke 24:31.

"The resurrection of Jesus was a type of the final resurrection of all who sleep in Him. The countenance of the risen Saviour, His manner, His speech, were all familiar to His disciples. As Jesus arose from the dead, so those who sleep in Him are to rise again."—*The Desire of Ages,* page 804.

He Holds the Keys

There is One who possesses the keys to the door of death. Jesus says, "I am He that liveth, and was dead; and, behold, I am alive for evermore, Amen; and have the keys of hell and of death." Revelation 1:18. To possess "the keys of hell and of death" is the symbol of the authority of the Son of God over these enemies of man. Jesus gained full control over hell and death by His victory over sin and Satan. When the King of kings comes in glory, these enemies shall be destroyed. 1 Corinthians 15:26.

Thank God, the keys are in His hands! No spirit medium can tamper with the dead. No earthly hand can desecrate the life or character of those who are now sleeping. Only the Son of God can take the keys and open the door. He alone can call the sleeping ones from their rest.

We sorrow not as those who have no hope, for Jesus is our assurance of resurrection and life. "Wherefore comfort one another with these words," says Paul. 1 Thessalonians 4:18. Death shall be forever wiped from the universe. "There can be no doubt that in the eyes of the apostle, and surely for the people to whom he wrote, death was a fearful calamity; it is an evening that threatens with oblivion all that we hold dear. How can it appear otherwise? What could give greater cause for rejoicing than the assurance, vindicated and justified by a resurrection which could only be ascribed to a God of righteousness and love and power, that death would finally be utterly vanquished?"—*The Interpreter's Bible,* vol. 10, pp. 249, 250.

Sometime ago I was driving in New Orleans in the vicinity of the cemeteries. I turned into one street that led to an iron fence—the boundary of the graveyard. My eye caught sight of a sign on a nearby telephone pole. It read: "Dead End." It seemed to symbolize the hopelessness of death for those who have not found the Life-giver.

The Christian belief in eternal life is a sacred trust that is not to be treated lightly. We believe that our talents and time are entrusted to us so that we will make the most of them. The child of God is not building merely for threescore years and ten. He is building both for time and for eternity. Yes, what we think about life, what we think about ourselves, and what we think about God, are all dependent upon our belief in the future—eternal life with our Redeemer and our God.

Let us give thanks that we live this side of the resurrection of our Lord. We can see down the highway of life, and it holds no "dead end" for us. The Pioneer of Life went before us and blazed the way to heaven. He calls to His trusting children, "Follow Me. . . . I am the way." With gratitude we can say, "Thanks be to God, who gives us the victory through our Lord Jesus Christ." 1 Corinthians 15:57, R.S.V.

FACING OUR SORROW

$\sim 9 \sim$

Strength to Endure

A WONDERFUL stained-glass window once adorned a famous cathedral in Southern Europe. Pilgrims from distant lands journeyed to the spot to gaze upon the masterpiece of art. One day a violent windstorm struck with such force it sent the window crashing to the marble floor, shattering it into hundreds of pieces. The caretakers gathered up the fragments, put them in a box, and stored them in the basement. Months passed and on a certain day a stranger came to town and inquired about the famous window. When told of its fate, he desired to see the fragments. When shown the box of shattered glass, the stranger asked, "Would you give these to me?"

"Take them along," said the caretaker; "they are no longer of value to the cathedral."

After many months had passed an invitation came to the custodians of the cathedral, asking them to visit the studio of a famous artist in a distant city. At the appointed hour the men arrived, and the artist ushered them into a room hung with a large canvas. When the curtain was dropped, the custodians saw a stained-glass window surpassing the beauty of the lost

(73)

masterpiece. As the visitors gazed in wonder, the artist said, "This window was created from the fragments of the shattered one in your cathedral. I return the broken pieces to you in the form of this picture. It is now ready to be transported to your church."

For many of us the pattern of life has been shattered by sorrow or tragedy. Broken pieces lie about us, and we feel as Job did when he said, "Wherefore is light given to him that is in misery, and life unto the bitter in soul?" Job 3:20. The complaint is a common one, for the despondent person frequently asks, "Why was I born?" But these moods will pass, especially when one's faith is anchored to the Rock of Ages. Out of the ruins of today can rise hope and happiness tomorrow.

"The longing for the rest of the grave is the mood of intense weariness and disease; and it is counteracted by the mood of restored health, which longs for activity, even in heaven."— *The Pulpit Commentary,* Job, page 60. When the heart is sad, the physical health is affected. Job said, "My eye has grown dim from grief, and all my members are like a shadow." Job 17:7, R.S.V.

To brood over one's disappointment, bereavement, or illness only clouds the mind and weakens the body. "It is a positive duty to resist melancholy, discontented thoughts and feelings,—as much a duty as it is to pray." "Let the burden of your own weakness and sorrow and pain be cast upon the compassionate Saviour."—*The Ministry of Healing,* pages 251, 257.

Concerning those who are burdened with pain or who have brought trouble to others, the apostle Paul wrote the Christians: "So you should rather turn to forgive and comfort him, or he may be overwhelmed by excessive sorrow." 2 Corinthians

2:7, R.S.V. Men and women need the helping hand of one
who has received courage and strength from God. A word
spoken at the right moment may lift a discouraged soul
from despair and set his feet on the road to new horizons.

When Mary Coburn lived in a New York apartment she
practiced her vocal lessons faithfully every day, not realizing
what the influence of her singing might bring. In *The Read-
er's Digest* she recounts her experience as she was at a dis-
couraging point in her career. "Almost panicky, I grabbed at
a piece of music. It was Albert Hay Malotte's beautiful setting
of 'The Lord's Prayer.' My courage returned. Jubilantly I
stood in the middle of the room and sang it with a full heart.
I must have sung it five or six times.

"Several days later I heard a rustle at my door, and turned to
see a note being slipped under it. It read: 'Dear Neighbor:
If ever you feel discouraged, perhaps this will hearten you.
Things have been going badly for me—so badly I didn't want
to live any longer. When I'd hear you practicing I'd snap out
of it a little, because you sounded as though you had something
to live for. Finally the other night I decided to end my life.
I went into the kitchen and turned on the gas. Then I heard
you singing. It was 'The Lord's Prayer.' Suddenly I realized
what I was doing. I turned off the gas, opened the windows
and drank in the fresh air. You sang that song several times.
Well—you saved my life. You gave me the courage to make a
decision I should have made long ago. Now life is all I could
hope it to be. Thanks always.' "

There is a prescription for spiritual morale in the thirty-
seventh psalm that never fails if it is diligently followed. The
fifth verse is particularly apropos, for we read, "Commit thy
way unto the Lord; trust also in Him; and He shall bring it to
pass." Our heavenly Father is a mender of broken hearts.

Trust Him, and He will take the fragments that have been scattered by sin and sorrow and create a new life that will shine as the stars forever in His eternal kingdom.

Only One Answer

For the ordeal of death and tears such as our world faces today there is only one answer—faith in the risen Christ and in His word. The hope of the resurrection takes away hopeless grief, for the Christian does "not grieve as others do who have no hope." 1 Thessalonians 4:13, R.S.V. Because we have suffered a stunning blow does not mean that we can sit down and quit. We face the dawn of each day with a God who loves us. "If we are called upon to meet bereavement, let us accept the bitter cup, remembering that a Father's hand holds it to our lips."—*The Ministry of Healing,* page 233.

Our heavenly Father does not want to see our lives ruined by sorrow and mourning. There is service to render to others; blessings to pass on to those in greater need. Let us accept the lesson and look up into the face of our loving Saviour. "Suffering is the emery wheel upon which the cutting edge of Christian character is sharpened. It is by our patience, patience under trial, that we are to 'win our souls.' For this reason we may 'triumph even in our troubles,' knowing that out of these is born endurance, character, and hope. 'The pain God is allowed to guide' ends in repentance and new character."— F. Olin Stockwell, in *The Christian Century,* Feb. 11, 1953.

In the farewell words of Moses to the children of Israel is the sublime promise:

"The eternal God is your dwelling place,
and underneath are the everlasting arms."
Deuteronomy 33:27, R.S.V.

The figure is that of a parent supporting a child who is attempting to walk. How well Moses knew the strength of God's "everlasting arms." The door had been closed on his hopes, and he was forced to renounce his dearest plans. Like Moses, let us take courage, for God is by us in the shadows. "Always underneath and round about are His everlasting arms. We never make our way alone through the world. Faces may change and conditions may alter, but God is the same yesterday, today, and forever."—*The Interpreter's Bible,* vol. 2, p. 556.

The Son of God trusted His Father, and He was willing to accept the bitter with the sweet in His earthly ministry. When we read the terrible story of Christ's death on the cross, we may feel that He was the victim of powers beyond His control. This is not true, for the Saviour suffered only because He *willed to suffer.* To His disciples He said: "For this reason the Father loves Me, because I lay down My life, that I may take it again. No one takes it from Me, but I lay it down of My own accord." John 10:17, 18, R.S.V. The ideal the Saviour set before us is perfect obedience to God's will. Jesus exemplified His submission to His Father when He said to Peter, "Shall I not drink the cup which the Father has given Me?"

As the potter takes the clay, wets it, and kneads it until it is pliable, so the Master Potter works upon our lives. When the clay is moist enough and perfectly pliable, the potter shapes it into a beautiful and useful vessel. In the same manner the Master of men molds and fashions us if we submit to His will. The trials, afflictions, and heartaches that seem cruel and to no purpose may be the essential experience to develop sympathy, patience, and love in the heart.

Can we not look back over some of the earlier experiences in our life and see how divine Providence was leading us when the way seemed mysterious and dark? Shall we not take heart when we are faced with perplexing moments today? Shall we not be submissive and teachable, learning that even the deepest tragedy does not come by chance?

Dr. Norman Vincent Peale recounts the experience of a skiing party in the Canadian Rockies who came to a dangerous transverse valley where avalanches threatened to destroy them. The guide told the group not to call, whistle, or talk in loud tones, for it might start the slide of death. In the party was a girl in her twenties who realized the danger. She began to whimper and cry, and said, "I can't do it. I'm terrified. I simply can't do it."

The leader of the party looked at the hysterical girl and said quietly, "The Lord has watched over you throughout you life hasn't He? You believe that, don't you?"

"Yes," sobbed the girl.

"Well, then can't you trust Him to take care of you for the next twenty minutes?" asked the leader.

The frightened girl came through the ordeal triumphantly, for she remembered how God had stood by her side through every experience.

In referring to the overwhelming disaster He faced, Jesus asked His disciples: " 'Are you able to drink the cup that I drink, or to be baptized with the baptism with which I am baptized?' And they said to Him, 'We are able' " Mark 10:38, 39, R.S.V., James and John were sincere in thinking they were able to drink from the cup of suffering and to receive the baptism of trial; but when the test came, "they all forsook Him, and fled." The disciples dreamed of doing great deeds for their Lord if He were a king; but they melted away from His side when a mob came with staves and sticks to take their Leader off to court. They could not face scorn, ridicule, and the jeers of the crowd. In like manner we might be ready to lay down our lives in heroic conquests for the cross, but we give up when petty trials, hardships, or light persecution come our way.

Courage to Carry On

There is an impressive lesson in seeing it through with God in the life of the prophet Ezekiel. Tragic loss came to him, for he wrote, "At even my wife died; and I did in the morning as I was commanded." Ezekiel 24:18. It was not that the man of God was insensible to his loss, for he said the light of his home went out and the desire of his heart had passed away; but he had spiritual stamina and a true perspective of life so that he could go on with his daily duties, even though his heart was broken.

A Christian woman who had lost her husband continued to mourn for weeks and months. Finally her little son came to her one day and asked, "Mother, is God dead?"

"No, dear," the woman replied; "but your father is."

The child's question challenged the woman's mind, however, and she put aside her grief and accepted life's responsibilities, knowing that her God still lived.

Our worth to our fellow men is measured, not by what we begin, but by what we complete. To carry on in the face of tragedy, to work in the face of failure, to pray in the face of defeat, to smile courageously through our tears—these come only as we have faith to look up and say, "Dear God, Thy will, not mine, be done."

To those who are in sorrow there are special words direct from the loving Saviour: "Blessed are they that mourn: for they shall be comforted." Matthew 5:4. The Greek word for *comfort* may be translated "to call to the side of." The English word *comfort* comes from the Latin root which has the idea of strength: *con-fortis,* or to endure with fortitude. God's comfort to the sorrowing is no anesthetic; it is a tender, reinforcing strength, when Christ comes to the side of the sufferer and enables him to go forward triumphant.

> "The Lord is near to the brokenhearted,
> and saves the crushed in spirit."
> Psalm 34:18, R.S.V.

Someday We'll Understand

The mirrors of the apostle Paul's day were made of polished metal, and the city of Corinth was famous for those made of silver or brass. However, they were not perfect reflectors, and since they were not they became an object lesson to the apostle of man's imperfect knowledge in this life. Writing to the church at Corinth, the apostle declared, "For now we see in a mirror dimly, but then face to face. Now I know in part; then I shall understand fully, even as I have been fully understood." 1 Corinthians 13:12, R.S.V. Moffatt translates the phrase, "the baffling reflections in a mirror."

Yes, often the reflections in the mirror of life are dim and baffling. Our faith is scarcely strong enough to see God. Yet we can be thankful for the dim reflection, since it is the promise that someday we shall see Him face to face!

Paul felt his physical resources ebbing away as he gave himself wholly to the preaching of the gospel. Tired and sometimes discouraged, yet he could say, "So we do not lose heart. Though our outer nature is wasting away, our inner nature is being renewed every day. For this slight momentary affliction is preparing for us an eternal weight of glory beyond all comparison." 2 Corinthians 4:16, 17, R.S.V.

"*Affliction* here is transmuted into glory beyond. . . . The affliction is *slight* and *momentary* by comparison with the *glory* which is massive and unfading. . . . Our judgment of things depends on the background against which we see them, as the background of a picture gives us perspective and qualifies the foreground. . . . If we have no belief in God or a future life, if we know nothing of Christ, if our view of the world is that it is merely a mechanical process without spiritual value or purpose, everything will be colored by this outlook. Trouble will be a disaster; pain will be a calamity; and sorrow a tragedy. But if we have the Christian view, the sufferings of earth will be no more than the chisel strokes of the Sculptor, forgotten in the beauty of the statue which He is shaping from the marble, or even welcomed as the means of His achievement."—*The Interpreter's Bible,* vol. 10, pp. 323, 324.

The mind can but faintly imagine the wonders of the earth restored to perfect beauty as God shall present it to those who love Him. Through our tears and blinding sorrow we hear the promise: "Eye hath not seen, nor ear heard, neither have entered into the heart of man, the things which God hath prepared for them that love Him." 1 Corinthians 2:9.

We will never be homesick for this better world, however, until we are dissatisfied with this one. Ellen G. White states, "We need to keep ever before us this vision of things unseen. It is thus that we shall be able to set a right value on the things of eternity and the things of time. It is this that will give us power to influence others for the higher life."—*The Ministry of Healing,* page 508.

TO KNOW GOD'S WILL

∽ 10 ∾

The Test of Discipleship

A WEALTHY manufacturer went to one of the ablest architects in America and asked him to prepare plans for a new factory to cost ten million dollars. The architect set to work studying and analyzing the requirements, the site of the building, and the necessary materials. Finally he completed the blueprints for the huge plant—a masterpiece of architectural engineering. When the manufacturer received the plans he studied them carefully, but soon he cast them aside and ordered carpenters, steelworkers, and bricklayers to work on a building he had crudely sketched. The structure was a hodgepodge of slovenly, poorly planned construction, inadequate for the needs of the company.

You say, "No smart businessman would be so stupid as to build such a structure."

Perhaps not, but this is a parable of what millions of human beings are doing with the temple of their lives. God has a perfect plan for each of us if we submit to His will. We can follow the divine blueprint or we can put it aside for our selfish, inadequate, poorly conceived ideas and attitudes. The choice is ours.

Those who are determined to have their own way follow

a stubborn course that ends in disaster. The wise man wrote, "There is a way which seemeth right unto a man, but the end thereof are the ways of death." Proverbs 14:12. When we persist in demanding our own way we are actually fighting against God. "Whenever men choose their own way, they place themselves in controversy with God. They will have no place in the kingdom of heaven, for they are at war with the very principles of heaven."—*Thoughts From the Mount of Blessing,* pages 82, 83.

Headstrong and rebellious, man does not want to obey or to submit to God's will. The heavenly Father is longing to teach us how to find happiness here and in the hereafter, but we lack faith and confidence in Him. It is essential, in these days of ruined dreams and perished hopes, to get back to the simple faith expressed by Isaiah:

> "Behold, God is my salvation;
>   I will trust, and will not be afraid;
>   for the Lord God is my strength and my song,
>   and He has become my salvation."
>   Isaiah 12:2, R.S.V.

The secret of victorious Christian living resides in the trusting heart. Warren Seabury, a missionary to China, wrote, "I do not know what is before me, but I am building my nest in the greatness of God." This confidence is supported by a knowledge of the Eternal One. We are instructed through His word and by the impressions that come to our minds by the Holy Spirit. Isaiah declared, "Though the Lord give you the bread of adversity and the water of affliction, yet your Teacher will not hid Himself any more, but your eyes shall see your Teacher. And your ears shall hear a word behind you, saying, 'This is the way, walk in

it,' when you turn to the right or when you turn to the left."
Isaiah 30:20, 21, R.S.V.

God speaks to man in various ways so that all may hear His
voice if they will only listen. Through His creative works He
communicates to us, for, as Paul states, "Ever since the creation
of the world His invisible nature, namely, His eternal power
and Deity, has been clearly perceived in the things that have
been made." Romans 1:20, R.S.V. Sin has marred the Creator's
handiwork, and the evolution theory robs God of His rightful
place in nature, yet to the discerning mind the universe is a
sublime expression of God's character.

The Eternal One speaks to humanity through His Son, the
Word "made flesh." Jesus Christ came to teach men and
women the eternal truths concerning salvation and to demon-
strate how much the Father loved His children. "We know
that the Son of God is come, and hath given us an understand-
ing, that we may know Him that is true." 1 John 5:20.

God communicates to us through chosen human beings. He
spoke "in time past unto the fathers by the prophets." Hebrews
1:1. These truths have been brought together in Holy Scripture
and become a guidebook for the Christian. As we delve into
the blessed Book, the wisdom and love of God in the plan of
redemption is revealed to us.

A Willingness to Accept God's Will

God speaks to man through the Holy Spirit. The conscience,
when subject to the divine will, is guided into the way of
truth. To His disciples Jesus made the promise that the Com-
forter would "teach you all things, and bring all things to your
remembrance, whatsoever I have said unto you." John 14:26.

With every prayer that we offer there must be a willingness
to accept God's answer. If we have the spirit of Jesus we will

pray as He did: "Thy will be done." The Scriptures are a defense against the foes that assail us. Doubt, discouragement, and despair are the enemy's instruments to destroy faith, but we have a tested and true weapon, "the sword of the Spirit, which is the word of God." Ephesians 6:17.

The man or woman who knows God's word and treasures it in his heart "shall not be afraid of evil tidings: his heart is fixed, trusting in the Lord." Paul desired every follower of Christ to be filled with "the knowledge of His will." Colossians 1:9. Suffering becomes more understandable as we accept God's blueprint for us.

"God reveals His will to us in His word, the Holy Scriptures. His voice is also revealed in His providential workings; and it will be recognized if we do not separate our souls from Him by walking in our own ways, doing according to our own wills, and following the promptings of an unsanctified heart, until the senses have become so confused that eternal things are not discerned, and the voice of Satan is so disguised that it is accepted as the voice of God."—*Messages to Young People,* page 156.

If we have not heard the voice of God saying, "This is the way, walk in it," it is because we have not trained ourselves to listen. It is possible for us to become so busy running here and there on God's service we never actually know what He wants us to do. Jesus warned His followers of such a tragic plight when He said, "Not everyone that saith unto Me, Lord, Lord, shall enter into the kingdom of heaven; but he that doeth the will of My Father which is in heaven." Matthew 7:21.

Obedience to God's commands is the acid test of discipleship. If we were left to follow our own whims and desires, we would lose our way. Therefore we are asked to accept God's will and keep His commandments. The motivation for our obedience must come from the heart, that is, the will, or it is worthless. The apostle Paul admonishes us to do "the will of God from the heart." Ephesians 6:6.

It is breath-taking to realize what can happen as we love Jesus Christ and obey His words. Here is the staggering promise: "If a man loves Me, he will keep My word, and My Father will love him, and We will come to him and make Our home with him." John 14:23, R.S.V. Yes, our heart can be God's home. It is a poor place we have to offer Him, not worthy of His entrance; yet He says He will come in and make it His *home!* Dwight L. Moody describes the effect of the abiding presence of our Lord in these words: "There are two lives for the Christian, one for the world, and one with God. If you dwell constantly at the feet of Jesus, it will save you many a painful hour."

God's negative answers sometimes carry with them His richest gifts. John Ellis Large, in *Think on These Things,* tells the well-known parable of the three trees that grew in the forest long ago: "The first tree prayed that, when it was hewn down, it might become part of the timbers of a noble palace, the most magnificent building ever shaped by the creative hands of men. . . . Instead, it was faced with the bitter fact that its lovely grain was being used to throw a rude stable together. But it was the stable in which the Christ Child was born!

"The second tree petitioned God that, when the ax should be laid to its roots, its planks might be fashioned into the hull of the lordliest vessel that ever sailed the seven seas. . . . Instead, when it was chopped down, it was used to form the hull of a lowly fishing vessel; and the tree resented the insult to its grandeur. But that insignificant schooner was the one from which Jesus preached His incomparable words at the edge of the little Sea of Galilee!

"The third tree beseeched God that it might *never* feel the bite of the cruel ax, but that it might go on for years pointing its proud finger toward the sky. . . . Instead, the dark day came when the woodsmen arrived and laid the sharp blade to its resisting roots; and it cried out against God with every blow. But the shaken tree was fated to become the crossarms and the upright of the cross of Calvary, destined to point its noble finger toward the sky forever!

"Not a single one of those trees lived to see its fondest wish come true. Not a single one got its deepest prayer answered, nor its own will fulfilled. But God, in fulfilling His will for those three trees, granted them a fulfillment infinitely beyond anything they could have desired or hoped for!"

To Do His Will

When Jesus struggled through the dark hours in the Garden of Gethsemane, He longed to be saved from crucifixion and death. Therefore He prayed, "O My Father, if it be possible, let this cup pass from Me: nevertheless not as I will, but as Thou wilt." Matthew 26:39. Three times Jesus uttered this petition. He might have rebelled against drinking the cup of sorrow, but He was submissive to the will of His Father. He turned His eyes once more toward heaven and breathed a prayer of submission to the divine will. "If this cup may not pass away from Me, except I drink it, Thy will be done." Verse 42. It was in Gethsemane that the Son of God prayed through to victory. He was triumphant in the hour of deepest trial and suffering! When the soldiers came into the garden to take Jesus, Peter was ready to fight; but the Saviour answered, "Put up thy sword into the sheath: the cup which My Father hath given Me, shall I not drink it?" John 18:11. Prayer had prepared the Master for the suffering before Him.

"The obedience that Christ rendered, God requires from human beings today. He served His Father with love, in willingness and freedom."—*Christ's Object Lessons,* page 282. At the foot of the Mount of Olives there is even today a spot among the gray-leaved olive trees called Gethsemane. It has become a shrine because here Jesus was willing to place everything in His Father's hands. This was where He trusted to the limit.

No wonder Paul declares that Jesus "became obedient unto death, even the death of the cross." Philippians 2:8. And the writer of the book of Hebrews emphasizes that Christ learned "obedience by the things which He suffered." Hebrews 5:8. The prayers of our Lord in Gethsemane are the key to all victorious Christian living, for they mean unconditional surrender. "When a man is in tune with Christ," says E. H. Pruden, "his lips will be saying and his hands will be doing what Christ wants."

We cannot answer all the questions concerning life and death, good and evil; but these become insignificant if only we have confidence in the eternal goodness of the Almighty. The history of much that has been called Christianity has often been a chronicle of distrust and fear; but when we say, as did Isaiah, "I will trust, and not be afraid," we will triumph gloriously. The end will ultimately explain and vindicate that which is darkness today. The experiences of life may be hard and harrowing, inscrutable and irreconcilable, but they are fertile soil in which the finest sort of faith can grow.

In a castle on the Rhine River once lived a baron who had grown bitter because of the hypocrisy of his supposed friends. To help pass the time in his rock-bound fortress he hung wires from one point to another to make an aeolian harp on which the winds might play. Days and nights came and winds blew, yet there was no music from the huge harp. The baron interpreted all of this to be a sign of God's displeasure. One evening, however, the sky was filled with storm clouds and a fierce tempest came with the darkness. As the lonely baron paced his halls, he suddenly heard it! The wild air was filled with music. His harp was singing with joy and passion above the roar of the storm. Then it was the baron knew the truth. The thick heavy wires could give out music only in a time of storm and tempestuous winds.

So it may be with our spiritual experience. The darkness falls, and hurricanes of doubt and suffering blow—and in those hours we discover the sweetest music of divine love.

> Our sweetest songs are those that tell
> of saddest thought.
> —Percy B. Shelley.

The soul that is sure of God and rests upon His will accepts the whole scheme of pain and trial. The more such a faith is tried, the deeper it will hide itself in God. "Therefore," says the apostle Peter, "let those who suffer according to God's will do right and entrust their souls to a faithful Creator." 1 Peter 4:19, R.S.V.

An anonymous Confederate soldier wrote this touching meditation in time of battle:

"I asked God for strength, that I might achieve—I was made weak, that I might learn humbly to obey. . . .

"I asked for help that I might do greater things—I was given infirmity, that I might do better things. . . .

"I asked for riches, that I might be happy—I was given poverty, that I might be wise. . . .

"I asked for power, that I might have the praise of men—I was given weakness, that I might feel the need of God. . . .

"I asked for all things, that I might enjoy life—I was given life, that I might enjoy all things. . . .

"I got nothing that I asked for—but everything I had hoped for. . . .

"Almost despite myself, my unspoken prayers were answered. I am, among all men, most richly blessed!"

Our Father has not minimized the trial and suffering we shall have to face. He tells us we will go through tribulations and trials, but He also promises to help us triumph over the worst of them. The beloved John heard the words of commendation that will be spoken to those who are victorious in the final conflict. Of these valiant sons of God the apostle wrote, "These are they which came out of great tribulation, and have washed their robes, and made them white in the blood of the Lamb." Revelation 7:14. Upon the sea of glass the conquerors will gather. They will have "gotten the victory" and will be able to sing a new song before the throne of God.

"When the earthly warfare is accomplished, and the saints are all gathered home, our first theme will be the song of Moses, the servant of God. The second theme will be the song of the Lamb, the song of grace and redemption. . . . This is the theme, this is the song,—Christ all and in all,—in anthems of praise resounding through heaven from thousands and ten thousand times ten thousand and an innumerable company of the redeemed host. All unite in this song of Moses and of the Lamb. It is a new song, for it was never before sung in heaven."
—*Testimonies to Ministers,* page 433.

These soldiers of the cross have learned discipline; they know how to obey. They have kept the commandments of God and have held firm in the faith of Jesus. It is of this hour that John was thinking when he wrote, "He that doeth the will of God abideth forever." 1 John 2:17.

Patient obedience will characterize Christ's remnant peo-
ple. They will obey God's law, honor Him as the Creator, and
remember His Sabbath. In the remnant group will be found
no hypocrisy, for no guile is in their mouths. They will follow
the example of their Lord as He prayed, "Thy will be done."

The victors will possess "the faith of Jesus." It is a faith that
looks beyond the wickedness, the depravity, the moral bank-
ruptcy, and the spiritual disillusionment of a lost civilization
to the light that shines brighter unto the perfect day. It is a
faith founded upon the word of God, for every Christian will
be able to answer, "It is written." It is a faith that surrenders
to the Eternal One and says, "Take me as I am and mold my
will to Thy pattern that I may be Your child forever."

COMFORTING THOSE WHO MOURN

⌁∘‖∘⌁

Hope for the Hopeless

"THERE is no home on earth but will have its hush," says an old Spanish proverb, describing the universal effect of sorrow. Yet no matter what our loss may be, we still have a duty to perform in life. Even though we may have sustained a stunning blow, we cannot sit down and quit. To carry on in the face of tragedy, to work in the face of defeat, to smile courageously through our tears—all these take faith in God and in His promises.

There is no more depressing experience for a minister than to be called to conduct the funeral of a loved one in a family that has no faith in God. The finality of the loss, the unrestrained agony, the bewildering bitterness, are beyond description. Paul told the Christian believers that they were not to sorrow "as others which have no hope." 1 Thessalonians 4:13. And to the hopeless and despairing we are to offer a genuine hope—Jesus Christ, "the resurrection, and the life."

The Saviour knew the lonely agony and despair that humanity experiences. In the prophetic words of Psalm 69:20 we see the suffering of the Messiah: "Reproach hath broken My heart; and I am full of heaviness: and I looked for some to take pity, but there was none; and for comforters, but I found none."

It is a source of strength to know that Jesus went through the deepest torrents of suffering without faltering, and as the result He is able to comfort the afflicted and brokenhearted.

The original Greek word for "sympathy" means "to suffer with" another person. Thus, when Jesus sympathizes with us He suffers with us in all our afflictions. The pain-wracked world needs Christians who "suffer with" their brother man. This experience comes only as we feel a kinship and a oneness with those who mourn. The prophet Ezekiel learned how to be tolerant and sympathetic when he visited the captives who lived by the Chebar River. He says, "I sat where they sat, and remained there astonished among them seven days." Ezekiel 3:15. As the prophet looked through the eyes of these people he became sensitive to their pathetic condition, and their need "overwhelmed" him. (R.S.V.)

We would be shocked out of our smugness and lethargy if we would leave our more sheltered existence and mingle for a time with the downtrodden, the outcast, the helpless, and the underprivileged. "Unless a helping hand is held out to them, they will sink lower and lower."—*The Ministry of Healing,* page 172. As ambassadors for Christ, we must minister to every class of people.

When we follow in the footsteps of the Master we will "rejoice with them that do rejoice, and weep with them that weep." Romans 12:15. Let us never forget that "there are multitudes struggling with poverty, compelled to labor hard for small wages, and able to secure but the barest necessities of life. Toil and deprivation, with no hope of better things, make their burden very heavy. When pain and sickness are added, the burden is almost insupportable. Careworn and oppressed, they know not where to turn for relief. Sympathize with them in their trials, their heartaches, and disappointments. This will open

the way for you to help them. Speak to them of God's prom-
ises, pray with and for them, inspire them with hope."—*The
Ministry of Healing,* page 158.

Helping Those Who Mourn

How shall we help a person in his hour of grief? We long
to do something to ease his pain and suffering, but we feel
incompetent and we are afraid we will do the wrong thing.
Howard Whitman recently gathered the suggestions of clergy-
men who had much experience in helping the bereaved, and he
sets forth the salient points in an excellent article in *The Chris-
tian Advocate.*

We should not attempt to minimize the grief of the indi-
vidual or try to divert him from his sorrow when it is fresh and
acute. Let the sorrowing one talk of his loss. It is often a good
thing to recount the life of the loved one who is gone. The one
who mourns should face the reality of the loss, accept the fact of
death, and go forward with God's help in a new and altered life.

To the sorrowing we can be good listeners. If they wish to
empty themselves of pent-up sorrow, let them do it, for grief
cannot long be harbored or cherished in the bosom without
damaging the outlook on life. Let us listen thoughtfully, and
when we do speak we will be ready to reassure the sorrowing
one that God loves him.

Do not allow your sympathy and interest in the sorrowing
one to be a thing of a moment. He may need help most acutely
after the lonely days have lengthened into months. Whitman
wisely suggests: "Keep in touch. See your friend more often
than you did before. See him for any purpose—for lunch to-
gether, for a drive in the country, for shopping, for an evening
visit. He has suffered a deep loss. Your job is to show him, by
implication, how much he still has left. Your being with him

is proof to him that he still has resources to draw upon."

We can show our love by little acts of kindness, helping lift the petty details until grief is assuaged. We can help the sorrowing get out of the vacuum by showing them how they are needed by others and how they can help the community and the church. Tennyson well said, "I must lose myself in action, lest I wither in despair."

The heart may be numb and the home desolate, but the mood of despair can be overcome. Let love find its way into the heart of the grief-stricken—love for the needy and love for those less fortunate. The authors of *When Sorrow Comes,* Grace Perkins Oursler and April Armstrong, give this prescription: "Fill the hours overbrimming, fill other hearts with the life-giving love you have lost. Don't let the wellspring of love dry up from lack of use. You have lost one outlet for those springs of human affection. Remember we were born to love and to give."—Page 88.

The Example of Jesus

As Jesus walked along the country roads or on the narrow streets of the cities of Palestine, He felt compassion for every person He met. "The word translated compassion is actually a much stronger word: it implies pain of love. He saw the people of His land as shepherdless people. They were as if wolves had harried them and left them bleeding, because they had none to lead and protect them."—*The Interpreter's Bible,* vol. 7, p. 360.

The "pain of love" caused the Master to pour out His life in service. He taught in the synagogues, He healed the sick, and He fed the hungry. Matthew depicts the sympathizing Saviour in these words: "When He saw the multitudes, He was moved with compassion on them, because they fainted, and were scattered abroad, as sheep having no shepherd." Matthew 9:36.

The Son of God never attended a funeral except to turn it into a time of rejoicing. One day as He was approaching the gate of the city of Nain, He saw a funeral procession for the only son of a widow. As the Saviour stood at the side of the sorrowing mother, His heart was touched with love and pity, and He said, "Weep not." Then He called the dead man back to life. This same Jesus is touched by our grief. To us who mourn, He says, "Weep not. I am the resurrection and the life." His heart has the same unchanging love for heartbroken mothers today that He had that day at Nain.

Our Lord was sorrowful as the time drew near when He must leave His disciples, for He realized they needed help and comfort from heaven. Therefore Jesus said, "I will pray the Father, and He shall give you another Comforter, that He may abide with you forever." John 14:16. "Another Comforter." Yes, Jesus had been the solace, the comfort of His followers, and to all His children through succeeding generations He sends the blessed Comforter, the Holy Spirit.

Pointing the Brokenhearted to Christ

When the church is filled with the power of the Holy Spirit, every member will lift the fallen and help bind up the wounds of the afflicted. While each person is to bear his own burdens as best he can, yet there are times when the load grows too heavy. Then Paul's admonition applies: "Bear ye one another's burdens, and so fulfill the law of Christ." Galatians 6:2. The best way to increase our faith and to strengthen our courage is to share them with others. Life to be happy must be shared; it smothers when it is shut up in itself.

The experience of a woman who had served the church for twenty years is recounted by Oscar F. Blackwelder. This Christian mother came to her pastor and asked, "Do you remember

the wretched health I had when you first learned to know me,
what a nervous wreck I was?" Then she added, "I have had
to bear so many burdens in my family that today I am a rela-
tively well woman." Helping to lift the burdens of her loved
ones had made her strong to bear her own.

The peace of the Christian is not an abstract idea or quality;
it is a Person. If we would correctly translate Ephesians 2:14
we would find that it is more than "He is our peace." The full
meaning is "He is the Author of our peace." When we have
learned of the Master and He has written His enduring peace
in our hearts, we can point the distressed and sorrowing to
Him. The weaker a soul may be, the stronger will be the arm
of the Saviour. The heavier the burden that is weighing upon
the heart, the greater the lifting power of our Burden Bearer.

In order to dramatize the need of the helpless and sorrowing,
Jesus identifies Himself with them, and He asks us to see not
their need but *His*. In the parable of the last judgment our
Lord described the humble, compassionate Christians who saw
the hunger, nakedness, loneliness, and sorrow of the masses,
and who did something to help them. To this group came the
King's blessing: "Inasmuch as ye have done it unto one of the
least of these My brethren, ye have done it unto Me." Mat-
thew 25:40.

These lowly followers of the Master were amazed to learn
that they were doing a personal service to their King. They
loved their fellow men, they saw a great need, and they acted
because the "pain of love" impelled them. In contrast to this
group there were the "professed Christians" who would have
done anything for Jesus if they could have served Him per-
sonally, but they would not stoop to help the poor and the
fallen. They had divorced their religion from daily life; it was
a theory, not a living, loving experience.

Our Saviour is willing to make humanity's need His own. He goes incognito in the poor, the helpless, the sorrowing. "He identifies Himself as being in person *the very sufferer*. Mark, selfish Christian: every neglect of the needy poor, the orphan, the fatherless, is a neglect of Jesus in their person."—*Testimonies,* vol. 2, p. 26. (Italics ours.)

Qualified to Serve

Alcoholics Anonymous is doing much good in helping release men and women from the throes of alcoholism. The organization is successful because those who have been delivered from the curse work to help those who are victims. Members visit the sick person and tell him how they gained the victory over alcohol. They can say, "I've been over the road and I know you can triumph, too."

In like manner the Christian can help the oppressed and fainthearted, for after he has experienced the comfort of God he can witness to what it has done for him. The comfort is founded upon a close fellowship with the heavenly Father. A missionary was teaching an Indian woman the Lord's Prayer. As he began with the first two words, "Our Father," her eyes lighted and she said, "I do not need to know any more. If God is our Father that changes everything."

Yes, everything is wonderfully changed because our Father comforts us. And "the Father of mercies and God of all comfort, who comforts us in all our affliction" is with us, "so that we may be able to comfort those who are in any affliction, with the comfort with which we ourselves are comforted." 2 Corinthians 1:3, 4, R.S.V. In commenting on this verse, *The Interpreter's Bible* declares, " 'The comfort with which we ourselves are comforted by God' is therefore the only form of comfort which is effective. Sympathy which merely assures people that we feel for them can do little. It may even increase their trouble by communicating a sense of our helplessness. It may feed their self-pity. The true comforter is one who can carry to others the strength of an experience in which God has given him the victory. This comfort is of universal application. It applies to all situations. It speaks to the hearts of people 'in any affliction.' All troubles find healing in a right relationship with God, and in the opening of the mind to His message."—Vol. 10, p. 281.

We never receive peace in wholesale quantities that will last for months or years; it is a daily possession. Thrilling are the words of the apostle Paul to the Christian: "God's peace, that surpasses all our dreams, keep guard over your hearts and minds in Christ Jesus." Philippians 4:7, Moffatt.

With a trusting heart as our precious possession, we can be a powerful influence upon those who are bewildered, helpless, and defeated. Isaiah pictures the mission of the child of God thus:

> "The Lord God has given me
>   the tongue of those who are taught,
> that I may know how to sustain with a word
>   him that is weary."

We are taught when we sit at the feet of Jesus. His words will become so much a part of our thinking that we will transmit them to others, and thus men will know we are the Saviour's disciples.

Since "no man is an island, entire of itself; every man is a piece of the continent, a part of the main," we are all bound together by our mutual needs. Intercessory prayer must be a part of the spiritual experience of every sincere Christian. When we pray for a soul in desperate need, we must be ready to go into action as God directs to help answer our petitions.

Jesus prayed for His disciples. To faltering Peter He said, "I have prayed for thee, that thy faith fail not." Luke 22:32. Furthermore, our High Priest "ever liveth to make intercession" for us. Hebrews 7:25. To follow the example of our Lord means that we will pray earnestly for the lost, the discouraged or downcast, and our enemies. We are to "pray one for another," and with our prayers link all our efforts to help our brother. Dr. George A. Buttrick explains the place of intercessory prayer in this way: "So we are called to live in sympathy. Sympathy means not only 'feeling with' our neighbor's sorrow, but communicating to him our confidence that if we were in some besetment we could lift a banner above it. How, save by prayer?"—*Prayer*, page 112.

All around us is a world in need. Let us search out the heartbroken and suffering, speaking words of hope, doing acts of kindness, praying for their physical and spiritual welfare. By kind words and gentle deeds let us make the pathway easier for weary, lost souls. We are to reveal the spirit of heaven as it was lived by Jesus Christ. "Speak as He would speak, act as He would act. Constantly reveal the sweetness of His character. Reveal that wealth of love which underlies all His teachings and all His dealings with men."—*The Ministry of Healing,* page 159.

PREPARING FOR THE
FINAL CRISIS

∽12∾

An All-Out Conflict Is Ahead

WHEN the conquering generals of ancient Rome returned from the wars, it was the custom of the populace to celebrate the victory with a triumphal procession. The soldiers marched through the streets while crowds shouted *"Io triumphe!"* At the head of the parade were magistrates and senators; after them came trumpeters, followed by wagons loaded with trophies of battle. Next came captives, humbled by their chains. Finally, the hero of the day appeared in regal splendor to receive the applause of the citizens. Thus was a returning conqueror lauded in olden times.

Soldiers of our American wars have been welcomed home by friends and loved ones with celebrations and parades. The victors of battle have received tribute from the nation for their heroic deeds.

But far exceeding the glory of any earthly triumph will be the homecoming that awaits God's faithful warriors who have been victorious in the conflict between good and evil. With eternal glory heaven will honor the heroes of the cross "who have come out of the great tribulation; they have washed their robes and made them white in the blood of the Lamb." Revelation 7:14, R.S.V.

We are called to fight an "all-out war" against the forces that destroy the soul. The church of Christ must awaken now, for a halfhearted preparation will never give us adequate defense against the enemy. "The eye of God, looking down the ages, was fixed upon the crisis which His people are to meet, when earthly powers shall be arrayed against them."—*The Great Controversy*, page 634. God has warned that "the devil is come down unto you, having great wrath, because he knoweth that he hath but a short time." Revelation 12:12. We must answer these questions: "Am I ready to endure the final crisis? Am I prepared to meet my Captain when He comes?"

God will step in to shake the church to its foundation. We are told that "soon everything that can be shaken will be shaken, that those things that cannot be shaken may remain." —*Testimonies*, vol. 9, pp. 15, 16. Yet the trial will strengthen the faith of those who are true to God, for "when the storm of persecution really breaks upon us, the true sheep will hear the true Shepherd's voice. . . . The people of God will draw together and present to the enemy a united front."—*Testimonies*, vol. 6, p. 401.

Prophecies in the Old and New Testaments warn us that "the day of the Lord will come." It is when Michael stands up that the dramatic events of the last crisis begin to take place, "and there shall be a time of trouble, such as never was since there was a nation even to that same time." Daniel 12:1. The time of trouble is a part of the great controversy that has been going on since Adam and Eve succumbed to Satan's temptation. Those who have stood unflinchingly for right, who have refused to receive the mark of the beast or believe false doctrines will suffer the wrath of the enemy. "When Christ shall cease His work as Mediator in man's behalf, then this time of trouble will begin. Then the case of every soul will have been decided, and there will be no atoning blood to cleanse from sin."—*Patriarchs and Prophets,* page 201.

"Great and terrible" is "the day of the Lord's vengeance." Joel 2:31; Isaiah 34:8. It is a "dreadful day," for man must stand alone as fiery trials sweep about him. Malachi 4:5. At this time the judgments of God fall upon sinners in the form of the seven last plagues. The prophet Jeremiah compares the ordeal of the remnant church to the long night of Jacob's wrestling. "Alas! for that day is great, so that none is like it: it is even the time of Jacob's trouble; but he shall be saved out of it." Jeremiah 30:7.

"Jacob's experience during that night of wrestling and anguish represents the trial through which the people of God must pass just before Christ's second coming. . . . As Jacob was threatened with death by his angry brother, so the people of God will be in peril from the wicked who are seeking to destroy them. And as the patriarch wrestled all night for deliverance from the hand of Esau, so the righteous will cry to God day and night for deliverance from the enemies that surround them."—*Patriarchs and Prophets,* page 201.

The Door of Mercy Closes

When the last opportunity for salvation has been given, a solemn edict from heaven comes to a judgment-bound world. The proclamation declares that every individual's case is to remain unchanged as of that moment: "He that is unjust, let him be unjust still: and he which is filthy, let him be filthy still: and he that is righteous, let him be righteous still: and he that is holy, let him be holy still. And, behold, I come quickly." Revelation 22:11, 12.

Daniel Webster once said that the most momentous question every human being must face is: "What is my personal accountability to God?" In the final crisis every human being is responsible for his own record. Our Saviour will have finished His ministration in the heavenly sanctuary, and in the time of trouble each person must stand alone. "Those who are living upon the earth when the intercession of Christ shall cease in the sanctuary above, are to stand in the sight of a holy God without a mediator."—*The Great Controversy*, page 425.

The word of God will be a citadel of strength to the remnant people in the day of temptation. Like their Saviour they will face the doubts and denials with "It is written." But the multitudes who have spurned truth in the day of opportunity will not find it though they search frantically. "Behold, the days come, saith the Lord God, that I will send a famine in the land, not a famine of bread, nor a thirst for water, but of hearing the words of the Lord: and they shall wander from sea to sea, and from the north even to the east, they shall run to and fro to seek the word of the Lord, and shall not find it." Amos 8:11, 12.

In the Hour of Trial

The Scriptures must become for men and women today what it was for their forefathers in earlier generations—the safeguard of Christian living. The admonition is given: "Study your Bible as you have never studied it before. Unless you arise to a higher, holier state in your religious life, you will not be ready for the appearing of our Lord."—*Testimonies*, vol. 5, p. 717.

The worth of a soldier is revealed in the way he faces the enemy, not how proud he is on the parade ground. In like manner, God's warriors receive their baptism of fire in the final conflict against evil. In that day neither position, degrees, nor wealth will keep us from disaster; we must depend wholly upon the promises of Jesus, for He has said, "My grace is sufficient for thee." 2 Corinthians 12:9.

A complaining Christian once said to a friend, "I simply cannot stand all the trials and sorrows that come to me. I wish I had never been made."

The wise friend replied, "You aren't made, my dear. You are only in the process of being made by all the experiences of life. That is how you develop character."

We become impatient with God's plan for us, and we rebel against the refining process; but this is a necessary part in the creation of character that will endure the last conflict. How difficult it is for us to be patient. It is not easy to "quietly wait for the salvation of the Lord." Yet God has been waiting thousands of years for men to finish His work in a sin-wearied world. To those who stand patiently, claiming the Lord's promise of salvation, come these words: "Because you have kept My word of patient endurance, I will keep you from the hour of trial which is coming on the whole world, to try those who dwell upon the earth." Revelation 3:10, R.S.V.

"Patient endurance." How few know the meaning of the words, yet how important it will be in the days ahead. When a traveler prepares to go on a journey, he is not waiting for his train or plane until he has purchased his ticket, checked his baggage, and made all final arrangements for leaving. Then, and only then, is he *waiting* for his train. In like manner we are not waiting for our Lord's return until we have every preparation completed and we are dedicated to that one event.

Our courage can be strong in the furnace of affliction, and we can have peace if the faith of Jesus possesses us. Not long ago I saw a dog chasing pigeons in a city park. The birds never seemed to be agitated or worried, for as danger approached they simply flew out of reach. Knowing they had wings they could well afford to be calm. Do we have wings of faith so that we may "mount up with wings as eagles"? Can we run and not be weary? Can we walk in the darkness and not be afraid? Isaiah 40:31.

"Though God's people will be surrounded by enemies who are bent upon their destruction, yet the anguish which they suffer is not a dread of persecution for the truth's sake; they fear that every sin has not been repented of, and that through some fault in themselves they will fail to realize the fulfillment of the Saviour's promise, 'I will keep thee from the hour of temptation, which shall come upon all the world.' "—*The Great Controversy,* page 619.

When all human help vanishes and the enemies of truth are ready to surround and destroy God's people, the Eternal One will shelter them in His pavilion. Sweet will be the promise: "There shall no evil befall thee, neither shall any plague come nigh thy dwelling." Psalm 91:10. Though the crisis may be fearful, yet the rainbow of God's love will be seen by every trusting child of God.

Wrestling With God

As we approach the time of Jacob's trouble we may be assured that God will not forget His children. "He that walketh righteously, and speaketh uprightly . . . shall dwell on high: his place of defense shall be the munitions of rocks: bread shall be given him; his waters shall be sure." Isaiah 33:15, 16. Yes, we shall know hunger and weariness; but as Jacob prevailed in the midnight struggle, so we may persevere and triumph.

"The people of God will not be free from suffering; but while persecuted and distressed, while they endure privation, and suffer for want of food, they will not be left to perish. That God who cared for Elijah, will not pass by one of His self-sacrificing children. He who numbers the hairs of their head, will care for them; and in time of famine they shall be satisfied. While the wicked are dying from hunger and pestilence, angels will shield the righteous, and supply their wants."—*The Great Controversy*, page 629.

As the plagues fall upon the world, leaders in governments will turn against God's remnant people and determine to destroy them. "A decree went forth to slay the saints, which caused them to cry day and night for deliverance. This was the time of Jacob's trouble."—*Life Sketches*, page 117. Again we are told that "when the protection of human laws shall be withdrawn from those who honor the law of God, there will be, in different lands, a simultaneous movement for their destruction. As the time appointed in the decree draws near, the people will conspire to root out the hated sect. It will be determined to strike in one night a decisive blow, which shall utterly silence the voice of dissent and reproof."—*The Great Controversy*, page 635.

In this hour, after probation has closed, the faithful remnant cling to the divine promises. They say, as did Jacob, "I will not let Thee go, except Thou bless me." They cannot comprehend why they must suffer; but, like Job, their faith surmounts the trial, and they hold fast to God. The patriarch of old was able to wrestle victoriously because he had confessed and forsaken his sins. "So, in the time of trouble, if the people of God had unconfessed sins to appear before them while tortured with fear and anguish, they would be overwhelmed; despair would cut off their faith, and they could not have confidence to plead with God for deliverance. But while they have a deep sense of their unworthiness, they have no concealed wrongs to reveal. Their

sins have gone beforehand to judgment, and have been blotted out; and they cannot bring them to remembrance."—
Ibid., p. 620.

The Hour of Deliverance

The midnight hour arrives, and, lo, it is the hour when the Almighty manifests His power to deliver His saints! There are upheavals in nature and a mighty earthquake "such as was not since men were upon the earth." The law of God is dramatically set forth to the inhabitants of the earth that all may know the eternal Ten Words, including the seventh-day Sabbath. Then the voice of God is heard proclaiming the hour of Christ's coming. In humble triumph the redeemed exclaim, "Lo, this is our God; we have waited for Him, and He will save us: this is the Lord; we have waited for Him, we will be glad and rejoice in His salvation." Isaiah 25:9.

The second coming of Jesus is a world-shaking event that will be witnessed by all earth's inhabitants. "Every eye shall see Him," echoes in our ears, and we remember that Paul said that the event would be heralded with a shout and a peal from "the trumpet of God." This is the triumphant appearing of the King of kings; for He comes in His own glory, with the glory of His Father, and the glory of all the heavenly beings. Victory over sin and death is a reality, and the universe is at peace once more.

Our Saviour is no longer "a Man of Sorrows, and acquainted with grief." Now He comes as the triumphant King who has redeemed His people from the slavery of sin. John presents the vivid picture in these words: "I saw heaven opened, and behold a white horse; and He that sat upon him was called Faithful and True, and in righteousness He doth judge and make war. His eyes were as a flame of fire, and on His head were many crowns; and He had a name written, that no man knew, but He Himself. . . . And the armies which were in heaven followed Him upon white horses, clothed in fine linen, white and clean. . . . And He hath on His vesture and on His thigh a name written, *King of kings, and Lord of lords.*" Revelation 19:11-16.

Those who have scoffed at the prophecies concerning our Lord's return will see Him in all His glory. Those who have mocked His claim to be the Son of God will be speechless in the hour of triumph. The words of the Master will be fulfilled: "Hereafter shall ye see the Son of man sitting on the right hand of power, and coming in the clouds of heaven." Matthew 26:64.

In this decisive hour the wheat will be separated from the chaff. Those who have accepted the sacrifice of Calvary, who have loved their Master and obeyed His commandments, will meet Him with joy. But human beings who have rejected every offer of divine love, who have spurned the messages of warning against sin, who have sought their own willful, lawless course, will hide in caves and mountain fastnesses. They will cry to the rocks and mountains: "Fall on us, and hide us from the face of Him that sitteth on the throne, and from the wrath of the Lamb: for the great day of His wrath is come; and who shall be able to stand?" Revelation 6:16, 17.

The redeemed are transported to heaven, where they gather upon the crystal sea before the throne of God. They have "gotten the victory" and now they become a mighty chorus to sing the song of Moses and the Lamb. Of this group one of the twenty-four elders has declared, "These are they which came out of great tribulation, and have washed their robes, and made them white in the blood of the Lamb." Revelation 7:14.

As the triumphant procession enters the city of God, Jesus bestows upon each one the emblems of victory. "The glittering ranks are drawn up, in the form of a hollow square, about their King, whose form rises in majesty high above saint and angel, whose countenance beams upon them full of benignant love. Throughout the unnumbered host of the redeemed, every glance is fixed upon Him, every eye beholds His glory whose 'visage was so marred more than any man, and His form more than the sons of men.' Upon the heads of the overcomers, Jesus with His own right hand places the crown of glory." Finally Jesus speaks, and a "voice, richer than any music that ever fell on mortal ear, is heard, saying, 'Your conflict is ended.' 'Come, ye blessed of My Father, inherit the kingdom prepared for you from the foundation of the world.' "—*The Great Controversy,* pages 645, 646.

As we think of the glories that await us, we long to be triumphant, and we ask: "How can I be sure of victory?" God's Guidebook tells us plainly we cannot conquer through our own efforts. God gives "us the victory through our Lord Jesus Christ." 1 Corinthians 15:57. The cross of Christ is the symbol of our salvation; His victory is ours.

Willing obedience is characteristic of the remnant people. They will obey the commandments of God and honor their Creator, who made the heavens and the earth. They will remember the Sabbath day to keep it holy. And in their mouth is found no guile, for they will walk daily with their Saviour.

The last generation of men will bear the burden of the weaknesses of their ancestors because of the long course of sin. Yet out of this age of chaos, God will bring a triumphant people. "Wrestling with God—how few know what it is! How few have ever had their souls drawn out after God with intensity of desire until every power is on the stretch. When waves of despair which no language can express sweep over the suppliant, how few cling with unyielding faith to the promises of God. Those who exercise but little faith now, are in the greatest danger of falling under the power of satanic delusions and the decree to compel the conscience. And even if they endure the test, they will be plunged into deeper distress and anguish in the time of trouble, because they have never made it a habit to trust in God. The lessons of faith which they have neglected, they will be forced to learn under a terrible pressure of discouragement."—*The Great Controversy,* pages 621, 622.

The hour of triumph is near. May we accept God's salvation through faith and be ready, standing loyally under the flag of our mighty Conqueror. He says, "Behold, I come quickly." With John we can respond, "Even so, come, Lord Jesus."

HOMESICK FOR HEAVEN

∽ 13 ∼

The End of Sorrow and Suffering

ONE four-letter word describes the dominant emotion of our generation—*fear*. We live in an age of crisis which the historian Arnold Toynbee calls "a time of troubles." Nothing fits the traditional pattern of living any more. War's end hasn't brought peace; more educational facilities have not produced better citizens; the H-bomb does not promise to scare civilization into being good any more than stories of hell-fire made everyone good in the days of the Puritans.

Science warns us that we are depleting many of our resources and that the world is waxing "old like a garment." By promise to free men from ancient beliefs, science led men away from the Bible and away from faith in God. Today we find civilization speeding down a dead-end street with the end in sight, as the nuclear scientists declare that it is possible to blow up the largest city with a single bomb. Thus we might well end all culture and destroy most of mankind. Truly our world is out of joint, and no man is wise enough to set it right.

Uncertainty and insecurity produce fear in men's hearts. Shortly before he died, H. G. Wells wrote, "A frightful queerness has come into life. Hitherto events have been held together by a certain logical consistency as the heavenly bodies have been held together by the golden cord of gravitation. Now it is as if the cord had vanished, and everything is driven anyhow, anywhere, at a steadily increasing velocity."—*The Mind at the End of Its Tether,* pages 4, 5.

Instead of faith directing action, many of us are trembling and weak-kneed. We are afraid of our children. Young married couples are afraid to have children because of the uncertain state of society and the responsibility demanded of them in raising a family. Children feel the fear that grips their elders. They do not understand what it is all about, but the future looks dark through their eyes. A teacher recently told what an eleven-year-old boy answered when asked what he planned to be when he grew up.

"I need not worry," said the boy, "as by that time there will be nowhere to grow up on."

Humanity dreams of beginning all over again. Instead of the blotted pages of history, the sordid stories of individual failures, we would like a new book with clean, white pages. Human nature grows weary of miserable disappointments and frustrations. Each new year is a symbol to millions of persons of the new beginning they long to make. They would give anything to forget the hideous past. God is ready for the human race to make a fresh start, for we have His plan stated plainly in these words: "Behold, I create new heavens and a new earth." Isaiah 65:17.

Through the ages men of God have been homesick for heaven. Implanted within each heart is the longing for freedom from fear and pain, and the coming of peace that only heaven can give. The apostle Peter had this desire, for he wrote, "We, according to His promise, look for new heavens and a new earth, wherein dwelleth righteousness." 2 Peter 3:13. And the heroes of the eleventh chapter of the book of Hebrews —sometimes called the Westminster Abbey of the Bible—were not satisfied with their world after they had caught a glimpse

of the heavenly home. "But now they desire a better coun-
try, that is, an heavenly: wherefore God is not ashamed to be
called their God: for He hath prepared for them a city."
Hebrews 11:16.

By faith every follower of Christ can claim an inheritance
in the new earth, for we are "heirs of salvation," "heirs of the
kingdom," "heirs according to the hope of eternal life." We can
claim "an inheritance incorruptible," beyond the insecurity of
a world of sin. Peter declares that it is "reserved in heaven for
you, who are kept by the power of God." 1 Peter 1:4, 5.

Although we dwell in the midst of sin and death, we can
look beyond the shadows and tears to the "new heavens and a
new earth" which is being prepared for those who love God.
"Let our faith pierce through every cloud of darkness and be-
hold Him who died for the sins of the world. He has opened
the gates of paradise to all who receive and believe on Him.
To them He gives power to become the sons and daughters of
God. Let the afflictions which pain us so grievously become
instructive lessons, teaching us to press forward toward the
mark of the prize of our high calling in Christ. Let us be en-
couraged by the thought that the Lord is soon to come."—
Testimonies, vol. 9, pp. 286, 287.

Heartaches and Tears Are Ended

Tomorrow need not be a dim mirage for humanity; God
will make it a glorious reality. Look at the fortune that awaits
us in God's new world. The capital city of Jerusalem will have
walls of transparent jasper, streets of pure gold, and gates of
pearl. In the heart of the city flows the river of life. John, the
beloved apostle, saw the glorious capital and describes it in
these words: "He showed me a pure river of water of life,
clear as crystal, proceeding out of the throne of God and of

the Lamb." Revelation 22:1 The tree of life is in the midst of
the city, and every month it bears twelve kinds of fruit.

A fortune which cannot be reckoned in silver or gold awaits
you and me in that better land, for there we shall have peace of
mind and enjoy perfect happiness. Most wonderful of all, we
learn that "the throne of God and of the Lamb shall be in it;
and His servants shall serve Him: and they shall see His face."
Verses 3, 4.

As M. L. Andreasen points out: "When Christ leaves to
come to this earth, God Himself comes with Him. Wonder of
wonders! God Himself shall be with us and be our God."—
The Faith of Jesus, page 566. This earth will become the capital
of the universe. The sin-cursed planet, so long darkened by the
powers of evil, will become the focal point for the inhabitants
of unnumbered worlds. Those who have triumphed over trial
and tribulation will have the privilege of ministering to the
Almighty and to Jesus, the Lamb. We shall see Him who re-
deemed us, and we shall reign with Him for ever and ever.

In our pain-wracked world, men would give every dollar
they possess to stop the suffering and to prevent the death of
their loved ones. In God's new earth eternal health will be the
gift for all. "God shall wipe away all tears from their eyes;
and there shall be no more death, neither sorrow, nor crying,
neither shall there be any more pain: for the former things are
passed away." Revelation 21:4.

Those who are afflicted with ailments so common today will
then be physically strong. "Pain cannot exist in the atmosphere
of heaven. There will be no more tears, no funeral trains, no
badges of mourning."—*The Great Controversy,* page 676. The
topic of conversation will no longer be the recent operation
or the new method of treating our diseases. That will have
passed away!

No disappointments, no heartaches, no suffering! "The voice of weeping shall be no more heard," and "the voice of crying" shall be turned to laughter. Isaiah 65:19. The long-cherished and unfulfilled dreams of this life will then be accomplished facts. Age will be meaningless, for in eternity we cannot mark time by years.

"And the city had no need of the sun, neither of the moon, to shine in it: for the glory of God did lighten it, and the Lamb is the light thereof." Revelation 21:23. Night will not exist in the world of tomorrow, since darkness and God's presence cannot dwell together. "In the city of God 'there shall be no night.' None will need or desire repose. There will be no weariness in doing the will of God and offering praise to His name. We shall ever feel the freshness of the morning, and shall ever be far from its close. . . . The light of the sun will be superseded by a radiance which is not painfully dazzling, yet which immeasurably surpasses the brightness of our noontide. The glory of God and the Lamb floods the Holy City with unfading light. The redeemed walk in the sunless glory of perpetual day."—*The Great Controversy,* page 676.

The Promise of Security

In an effort to find security, men buy every type of insurance: life, fire, theft, health, accident, disaster, and old age. The fear of facing a bleak, hopeless future haunts every home in our world; but in God's better world that fear will vanish. We shall build houses and enjoy them; we shall plant and cultivate as we desire and reap the harvest without damage or loss. We will be able to make plans and see them completed. Today we are afraid of crop failures. The homes we build and the businesses we start soon pass to other hands. But in Heaven's new order there will be certainty and stability. God's promise of permanency is set forth by Isaiah when he says of the redeemed, "They shall build houses, and inhabit them; and they shall plant vineyards, and eat the fruit of them. They shall not build, and another inhabit; they shall not plant, and another eat: for as the days of a tree are the days of My people, and Mine elect shall long enjoy the work of their hands." Isaiah 65:21, 22.

Millions of weary, homeless refugees have wandered from country to country since war's ending, seeking a permanent dwelling place. They are the flotsam and jetsam of the tides of modern global warfare. Orphans and helpless aged persons feel the agony of being displaced persons who will never again on earth know the meaning of "home." Such suffering will be unknown in God's new earth. He promises:

> "My people will abide in a peaceful habitation,
>   in secure dwellings, and in quiet resting places."
>   Isaiah 32:18, R.S.V.

No more bloodshed or violence will break out in the home of the redeemed.

The three words, "I am sick," will never again be heard. Isaiah 33:24. No hospitals will be found in that wondrous city; no institutions for the blind, the deaf, the dumb, and the crippled will be needed. "Then the eyes of the blind shall be opened, and the ears of the deaf shall be unstopped. Then shall the lame man leap as an hart, and the tongue of the dumb sing: for in the wilderness shall waters break out, and streams in the desert." Isaiah 35:5, 6.

Emil Brunner well says, "We do not know what lies on the other side of death . . . we cannot imagine what life would look like which was not marked with the stamp of death. We can only express what we think in futile negations, which say nothing, save that we have become aware to some extent of the negations which death brings into our life. A negation of negations, that is the formula for ideas of eternal life. 'And God shall wipe away all tears from their eyes, and there shall be no more death, neither sorrow, nor crying, neither shall there be any more pain, for the former things are ·passed away.'

"Life without cessation, joy without sorrow, power without limitations, fellowship with God without disturbance, time without passing away, physical life without the flesh, sight without the pale cast of thought, without the paradoxes of faith, knowledge no longer 'as in a glass darkly' or in a riddle, but 'face to face, even as we are known'—all this might be expressed in one sentence: God will be there, and we shall be with Him. He will be our God, and we shall be His people."
—*The Mediator.*

Insured Against Sin

There is one insurance policy that is given to every citizen of the city of God. The underwriter is our heavenly Father, and the guarantee is sure. The wording of God's promise is simple and pointed: "He will make an utter end: affliction shall not rise up the second time." Nahum 1:9. No pain, no sorrow, no death, mean only one thing—no more sin. Certain restrictions are placed upon citizenship in the new earth to protect the redeemed from sin. Of the New Jerusalem we read, "And there shall in no wise enter into it anything that defileth, neither whatsoever worketh abomination, or maketh a lie: but they which are written in the Lamb's book of life." Revelation 21:27.

God's law will be forever honored, and all who enter the city will keep the commandments of God. Revelation 22:14. We are told that "the nations of the saved will know no other law than the law of heaven."—*Prophets and Kings,* page 732.

The wonder city will be open to all nations of the earth; but only those who are victors over sin, who have followed Jesus Christ, and have allowed Him to rule their lives, will have a right to this Utopia. As the redeemed obey their Saviour they will learn more and more of His will for them. Heaven will be a school in which we are ever learning. To the student will be opened the wonders of true science, not seen merely in laboratory experiments or test tubes; but in the firsthand glories of all creation.

There we shall learn the full story of the plan for man's salvation, the ministry of angels, and the mystery of godliness. In the divine school we shall learn why the great controversy between good and evil was permitted and how God's love was manifest in every page of human history.

"In the plan of redemption there are heights and depths that eternity itself can never exhaust, marvels into which the angels desire to look. The redeemed only, of all created beings, have in their own experience known the actual conflict with sin; they have wrought with Christ, and, as even the angels could not do, have entered into the fellowship of His sufferings." —*Education,* page 308.

One course of study will be of great interest in the school of heaven. There "all the perplexities of life's experience will then be made plain. Where to us have appeared only confusion and disappointment, broken purposes and thwarted plans, will be seen a grand, overruling, victorious purpose, a divine harmony."—*Ibid.,* p. 305. I want to take that course and learn God's reason for our trials and sorrows, don't you?

The conflict is forever ended, and we can give eternal thanks "to the Father, who has qualified us to share in the inheritance of the saints in light. He has delivered us from the dominion of darkness and transferred us to the kingdom of His beloved

Son." Colossians 1:12, 13, R.S.V. If this home is to be a reality to us, we must bend every effort now to reach it.

If faith grips your life and mine, then we will never give up the eternal interests of tomorrow for the small, fading baubles of today. Let faith grip our hearts and fear will vanish, for "perfect love casteth out fear."

The most precious gift to be bestowed upon the redeemed is eternal life. Jesus Christ will present this blood-bought gift to us. If we accept His forgiveness for our sins and claim His salvation, we shall hear His words: "Come, ye blessed of My Father, inherit the kingdom prepared for you from the foundation of the world." Matthew 25:34.

Jesus has a plan for your life and mine. He will give us power to be triumphant in suffering. He will deliver us from this chaotic, sin-cursed earth and bestow a fortune upon us— a home in a perfect world surrounded by peace and security where we shall see our Redeemer face to face!